D0998401

Samuel DANIEL
and
Michael DRAYTON

a reference guide

A
Reference
Guide
to
Literature

James Harner
Editor

Samuel DANIEL
and
Michael DRAYTON

a reference guide

JAMES L. HARNER

G.K. HALL & CO.

70 LINCOLN STREET, BOSTON, MASS.

Z2014
P7
H37

'Copyright © 1980 by James Lowell Harner

Library of Congress Cataloging in Publication Data

Harner, James L
  Samuel Daniel and Michael Drayton.

  (A Reference guide to literature)
  Includes indexes.
  1. English poetry—Early modern, 1500—1700—
Bibliography. 2. Daniel, Samuel, 1562-1619—
Bibliography. 3. Drayton, Michael, 1563-1631—
Bibliography. I. Series: Reference guide to literature.
Z2014.P7H37   [PR531]   016.821'3'09   80-22655
ISBN 0-8161-8322-8

This publication is printed on permanent/durable acid-free paper
MANUFACTURED IN THE UNITED STATES OF AMERICA

Contents

MAY 1 5 1981

MAY 3 1 1961

Introduction

Samuel Daniel (1562-1619) and Michael Drayton (1563-1631) are tradi-
tionally linked in literary histories and anthologies as representa-
tives of the achievements and shortcomings as well as the range of
English Renaissance literature. As professional[1] poets who were much
admired by their contemporaries, as practitioners in a majority of
the forms and genres popular during their time, and as authors who
share many of the same topics, they are indeed similar. Though both
retained an essentially Elizabethan attitude toward life and literature well into the seventeenth century and though both were accomplished historical, lyric, and epic poets as well as perceptive
critics, the achievement of each is distinct. While both are frequently described as mirrors of their age, Daniel more precisely
reflects the Compleat Elizabethan Poet and Drayton the Compleat
Renaissance Poet.

   William Browne's epithet "well-languaged Daniel" and Drayton's
observation that his fellow poet was "too much historian in verse"
characterize the range of Daniel criticism from the sixteenth century
to the present. As Cecil Seronsy, one of the most productive and
able of Daniel scholars, pointed out in 1957:

> Critical evaluation of Samuel Daniel as poet has remained
> fairly constant for well over three centuries, oscillating
> between two rather familiar poles of praise and censure ini-
> tially marked by Daniel's contemporaries. Nashe, Barnfield,
> and many others eulogized him. William Browne called him
> 'well-languaged Daniel' and to William Drummond of Hawthorn-
> den he was 'for sweetness in rhyming second to none.' On
> the other hand, Spenser, while recognizing Daniel's gifts,
> admonished him to rouse the feathers of his low-flying muse,
> and Drayton, who at first wrote under the influence of 'the
> sweet Musaeus of these times,' later found Daniel to be 'too
> much historian in verse.' Ben Jonson's harsh judgment that
> Daniel was no poet was in part balanced by Edmund Bolton's
> comment that 'the works of Samuel Daniel contained somewhat
> a flat but yet withal a very pure and copious English, and
> words as warrantable as any man's, and fitter perhaps for
> Prose than measure.' (1957.10)

Introduction

Daniel's reputation has fluctuated widely since his own day. The numerous attempts to rescue him from undeserved neglect have met with indifference in many of the twentieth-century reassessments of Elizabethan poetry, especially those of Winters (1939.7) and Hobsbaum (1965.10). Those who appreciate his purity of language, restraint, "grave ethical passion" (1962.2), and defense of the value of culture and literature are countered by others who find him boring because of evenness of tone, abstractness, and lack of passion. There are few, however, who have gone so far as to agree with Jonson that Daniel was "no poet."

Daniel's importance lies not merely in the range of his accomplishments in sonnet sequence, epic, drama (Senecan, pastoral, and masque), tragic complaint, translation, criticism, verse epistle, and prose history, but also in the influence he exerted on many of these forms and genres. His place in the development of the sonnet, tragic complaint, and verse epistle has been recognized since the early part of this century, as has the importance of Defense of Rhyme in the history of criticism. Common to much of the writing on Daniel is the praise of his language, especially its purity and "modern" quality. Although Daniel's contribution to the development of the English language was noted by Child as early as 1909 (1909.4), a detailed examination of his influence is still lacking; in fact, it was not until Seronsy's "Well-Languaged Daniel: A Reconsideration" (1957.10) that there was an adequate exposition of Daniel's frequently praised but rarely analyzed style. Finally, Daniel's influence on his fellow writers (e.g., Drayton and Shakespeare) as well as on later ones (Coleridge, Thoreau, Milton, and particularly Wordsworth) is well documented, as is the praise accorded him by Eliot and Housman. In fact, before 1940 one might have appropriately described Daniel as a poets' poet.

Of Daniel's individual works, Delia, Civil Wars, and Cleopatra have received the most attention. Much of the early emphasis on these was the result of investigations into the nature of their relationship to Shakespeare's works and of source studies in general. More recently, however, Delia and Civil Wars are being treated as works which in themselves are worthy of examination. This is particularly true of Civil Wars, which has been at the center of the investigation of Daniel's importance as a historian as well as the analysis of his philosophy of history. This emphasis on Daniel as historian and detailed analyses of his craftsmanship which are beginning to modify the clichés of the past 350 years of Daniel criticism mark the two major focuses of current scholarship.[2]

Scholarly and critical commentary on Daniel, as well as an adequate appreciation by modern readers of his merit, is hampered by the lack of a textually sound, complete edition. Several attempts have been made during the twentieth century to produce one, but none has ever been brought to completion. Only Civil Wars (1958.4) has appeared in the projected Yale edition, and this volume was greeted

by reviewers with considerable reservation about the soundness of
the text. Nothing has been heard of the progress of the edition
since 1960 (see 1960.13).[3]

Drayton has not been subjected to the same extremes of critical
reaction as has Daniel. A more prolific writer, Drayton was also a
more uneven one. He produced acknowledged masterpieces that are
still enthusiastically and widely read--notably Idea 61, "Ballad of
Agincourt," and Nymphidia--but many of his works are marred by awkward syntax, prosaic verse, and a lack of selectivity in detail.
Both he and Daniel worked in several of the same genres and forms,
but Drayton's range is greater. Though he wrote no prose history and
translated no treatise on emblems, he did produce biblical epics,
pastoral eclogues, satires, epyllia, fairy poems, and the unclassi-
fiable Polyolbion. Though not to the same extent as Daniel's,
Drayton's works were influential, particularly in the development of
the heroic couplet, dramatic monologue, heroic epistle, and ode. He
was more susceptible to literary fads than Daniel, but his range of
style--from Spenserian through Metaphysical to Caroline--is greater.
In fact, as Bush points out, Drayton's experimentation in various
styles and forms, along with his revisions, mirrors "the poetic history of an entire period" (1932.5). As one might expect, he mirrors
its excesses as well as its accomplishments.

Drayton's reputation has also been the subject of a number of
attempts at rehabilitation, and currently he is sharing in the renewed interest in the Spenserians. As Noyes has shown in his study
of Drayton's Literary Vogue since 1631 (1935.4), his reputation de-
clined after his death until 1748, though England's Heroical
Epistles, one of his most frequently acclaimed works until the middle of this century, occasioned a number of imitations. From 1748
to the twentieth century his poetry has exerted some influence--most
notably Endymion and Phoebe on Keats and "Ballad of Agincourt" on
Tennyson--though never to the extent that Daniel's has.

Drayton has been most consistently praised for his pastoral and
fairy poetry, and generally accounted to be at his best in his
lyrics and at his worst in his long poems. And, he has not infre-
quently been admired as much for his character as for his art: his
staunch defense of Elizabethan values, together with the patriotism
and love of England which permeate his works, has attracted readers
(and composers in the case of "To the Virginian Voyage").

Polyolbion, the work most commonly and unfortunately (in terms
of his stature as a poet) associated with Drayton, has been the subject of most debate among his critics. Many acknowledge the labor,
the dedication, and sometimes the learning that went into the poem,
but few accord to the work any poetic merit. Criticized for the
alexandrines and the excessive personification, Polyolbion is frequently pronounced unreadable; yet it has found staunch defenders
who continually predict a rekindling of interest in the poem. Its

appeal to the antiquarian and the lover of the British countryside and the renewed interest among academic critics during the last decade indicate that Polyolbion will not soon be consigned totally to the ranks of the curiosities of literature.

Among other perennial subjects of Drayton criticism are Idea (with Walter Davis's interpretation of the work as a comic sequence dominating current scholarship [1969.3]), his sources (a particularly fertile area because of the subject matter of the poems), and his revisions, especially of the sonnets and Shepherd's Garland. More recently, Drayton's philosophy of history and his theory of poetry are receiving attention.

Drayton's reputation has always been more secure than Daniel's. Unlike Daniel, he has been well served by a fine collected Works (as well as by several editions of individual poems and selections from the eighteenth century to the present), and his acknowledged master-pieces have continued to attract new generations of readers.

Neither will ever likely regain the popularity he once had or become again an influence on a new generation of poets, but both will continue to be read, admired, and discussed as long as there are lovers of good poetry.

In the following pages I have attempted to gather, within the limits outlined below, all the scholarship on Drayton and Daniel from 1684 through 1978 (along with a few works that appeared early in 1979). The few items I have not seen are marked with an asterisk, and some of these are annotated from reviews or published abstracts. I would, of course, appreciate information on works overlooked or not seen.

I have not attempted to catalogue all the passing mentions of either poet, especially those from the sixteenth through eighteenth centuries.[4] Although Drayton and Daniel are mentioned in a large portion of the many books on Renaissance literature, I have generally included only those that offer at least three continuous pages of discussion. I have included new editions and reprints of books com-pletely devoted to Daniel or Drayton, but I have omitted new editions of other books unless the discussion of either poet has been signi-ficantly revised. I have also included reviews of books about and editions of Drayton and Daniel: I have annotated separately the reviews that offer a significant contribution to the study of the respective poet; I have listed others with the book(s) under review. I have included all articles, no matter how brief, that are devoted solely to or that include a significant discussion of either poet. I have listed editions of single works or selections, but have made no attempt to track down all reprintings in anthologies. I have included doctoral dissertations,[5] but not masters' theses. I have excluded entries in literary handbooks and encyclopedias. In the annotations my aim has been to summarize content and, when appropri-ate, conclusions; I have therefore used when possible the author's own words.

NOTES

[1]Richard Helgerson's "laureate" may prove a more accurate epithet; see 1979.2 (Daniel) and 1979.2 (Drayton).

[2]On Daniel as historian see, for example, 1947.7, 1954.7, 1956.3, 1957.9, 1965.5, 1970.10, 1971.8, 1977.5, and 1979.3; on his craftsmanship see, for example, 1974.8, 1974.9, 1977.7, and 1979.4.

[3]In a recent letter, Laurence Michel reported that the edition is dormant.

[4]For Daniel, see 1942.3; for Drayton, see 1935.4 and 1941.10. I have not included all works listed in previous bibliographies of Daniel (1942.3, 1967.6, and 1977.6) and Drayton (1941.10, 1967.7, and 1975.6). Those omitted include only a passing mention of either poet or are general background studies.

[5]Dissertations for which no abstract is cited are listed in one of the following: Lawrence F. McNamee, Dissertations in English and American Literature: Theses Accepted by American, British, and German Universities, 1865-1964 (New York: R. R. Bowker, 1968), Supplement I, 1964-1968 (1969), Supplement II, 1969-1973 (1974); Comprehensive Dissertation Index (Ann Arbor: Xerox University Microfilms, 1973-); Index to Theses Accepted for Higher Degrees in the Universities of Great Britain and Ireland (London: Aslib, 1953-); Roger R. Bilboul, ed., Retrospective Index to Theses of Great Britain and Ireland, 1716-1950. Vol. I: Social Sciences and Humanities (Oxford: European Bibliographical Center, 1975); Gernot U. Gabel and Gisela R. Gabel, comps., Dissertations in English and American Literature: Theses Accepted by Austrian, French, and Swiss Universities, 1875-1970 (Hamburg: Gernot Gabel, 1977); and Hans Walter Gabler, English Renaissance Studies in German, 1945-1967: A Check-List of German, Austrian, and Swiss Academic Theses, Monographs, and Book Publications on English Language and Literature, c. 1500-1650, Schriftenreihe der Deutschen Shakespeare-Gesellschaft West, NS 11 (Heidelberg: Quelle & Mayer, 1971).

Acknowledgments

In the composition of a bibliography one necessarily incurs many debts. One of the pleasures of bringing this work to a conclusion is the opportunity to acknowledge those who have in some way provided assistance.

Librarians, both here and abroad, were invariably helpful in locating items and answering queries. The staffs of the libraries at the University of Michigan, Toledo University, Ohio State University, Indiana University, and Bowling Green State University deserve special notice. In particular Kausalya Raj and Kay Sandy of the inter-library loan office at Bowling Green efficiently and expeditiously handled a mound of requests, many of which were for obscure periodicals and books.

Many of the authors listed herein graciously answered questions, sent offprints, and offered encouragement. Brownell Salomon offered helpful comments on a portion of the manuscript.

I am grateful to the Faculty Improvement Leave Program at Bowling Green for a leave which allowed the time to complete my research. The English Department provided a research assistant, Willard Fox III, who patiently, conscientiously, and good-naturedly checked stacks of note cards and scanned runs of journals.

Susan Gross helped with much of the preliminary typing, and Lenée Harner had a hand in various stages of the work.

Once again Darinda Harner gave up a disproportionate share of her time to turn boxes of heavily edited note cards into a finished typescript.

Abbreviations

AF	Anglistische Forschungen
AL	American Literature
AN&Q	American Notes and Queries
Anglia	Anglia: Zeitschrift für Englische Philologie
Archiv	Archiv für das Studium der Neueren Sprachen und Literaturen
BC	Book Collector
BLR	Bodleian Library Record
BNL	Beiträge zur Neueren Literaturgeschichte
BNYPL	Bulletin of the New York Public Library
CEA	CEA Critic
ChauR	Chaucer Review
ChildL	Children's Literature
CHum	Computers and the Humanities
CL	Comparative Literature
CLAJ	College Language Association Journal
CSE	Cornell Studies in English
DA	Dissertation Abstracts
DAI	Dissertation Abstracts International
DPL	De Proprietatibus Litterarum

DR	Dalhousie Review
DUJ	Durham University Journal
DVLG	Deutsche Vierteljahrsschrift für Literaturwissenschaft und Geistesgeschichte
EA	Études Anglaises
E&S	Essays and Studies by Members of the English Association
EDH	Essays by Divers Hands
EIC	Essays in Criticism
ELH	ELH: Journal of English Literary History
ElizS	Elizabethan & Renaissance Studies
ELN	English Language Notes
ES	English Studies
ESA	English Studies in Africa
Expl	Explicator
HLB	Harvard Library Bulletin
HLQ	Huntington Library Quarterly
HSE	Hungarian Studies in English
ISLL	Illinois Studies in Language and Literature
JEGP	Journal of English and Germanic Philology
JES	Journal of European Studies
JHI	Journal of the History of Ideas
JWCI	Journal of the Warburg and Courtauld Institutes
KBAA	Kieler Beiträge zur Anglistik und Amerikanistik
Library	The Library
LSE	Lund Studies in English
M&L	Music and Letters

MLN	Modern Language Notes
MLQ	Modern Language Quarterly
MLR	Modern Language Review
MP	Modern Philology
N&Q	Notes and Queries
PBSA	Papers of the Bibliographical Society of America
PLPLS-LHS	Proceedings of the Leeds Philosophical and Literary Society, Literary & Historical Section
PMLA	PMLA: Publications of the Modern Language Association of America
Poetics	Poetics: International Review for the Theory of Literature
PoetryR	Poetry Review
PQ	Philological Quarterly
QFSK	Quellen und Forschungen zur Sprach- und Kulturgeschichte der Germanischen Völker
QQ	Queen's Quarterly
RBPH	Revue Belge de Philologie et d'Histoire
Ren&R	Renaissance and Reformation/Renaissance et Réforme
RenB	Renaissance Bulletin
RenD	Renaissance Drama
RenP	Renaissance Papers
RenQ	Renaissance Quarterly
RES	Review of English Studies
RLC	Revue de Littérature Comparée
RLV	Revue des Langues Vivantes
RR	Romanic Review
SAVL	Studien zur Allgemeinen und Vergleichenden Literaturwissenschaft

Abbreviations

SB	Studies in Bibliography
SCN	Seventeenty-Century News
SEL	Studies in English Literature, 1500–1900
SEngL	Studies in English Literature (The Hague)
ShakS	Shakespeare Studies
ShS	Shakespeare Survey
SJH	Shakespeare-Jahrbuch (Heidelberg)
SLitI	Studies in the Literary Imagination
SN	Studia Neophilologica
SP	Studies in Philology
SPGL	Studien zur Poetik und Geschichte der Literatur
SQ	Shakespeare Quarterly
SR	Sewanee Review
SzEP	Studien zur Englischen Philologie
TCI	Twentieth Century Interpretations
TEAS	Twayne's English Author Series
TLS	[London] Times Literary Supplement
TSE	Tulane Studies in English
UCPES	University of California Publications, English Studies
UDR	University of Dayton Review
UNCSCL	University of North Carolina Studies in Comparative Literature
WBEP	Wiener Beiträge zur Englischen Philologie
YES	Yearbook of English Studies
YSE	Yale Studies in English

Samuel Daniel

Major Works

Annotated Bibliography

1684

1   WINSTANLEY, WILLIAM. ["The Life of Mr. Samuel Daniel,"] in his <u>Englands Worthies: The Lives of the Most Eminent Persons from Constantine the Great to This Presant Time</u>. [London:] Obadiak Blagrave, pp. 337–40.
       Provides biographical sketch and brief critical appraisal.

1687

1   WINSTANLEY, WILLIAM. "Mr. Samuel Daniel," in his <u>The Lives of the Most Famous English Poets</u>. London: Samuel Manship, pp. 109–12.
       Provides biographical notice and critical appreciation; praises Daniel as both poet and historian.

1691

1   LANGBAINE, GERARD. "Samuel Daniel, Esq.," in his <u>An Account of the English Dramatick Poets</u>. Oxford: George West and Henry Clements, pp. 100–106.
       Provides biographical sketch and critical appraisal of Daniel's plays; identifies sources.

2   [WOOD, ANTHONY À.] "Samuel Daniel," in his <u>Athenae Oxonienses: An Exact History of All the Writers and Bishops Who Have Had Their Education in the Most Ancient and Famous University of Oxford</u>. Vol. I. London: Tho. Bennet, columns 379–80.
       Provides biographical sketch, a brief critical appraisal, and a list of works. Revised 1815.2.

5

1706

1 DANIEL, SAMUEL. [A Collection of the History of England,] in
A Complete History of England. Vol. I. [Edited by John
Hughes.] London: Brab. Aylmer et.al., pp. 83-427.
   Reprints History of England along with a revised version
of Trussell's continuation. Observes that the latter "was
so meanly perform'd by Mr. Trussel, and the stile so
wretched, that there was a Necessity to have those Reigns
[Richard II, Henry IV, Henry V, and Henry VI] new writ,
which have therefore been done much larger and more exact,
and after Mr. Daniel's Method."

1718

1 DANIEL, SAMUEL. The Poetical Works of Mr. Samuel Daniel.
2 volumes. London: Robert Gosling, W. Mears, and Jonas
Browne, 388, 456 pp.
   Includes modernized texts of most of Daniel's works.
In "Some Account of the Life and Writings of Mr. Samuel
Daniel" (I, ix-xxii), an anonymous writer provides a biography and critical commentary. Praises the purity and
elegance of Daniel's style and versification. Reviewed in
1823.1.

1737

1 COOPER, ELIZABETH. The Muses Library; or, A Series of English
Poetry. London: J. Wilcox, 416 pp.
   Includes extracts from Daniel's works. In a brief
introductory note, characterizes him as "a Person of great
Good-Sense, and unbias'd Integrity; both Clear and Concise
in his Expression; rather too simple and void of Ornament,
and not comparable in his Numbers either to Fairfax or
Spencer; But, on the whole, highly worthy of Esteem and
Reputation" (pp. 381-400).

1751

1 DANIEL, SAMUEL. The Tragedy of Cleopatra. Glasgow: Robert &
Andrew Foulis, 34 pp.
   Provides modernized reprint of unidentified edition.

1753

1   CIBBER, [THEOPHILUS]. "Samuel Daniel," in his The Lives of
the Poets of Great Britain and Ireland to the Time of Dean
Swift. Vol. I. London: R. Griffiths, pp. 145-49.
      Provides biographical sketch and list of works. Ob-
serves that Daniel "seems to have been a second rate genius, and a tolerable versifier; his poetry in some places
is tender, but want of fire is his characteristical fault."

1787

1   HEADLEY, HENRY, ed. Select Beauties of Ancient English
Poetry: With Remarks. 2 volumes. London: T. Cadell,
215, 200 pp.
      Includes an appreciative "Biographical Sketch" of
Daniel, "the Atticus of his day." Observes: "Though very
rarely sublime, he has skill in the pathetic, and his
pages are disgraced with neither pedantry or conceit" (I,
xlii-xliv). Provides several annotated extracts arranged
under various headings, for example, "Pathetic Pieces,"
"Descriptive Pieces" (passim). (For the importance of
Headley's collection, see Earl R[eeves] Wasserman, "Henry
Headley and the Elizabethan Revival," SP, 36 [July 1939],
491-502.)

1793

1   DANIEL, SAMUEL. "The Poetical Works of Samuel Daniel," in
The Works of the British Poets, with Prefaces, Biographical
and Critical. Vol. IV. Edited by Robert Anderson.
London: John & Arthur Arch et al., pp. 109-251.
      Provides modernized reprints of Civil Wars, Funeral
Poem upon the Death of the Earl of Devonshire, Panegyric
Congratulatory, Epistles, Musophilus, Delia, "Ulysses and
the Siren," Rosamond, Letter from Octavia, and other
lyrics. In "The Life of Daniel" (pp. 111-14), presents a
basic chronological overview of his life and works. Comments in particular on his style, which "is distinguished
from that of his contemporaries, by a peculiar neatness
and simplicity." (The general title page to the volume is
dated 1795; the title page for Daniel's works is dated
1793.)

<u>1800</u>

1   PHILLIPS, EDWARD. <u>Theatrum Poetarum Anglicanorum: Contain-</u>
     <u>ing the Names and Characters of All the English Poets from</u>
     <u>the Reign of Henry III. to the Close of the Reign of Queen</u>
     <u>Elizabeth</u>. Revised by S[amuel] E[gerton] Brydges. Canter-
     bury: J. White, 422 pp.
        Enlarges the very brief entry in the 1675 edition with
     critical and biographical extracts from various sources
     and a list of works. Concludes: "The character of Dan-
     iel's genius seems to be propriety, rather than elevation.
     His language is generally pure and harmonious; and his
     reflections are just. But his thoughts are too abstract,
     and appeal rather to the understanding, than to the imagi-
     nation or the heart" (pp. 258-61).

<u>1808</u>

1   BRYDGES, SAMUEL EGERTON. "Original Letter of Samuel Danyell,
     the Poet," in his <u>Censura Literaria: Containing Titles,</u>
     <u>Extracts, and Opinions of Old English Books</u>. Vol. VI.
     London: Longman, Hurst, Rees, and Orme, and J. White,
     pp. 391-93.
        Transcribes "An Original Letter of Samuel Danyel, sent
     to Lord Keeper Egerton with a present of his 'Works, newly
     augmented, 1601;' extant in the Bridgewater Library." On
     the question of authenticity <u>see</u> 1965.13.

<u>1809</u>

1   DANIEL, SAMUEL. <u>Tethys Festival; or, The Queenes Wake</u>, in <u>A</u>
     <u>Collection of Scarce and Valuable Tracts, on the Most</u>
     <u>Interesting and Entertaining Subjects: But Chiefly Such</u>
     <u>as Relate to the History and Constitution of These King-</u>
     <u>doms</u>. Vol. II. Second edition. Edited by Walter Scott.
     London: T. Cadell and W. Davies et al., pp. 191-99.
     [Somers Tracts.]
        Reprints 1610 edition. (The <u>Collection</u> was first pub-
     lished 1748-1752; however, the 1809 edition is the one
     most frequently cited and generally available.)

<u>1810</u>

1   DANIEL, SAMUEL. "The Poems of Samuel Daniel," in <u>The Works</u>
     <u>of the English Poets, from Chaucer to Cowper</u>. Vol. III.

Edited by Alexander Chalmers. London: J. Johnson et al., pp. 445-581.

Provides modernized texts of much of Daniel's poetry. In "The Life of Daniel" (pp. 447-51), gives an overview of his life, works, and critical reputation. Concludes: "[H]is language is every where so much more harmonious than that of his contemporaries, that he deserves his place in every collection of English poetry, as one who had the taste or genius to anticipate the improvements of a more refined age."

1814

1   BRYDGES, [SAMUEL] EGERTON. ["Tethys' Festival,"] in his Restituta; or, Titles, Extracts, and Characters of Old Books in English Literature, Revived. Vol. I. London: Longman, Hurst, Rees, Orme, and Brown, pp. 238-39, 366.

Notes text of Tethys' Festival in The Order and Solemnity of the Creation of Prince Henry and lists the names of those who represented the various characters.

1815

1   DANIEL, SAMUEL. A Defence of Ryme, in Ancient Critical Essays upon English Poets and Poësy. Vol. II. Edited by Joseph Haslewood. London: Robert Triphook, pp. 191-219.

Reprints 1603 edition.

2   WOOD, ANTHONY A. "Samuel Daniel," in Athenae Oxonienses. Vol. II. Edited by Philip Bliss. London: F. C. Rivington et al., columns 267-74.

Revises and expands 1691.2.

1817

1   COLERIDGE, S[AMUEL] T[AYLOR]. Biographia Literaria; or, Biographical Sketches of My Literary Life and Opinions. 2 volumes. New York: C. Wiley, 183, 196 pp.

In chapter 18 (II, 39-62), praises Daniel's diction and style, "which, as the neutral ground of prose and verse, is common to both." In chapter 22 (II, 87-119), points out resemblances in diction between Wordsworth and Daniel (passim).

1817

2   DRAKE, NATHAN. Shakspeare and His Times: Including the Bio-
    graphy of the Poet; Criticisms on His Genius and Writings;
    a New Chronology of His Plays; a Disquisition on the Object
    of His Sonnets; and a History of the Manners, Customs, and
    Amusements, Superstitions, Poetry, and Elegant Literature
    of His Age. 2 volumes. London: T. Cadell and W. Davies,
    747, 683 pp.
        Provides brief critical estimate of major works of Dan-
    iel, "the most correct poet of his age." Comments on the
    influence of Delia on Shakespeare's sonnets, and identifies
    "the merits of Daniel" as "purity of language, elegance of
    style, . . . harmony of versification, . . . an almost
    perfect freedom from pedantry and affectation, and a con-
    tinual flow of good sense and just reflection" (I, 611-12,
    passim).

1819

1   DANIEL, SAMUEL. "Select Poems of Samuel Daniel with a Life
    of the Author," in The Works of the British Poets: With
    Lives of the Authors. Vol. II. Edited by Ezekiel Sanford.
    Philadelphia: Mitchell, Ames, and White, pp. 281-320.
        Provides modernized texts of Rosamond and "Ulysses and
    the Siren." In "Life of Daniel" (pp. 283-85), offers a
    brief critical appreciation, concluding: "Daniel is dis-
    tinguished for the justness and good sense of his thoughts,
    and the neatness and harmony of his verse."

1823

1   ANON. Review of The Poetical Works of Mr. Samuel Daniel.
    Retrospective Review, 8, part 2, 227-46.
        In review of 1718.1 offers a generally unfavorable ap-
    praisal of Daniel, for example, calls Civil Wars "tire-
    somely monotonous, . . . dry and antipoetical" and the
    plays "equally jejune and unimpassioned." Finds that only
    Delia merits qualified praise. Includes extracts.

2   HOOD, EU. "Fly Leaves, No. XIV." Gentleman's Magazine, 93
    (August), 109-11.
        Notes lack of a standard edition of Daniel and of crit-
    ical attention to his revisions.

1828

1 NICHOLS, JOHN. The Progresses, Processions, and Magnificent Festivities of King James the First. 4 volumes. London: J. B. Nichols, 653, 762, 594, 595 pp.
    Provides annotated texts of Panegyric Congratulatory (I, 21-34), Vision of the Twelve Goddesses (from True Description of a Royal Masque) and the dedication from the 1604 authorized edition (I, 305-*314), Tethys' Festival (II, 346-58), and portions of Hymen's Triumph (II, 749-53). Includes several contemporary documents and manuscripts related to the above works (passim).

1830

1 K., T. H. "Notices of the Lives and Writings of Our Early Dramatists, No. VIII: Samuel Daniel." Dramatic Magazine, 2 (December), 340-43.
    Provides biographical sketch, list of major works, brief general critical estimate, and extract from Hymen's Triumph.

1831

1 COLLIER, J[OHN] PAYNE. The History of English Dramatic Poetry to the Time of Shakespeare and Annals of the Stage to the Restoration. 3 volumes. London: J. Murray, 490, 494, 604 pp.
    Traces briefly Daniel's career as licenser of the Children of the Queen's Revels, discusses him as "a decided opponent of the romantic drama," and provides a critical estimate of Cleopatra and Philotas (passim).

2 DANIEL, SAMUEL. "Samuel Daniel, 1562-1619," in Select Works of the British Poets from Chaucer to Jonson, with Biographical Sketches. Edited by Robert Southey. London: Longman, Rees, Orme, Brown, and Green, pp. 572-95.
    Prints modernized selections from Daniel's poetry. In headnote, praises his diction and amiability.

1832

1 B[OADEN], J[AMES]. "To What Person the Sonnets of Shakespeare
Were Actually Addressed." Gentleman's Magazine, 102 (September), 217-21; (October), 308-14.
        Identifies Daniel as the Rival Poet. Revised as 1837.1

1833

1 U. "Samuel Daniel." Bath and Bristol Magazine; or, Western
Miscellany, 2, no. 1, 1-13.
        Provides appreciative biographical and critical over-
view in an attempt to rescue Daniel from neglect.

1837

1 BOADEN, JAMES. On the Sonnets of Shakespeare: Identifying
the Person to Whom They Are Addressed; and Elucidating
Several Points in the Poet's History. London: Thomas
Rodd, 66 pp.
        In revision of 1832.1 argues that Daniel is the Rival
Poet and discusses the influence of Delia on the Sonnets
and Rosamond on Rape of Lucrece (pp. 46-55).

2 COLLIER, J[OHN] PAYNE. A Catalogue, Bibliographical and
Critical, of Early English Literature; Forming a Portion
of the Library at Bridgewater House, the Property of the
Rt. Hon. Lord Francis Egerton, M.P. London: Thomas Rodd,
370 pp. [Bridgewater Catalogue.]
        Describes several editions of Daniel's works (STC 6236,
6239, 6244, 6245, 6246, 6248, 6259, 6260) with notes on
revisions and bibliographical and critical matters
(pp. 78-84). Incorporated in 1866.1.

1839

1 BELL, ROBERT. "Michael Drayton, 1563-1631: With Notices of
His Contemporaries," in his Lives of the Most Eminent
Literary and Scientific Men of Great Britain, I: English
Poets. London: Longman, Orme, Brown, Green, & Longmans,
and John Taylor, pp. 1-37.
        Provides brief overview of Daniel's life and works;
in comparing him with Drayton, concludes "that Daniel had
more tenderness and elegance, and Drayton more strength
and variety" (pp. 26-29).

2 KNIGHT, CHARLES. "Introductory Notice [to Richard II]," in
   his edition of The Pictorial Edition of the Works of
   Shakspere: Histories. Vol. I. London: Charles Knight,
   pp. 81-87.
       Discusses Shakespeare's use of Civil Wars (1595) as a
   source. Finds that the work fails because Daniel "attempts
   an impossible mixture of the Poem and Chronicle" and because "Daniel's mind wanted the true poetical elevation."

1845

1 CRAIK, GEORGE L[ILLIE]. Sketches of the History of Literature and Learning in England with Specimens of the Principal Writers, Series Second: From the Accession of
   Elizabeth to the Revolution of 1688. Vol. III. London:
   Charles Knight, 228 pp.
       Includes general critical estimate of Daniel: calls
   Civil Wars his "great work" and Musophilus "his finest
   piece." Comments on the "modern air" and the "easy and
   natural flow" of Daniel's style, and asserts that "[t]he
   highest quality of his poetry is a tone of quiet, pensive
   reflection . . . which often rises to dignity and eloquence, and has at times even something of depth and
   originality" (pp. 142-49).

2 HUNTER, JOSEPH. "Chorus Vatum Anglicanorum: Collections
   Concerning the Poets and Verse-Writers of the English
   Nation." Vol. III. British Library Add. MS. 24,489.
       Collects notes from various sources on Daniel's life
   and works (pp. 223-45, 601).

1849

1 CUNNINGHAM, PETER. "Will of Samuel Daniel, the Poet:
   Shakespeare's Rival and Contemporary." Shakespeare Society's Papers, 4: 156-58.
       Transcribes and describes Daniel's will.

1851

1 COLERIDGE, HARTLEY. "Daniel," in his Essays and Marginalia.
   Vol. II. Edited by Derwent Coleridge. London: Edward
   Moxon, pp. 12-16.
       Transcribes several of Samuel Taylor Coleridge's manu-
   script notes on Daniel's style and language in a copy of
   1793.1.

1852

1 [THOMS, WILLIAM J.] "Coleridge: Letters to Lamb, and Notes
   on Samuel Daniel's Poems." N&Q, 6 (7 August), 117-18.
       Transcribes Coleridge's letters and notes in Lamb's
   copy of 1718.1.

1853

1 RIMBAULT, EDWARD F. "Samuel Daniel." N&Q, 7 (2 April), 344.
       In response to an earlier query (6 [25 December 1852],
   603), supplies miscellaneous biographical and bibliographical information.

1854

1 ANON. "Manuscripts of the Poet Gray." Athenaeum, no. 1396
   (29 July), pp. 941-42.
       In a report of the sale of Thomas Gray's manuscripts,
   prints "an unpublished character of Daniel--part of the
   Poet's intended History of English Poetry." In the manuscript, Gray provides an appreciative estimate of Daniel.
   See 1911.2.

2 HAZLITT, WILLIAM. "Samuel Daniel," in his Johnson's Lives of
   the British Poets Completed. Vol. I. London: Nathaniel
   Cooke, pp. 177-80.
       Provides a brief biography with a list of works.
   Quotes from Coleridge's manuscript notes in Lamb's copy
   of 1718.1.

1855

1 DANIEL, SAMUEL. Selections from the Poetical Works of Samuel
   Daniel. Edited by John Morris. Bath: Charles Clark,
   296 pp.
       Provides annotated, modernized selections. In "Bio-
   graphical Introduction" (pp. xi-xxxix), offers an overview
   of Daniel's life and works; emphasizes his connections
   with the court of James I.

1856

1   SIMEON, JOHN. "Inedited Poems of Daniel." <u>Miscellanies of
the Philobiblion Society</u>, 2, no. 13, 1-12.
      Prints two poems--"The Bodie" and "The Minde"--ascribed
to Daniel in a commonplace book in his possession. <u>See</u>
1938.6

1858

1   LOWNDES, WILLIAM THOMAS. <u>The Bibliographer's Manual of English Literature</u>. Vol. II, part III. Revised by Henry
G[eorge] Bohn. London: Henry G. Bohn, pp. i-iv, 577-850.
      Includes several listings, with bibliographical notes,
for editions of Daniel's works (pp. 586-87). <u>See</u> 1862.1.

1859

1   ROBINSON, C. J. "Somersetshire Poets." <u>N&Q</u>, 20 (10 September), 204.
      Notes that according "to the poet's own epitaph" Daniel
was born in Wiltshire. <u>See</u> 1860.1, 1860.2, 1860.3, 1860.4,
and 1860.5.

1860

1   D., E. "Samuel Daniel." <u>N&Q</u>, 21 (14 April), 286.
      In response to Robinson (1859.1) and G. H. K. (1860.2),
transcribes Daniel's epitaph from 1855.1. <u>See</u> 1860.3,
1860.4, and 1860.5.

2   K., G. H. "Samuel Daniel." <u>N&Q</u>, 21 (4 February), 90.
      Requests Robinson's source for Daniel's "epitaph"
(1859.1) since the one he quotes is not that at Beckington.
<u>See</u> 1860.1, 1860.3, 1860.4, and 1860.5.

3   _____. "Samuel Daniel." <u>N&Q</u>, 21 (17 March), 208.
      Reaffirms that Daniel's "epitaph" quoted by Robinson
(1860.5) is not the one "at this present" at Beckington.
<u>See</u> 1859.1, 1860.1, 1860.2, and 1860.4.

1860

4 _____. "Samuel Daniel." N&Q, 21 (26 May), 404.
   Affirms that E. D.'s transcription of Daniel's epitaph
   (1860.1) is the same as that sent "by the rector Beckington." See 1859.1, 1860.2, 1860.3, and 1860.5.

5 ROBINSON, C. J. "Samuel Daniel." N&Q, 21 (25 February), 152.
   Responds to G. H. K. (1860.2) by identifying his source
   as "a printed collection in three volumes octavo, which I
   saw in the British Museum, but the exact title of which I
   do not remember." Quotes "epitaph." See 1859.1, 1860.1,
   1860.3, and 1860.4.

1862

1 HAZLITT, W[ILLIAM] CAREW. "Lowndes's Bibliographer's Manual:
   Notes on the New Edition, No. V." N&Q, 26 (4 October),
   266-69.
   Includes additions and corrections to entries on Daniel
   in 1858.1.

1863

1 WHITE, RICHARD GRANT. "Introduction [to Richard II]," in his
   edition of The Works of William Shakespeare. Vol. VI.
   Boston: Little, Brown, pp. 137-45.
   Idenfifies a "second edition" of Civil Wars in 1595 and
   argues that Daniel was indebted to Richard II in the revisions. (On White's mistaken identification of a second
   edition, see 1958.4.)

1864

1 [THOMS, WILLIAM J.]. "Hymen's Triumph." N&Q, 29 (23 April),
   347.
   In reply to a query by W. R. C. on the authorship of
   Hymen's Triumph, identifies Daniel as the author and provides miscellaneous information about the play.

1865

1 CORNEY, BOLTON. "Samuel Daniel and John Florio." N&Q, 32
   (1 July), 4.
   Argues that Daniel and Florio were not brothers-in-law.
   Interprets "brother" in Daniel's commendatory sonnet

(Queen Anna's New World of Words) to mean "brother-officers"
of the Queen's Privy Chamber. See notes by J. S. (8 July,
pp. 35-36), Corney (8 July, p. 40; 15 July, pp. 52-53), and
W[illiam] Aldis Wright (29 July, p. 97).

2   NICHOLSON, B[RINSLEY]. "Parallel Passages in Shakspeare and
       Daniel." N&Q, 31 (29 April), 337.
         Notes parallel between "To Henry Wriothesley" and
       Coriolanus and Cymbeline.

1866

1   COLLIER, J[OHN] PAYNE. A Bibliographical and Critical Account
       of the Rarest Books in the English Language. Vol. I. New
       York: D. G. Francis, 335 pp.
         Incorporates, with revisions, material from 1837.2; adds
       entries on STC 6253 and 11900 (pp. 208-20).

1867

1   HAZLITT, W[ILLIAM] CAREW. Hand-Book to the Popular, Poetical,
       and Dramatic Literature of Great Britain, from the Inven-
       tion of Printing to the Restoration. London: John Russell
       Smith, 716 pp.
         Provides bibliographical description of and notes on
       various editions of Daniel's works (pp. 137-40). See
       1876.2, 1882.1, 1892.3, and 1903.6 for additions and cor-
       rections.

1868

1   EDWARDS, EDWARD. The Life of Sir Walter Ralegh. Vol. I.
       London: Macmillan, 779 pp.
         Examines question of authorship of Breviary of the
       History of England; inclines toward Ralegh (pp. 513-15).

2   WHIPPLE, E[DWIN] P[ERCY]. "Minor Elizabethan Poets." Atlan-
       tic Monthly, 22 (July), 26-35.
         Includes appreciative estimate of Daniel, praising his
       diction. Concludes: "Amiable in character, gentle in
       disposition, and with a genius meditative rather than
       energetic, he appears to have possessed that combination
       of qualities which makes men personally pleasing if it
       does not make them permanently famous." Reprinted 1869.1.

<u>1869</u>

1   WHIPPLE, EDWIN P[ERCY]. "Minor Elizabethan Poets," in his
        <u>The Literature of the Age of Elizabeth</u>. Boston: Fields,
        Osgood, pp. 221-49.
            Reprints 1868.2.

<u>1870</u>

1   DANIEL, SAMUEL. "<u>The Complaint of Rosamond</u>" by Samuel Daniel:
        <u>An Exact Reproduction of the Earliest Known Edition</u>.
        Edited by J[ohn] Payne Collier. London: privately
        printed, n.p.
            Provides a "typographical facsimile" of the "first im-
        pression" of the 1592 edition, the "oldest known copy"
        of the work. In "Introduction," corrects his comments in
        1870.2 and dates the composition 1585-1591. Included in
        1870.3.

2   _____. <u>Delia. Containing Certayne Sonnets: With the Com-</u>
        <u>plaint of Rosamond</u>. Edited by J[ohn] P[ayne] C[ollier].
        [London: T. Richards, 100 pp.]
            Provides type facsimile of the 1592 edition (with the
        sixth edition of <u>Rosamond</u>). In "Introduction" suggests
        that "there was a still older edition of" <u>Rosamond</u> and
        that the two works were originally published separately.
        See 1870.1; included in 1870.3.

3   _____, and MICHAEL DRAYTON. <u>Early Poems of Daniel and Dray-</u>
        <u>ton</u>. Edited by J[ohn] Payne Collier. London: privately
        printed, n.p.
            Provides type facsimiles of <u>Delia and Rosamond</u> (1592)
        and <u>Rosamond</u> (1592). Made up from copies of 1870.1 and
        1870.2.

<u>1873</u>

1   BROWNE, C. ELLIOT. "The Earliest Mention of Shakspeare."
        <u>N&Q</u>, 47 (10 May), 378-79.
            Rejects the identification of Daniel with "Watson's
        heir" in <u>Polimanteia</u>.

2   CORSER, THOMAS. <u>Collectanea Anglo-Poetica: or, A Biblio-</u>
        <u>graphical and Descriptive Catalogue of a Portion of a</u>

18

Collection of Early English Poetry, with Occasional Extracts and Remarks Biographical and Critical. Part V.
Chetham Society, vol. 91. [Manchester:] Chetham Society,
pp. 8-65.

Classifies Daniel as "one of the foremost and most
pleasing of our second class of poets." Provides extensive
notes on several early editions of Daniel's works: annotations frequently give description of content, auction
record of copies, locations, collation, extracts, variant
readings, references to scholarship, and critical estimate.
(Includes the following editions: STC 6236, 6237, 6238,
6239, 6240, 6244 [2 states], 6245, 6253 [2 states], 6254,
6256, 6257, 6259, 6260, 6261 [2 states], 11900, and
13162.)

3 JONES, W. H. "St. Audoen's, South Wraxall." Wiltshire Ar-
chaeological and Natural History Magazine, 14 (September),
100-107.

Points out that Daniel "seems to have held some situation as Bailiff under the Earl of Hertford . . . connected
with" St. Audoen's. Also calls attention to "an original
letter at Longleat, endorsed 'Mr. Danyell the Poet 26 May,
1608,' written to Mr. James Kirten."

1874

1 MINTO, WILLIAM. Characteristics of English Poets from Chaucer
to Shirley. Edinburgh: William Blackwood and Sons,
495 pp.

Provides general critical appreciation of Daniel; notes
that "[h]e was no master of strong passions," that the
importance of Delia lies in his use of the English sonnet
form, and that "Daniel's genius is best shown in the expression of bereaved love in" Rosamond (pp. 250-55).

1875

1 WARD, ADOLPHUS WILLIAM. A History of English Dramatic Literature to the Death of Queen Anne. Vol. II. London:
Macmillan, 647 pp.

Gives overview of Daniel's plays, pointing out that he
was a better poet than dramatist and that his pastorals
are better than his tragedies (pp. 141-43). Revised
1899.13.

1876

1 GROSART, ALEXANDER B[ALLOCH]. "Spenser and Daniel, and the
Towneley Mss." Athenaeum, no. 2534 (20 May), p. 697.
Provides information on format and proposed contributors
to his projected edition of Daniel's works (1885.1, 1885.2,
1885.3, 1896.2, and 1896.3). Announces that his "ambition . . . is to make the new Spenser and Daniel landmarks
in critical and worthy editing."

2 HAZLITT, W[ILLIAM] CAREW. Collections and Notes, 1867-1876.
London: Reeves and Turner, 510 pp.
Provides additions and corrections to 1867.1 (pp. 115-
17). See 1882.1, 1892.3, and 1903.6 for further additions
and corrections.

1877

1 SIDNEY, PHILIP. Astrophel and Stella, in An English Garner:
Ingatherings from Our History and Literature. Vol. I.
Edited by Edward Arber. London: E. Arber, pp. 467-600.
Provides modernized reprint of 1591 edition, which
includes the unauthorized publication of several of
Daniel's sonnets (pp. 580-94). Reprinted 1904.2.

1879

1 DESHLER, CHARLES D. Afternoons with the Poets. New York:
Harper & Brothers, 320 pp.
Gives a general overview of critical estimates of Dan-
iel as poet and comments appreciatively on Delia. Finds
Daniel's sonnets superior to Drayton's (pp. 100-108).

2 HAMILTON, WALTER. The Poets Laureate of England: Being a
History of the Office of Poet Laureate. London: Elliot
Stock, 336 pp.
In chapter on "The Volunteer Laureates" (pp. 18-41),
includes a brief overview of Daniel's life and works
(pp. 38-41).

3 JACKSON, J. E. "Longleat Papers, No. 4." Wiltshire Archae-
ological and Natural History Magazine, 18 (November),
257-85.
Prints the two letters (20 May and 31 May 1608) from
Daniel to James Kirton, Steward to the Earl of Hertford.
Points out that the earlier letter seems to indicate that
Daniel was "acting as farm-bailiff" to the Earl.

1880

1 DANIEL, SAMUEL. Delia, in An English Garner: Ingatherings from Our History and Literature. Vol. III. Edited by Edward Arber. Birmingham: E. Arber, pp. 599-620.
  Provides modernized reprint of 1594 edition, omitting those sonnets printed in volume I (1877.1). Reprinted 1904.2.

2 _____. The Vision of the Tvvelve Goddesses: A Royall Masque. Edited by Ernest Law. London: Bernard Quaritch, 81 pp.
  Provides "exact reproduction" (annotated) of the 1623 edition. In "Introduction" (pp. 5-54), transcribes references to the work in contemporary documents, discusses the court environment, and attempts to re-create the setting for and performance of the masque.

3 SAINTSBURY, G[EORGE EDWARD BATEMAN]. "Samuel Daniel," in The English Poets: Selections with Critical Introductions by Various Writers. Vol. I. Edited by Thomas Humphry Ward. London: Macmillan, pp. 467-68.
  Praises Daniel's language, his "power of dignified moral reflection," and "his combination of moral elevation with a certain picturesque peacefulness of spirit."

1882

1 HAZLITT, W[ILLIAM] CAREW. Second Series of Bibliographical Collections and Notes on Early English Literature, 1474-1700. London: Bernard Quaritch, 727 pp.
  Provides additions and corrections to 1867.1 and 1876.2 (p. 157). See 1892.3 and 1903.6 for further additions and corrections.

2 ISAAC, HERMANN. "Wie weit geht die Abhängigkeit Shakespeare's von Daniel als Lyriker? Eine Studie zur englischen Renaissance-Lyrik." Shakespeare-Jahrbuch, 17: 165-200.
  Argues that Delia had little influence on Shakespeare's sonnets; in the process, provides detailed analysis of Daniel's style. See 1912.2.

3 SOERGEL, ALFRED. Die englischen Maskenspiele. Ph.D. dissertation, Vereinigten Friedrichs-Universität, Halle--Wittenberg. Halle: n.p., 92 pp.
  Draws on Daniel's masques in providing a history and analysis of the characteristics of the form (passim).

1884

1 M., A. J. "Samuel Daniel." N&Q, 69 (19 April), 306.
   Points out indebtedness of Charles Kingsley to "To the
   Countess of Cumberland." See 1884.2.

2 SHELLY, J. "Samuel Daniel." N&Q, 69 (28 June), 515.
   Suggests that Kingsley took Daniel's lines from the
   motto to Coleridge's Aids to Reflection. See 1884.1.

3 WALFORD, E. "Samuel Daniel." N&Q, 69 (3 May), 359.
   Points out Latin analogues to two lines in "To the
   Countess of Cumberland."

1885

1 DANIEL, SAMUEL. The Complete Works in Verse and Prose of
   Samuel Daniel. Vol. I. Edited by Alexander B[alloch]
   Grosart. N.p.: printed for private circulation, 324 pp.
      Includes inedited poems from various sources; Delia
   (1623 edition, with prefatory note on the various editions
   and revisions); Rosamond (1623); Letter from Octavia
   (1623); Panegyric Congratulatory (1623); Funeral Poem upon
   the Death of the Earl of Devonshire (1623); Epistles
   (1623); Musophilus (1623); and occasional poems from various sources. Provides textual notes and brief bibliographical preface for each work. In "Memorial-Introduction, I:
   Biographical" (pp. xi-xxviii), gives overview of Daniel's
   life, concluding: "The impression left on one, after
   pondering the facts, is that he was an infirm, over-
   sensitive man, physically and intellectually, though . . .
   he led observers to conclude that he was capable of far
   greater things than ever he wrote." See 1903.9 and 1944.1.
   Reprinted 1963.4.

2 _____. The Complete Works in Verse and Prose of Samuel Daniel.
   Vol. II. Edited by Alexander B[alloch] Grosart. N.p.:
   printed for private circulation, 339 pp.
      Includes Civil Wars (1623); provides textual notes and
   brief prefatory bibliographical note. See 1944.1. Reprinted 1963.4.

3 _____. The Complete Works in Verse and Prose of Samuel Daniel.
   Vol. III. Edited by Alexander B[alloch] Grosart. N.p.:
   printed for private circulation, 409 pp.
      Includes Cleopatra (1623, with prefatory discussion of
   of Daniel's revisions); Philotas (1623); Vision of the

Twelve Goddesses (1623); Queen's Arcadia (1623); Tethys' Festival (1610); and Hymen's Triumph (1623). Provides textual notes and brief bibliographical preface for each work. In "Preliminary Note on the Position of Daniel's Tragedies in English Literature" (pp. vii-xi), Saintsbury points out that Daniel stands almost alone among Elizabethan dramatists in his adoption of Senecan tragedy. See 1944.1. Reprinted 1963.4.

4 PRIDEAUX, W. F. "Samuel Daniel." N&Q, 71 (7 March), 186.
    Observes that "[t]he advance of the British troops along the Nile recalls to mind the fine ode with which The Tragedy of Cleopatra concludes."

1887

1 DANIEL, SAMUEL. The Complaynt of Rosamond. [Edited by Edmund Goldsmid.] Bookworm's Garner, 2. Edinburgh: E. & G. Goldsmid, 75 pp.
    Reprints 1623 edition.

2 SAINTSBURY, GEORGE [EDWARD BATEMAN]. A History of Elizabethan Literature. London: Macmillan, 485 pp.
    In an appreciative overview of Daniel's works, praises his diction and versification. Observes: "The poetical value of Daniel may almost be summed up in two words—sweetness and dignity. He is decidedly wanting in strength, and, despite Delia, can hardly be said to have had a spark of passion" (pp. 135-39, passim).

1888

1 L[EE], S[IDNEY]. "Samuel Daniel," in The Dictionary of National Biography. Vol. XIV. Edited by Leslie Stephen. New York: Macmillan; London: Smith, Elder, pp. 25-31.
    Provides overview of life and works, with brief critical estimates.

2 Z., A. "Samuel Daniel, the Poet." N&Q, 78 (29 September), 248-49.
    Queries relationship between Daniel and James Daniel, a participant in the Monmouth rebellion. Points out that "the tradition is that they were related." (For a similar query, see F. S. A., "Samuel and James Daniel," N&Q, 82 [20 December 1890], 488.)

1889

1   COOK, ALBERT S.   "The Elizabethan Invocations to Sleep."   MLN,
      4 (December), 229–31.
         Traces sources of the various invocations to sleep (in-
      cluding Delia 45) to Seneca, Ovid, and "the so-called Orphic
      hymn to sleep."

2   FLEAY, F[REDERICK] G[ARD].   "On the Career of Samuel Daniel."
      Anglia, 11: 619–30.
         In a chronological overview of Daniel's life and works,
      identifies Delia as Elizabeth Carey and discusses the enmity
      between Daniel and Jonson (identifying Daniel with Littlewit
      in Bartholomew Fair and with Hedon in Cynthia's Revels).
      Revised 1891.1.

1891

1   FLEAY, FREDERICK GARD.   "Samuel Daniel," in his A Biographical
      Chronicle of the English Drama, 1559–1642.   Vol. I.   London:
      Reeves and Turner, pp. 84–99.
         Reprints, with a few additions, 1889.2.   The additions
      include an allusion to Daniel in Northward Ho and a list of
      his plays.   See 1899.10 and 1926.2.

2   SCHELLING, FELIX E[MMANUEL].   Poetic and Verse Criticism of
      the Reign of Elizabeth.   Publications of the University of
      Pennsylvania, Series in Philology, Literature, and Archae-
      ology, vol. 1, no. 1.   Philadelphia: University of Pennsyl-
      vania Press, 97 pp.
         Provides detailed synopsis of Defense of Rhyme, espe-
      cially as it answers Campion's Observations.   Concludes
      "that a careful reading of Daniel's Defence of Ryme will
      leave a better impression of the real weight of that able
      and thoughtful author than too continued a perusal of much
      of his 'chaste and correct' poetry" (pp. 83–91).

1892

1   CHOATE, ISAAC BASSETT.   Wells of English.   Boston: Roberts
      Brothers, 310 pp.
         In chapter 18 ("Samuel Daniel, 1563–1619," pp. 139–45),
      discusses his contemporary reputation, the clarity of his
      language, his use of various stanza forms, and the influ-
      ence of Giambattista Marino on his works.

2   HANSEN, ADOLF. "Engelske Sonetter indtil Milton." Tilskueren
    (February), pp. 195-222.
        Includes Delia in overview of the development of the
    sonnet from Wyatt through Milton. Translates three son-
    nets.

3   HAZLITT, W[ILLIAM] CAREW. Bibliographical Collections and
    Notes (1474-1700): Third and Final Series, Second Supple-
    ment. London: Bernard Quaritch, 110 pp.
        Provides addition to 1867.1, 1876.2, and 1882.1 (p. 22).
    See 1903.6 for further additions and corrections.

1893

1   ANON. Catalogue of Original and Early Editions of Some of
    the Poetical and Prose Works of English Writers from
    Langland to Wither. New York: Grolier Club, 254 pp.
    [Langland to Wither.]
        Includes annotated bibliographical descriptions of STC
    6237, 6238, 6239, 6240, 6242, 6244 (2 issues), 6245, 6254,
    6259, 6260, 6261, and 11900 (pp. 42-56). See 1907.2.

2   ANON. "The Hazlitt Papers." Athenaeum, no. 3447 (18 Novem-
    ber), pp. 697-98.
        In discussing the forthcoming sale of W. C. Hazlitt's
    library, prints for the first time some of Coleridge's
    marginalia in Lamb's copy of 1718.1.

3   ANON. "Samuel Daniel." Macmillan's Magazine, 68 (October),
    433-40.
        In an appreciative overview of Daniel's life and works,
    singles out Delia and some of the epistles as his best
    poems, traces contemporary estimates, and comments on the
    un-Elizabethan qualities of his verse.

4   MORLEY, HENRY. English Writers, X: Shakespeare and His Time:
    Under Elizabeth. London: Cassell, 523 pp.
        Traces early career of Daniel, giving a brief critical
    estimate and summary of major works (to c. 1603). Pro-
    vides synopsis of Civil Wars and compares it to Drayton's
    Barons' Wars (pp. 208-11, 310-14, 322-30). Continued
    1895.1.

<u>1894</u>

1 GOSSE, EDMUND [WILLIAM]. <u>The Jacobean Poets</u>. University
   Extension Manuals. London: John Murray, 234 pp.
   In chapter 1 ("The Last Elizabethans," pp. 1-22), discusses Daniel as a transitional poet. Provides a brief
   critical estimate of his works published after 1603. Concludes: "The almost unrelieved excision of all ornament
   and colour, the uniform stateliness, the lack of passion,
   which render Daniel admirable and sometimes even charming
   in a short poem, weary us in his long productions, and so
   invariably sententious is he that we are tempted to call
   him a Polonius among poets" (pp. 9-14).

2 Q[UILLER-] C[OUCH], A[RTHUR] T[HOMAS]. "A Literary Causerie:
   Samuel Daniel." <u>Speaker</u>, 9 (24 February), 224-25.
   Attempts to redress the current neglect of Daniel by
   showing "the gentleness and dignified melancholy of his
   life" and by illustrating "that Daniel had done much,
   though quietly, to train the growth of English verse."
   Suggests that he was a "'poets' poet'" and that his work
   sometimes suffers from a "'donnish' timidity . . . a certain distrust of his own genius." Reprinted 1896.5.

<u>1895</u>

1 MORLEY, HENRY, and W[ILLIAM] HALL GRIFFIN. <u>English Writers,
   XI: Shakespeare and His Time: Under James I</u>. London:
   Cassell, 484 pp.
   Continue overview of Daniel's career from 1893.4. Ob-
   serve: "It is in his sonnets alone that Daniel is really
   great." Include bibliography (pp. 322-26, 365-66).

<u>1896</u>

1 ANON. "Sonnets to Delia." <u>Poet-Lore</u>, 8 (October), 473-76.
   Provides pastiche of quotations from introduction to
   1885.1 on the "'human passion'" in <u>Delia</u> and on Daniel's
   life.

2 DANIEL, SAMUEL. <u>The Complete Works in Verse and Prose of
   Samuel Daniel</u>. Vol. IV. Edited by Alexander B[alloch]
   Grosart. N.p.: printed for private circulation, 357 pp.
   Includes prefatory matter to <u>Worthy Tract</u> (1585),
   <u>Defense of Rhyme</u> (1607), and <u>History of England</u> (1626).
   Provides prefatory bibliographical note to each work. In

"Memorial-Introduction, II: Critical" (pp. vii-lvii), traces criticism on Daniel (1594-1876) and offers a general critical estimate of him as a poet. Also includes some additional biographical information and prints some passages from the manuscript of Hymen's Triumph. See 1944.1. Reprinted 1963.4.

3 _____. The Complete Works in Verse and Prose of Samuel Daniel. Vol. V. Edited by Alexander B[alloch] Grosart. N.p.: printed for private circulation, 331 pp.
Continues History of England from 1896.3, providing additional notes on the work; prints the supplementary chapter of Worthy Tract; and supplies a "Glossarial-Index, Incorporating Notes and Illustrations of the Works." See 1944.1. Reprinted 1963.4.

4 _____. Delia, in Elizabethan Sonnet-Cycles. Edited by Martha Foote Crow. Chicago: A. C. McClurg, pp. 1-79.
Provides modernized reprint of 1623 edition (plus seven sonnets not reprinted from earlier editions). In introductory note, points out that Daniel's influence on the themes and form of Shakespeare's sonnets is not as great as is usually assumed, discusses the influence of Petrarch on Delia, identifies Delia as the Countess of Pembroke, and provides a general critical assessment of Daniel.

5 QUILLER-COUCH, A[RTHUR] T[HOMAS]. "Samuel Daniel," in his Adventures in Criticism. London: Cassell, pp. 50-60.
Reprints, "with few alterations," 1894.2.

1897

1 DANIEL, SAMUEL. A Defence of Ryme, in Literary Pamphlets Chiefly Relating to Poetry from Sidney to Byron. Vol. I. Edited by Ernest Rhys. The Pamphlet Library. London: Kegan Paul, Trench, Trübner, pp. 190-237.
Provides annotated reprint based on 1607 edition.

2 _____. The Vision of the Twelve Goddesses, in English Masques. Edited by Herbert Arthur Evans. Warwick Library. London: Blackie & Son, pp. 1-16.
Provides modernized reprint of 1623 edition (?). In "Introduction" (pp. xi-lviii), comments briefly on Daniel in overview of development of the masque and its characteristics.

1897

3 HAZLITT, WILLIAM CAREW. The Lambs: Their Lives, Their
Friends, and Their Correspondence: New Particulars and
New Material. London: Elkin Mathews; New York: Charles
Scribner's Sons, 246 pp.
Prints Coleridge's two letters on Daniel (in Lamb's
copy of 1718.1) "for the first time in an accurate form"
(pp. 219-24).

4 PENNIMAN, JOSIAH H[ARMAR]. The War of the Theatres. Publi-
cations of the University of Pennsylvania, Series in
Philology, Literature, and Archaeology, vol. 4, no. 3.
Boston: Ginn, 172 pp.
Examines Jonson's attack on Daniel as Matthew in Every
Man in His Humor, as Brisk in Every Man out of His Humor,
and as Hedon in Cynthia's Revels (pp. 24-30, 52-56, 81-84,
passim). See 1899.10.

5 SARRAZIN, GREGOR. William Shakespeares Lehrjahre: Eine
litterarhistorische Studie. Litterarhistorische
Forschungen, vol. 5. Weimar: Emil Felber, 246 pp.
Examines the influence of Delia on style and structure
of Shakespeare's sonnets and considers briefly the influence of Rosamond on various works by Shakespeare (pp. 149-
74).

*6 SMALL, ROSCOE ADDISON. "The Stage-Quarrel between Ben Jonson
and the So-Called Poetasters." Ph.D. dissertation, Harvard University.
Published as 1899.10.

7 SMITH, HOMER. "Pastoral Influence in the English Drama."
PMLA, 12, no. 3, 355-460.
Discusses influence of Tasso and Guarini, characteriza-
tion, versification, satire, and Daniel's theory and
practice of pastoral drama in Queen's Arcadia and Hymen's
Triumph.

<u>1898</u>

1 GUGGENHEIM, JOSEF. Quellenstudien zu Samuel Daniels
Sonettencyklus "Delia." Ph.D. dissertation, University of
Berlin. Berlin: E. Ebering, 67 pp.
Traces influences on and sources of Delia; examines,
in particular, Daniel's use of Petrarch. See 1912.2.

2   HANNAY, DAVID. <u>The Later Renaissance</u>. Periods of European
    Literature, 6. Edinburgh: William Blackwood and Sons,
    395 pp.
        Provides a brief critical assessment of Daniel, em-
    phasizing the purity of his language (pp. 213-15).

3   SPENCER, VIRGINIA EVILINE. <u>Alliteration in Spenser's Poetry:</u>
    <u>Discussed and Compared with the Alliteration as Employed</u>
    <u>by Drayton and Daniel</u>. 2 parts. Ph.D. dissertation,
    University of Zurich. N.p.: n.p., 96, 48 pp.
        Gives classified tabular comparison of the use of
    alliteration by the three. Concludes that Daniel, in
    contrast to Drayton and Spenser, made "sparing use of
    alliteration."

                            <u>1899</u>

1   ANON. "Daniel and Drayton." <u>Academy</u>, 56 (19 August), 175-76.
        In review of 1899.5 points out that "Daniel resembles
    Drayton only in manliness." Characterizes Daniel's style
    as "extremely clear and carefully finished" and identifies
    "grave and dignified reflection" as "[h]is characteristic
    vein."

2   B., C. C. "Daniel's <u>Sonnets to Delia</u>." <u>N&Q</u>, 100 (26 August),
    170-71.
        In response to Prideaux (1899.8), discusses several
    readings from the <u>Delia</u> sonnets in the 1591 edition of
    <u>Astrophel and Stella</u>. <u>See</u> 1899.3, 1899.9, and 1899.11.

3   BEECHING, H[ENRY] C[HARLES]. "Daniel's <u>Sonnets to Delia</u>."
    <u>N&Q</u>, 100 (26 August), 170.
        Defends choice of copy-text in 1899.5 by arguing that
    since Daniel was "so severe a castigator of his verses . .
    . , it became an editor's duty to abide by the form the
    poet last gave them." Also responds to Prideaux's cor-
    rections and emendations (1899.8). <u>See</u> 1899.2, 1899.9,
    and 1899.11.

4   _____. "The Sonnets of Michael Drayton." <u>Literature</u>, NS,
    no. 31 (11 August), pp. 107-109.
        Traces influence of Daniel on Drayton's sonnets.

5   DANIEL, SAMUEL, and MICHAEL DRAYTON. <u>A Selection from the</u>
    <u>Poetry of Samuel Daniel & Michael Drayton</u>. Edited by
    H[enry] C[harles] Beeching. London: J. M. Dent, 219 pp.

1899

Provides annotated, modernized selections from Daniel's
works (pp. 1-56). In "Introduction" (pp. ix-xxi), compares
the careers and works of the two poets. See 1899.2,
1899.3, 1899.8, 1899.9, and 1899.11. Reviewed in Anon.,
Athenaeum, no. 3751 (16 September 1899), pp. 379-80;
1899.1.

6   EWIG, WILHELM. "Shakespeare's Lucrece: Eine litterarhisto-
     rische Untersuchung, III." Anglia, 22: 393-455.
         In Anhang I ("Shakespeare und Daniel's Complaint of
     Rosamond," pp. 436-48), examines the influence of Rosamond
     on Lucrece; gives particular attention to parallels in
     language and style.

7   HARTSHORNE, ALBERT. "Samuel Daniel and Anne Clifford, Count-
     ess of Pembroke, Dorset, and Montgomery." Archaeological
     Journal, 56: 187-210.
         Provides a general overview of Daniel's life and a brief
     critical assessment of his works. Discusses his retirement
     to "Cliffords Farm" (with a description of the remains) and
     his position from 1596 to 1610 as tutor to Anne Clifford.

8   PRIDEAUX, W. F. "Daniel's Sonnets to Delia." N&Q, 100
     (5 August), 101-103.
         Criticizes Beeching for not following the 1592 edition
     ("the oldest and purest text"); discusses several of
     Daniel's revisions and offers corrections and emendations
     (especially "Pant in" for "Paint on" in Delia 9) to Beech-
     ing's edition (1899.5). See 1899.2, 1899.3, 1899.9, and
     1899.11.

9   _____. "Daniel's Sonnets to Delia." N&Q, 100 (9 September),
     209-10.
         Responds to Beeching (1899.3), defending some of his
     earlier emendations (1899.8); responds to C. C. B.
     (1899.2), arguing that the 1591 text is not "authoritative."
     See 1899.11.

10   SMALL, ROSCOE ADDISON. The Stage-Quarrel between Ben Jonson
     and the So-Called Poetasters. Forschungen zur Englischen
     Sprache und Litteratur, vol. 1. Breslau: M. & H.
     Marcus, 214 pp.
         In revision of 1897.6 argues, contra Fleay (1891.1) and
     Penniman (1897.4), that Daniel took no part in the quarrel.
     Examines Daniel's relationship with Jonson and refutes
     Fleay's identification of Daniel with various characters

in Jonson's plays, his identification of Delia with Elizabeth Carey, and his theory that "Daniel and Drayton had a
violent quarrel with regard to the patronage of" the
Countess of Bedford (pp. 181-97, passim).

11   THISELTON, ALFRED E. "Daniel's Sonnets to Delia." N&Q, 100
      (7 October), 293.
          Suggests possible meaning of both "Paint" and "Pant" in
      Delia 9. See 1899.2, 1899.3, 1899.8, and 1899.9.

12   THORNDIKE, ASHLEY H. "The Pastoral Element in the English
      Drama before 1605." MLN, 14 (April), 114-23.
          Surveys pastoral elements in royal entertainments and
      the public theater to argue that in Queen's Arcadia Daniel
      "can hardly have seemed wholly an innovator."

13   WARD, ADOLPHUS WILLIAM. A History of English Dramatic Liter-
      ature to the Death of Queen Anne. Vol. II. Revised
      edition. London: Macmillan; New York: Macmillan, 778 pp.
          Expands his earlier discussion of Daniel (1875.1), but
      retains essentially the same estimate of his dramatic
      works (pp. 617-23).

1900

*1   KARIGL, FERDINAND. "Samuel Daniels dramatische Werke."
      Ph.D. dissertation, University of Vienna.
          Cited in Gernot U. Gabel and Gisela R. Gabel, Disserta-
      tions in English and American Literature: Theses Accepted
      by Austrian, French, and Swiss Universities, 1875-1970
      (Hamburg: Gernot Gabel, 1977), p. 23, item 281.

*2   LESTER, JOHN ASHBY. "Connections between the Drama of France
      and Great Britain, Particularly in the Elizabethan Period."
      Ph.D. dissertation, Harvard University.
          Discusses Cleopatra.

1901

1   [CREIGHTON, CHARLES]. "Shakespeare and the Earl of Pembroke,
     I: The Key to the Sonnets Enigma." Blackwood's Magazine,
     169 (May), 668-83.
          Identifies Daniel as the Rival Poet and argues that "the
     rivalry was really a struggle to gain the Pembroke interest
     in the competition for the office of Poet-Laureate and its

1901

substantial pension, vacant on the death of Spenser."
Finds "sufficient evidence in Daniel's own works that he
became, in effect, the Laureate in 1599." Revised 1904.3.

1902

1   BROTANEK, RUDOLF. Die englischen Maskenspiele. WBEP, vol.
15. Vienna: Wilhelm Braumüller, 387 pp.
Provides general critical estimate of Vision of the
Twelve Goddesses and Tethys' Festival, and compare them
to Jonson's masques. Comments on the antagonism between
Daniel and Jonson (pp. 130-33, passim).

2   LANIER, SIDNEY. Shakspere and His Forerunners: Studies in
Elizabethan Poetry and Its Development from Early English.
Vol. I. New York: Doubleday, Page, 348 pp.
In examining "The Sonnet-Makers from Surrey to Shakspere" (chapters 7-10, pp. 160-270), classes Daniel as one
of the "four . . . greatest artists among all the sonnet-
writers." Offers an appreciative discussion of Delia,
stressing Daniel's manliness and dignity (pp. 216-25,
passim).

3   LUTZ, ERNST. Samuel Daniel's historisches Gedicht "The Civil
Wars between the Houses of Lancaster and York" und Shake-
speare's historische Dramen. Programm zum Jahresbericht
der Königlichen Realschule Memmingen. Memmingen: Jos.
Feiner, 38 pp.
Traces Daniel's sources and provides a detailed com-
parison of Daniel's treatment of historical events with
Shakespeare's in his history plays.

4   MOULTON, CHARLES WELLS. "Samuel Daniel," in his edition of
The Library of Literary Criticism of English and American
Authors, I: 680-1638. Buffalo: Moulton, pp. 611-17.
Prints extracts from criticism, sixteenth to nineteenth
centuries.

5   PROBST, ALBERT. Samuel Daniel's "Civil Wars between the Two
Houses of Lancaster and York" und Michael Drayton's "Barons'
Wars:" Eine Quellenstudie. Ph.D. dissertation, Kaiser-
Wilhelms-Universität. Strasbourg: M. DuMont-Schauberg,
134 pp.
Provides overview of Daniel's sources (particularly
the chronicles and Mirror for Magistrates) and the influ-
ence of Civil Wars on Shakespeare's history plays. Exam-
ines Daniel's metaphoric language, comparing it with
Spenser's in The Faerie Queene.

6 SAINTSBURY, GEORGE [EDWARD BATEMAN]. <u>A History of Criticism
   and Literary Taste in Europe from the Earliest Texts to
   the Present Day, II: From the Renaissance to the Decline
   of Eighteenth Century Orthodoxy</u>. Edinburgh: William
   Blackwood & Sons, 611 pp.
       Discusses <u>Defense of Rhyme</u> as an answer to Campion's
   <u>Observations</u>. Praises Daniel's "combination of solid good
   sense with eager poetic sentiment, of sound scholarship
   with wide-glancing intelligence" (pp. 189-91). <u>See</u> 1911.5.

<u>1903</u>

1 COURTHOPE, W[ILLIAM] J[OHN]. <u>A History of English Poetry,
   III: The Intellectual Conflict of the Seventeenth Century;
   Decadent Influence of the Feudal Monarch; Growth of the
   National Genius</u>. London: Macmillan, 565 pp.
       Devotes chapter 2 ("Spenser's Successors," pp. 9-26) to
   Daniel. Provides chronological overview of his life and
   works; discusses contemporary opinions of his poetry;
   compares him to Wordsworth, noting that, like him, Daniel
   was more philosopher than poet. Examines the English
   humanism which informs Daniel's works and observes that
   he lacks "individuality in his style of metrical expression."

2 CROLL, MORRIS W[ILLIAM]. <u>The Works of Fulke Greville</u>. Philadelphia: J. B. Lippincott, 59 pp. [Also submitted as
   Ph.D. dissertation, University of Pennsylvania, 1901.]
       Discusses friendship between Daniel and Greville and
   relationships between various works, especially <u>Philotas</u>
   and <u>Alaham</u> and <u>Mustapha</u> (passim).

3 DANIEL, F. "Samuel Daniel." <u>N&Q</u>, 108 (17 October), 308-309.
       Suggests that parish registers of Nynehead be checked
   for entry of Daniel's birth.

4 ERSKINE, JOHN. <u>The Elizabethan Lyric: A Study</u>. Columbia
   University Studies in English, vol. 2. New York: Macmillan, 362 pp. [Also submitted as Ph.D. dissertation,
   Columbia University.]
       Discusses <u>Delia</u> in a "chronological survey of the Eng-
   lish lyric in Elizabeth's time." Identifies Delia as the
   Countess of Pembroke and attributes the tone of the work
   to Daniel's need "to dwell on her intellectual and spirit-
   ual beauty rather than on physical charms." Briefly discusses Daniel's themes and use of the English sonnet form
   as well as influences on <u>Delia</u> (pp. 134-40).

1903

5   GREG, W[ALTER] W[ILSON]. "Hymen's Triumph and the Drummond
     MS." Modern Language Quarterly, 6: 59-64.
          Identifies manuscript as presentation copy to Jean
     Drummond, bride of Robert Ker of Cessfurd, whose wedding
     the play celebrated. Points out that the manuscript rep-
     resents an early draft of the work and discusses variants
     between the manuscript and printed versions.

6   HAZLITT, W[ILLIAM] CAREW. Bibliographical Collections and
     Notes on Early English Literature Made during the Years
     1893-1903. London: Bernard Quaritch, 450 pp.
          Provides additions and corrections to 1867.1, 1876.2,
     1882.1, and 1892.3 (p. 96).

7   MAIBERGER, MAX. Studien über den Einfluss frankreichs auf
     die elisabethanische Literatur, erster Teil: Die Lyrik
     in der zweiten Hälfte des XVI. Jahrhunderts. Ph.D. dis-
     sertation, Ludwig-Maximilians-Universität, Munich.
     Frankfurt: Knauer, 55 pp.
          Discusses Delia in an overview of French influence on
     Elizabethan sonnets (pp. 26-30, passim).

8   OWEN, DANIEL E[DWARD]. Relations of the Elizabethan Sonnet
     Sequences to Earlier English Verse, Especially That of
     Chaucer. Ph.D. dissertation, University of Pennsylvania.
     Philadelphia: Chilton Printing Co., 34 pp.
          Draws on Delia in analyzing resemblances in conceits
     and in subject matter and its treatment between Elizabethan
     sonnets and Middle English love poetry (passim).

9   PRIDEAUX, W. F. "Daniel's Delia, 1592." Athenaeum, no.
     3952 (25 July), pp. 126-27.
          Argues "that in 1592 two editions of 'Delia' were pub-
     lished, and three editions of 'The Complaint of Rosamond.'"
     Provides bibliographical description and locates copies of
     each. Corrects Grosart's description of editions in
     1885.1. See 1904.7.

10   ZUBERBÜHLER, ARNOLD. Daniel's "Civile Wars between the Two
     Houses of Lancaster and Yorke" und seine historischen
     Quellen. Ph.D. dissertation, University of Zurich.
     Zurich: Meyer & Hendess, 91 pp.
          Provides book-by-book analysis of Daniel's sources.

1904

1 ANDERS, H[ENRY] R. D. Shakespeare's Books: A Dissertation
on Shakespeare's Reading and the Immediate Sources of His
Works. Schriften der Deutschen Shakespeare-Gesellschaft,
1. Berlin: Georg Reimer, 336 pp.
Examines influence of Rosamond, Delia, and Civil Wars
(1595) on Shakespeare's works. Asserts that Cleopatra
had no influence on Shakespeare (pp. 85-89, passim).

2 [ARBER, EDWARD, ed.] Elizabethan Sonnets: Newly Arranged
and Indexed. 2 volumes. Introduction by Sidney Lee.
Westminster: Archibald Constable, 426, 450 pp.
Reprints Delia (II, 115-36) from 1880.1 and sonnets
published with Astrophel and Stella (I, 88-102) from
1877.1. In "Introduction" (I, ix-cx), devoted to "illus-
trat[ing] the close dependence of the Elizabethan sonnet
on foreign models," traces Daniel's sources. Gives particular attention to . . . borrowings from Ronsard, Du Bellay,
and (especially) Desportes. Argues that "Delia is a mere
shadow of a shadow--a mere embodiment of what Petrarch
wrote of Laura, and Ronsard wrote of Marie, and the other
ladies of his poetic fancy." See 1934.4.

3 CREIGHTON, C[HARLES]. Shakespeare's Story of His Life. London: Grant Richards, 459 pp.
Incorporates, "with alterations and additions," 1901.1.
Identifies Daniel as the S. D. who "edited" Willoby His
Avisa, as the Master of the ship in Shakespeare's Tempest,
and as Agamemnon in Troilus and Cressida. Also believes
that Musophilus influenced Troilus and Cressida (pp. 32-
37, passim).

4 DANIEL, SAMUEL. A Defence of Ryme, in Elizabethan Critical
Essays. Vol. II. Edited by G[eorge] Gregory Smith.
Oxford: Clarendon Press, pp. 356-84.
Provides annotated reprint of 1603 edition. In "Introduction" (I, xi-xcii), refers frequently to Daniel in an
examination of the concerns, characteristics, and sources
of Elizabethan criticism. Discusses how he "foreshadows
the modern conception of historical process in literature"
and how Defense of Rhyme represents a "movement in the
direction of romantic taste." See 1977.10.

5 [ELTON, OLIVER]. "Literary Fame: A Renaissance Study."
Otia Merseiana, 4: 24-52.
Discusses Musophilus, which he characterizes as "a kind
of judicial charge to clear the character of Fame," in a

1904

survey of the treatment of literary fame in Renaissance
literature. Revised 1907.1; reprinted 1924.3.

6   MOORMAN, F[REDERIC] W[ILLIAM]. "Shakespeare's History-Plays
and Daniel's <u>Civile Wars</u>." <u>Shakespeare-Jahrbuch</u>, 40: 69-
83.
    Compares <u>Civil Wars</u> and <u>Richard II</u> to "gain an insight
into the way in which the prose story of the Chroniclers
was altered and embellished in order to fulfil the requirements of an historic play and an historic poem."
Finds no influence between the two works. Examines
Shakespeare's use of Daniel in <u>Henry IV</u>.

7   SHIPMAN, CAROLYN. "Daniel's <u>Delia</u>, 1592." <u>Athenaeum</u>,
no. 3975 (2 January), p. 18.
    Offers additions to Prideaux's discussion of editions
of <u>Delia</u> and <u>Rosamond</u> (1903.9).

8   STOTSENBURG, JOHN H[AWLEY]. <u>An Impartial Study of the Shakespeare Title</u>. Louisville: John P. Morton, 542 pp.
    In chapter 11 ("Daniel's Letter to Egerton Does not
Refer to Shaksper," pp. 108-15), argues that the phrase
"the author of plays now daily presented" refers to Drayton, not Shakespeare.

1905

1   LAIDLER, JOSEPHINE. "A History of Pastoral Drama in England
until 1700." <u>Englische Studien</u>, 35: 193-257.
    In sections on <u>Queen's Arcadia</u> and <u>Hymen's Triumph</u>,
discusses Italian influence--particularly that of Guarini
and Tasso--on Daniel.

1906

1   CASE, R[OBERT] H[OPE]. "Introduction," in his edition of
William Shakespeare's <u>The Tragedy of Antony and Cleopatra</u>.
Arden Shakespeare. London: Methuen, pp. vii-xxvi.
    Traces parallels between 1607 <u>Cleopatra</u> and <u>Antony and
Cleopatra</u> to suggest "that Daniel re-wrote his play because
he had seen another treatment of the theme, namely,
Shakespeare's." Observes that the revisions make Daniel's
play "more dramatic" (pp. vii-xii). (Maurice Roy Ridley,
in his revised edition [Cambridge: Harvard University
Press, 1954], retains Case's "Introduction," making no
revisions in the discussion of <u>Cleopatra</u>.)

2   DANIEL, SAMUEL. "Samuel Daniel," in <u>Thomas Lodge, Songs and
    Sonnets; Robert Greene, Lyrics from Romances, etc.; Samuel
    Daniel, Selected Verse</u>. Edited by H. Kelsey White. Pem-
    broke Booklets, 1st ser., 6. Hull: J. R. Tutin, pp. 49-
    64.
        Provides modernized selection from Daniel's poetry. In
    "Prefatory Note" (pp. 5-6), identifies the "'common denomi-
    nator'" among the three poets as "the lyric note which
    pervades" their verse.

3   GREG, WALTER W[ILSON]. <u>Pastoral Poetry & Pastoral Drama:
    A Literary Inquiry, with Special Reference to the Pre-
    Restoration Stage in England</u>. London: A. H. Bullen,
    476 pp.
        In chapter 4 ("Dramatic Origins of the English Pastoral
    Drama," pp. 215-63), examines the influence of Guarini and
    Tasso on <u>Queen's Arcadia</u> and <u>Hymen's Triumph</u>. Discusses
    the historical importance of the works ("[w]ith Daniel
    begins and ends in English literature the dominant influ-
    ence of the Italian pastoral drama"). Characterizes
    <u>Queen's Arcadia</u>, the lesser of the two plays, as "a patch-
    work of motives and situations borrowed from the Italian,
    and pieced together with more or less ingenuity." Finds
    <u>Hymen's Triumph</u>, the better work, "an original composi-
    tion," but criticizes Daniel for taking "himself and his
    subject with a distressing seriousness wholly unsuited to
    the style." Examines Daniel's style in both plays. Con-
    cludes that in his pastoral dramas Daniel is a "poet of
    considerable taste, of great sweetness and some real feel-
    ing, but deficient in passion, in power of conception and
    strength of execution" (pp. 251-63).

4   JERRAM, C. S. "'Rime' v. 'Rhyme.'" <u>N&Q</u>, 114 (18 August),
    132.
        Notes Daniel's use of "rhyme" in <u>Civil Wars</u> and <u>Muso-
    philus</u> in response to a query by Walter W[illiam] Skeat
    (4 August, pp. 90-91) about the earliest use of "rhyme."
    See John T. Curry (8 September, pp. 192-95) and 1906.5.

5   PRIDEAUX, W. F. "'Rime' v. 'Rhyme.'" <u>N&Q</u>, 114 (22 Septem-
    ber), 233.
        In response to John T. Curry (8 September, pp. 192-95)
    corrects Jerram (1906.5) by noting that Daniel uses "rime"
    not "rhyme."

6   SMITH, G[EORGE] C[HARLES] MOORE. "Seneca, Jonson, Daniel,
    and Wordsworth." <u>MLR</u>, 1 (April), 232.
        Identifies Daniel's source in Seneca for "To the Count-
    ess of Cumberland," 11. 98-99.

1907

1   ELTON, OLIVER. "Literary Fame: A Renaissance Note," in his
    Modern Studies. London: Edward Arnold, pp. 37-66.
        In revision of 1904.5, makes only minor stylistic
    changes in discussion of Daniel. See 1924.3.

2   PRIDEAUX, W. F. "Daniel's Civil Wars, 1595." N&Q, 116
    (23 November), 405-406.
        Provides bibliographical particulars on copy of 1595
    edition of Civil Wars, noting variations from the descrip-
    tion in 1893.1.

1908

1   [COLERIDGE, SAMUEL TAYLOR]. Coleridge's Literary Criticism.
    Edited by J[ohn] W[illiam] Mackail. London: Henry
    Frowde, 286 pp.
        Reprints various passages on Daniel from Coleridge's
    writings (passim).

2   CRAWFORD, CHARLES. "Englands Parnassus, 1600." N&Q, 118
    (2 May), 341-43; (23 May), 401-403; 119 (4 July), 4-6;
    (1 August), 84-85; (5 September), 182-83; (3 October),
    262-63; (7 November), 362-63; (5 December), 444-45; 120
    (2 January 1909), 4-5; (13 February), 123-24; (13 March),
    204-205; (10 April), 283-85; (15 May), 383-84; (5 June),
    443-45; (26 June), 502-503.
        Identifies several passages from Daniel's works, cor-
    recting and supplementing Collier's edition (London,
    1867).

3   DANIEL, SAMUEL, and MICHAEL DRAYTON. Daniel's "Delia" and
    Drayton's "Idea." Edited by Arundell [James Kennedy]
    Esdaile. King's Classics. London: Chatto and Windus,
    219 pp.
        Reprints 1623 edition of Delia (pp. 1-66) and provides
    "Bibliography of the Early Editions" (pp. 145-50). In
    "Introduction" (pp. ix-xlii), places Delia in the context
    of the early history of the sonnet. Praises the work "for
    the easy melody of the verse" and for Daniel's ability to
    give "expression to a poignant sense of the pathos of
    fair things doomed to age and death."

4 KABEL, PAUL. <u>Die Sage von Heinrich V. bis zu Shakespeare.</u>
   Palaestra, vol. 69. Berlin: Mayer & Müller, 148 pp.
   Discusses treatment of Henry V in <u>Civil Wars</u> (1595) in
   an analysis of historical and literary treatments of the
   king. Examines influence of Daniel's work on Shakespeare's
   representation of Henry (pp. 91-94, passim).

5 KASTNER, L[EON] E[MILE]. "The Elizabethan Sonneteers and the
   French Poets." <u>MLR</u>, 3 (April), 268-77.
   Traces influence of Du Bellay's <u>L'Olive</u> and other French
   and Italian sonneteers on <u>Delia</u>. Argues that <u>Delia</u> 14,
   19, 23, and "The only bird alone that Nature frames" (from
   the sonnets published with <u>Astrophel and Stella</u>) "are re-
   produced almost verbatim" from Du Bellay.

6 LEE, SIDNEY. "The Elizabethan Sonnet," in <u>The Cambridge History of English Literature, III: Renascence and Reforma-
   tion</u>. Edited by A[dolphus] W[illiam] Ward and A[lfred]
   R[ayney] Waller. Cambridge: Cambridge University Press,
   pp. 247-72.
   Discusses <u>Delia</u> as it exemplifies the sonneteers'
   "practice of literal translation." Finds Daniel's "servil-
   ity" to Desportes "startling."

7 SAINTSBURY, GEORGE [EDWARD BATEMAN]. <u>A History of English
   Prosody from the Twelfth Century to the Present Day, II:
   From Shakespeare to Crabbe</u>. London: Macmillan; New York:
   Macmillan, 593 pp.
   Comments briefly on Daniel's prosody (noting "he was
   almost an impeccable metrist and rhythmist") and places
   <u>Defense of Rhyme</u> in the context of works on prosody
   (pp. 104-105, 185-87).

8 SCHELLING, FELIX E[MMANUEL]. <u>Elizabethan Drama, 1558-1642:
   A History of the Drama in England from the Accession of
   Queen Elizabeth to the Closing of the Theaters, to Which
   Is Prefixed a Résumé of the Earlier Drama from Its Be-
   ginnings</u>. 2 volumes. Boston: Houghton, Mifflin, 652,
   697 pp.
   Provides general discussion of Daniel's plays under the
   appropriate heads (pastoral, Senecan, masque) and examines
   Daniel's relationship with Jonson (passim).

9 UPHAM, ALFRED HORATIO. <u>The French Influence in English Literature from the Accession of Elizabeth to the Restoration</u>.
   Columbia University Studies in Comparative Literature.
   New York: Columbia University Press, 570 pp. [Also submitted as Ph.D. dissertation, Columbia University.]

1909

Discusses French influence (particularly that of Scève,
Desportes, and Du Bellay) on Delia and Daniel's relationship with the Countess of Pembroke (pp. 113-20, passim).

1909

1   BALLWEG, OSKAR. Das klassizistische Drama zur Zeit Shake-
    speares. BNL, vol. 1, no. 3. Heidelberg: Carl Winter,
    126 pp.
       In chapter 3 ("Samuel Daniel," pp. 13-34), discusses
    classical elements in Cleopatra and Philotas. Traces in-
    fluence of Plutarch, Jodelle, and Garnier on Cleopatra,
    and examines political undertone of Philotas.

2   BOAS, F[REDERICK] S[AMUEL, and WALTER WILSON GREG]. "James I
    at Oxford in 1605," in [Malone Society] Collections.
    Vol. 1, part 3. Edited by W[alter] W[ilson] Greg.
    [Oxford:] Oxford University Press for The Malone Society,
    pp. 247-59.
       Transcribes document from Oxford University Archives
    (P. Fasic. 5. 3.) which lists properties and garments
    purchased for plays (including Queen's Arcadia) given
    during James's visit.

3   CHAMBERS, E[DMUND] K[ERCHEVER]. "Court Performances under
    James the First." MLR, 4 (January), 153-66.
       Discusses events surrounding Daniel's tenure as licenser
    to the Children of the Queen's Revels. Suggests that the
    production of Philotas in 1604 was one of the "indiscre-
    tions" of the company.

4   CHILD, HAROLD H[ANNYNGTON]. "Robert Southwell; Samuel
    Daniel," in The Cambridge History of English Literature,
    IV: Prose and Poetry, Sir Thomas North to Michael Drayton.
    Edited by A[dolphus] W[illiam] Ward and A[lfred] R[ayney]
    Waller. Cambridge: Cambridge University Press, pp. 127-
    40.
       Discusses Daniel as the representative of "humanistic
    and historical" poetry and as "the leading example of the
    graver, reflective poetry" of the 1590s. Provides over-
    view of his career, with critical estimates of Rosamond
    ("Daniel in his most characteristic mood"), Musophilus,
    and, in particular, Civil Wars. Examines Daniel's style,
    suggesting that he "did more to establish [English] . . .
    as a classical and polite tongue than has, perhaps, been
    commonly recognised." Concludes that Daniel "was eminent as
    a poet, as Matthew Arnold was eminent, because he was first
    of all a critic of life and letters" (pp. 132-40).

5   REYHER, PAUL. Les Masques anglais: Étude sur les ballets et
    la vie de cour en Angleterre (1512-1640). Paris:
    Hachette, 573 pp.
        Draws frequently on Daniel's masques in a comprehensive
    analysis of the form and its history (passim).

6   RUUTZ-REES, C. "Some Debts of Samuel Daniel to Du Bellay."
    MLN, 24 (May), 134-37.
        Examines influence of Du Bellay's L'Olive on Delia 14,
    18, 38, and "The only bird alone that Nature frames" (pub-
    lished with Astrophel and Stella). Concludes "that Dan-
    iel's admiration of Du Bellay appears rather in closeness
    of imitation in special cases, than in the diffusion
    throughout his poems of any general influence."

7   SHEAVYN, PHOEBE. The Literary Profession in the Elizabethan
    Age. Publications of the University of Manchester, Eng-
    lish Series, 1. Manchester: Manchester University Press,
    234 pp.
        Draws frequently on Daniel in analyzing various aspects
    of the profession of letters (passim). Revised 1967.16.

1910

1   LEE, SIDNEY. The French Renaissance in England: An Account
    of the Literary Relations of England and France in the
    Sixteenth Century. New York: Charles Scribner's Sons,
    518 pp.
        Examines Daniel's debts in Delia and Cleopatra to French
    writers; comes near to calling Daniel a plagiarist (passim).

1A PORTER, CHARLOTTE. "Introduction," in her edition of William
    Shakespeare's The Life and Death of King Richard the
    Second. First Folio Edition. New York: Thomas Y. Crow-
    ell, pp. vii-xvii.
        Demonstrates that White (1863.1) was mistaken in his
    identification of a "second edition" of Civil Wars
    (pp. xiv-xvii).

2   SCHELLING, FELIX E[MMANUEL]. English Literature during the
    Lifetime of Shakespeare. New York: Henry Holt, 501 pp.
        Provides general critical overview of Daniel, particu-
    larly as sonneteer, historical poet, and dramatist (passim).
    (The discussion of Daniel is essentially the same in the
    revised edition [New York: Henry Holt, 1927].)

1910

3   WESTCOTT, ALLAN F. "Was Samuel Daniel an Italian?" <u>Nation</u>,
    91 (22 December), 603-604.
        Suggests on the basis of entries in the Exchequer Ac-
    counts and Daniel's travels, works, and friendships that
    he was "an Italian by parentage" though "an Englishman by
    allegiance and perhaps by birth." Further suggests "that
    the stylistic purity of 'well-languaged' Daniel is that
    of a writer for whom English was not strictly the mother
    tongue."

1911

1   DANIEL, SAMUEL. <u>Daniel's "The Tragedie of Cleopatra" nach dem
    Drucke von 1611</u>. Edited by M[ax] Lederer. Materialien
    zur Kunde des Älteren Englischen Dramas, 31. Louvain:
    A. Uystpruyst, 115 pp.
        Provides critical edition based on 1611 edition. In
    "Einleitung" (pp. ix-xvi), discusses publishing history,
    relationship among editions, Daniel's use of North's
    translation of Plutarch, and metrics. Reprinted 1963.5.

2   GRAY, THOMAS. "Samuel Daniel," in his <u>Essays and Criticisms</u>.
    Edited by Clark Sutherland Northup. Belles-Lettres
    Series, Section IV: Literary Criticism and Critical
    Theory. Boston: D. C. Heath, pp. 118-21.
        Prints Gray's manuscript essay, which was to be part of
    a projected history of English poetry. <u>See</u> 1854.1.

3   LEGOUIS, ÉMILE [HYACINTHE]. "Poésie historique de la
    Renaissance--Samuel Daniel (1562-1619)." <u>Revue des Cours
    et Conférences</u>, 2d ser., 19 (23 March), 72-79.
        In a general overview of Daniel's works, stresses the
    clarity and classical nature of his language and discusses
    his patriotism. Calls <u>Civil Wars</u> his great work.

4   PRIDEAUX, W. F. "Daniel's <u>Whole Workes</u>, 1623." <u>N&Q</u>, 124
    (28 October), 344-45.
        Offers bibliographical information, particularly on the
    portrait which is sometimes present.

5   SAINTSBURY, GEORGE [EDWARD BATEMAN]. <u>A History of English
    Criticism: Being the English Chapters of "A History of
    Criticism and Literary Taste in Europe" Revised, Adapted,
    and Supplemented</u>. Edinburgh: William Blackwood & Sons,
    567 pp.
        Reprints section on Daniel from 1902.6 (<u>see</u> pp. 72-74,
    passim).

1912

1   DIXON, W[ILLIAM] MACNEILE. English Epic and Heroic Poetry.
London: J. M. Dent; New York: E. P. Dutton, 351 pp.
    Argues that Daniel fails as a heroic poet because he
lacks "imagination" and cannot maintain continuity of
"style." Characterizes him as "one of the founders in
truth of the classical style in English, a forerunner of
the Augustans, a correct poet before Pope" (pp. 176–80,
passim).

2   KASTNER, L[EON] E[MILE]. "The Italian Sources of Daniel's
Delia." MLR, 7 (April), 153–56.
    Identifies Daniel's use of Guarini, Tasso, other minor
Italian poets, and Desportes as sources. Focuses on Delia
27, 34, and 42. Provides additions and corrections to
1898.1 and 1882.2.

3   MILLER, GEORGE MOREY. The Historical Point of View in Elizabethan Criticism. Ph.D. dissertaion, University of Heidelberg. Heidelberg: Carl Winter, 69 pp.
    Discusses influences on Defense of Rhyme and provides a
running synopsis to illustrate "the historical point of
view" in the work. Concludes: "Daniel not only gave the
death blow to the craze for foreign meters, but he also
re-established the credit of the Middle Ages. He affirmed
a century before Du Bos that delight is the one test for
poetry, and he showed finally that any successful poetry
can only be composed in harmony with the spirit of its
own age and its own national tradition and character.
With this assertion of a relative standard of judgment he
exhibited a tolerance wholly in keeping with such a breadth
of view. With Daniel, then, Elizabethan criticism reached
both its end and its climax" (pp. 57–65). Reprinted in
1913.3.

4   REDGRAVE, GILBERT R[ICHARD]. "Daniel and the Emblem Literature." Transactions of the Bibliographical Society, 11
(March), 39–58.
    Provides running commentary on Worthy Tract in "showing
what was understood by the Emblem and the Impresa among
our early writers on this subject." Comments briefly on
Daniel's possible sources.

5   REED, EDWARD BLISS. English Lyrical Poetry: From Its Origins
to the Present Time. New Haven: Yale University Press;
London: Oxford University Press, 626 pp.
    In a history of the lyric, offers a general critical es-
timate of Delia, with comments on Daniel's style (pp. 159–62).

1913

1 BUBERT, ALEXANDER. <u>Samuel Daniels "Cleopatra" u[nd] "Philotas"</u>
<u>und Samuel Brandons "The Virtuous Octavia."</u> Ph.D. disserta-
tion, Königlichen Albertus-Universität, Königsberg.
Königsberg: Karg and Manneck, 95 pp.
    Provides act-by-act analysis of sources of <u>Cleopatra</u>
and <u>Philotas</u>, examines the question of influence of Senecan
drama on the two plays, and discusses the influence of
<u>Cleopatra</u> on Brandon's <u>The Virtuous Octavia</u>.

*2 FRANK, RUDOLPH. "Samuel Daniel und seine Stellung in der
englischen Literatur auf einer Analyse und kritischen
Besprechung seiner Werke." Ph.D. dissertation, University
of Vienna.
    Manuscript dissertation; cited in Gernot U. Gabel and
Gisela R. Gabel, <u>Dissertations in English and American</u>
<u>Literature: Theses Accepted by Austrian, French, and Swiss</u>
<u>Universities, 1875-1970</u> (Hamburg: Gernot Gabel, 1977),
p. 23, item 283.

3 MILLER, G[EORGE] M[OREY]. <u>The Historical Point of View in</u>
<u>English Literary Criticism from 1570-1770</u>. AF, 35.
Heidelberg: Carl Winter, 164 pp.
    Includes reprint of 1912.3; <u>see</u> pp. 57-65.

4 PENNIMAN, JOSIAH H[ARMAR]. "Introduction," in his edition of
<u>"Poetaster" by Ben Jonson and "Satiromastix" by Thomas Dek-</u>
<u>ker</u>. Belles-Lettres Series, Section III: English Drama.
Boston: D. C. Heath, pp. xiii-lxviii.
    Argues for the following identifications with Daniel:
Matthew (<u>Every Man in His Humor</u>), Gullio (<u>Return from</u>
<u>Parnassus</u>), Brisk (<u>Every Man out of His Humor</u>), Emulo
(<u>Patient Grissil</u>), and especially Hedon (<u>Cynthia's Revels</u>).

1914

1 MÜLLER, AMANDUS. <u>Studien zu Samuel Daniels Tragödie "Cleo-</u>
<u>patra": Quellenfrage und literarischer Charakter</u>. Ph.D.
dissertation, University of Leipzig. Borna-Leipzig:
Robert Noske, 67 pp.
    Provides detailed analysis of sources; examines Daniel's
handling of time, place, and action, his use of the chorus,
and his treatment of dramatic speech.

2 ROBERTSON, JOHN MACKINNON. Elizabethan Literature. Home
   University Library of Modern Knowledge, 89. New York:
   Henry Holt; London: Williams and Norgate, 256 pp.
       In chapter 7 ("Poetry after Spenser," pp. 140-75),
   offers a general appreciation of Daniel (with emphasis on
   his style); notes that "he is at his best in gravely im-
   passioned argument" (pp. 153-55).

3 THOMPSON, GUY ANDREW. Elizabethan Criticism of Poetry.
   Ph.D. dissertation, University of Chicago, 1912. Menasha,
   Wis.: Collegiate Press (George Banta), 222 pp.
       Draws frequently on Defense of Rhyme in topical analysis
   of major concerns of Elizabethan critics (passim).

1915

1 HÜDEPOHL, ADOLF. Die tragische Ironie in der englischen
   Tragödie und Historie vor Shakespeare. Ph.D. dissertation,
   Friedrichs-Universität, Halle--Wittenberg. Halle:
   Ehrhardt Karras, 173 pp.
       Comments on the influence of Jodelle on Cleopatra and
   points out examples of tragic irony in the play (pp. 120-
   24).

2 KAUN, ERNST. Konventionelles in den elisabethanischen
   Sonetten mit Berücksichtigung der französischen und
   italienischen Quellen. Ph.D. dissertation, University of
   Greifswald, 1914. Greifswald: Hans Adler, 122 pp.
       Includes several examples from Delia in a classification
   of conventional elements in Elizabethan sonnets. Arranges
   passages under the following categories (which are then
   subdivided): praise of mistress's beauty, poet's assertion of his love, mistress's refusal of love, psychological
   condition of the unrequited lover, poet's attempt to ex-
   tricate himself from the relationship, poet's censure of
   his mistress, and parting (passim).

3 SMITH, ROBERT METCALF. Froissart and the English Chronicle
   Play. Columbia University Studies in English and Comparative Literature. New York: Columbia University Press,
   179 pp. [Also submitted as Ph.D. dissertation, Columbia
   University.]
       In chapter 8 ("Daniel's Civil Wars," pp. 131-42), exam-
   ines Daniel's use of Froissart as the main source of books
   I-II. In chapter 9 ("Daniel's Civil Wars and Shakespeare's
   Richard II," pp. 143-57), argues that Shakespeare was indebted to Daniel.

1916

1   ALDEN, RAYMOND MACDONALD, ed. The Sonnets of Shakespeare:
    From the Quarto of 1609 with Variorum Readings and Com-
    mentary. Boston: Houghton, Mifflin, 562 pp.
        Provides overview of scholarship on identification of
    Daniel with the Rival Poet and on the influence of Delia
    on the Sonnets ("the hypothesis of Daniel's influence is
    not improbable"). Cites in the variorum notes several
    parallels between Daniel's poems and the Sonnets (passim).

2   CLARK, J[OHN] SCOTT. "Samuel Daniel (1562-1619)," in his
    A Study of English and American Writers, III: A Laboratory
    Method. With additions by John Price Odell. Chicago:
    Row, Peterson, pp. 27-30.
        In a work designed to assist teachers in "determining
    the particular and distinctive features of a writer's
    style," classifies previous critical opinions on the
    "distinctive characteristics" of Daniel's style ("Pure
    Diction," "Gentleness--Dignity--Mildness," "Metrical
    Skill," and "Didacticism--Tediousness").

3   REINECKE, KURT. Der Chor in den wichtigsten Tragödien der
    englischen Renaissance-Literatur. Ph.D. dissertation,
    University of Leipzig. Leipzig: Oscar Brandstetter, 96
    pp.
        Analyzes characteristics and function of the chorus in
    Cleopatra and Philotas (passim).

4   SELLERS, H[ARRY]. "Samuel Daniel: Additions to the Text."
    MLR, 11 (January), 28-32.
        Draws attention to several works not printed in modern
    editions: "A Letter Written to a Worthy Countess,"
    probably to Anne Clifford and printed in 1623 Works; "To
    the Right Noble Anne Lady Clifford" from Certain Small
    Works, 1607; "To Fulke Greville," prefatory poem to
    Musophilus in Certain Small Works, 1611; additional lines
    in Musophilus in Poetical Essays, 1599; Latin verses ad-
    dressed to Florio in British Library MS. Add. 15,214;
    commendatory poem in Pierre Erondelle's The French Garden;
    and two versions of Delia sonnets in John Daniel's Songs
    for the Lute.

5   WIETFELD, ALBERT. Die Bildersprache in Shakespeare's Sonet-
    ten. SzEP, 54. Halle: Max Niemeyer, 144 pp.
        Draws frequently on Delia and Rosamond for parallels in
    analyzing Shakespeare's metaphoric language. Notes thirty

parallels (the most of any writer discussed) between Daniel's poems and the Sonnets (passim).

1918

1 EAGLE, R[ODERICK] L[EWIS]. "Shakespeare in Contemporary Satire." TLS (21 February), p. 94.
      Responds to 1918.2: denies identification of Daniel with Hall's Labeo and allusion to Delia 13 in Marston's Pygmalion's Image.

2 L., H. "Shakespeare in Contemporary Satire." TLS (7 February), p. 70.
      Suggests allusion to Delia 13 in Marston's Pygmalion's Image. See R[oderick] L[ewis] Eagle, 24 January, p. 46; and 1918.1.

1919

1 ANON. "A Mighty Prophecy." Spectator, 123 (2 August), 141-42.
      Points out the "modern quality" of Daniel's subject matter in Civil Wars by suggesting parallels with World War I. Asserts that "where he leaves the trodden path of historical fact and dons the mantle of the seer . . . we find Daniel at his poetic best."

2 CREIGHTON, C[HARLES]. "Shakespeare's Sonnets: A Reading." TLS (23 January), p. 46.
      Discusses Daniel's dedications in gift copies of his works. Suggests that if providing decorated calligraphic dedications were his practice, this is evidence to support his identification as the Rival Poet.

1920

1 GUINEY, L. I. "Elizabethan Guesses." N&Q, 138 (February), 32-33.
      Identifies allusion to Daniel in Samuel Sheppard's A Mausolean Lament, 1651.

2 LAWRENCE, W[ILLIAM] J[OHN]. "The Casting-Out of Ben Jonson." TLS (8 July), p. 438.
      Argues that Jonson's report of being "'ushered by my Lord Suffolk from a Mask'" (Drummond, Conversations)

1920

refers to the ejection of Jonson and Sir John Roe from the 8 January 1604 performance of Vision of the Twelve Goddesses. Discusses the relationship of the incident to the enmity between Jonson and Daniel, and suggests that the final paragraph of the dedicatory epistle to the masque refers to the incident. See 1920.3, 1920.4, and 1920.5.

3   ____. "The Casting-Out of Ben Jonson." TLS (22 July), p. 472.
         Responds to 1920.4 by citing published arguments identifying Daniel with Matthew and Brisk. See 1920.2 and 1920.5.

4   SIMPSON, PERCY. "The Casting-Out of Ben Jonson." TLS (15 July), p. 456.
         Offers additions and corrections to 1920.2. Argues that Matthew (Every Man in His Humor) and Brisk (Every Man out of His Humor) should not be identified with Daniel. See 1920.3 and 1920.5.

5   ____. "The Casting-Out of Ben Jonson." TLS (5 August), pp. 504-505.
         Responds to 1920.3, arguing against the identification of Daniel with Matthew and Gullio (Return from Parnassus). See 1920.2 and 1920.4.

1921

1   BROADUS, EDMUND KEMPER. The Laureateship: A Study of the Office of Poet Laureate in England with Some Account of the Poets. Oxford: Clarendon Press, 247 pp.
         In chapter 4 ("Spenser, Drayton, and Daniel as Traditional Poets Laureate," pp. 33-39), examines the tradition that Daniel was poet laureate but notes "that there is no documentary warrant for it." Suggests that Daniel's appointment as licenser to the Children of the Queen's Revels, his position "as Groom of the Privy Chamber, and his activity as a writer of court masques . . . account for the tradition that he was official poet laureate to Elizabeth and James."

2   CHAMBRUN, [CLARA] LONGWORTH. Giovanni Florio: Un Apôtre de la Renaissance en Angleterre a 1'époque de Shakespeare. Paris: Payot, 227 pp.
         Argues that Florio was Daniel's brother-in-law (pp. 28-31).

3   KASTNER, L[EON] E[MILE], and H[ENRY] B[UCKLEY] CHARLTON.
     "Introduction," in their edition of The Poetical Works of
     Sir William Alexander Earl of Stirling. Vol. I. Scottish
     Text Society, NS, no. 11. Edinburgh: William Blackwood
     and Sons for the Scottish Text Society, pp. xvii-cc.
          Charlton examines Daniel's tragedies in an overview of
     French Senecan drama in England. Discusses Philotas as
     the one work of the type for which a performance was given
     (pp. clxxvii-clxxxii). See 1946.1.

                            1922

1   BARTLETT, HENRIETTA C[OLLINS]. Mr. William Shakespeare:
     Original and Early Editions of His Quartos and Folios, His
     Source Books, and Those Containing Contemporary Notices.
     New Haven: Yale University Press; London: Oxford Uni-
     versity Press, 247 pp.
          Notes several references to Daniel in sixteenth- and
     seventeenth-century works; provides bibliographical de-
     scription of Delia, 1595 (passim).

2   DANIEL, SAMUEL. A Defence of Rhyme, in English Critical
     Essays (Sixteenth, Seventeenth, and Eighteenth Centuries).
     Edited by Edmund D[avid] Jones. World's Classics, 240.
     London: Oxford University Press, pp. 72-103.
          Provides modernized reprint of unidentified edition.

3   RAUSCH, HEINRICH. Der "Chorus" im englischen Drama bis 1642.
     Giessen: Englischen Seminars der Universität Giessen,
     52 pp.
          Discusses Daniel's use of the chorus in Cleopatra and
     Philotas (pp. 20-21, 31-32).

                            1923

1   BRADY, GEORGE KEYPORTS. "Samuel Daniel: A Critical Study."
     Ph.D. dissertation, University of Illinois. [Separately
     published abstract: Urbana: (University of Illinois
     Press, 1923), 38 pp.]
          Provides detailed analysis of Delia: traces sources,
     method of composition, and influence on later poets in
     investigating the degree of sincerity in the work and the
     identity of Delia. Analyzes language, sonnet structure,
     rhymes, and rhythm.

1923

2   CHAMBERS, E[DMUND] K[ERCHEVER]. The Elizabethan Stage.
       Vol. III. Oxford: Clarendon Press, 524 pp.
          Provides biographical sketch and list of Daniel's plays,
       with bibliographical, critical, and historical notes
       (pp. 272-83).

3   FORREST, H[ENRY] T[ELFORD] S[TONOR]. The Five Authors of
       "Shake-speares Sonnets." London: Chapman & Dodd, 271 pp.
          Argues that Daniel is one of five authors (the others
       being Shakespeare, Barnes, Warner, and Donne) who wrote
       the Sonnets as part of a series of competitive "private
       sonnet-tournaments." Assigns ten sonnets to Daniel
       (passim).

*4 KÜHL, PAUL. "Das Verhältnis von Shakespeares Richard II zu
       Marlowes Edward II." Ph.D. dissertation, University of
       Greifswald, 56 pp. [Separately published abstract:
       Neubrandenberg: n.p., 1923.]
          Discusses relationship between Civil Wars and Richard II
       (reviewed by Wolfgang Keller, Shakespeare-Jahrbuch, 59-60
       [1924], 178).

                             1924

1   BALD, R[OBERT] C[ECIL]. "Shakespeare and Daniel." TLS
       (20 November), p. 776.
          Suggests influence of Letter from Octavia (Argument)
       on Antony and Cleopatra.

2   BULLEN, A[RTHUR] H[ENRY]. "Samuel Daniel," in his Elizabe-
       thans. New York: E. P. Dutton, pp. 25-46.
          Provides appreciative overview of Daniel's life and
       works, singling out Musophilus for special praise. Ob-
       serves that "[f]ew men have ever cultivated literature
       with the frank, whole-hearted devotion of Samuel Daniel"
       but concludes that is is unlikely he "will ever be popular
       again" except among "students and men of letters."

3   [ELTON, OLIVER]. Literary Fame: A Renaissance Study. N.p.:
       privately printed, 31 pp.
          Reprints 1904.5. See 1907.1.

4   FORBIS, JOHN F. The Shakespearean Enigma and an Elizabethan
       Mania. New York: American Library Service, 348 pp.
          Discusses Delia in arguing that Daniel, Sidney, Shake-
       speare, Drayton, and a host of other sonneteers were
       actually writing about the intoxicating effects of wine.

                             50

Asserts: "All of Daniel's sonnets are unmistakably Petrarchan, and readily yield their meaning when Wine is taken as their subject" (pp. 292-93, passim).

5 HAINES, C. R. "Shakespeare Allusions." TLS (5 June), p. 356.
    Points out allusions to Daniel and (possibly) Drayton in Sylvester's translation of Du Bartas (2d Week).

6 HEBEL, J[OHN] WILLIAM. "Drayton's Sirena." PMLA, 39 (December), 814-36.
    Identifies Daniel with Olcon of Eclogue 8 in Drayton's Poems Lyric and Pastoral; discusses reasons for Drayton's jealousy of Daniel.

7 JEFFERY, V[IOLET] M[AY]. "Italian and English Pastoral Drama of the Renaissance, III: Sources of Daniel's Queen's Arcadia and Randolph's Amyntas." MLR, 19 (October), 435-44.
    Traces Daniel's "precise and deliberate" borrowing from Luigi Groto's Pentimento amoroso, Guarini's Pastor fido, and Tasso's Aminta.

8 LEGOUIS, É[MILE HYACINTHE] and L[OUIS] CAZAMIAN. Histoire de la littérature anglaise. Paris: Hachette, 1340 pp.
    In book 4, chapter 3 ("La Poésie de 1590 à 1625," pp. 286-33), Legouis provides an appreciative overview of Daniel's works, stressing his role as a moralist and historian, a poet of reflection rather than passion (pp. 287-90, passim). Translated 1927.7.

9 REYHER, PAUL. "Notes sur les sources des Richard II." Revue de l'Enseignement des Langues Vivantes, 41: 1-13, 54-64, 106-14, 158-68.
    Notes parallels between Civil Wars and Richard II; concludes that the direction of the influence is impossible to determine.

10 WELLS, HENRY W[ILLIS]. Poetic Imagery Illustrated from Elizabethan Literature. Columbia University Studies in English and Comparative Literature. New York: Columbia University Press, 239 pp. [Also submitted as Ph.D. dissertation, Columbia University.]
    Draws frequently on Daniel's poetry in analyzing types of images (decorative, sunken, violent, radical, intensive, expansive, and exuberant). Notes that Daniel is associated particularly with the sunken image (passim).

1924

11 WITHERSPOON, ALEXANDER MACLAREN. <u>The Influence of Robert
    Garnier on Elizabethan Drama</u>. YSE, 65. Ph.D. disserta-
    tion, Yale University, 1923. New Haven: Yale University
    Press; Oxford: Oxford University Press, 203 pp.
        Analyzes the influence of Garnier on <u>Cleopatra</u> and, to
    a lesser extent, on <u>Philotas</u>; examines Daniel's revision
    of <u>Cleopatra</u>; and traces his influence on Brandon and
    Alexander (pp. 99-117, 126-33, passim).

1925

1 DANIEL, MARY SAMUEL. "Two Elizabethans: I. An Elizabethan
    Wordsworth." <u>Dublin Review</u>, 176 (January), 108-17.
        In appreciative overview of Daniel's life and career,
    praises him for his "contemplative reflectiveness, [and]
    quiet, restrained expression of deeply brooding thought";
    notes that he "was in many ways a Wordsworth, born out of
    due time."

2 DANIEL, SAMUEL. <u>A Defense of Ryme</u>, in <u>Samuel Daniel</u> <u>A De-
    fence of Ryme</u>; <u>Thomas Campion, Observations in the Art of
    English Poesie</u>. Edited by G[eorge] B[agshawe] Harrison.
    Bodley Head Quartos, 14. London: John Lane; New York:
    E. P. Dutton, pp. 1-46.
        Reprints 1603 edition. Reviewed in Anon. "English
    Poesie," <u>Nation and Athenaeum</u>, 37 (29 August 1925), 651-
    52; Anon., "Elizabethan Pamphlets," <u>New Statesman</u>, 25
    (26 September 1925), 666, 668; J. St. Loe Strachey,
    <u>Spectator</u>, 135 (5 September 1925), 370-71.

3 GREG, W[ALTER] W[ILSON], ed. <u>English Literary Autographs,
    1550-1650: Part I--Dramatists</u>. [London:] Oxford Uni-
    versity Press, n.p.
        Reproduces (with transcriptions) three examples of
    Daniel's handwriting in plate XXI.

*4 PARADISE, NATHANIEL BURTON. "Thomas Lodge: The History of
    an Elizabethan." Ph.D. dissertation, Yale University,
    254 pp.
        Revised 1931.1.

5 THORN-DRURY, G[EORGE]. "Some Notes on Dryden." <u>RES</u>, 1
    (January), 79-83.
        Traces Dryden's use of <u>Cleopatra</u> as a source for <u>All
    for Love</u>.

1926

1 FLOOD, W. H. GRATTAN. "Was Samuel Daniel in France in 1584-1586?" RES, 2 (January), 98-99.

   Points out that the two letters (in the Public Record Office) from a Samuel Daniel in France are not, according to W. W. Greg, in Daniel's hand.

2 GOLDING, S. R. "The Authorship of The Maid's Metamorphosis." RES, 2 (July), 270-79.

   Denies Fleay's ascription of "the major portion of the play to Daniel" (1891.1).

3 HILLEBRAND, HAROLD NEWCOMB. The Child Actors: A Chapter in Elizabethan Stage History. ISLL, vol. 11, nos. 1-2. Urbana: University of Illinois, 355 pp.

   Discusses Daniel as licenser to the Children of the Queen's Revels and his litigation against Edward Kirkham (transcribes Chancery documents regarding the latter). Also discusses problems surrounding the staging of Philotas (passim).

4 POLLARD, A[LFRED] W[ILLIAM], and G[ILBERT] R[ICHARD] REDGRAVE, comps. A Short-Title Catalogue of Books Printed in England, Scotland, & Ireland and of English Books Printed Abroad, 1475-1640. London: The Bibliographical Society, 625 pp.

   Provide list of extant editions (with locations) of Daniel's works (pp. 139-40). (New edition in progress.)

5 ROBERTS, JOHN HAWLEY. "A Note on Samuel Daniel's Civile Wars." MLN, 41 (January), 48-50.

   Suggests that the influence of Mirror for Magistrates and the 1595 Lambeth Conference "where the issue of predestination was clearly defined" led to Daniel's confusion of "the idea of righteous retribution with predestinated evil" in Civil Wars, book 6.

6 _____. "Samuel Daniel's Relation to the Histories and Historical Poetry of the Sixteenth Century." Ph.D. dissertation, University of Chicago. [Abstract in University of Chicago Abstracts of Theses, Humanistic Ser., 2 (1926), 401-404.]

   Examines Daniel's indebtedness in Rosamond and Civil Wars to "the chronicles and metrical histories which had appeared during the sixteenth century" and "to the general trend of critical theories current during that period." Analyzes influence of the Mirror for Magistrates tradition

1926

on Rosamond and of Lucan's Pharsalia on the form, of
Holinshed's Chronicles on the subject matter, and of the
Mirror for Magistrates on Daniel's "philosophical contri-
butions to the story" in Civil Wars.

7   SCOTT, JANET G[IRVAN]. "Minor Elizabethan Sonneteers and
     Their Greater Predecessors." RES, 2 (October), 423-27.
         Outlines Griffin's "plagiarism" of language from Delia
     in Fidessa.

8   _____. "The Names of the Heroines of Elizabethan Sonnet-
     Sequences." RES, 2 (April), 159-62.
         Points out "that the utmost we can say about Daniel's
     debt to Scève [for Delia] is that the English poet may
     have heard of Scève's title." As for Cynthia, the name in
     the sonnets published with Astrophel and Stella, finds
     that Daniel "was working on parallel lines to Scève, and
     was not necessarily indebted to him."

9   SNEATH, GEORGE MARK. "The Influence of the English Literary
     Critics of the Sixteenth Century on English Verse from
     1590 to 1599." Ph.D. dissertation, Boston University.
         Includes discussion of Defense of Rhyme as well as
     Daniel's poetry.

10   STEELE, MARY SUSAN. Plays & Masques at Court during the
     Reigns of Elizabeth, James, and Charles. CSE, 20.
     Ithaca: Cornell University Press, 310 pp.
         Includes Daniel's masques in a list of court plays and
     masques 1558-1642.

11   TRENEER, ANNE. The Sea in English Literature from "Beowulf"
     to Donne. Liverpool: University Press of Liverpool;
     London: Hodder and Stoughton, 317 pp.
         Discusses Daniel's references to the sea, which "gave
     [him] a sense of security." Observes that Daniel "is a
     strangely consistent poet, possessed by a clear, steady
     desire for immortality" (pp. 223-25).

1927

1   ALBRIGHT, EVELYN MAY. "Shakespeare's Richard II and the
     Essex Conspiracy." PMLA, 42 (September), 686-720.
         Compares Daniel's treatment (and its relationship to
     the Essex conspiracy) of Henry IV and Richard II in Civil
     Wars to that of John Hayward's in Life and Reign of King

Henry IV. Concludes that "although Daniel was an enthusiastic admirer of Essex . . . , he disapproved of any act
of violence to bring Essex into power. He 'played safe'
in his whole history of Richard and Henry."

2   BRAY, DENYS [DE SAUMAREZ]. "The Art Form of the Elizabethan
    Sonnet Sequence and Shakespeare's Sonnets." Shakespeare-
    Jahrbuch, 63: 159-82.
        In arguing that Elizabethan sonnets should be read as
    part of a sequence, not as individual poems, draws upon
    Delia to illustrate the structuring devices of "line-link"
    and "half-line link." Revised 1938.1.

3   BRETTLE, R. E. "Samuel Daniel and the Children of the Queen's
    Revels, 1604-5." RES, 3 (April), 162-68.
        Prints two documents (complaint of Edward Kirkham and
    Anne Kendall, and Daniel's answer) relating to Daniel's
    position as licenser to the Children of the Queen's
    Revels.

4   DANIEL, SAMUEL. A Defence of Ryme, in The Prelude to Poetry:
    The English Poets in Defence and Praise of Their Own Art.
    Edited by Ernest Rhys. Everyman's Library, 789. London:
    J. M. Dent; New York: E. P. Dutton, pp. 86-111.
        Reprints 1602 edition.

5   ELIOT, T[HOMAS] S[TEARNS]. "Introduction," in Seneca His
    Tenne Tragedies Translated into English. Vol. I. Tudor
    Translations, 2d ser., 11. London: Constable; New York:
    Alfred A. Knopf, pp. v-liv.
        To refute Seneca's "supposed bad influence upon the
    language," points out that Daniel's language "is pure and
    restrained; the vocabulary choice, the expression clear;
    there is nothing far-fetched, conceited, or perverse."
    (The "Introduction" has been reprinted several times.)

6   HASSELKUSS, HERMANN KARL. Der Petrarkismus in der Sprache
    der englischen Sonettdichter der Renaissance. Ph.D. dis-
    sertation, Westfälischen Wilhelms-Universität, Münster.
    [Barmen: Montanus and Ehrenstein,] 249 pp.
        Includes Delia in analysis of influences on, stylistic
    traits of, and thematic concerns in Elizabethan sonnets.
    Lists parallels between lines in Delia and in Petrarch's
    sonnets (pp. 46-50, passim).

1927

7 LEGOUIS, ÉMILE [HYACINTHE], and LOUIS CAZAMIAN. <u>A History of</u>
<u>English Literature</u>, I: <u>The Middle Ages & the Renascence</u>
<u>(650-1660)</u>. Translated by Helen Douglas Irvine. New
York: Macmillan, 399 pp. [Volume I is by Legouis.]
    Translation of 1924.8; <u>see</u> pp. 187-90, passim.

8 SELLERS, H[ARRY]. "A Bibliography of the Works of Samuel
Daniel, 1585-1623: With an Appendix of Daniel's Letters."
<u>Proceedings and Papers of the Oxford Bibliographical Soci-</u>
<u>ety</u>, 2, part 1, 29-54.
    Provides full bibliographical descriptions of Daniel's
printed works, lists works which include commendatory
poems by him, describes manuscripts, and prints extant
letters and will. Supplement, 1930.6.
    Reviewed in Floris Delattre, <u>RBPH</u>, 12 (1933), 307-308.

9 _____. "Two New Letters of Samuel Daniel." <u>TLS</u> (24 March),
p. 215.
    Transcribes two letters to James Kirton (20 May, 31 May
1608) from the collection at Longleat.

10 WELSFORD, ENID. <u>The Court Masque: A Study in the Relation-</u>
<u>ship between Poetry & the Revels</u>. Cambridge: Cambridge
University Press, 450 pp.
    Discusses the "literary defects" of <u>Vision of the Twelve</u>
<u>Goddesses</u> and <u>Tethys' Festival</u> and places the works in the
evolution of the masque (pp. 171-73, 188-91, passim).

1928

1 [DOBREE, BONAMY]. "Cleopatra and 'That Criticall Warr.'"
<u>TLS</u> (11 October), pp. 717-18.
    Examines theme, method of telling the story (relation),
verse form, and diction in <u>Cleopatra</u> in a comparison of
Daniel's play, <u>Antony and Cleopatra</u>, and <u>All for Love</u>.
Reprinted 1929.2 and 1968.4.

2 ECKHARDT, EDUARD. <u>Das englische Drama im Zeitalter der</u>
<u>Reformation und der Hochrenaissance: Vorstufen Shake-</u>
<u>speare und seine Zeit</u>. Berlin: Walter de Gruyter,
305 pp.
    Discusses <u>Cleopatra</u> and <u>Philotas</u> as examples of the
influence of <u>Seneca</u> and <u>Garnier</u> on Elizabethan drama;
includes notes on sources and style for each play
(pp. 247-49).

3   EMPEROR, JOHN BERNARD. The Catullian Influence in English
    Lyric Poetry, Circa 1600-1650. University of Missouri
    Studies, vol. 3, no. 3. Columbia: University of
    Missouri, 133 pp.
        Lists passages illustrating influence of Catullus on
    Daniel's poetry. Observes that "where Daniel was most
    lyrical he was least imitative" (pp. 30-32).

4   GENOUY, HECTOR. L'Élément pastoral dans la poésie narrative
    et le drame en Angleterre, de 1579 à 1640. Paris: Henri
    Didier, 448 pp.
        Discusses Italian influence on and satire in Queen's
    Arcadia and Italian influence on and the superior quality
    of Hymen's Triumph, classing it among the best pastoral
    dramas (pp. 360-62, 372-75).

1929

1   BARTLETT, HENRIETTA C[OLLINS]. "Extant Autograph Material by
    Shakespeare's Fellow Dramatists." Library, 4th ser., 10
    (December), 308-12.
        Lists Daniel's manuscripts (portions of Hymen's Tri-
    umph, stanza from Panegyric Congratulatory, and two let-
    ters) located in a 1925 survey of "the more important
    libraries in England and America."

2   DOBRÉE, BONAMY. Restoration Tragedy, 1660-1720. Oxford:
    Clarendon Press, 189 pp.
        Reprints 1928.1 as chapter 4 ("Cleopatra and 'That
    Criticall War,'" pp. 66-90). See 1968.4.

3   PEARSON, LU EMILY HESS. "The Love Conventions of the English
    Sonnet: A Study of the Elizabethan Protest against
    Petrarchism." Ph.D. dissertation, Stanford University.
    [Abstract in Stanford University Abstracts of Disserta-
    tions, 5 (1929-1930), 50-57.]
        Includes discussion of Delia. Revised as 1933.4.

4   SCOTT, JANET G[IRVAN]. Les Sonnets élisabéthains: Les
    Sources et l'apport personnel. Bibliothèque de la Revue
    de Littérature Comparée, 60. Paris: Honoré Champion,
    344 pp.
        In chapter 8 ("Samuel Daniel," pp. 115-28), discusses
    identity of Delia, themes, style, and versification. De-
    votes major portion of chapter to identification of for-
    eign sources of and influences on Delia. In "Appendice"
    provides list of sources (p. 314). See 1934.4 and 1935.2.

1929

5   WECTER, DIXON. "Elizabeth and Essex." <u>TLS</u> (31 January),
        p. 80.
            Corrects Lessing's comments on <u>Philotas</u> in <u>Hamburgische</u>
        <u>Dramaturgie</u>. Suggests that it "is indeed unlikely" that
        "Daniel had intended any political allegory in his plot."

                                1930

1   ANON. "Samuel Daniel and Fulke Greville." <u>TLS</u> (5 June),
        p. 475.
            In review of 1930.2 discusses Daniel's restraint, the
        reciprocal influence of Shakespeare and Daniel, and (in
        particular) Greville's influence on Daniel, especially in
        <u>Musophilus</u> and <u>Defense of Rhyme</u>. Also observes that
        Daniel's personality is of more interest to the present
        age than is his poetry.

2   DANIEL, SAMUEL. <u>Poems and "A Defence of Ryme</u>." Edited by
        Arthur Colby Sprague. Cambridge: Harvard University
        Press, 254 pp.
            Provides critical texts of <u>Delia</u>, <u>Rosamond</u>, <u>Musophilus</u>,
        <u>Epistles</u>, <u>Defense of Rhyme</u>, and "Ulysses and the Siren"
        in an effort "to represent Daniel at his best." In "Intro-
        duction" (pp. xiii-xxxvii), provides critical overview of
        Daniel's works and discusses his revisions, patriotism,
        and love of the past. Reprinted 1950.2 and 1965.6. Re-
        viewed in: A. B[randl], <u>Archiv</u>, 165 (1934), 302; Floris
        Delattre, <u>RBPH</u>, 12 (1933), 307-308; Edwin [Almiron]
        Greenlaw, <u>MLN</u>, 46 (December 1931), 559-60; H[arrie]
        S[tuart] V[edder] Jones, <u>JEGP</u>, 30 (April 1931), 323;
        W[illiam] L[indsay] Renwick, <u>RES</u>, 7 (October 1931), 470-
        71; 1930.1.

3   [DANIEL, SAMUEL ?] <u>The Prayse of Private Life</u>, in <u>The Let-</u>
        <u>ters and Epigrams of Sir John Harington Together with "The</u>
        <u>Prayse of Private Life</u>." Edited by Norman Egbert McClure.
        Philadelphia: University of Pennsylvania Press, pp. 323-
        78.
            Prints British Library MS. Add. 30,161, a transcript of
        the copy presented by Daniel to the Countess of Cumberland
        in 1605. In "Introduction" (pp. 1-58), attributes the
        work to Harington and discusses its relationship to
        Petrarch's <u>De Vita Solitaria</u> (pp. 44-46). <u>See also</u> the
        notes, pp. 428-32. (Seronsy [1967.15] and Sellers
        [1930.6] suggest that Daniel is possibly the author.)

4   FARRAND, MARGARET L.   "Samuel Daniel and His 'Worthy Lord.'"
    MLN, 45 (January), 23-24.
        Suggests that the publication of Worthy Tract brought
    Daniel to the attention of the Earl of Pembroke, who was
    interested in heraldry.

5   HÖHNA, HEINRICH.   Der Physiologus in der elisabethanischen
    Literatur.   Ph.D. dissertation, Friedrich-Alexander-
    Universität, Erlangen.   Erlangen: Höfer & Limmert,
    96 pp.
        Catalogues and suggests sources for selected natural
    history references in Daniel's works (pp. 32-37, passim).

6   SELLERS, H[ARRY].   "Supplementary Note to 'A Bibliography
    of the Works of Samuel Daniel.'"   Proceedings and Papers
    of the Oxford Bibliographical Society, 2, part 4, 341-42.
        Adds information on Delia and Rosamond Augmented;
    Cleopatra (1598), which was not included in 1927.8.   Sug-
    gests that Praise of Private Life, attributed to Sir John
    Harington, is by Daniel.

1931

1   PARADISE, N[ATHANIEL] BURTON.   Thomas Lodge: The History of
    an Elizabethan.   New Haven: Yale University Press,
    264 pp.
        In revision of 1925.4 suggests that Alcon of Queen's
    Arcadia is possibly Lodge; discusses the relationship
    between Daniel and Lodge (passim).

1932

1   AIKEN, PAULINE.   The Influence of the Latin Elegists on Eng-
    lish Lyric Poetry, 1600-1650, with Particular Reference to
    the Works of Robert Herrick.   University of Maine Studies,
    2d ser., 22 [Maine Bulletin, 34, no. 6].   Orono: Univer-
    sity Press, 115 pp.
        Notes that although Daniel "wrote in the conventions of
    courtly and Platonic love, rather than in the Latin erotic
    strain . . . some traces of elegiac influence may be
    found."   Suggests parallels in Daniel's poetry with that
    of Latin elegists but points out that the influence was
    indirect, perhaps through Marino.   Suggests that Daniel
    derived "Delia" from the name of Tibullus's mistress
    (pp. 31-32, passim).

1932

2   DANIEL, SAMUEL. A Defence of Ryme, in The Great Critics:
    An Anthology of Literary Criticism. Edited by James Harry
    Smith and Edd Winfield Parks. New York: W. W. Norton,
    pp. 188-211.
        Reprint 1602 edition. In brief introductory note dis-
    cuss Defense of Rhyme as a response to Campion.

1933

1   BALL, LEWIS F[RANKLIN]. "Studies in the Structure of the
    Minor English Renaissance Epics." Ph.D. dissertation,
    Johns Hopkins University.
        See 1934.1, which was also published separately as a
    "Summary" of the dissertation (Baltimore: n.p., 1934).

2   CONSTABLE, KATHLEEN M[ARY]. "The Rival Poet and the Youth
    of the Sonnets." TLS (9 November), p. 774.
        Suggests that Meredian of Drayton's Gaveston (1. 1736)
    is a rival poet, perhaps Daniel.

3   HOUSMAN, A[LFRED] E[DWARD]. The Name and Nature of Poetry.
    The Leslie Stephen Lecture Delivered at Cambridge, 9 May
    1933. Cambridge: Cambridge University Press, 54 pp.
        Cites lines 1-9 of "Ulysses and the Siren" as "a typi-
    cal example of poetry": "Indeed a promising young poetaster
    could not do better than lay up that stanza in his memory,
    not necessarily as a pattern to set before him, but as a
    touchstone to keep at his side. Diction and movement
    alike, it is perfect. It is made out of the most ordinary
    words, yet it is pure from the least alloy of prose; and
    however much nearer heaven the art of poetry may have
    mounted, it has never flown on a surer or a lighter wing"
    (pp. 6-8).

4   PEARSON, LU EMILY [HESS]. Elizabethan Love Conventions.
    Berkeley: University of California Press, 375 pp.
        In revision of 1929.3 devotes section to the examina-
    tion of "form and cadence of . . . Daniel's sonnets,"
    suggesting that "Daniel, more than any other Elizabethan,
    prepared the way for the form and cadence of Shakespeare's
    sonnets." Examines influences (especially that of
    Petrarch) on Delia, pointing out that "since he was not
    creative by nature, or born a master of passion, Daniel
    gathered unto himself the ideas of others, and . . .
    wrought them into his own thought and feeling." Concludes

that Daniel "made use of the fashion [for writing sonnets] in order to refine the language of his time, and through the language, the manners, and through the manners, the morals" (pp. 151-58).

5   POTTER, GEORGE REUBEN. "Isis' Ass and the Elizabethans." MLN, 48 (February), 101.

Points out reference to Isis's ass in Musophilus and suggests that Daniel's poem might be Herrick's source for the allusion in "Epigram upon Spur."

6   STEWART, J. I. M. "Montaigne's Essays and A Defence of Ryme." RES, 9 (July), 311-12.

Points out Daniel's indebtedness to Florio's translation.

1934

1   BALL, LEWIS F[RANKLIN]. "The Background of the Minor English Renaissance Epics." ELH, 1 (April), 63-89. [Also published separately (Baltimore: n.p., 1934) as a "Summary" of 1933.1.]

Argues that Civil Wars "should be regarded as . . . [an epic] on the basis of classical and Renaissance theory and practice, and that . . . [it was] considered as such by the Elizabethans." Discusses how in Daniel's poem "[e]pic breadth and dignity are secured by the sustained tone of high seriousness, the magnitude of the action, and by such minor devices as occasional extended similes and parallels between modern and ancient story."

2   MEOZZI, ANTÈRO. Il Petrarchismo europeo (secolo XVI). Volume II of his Azione e diffusione della letteratura italiana in Europa (secolo XV-XVII). Pisa: Vallerini, 436 pp.

Traces French and Italian influences on Delia and comments on the musicality of Daniel's verse (pp. 224-27).

3   PRIEST, HAROLD MARTIN. "Tasso in English Literature, 1575-1675." Ph.D. dissertation, Northwestern University. [Abstract in Northwestern University Summaries of Ph.D. Dissertations, 1 (1933), 5-9.]

Investigates influence of Tasso on Delia and, in particular, of his Aminta and Guarini's Pastor fido on Queen's Arcadia. Of the latter, notes: "Not only was there a wholesale borrowing of characters and episodes from those two models; there was also a conscious effort to reproduce

1934

the poetic tone and even a witless imitation of the
dramatic technique" of the two works.

4   VAGANAY, HUGHES. "Les Sonnets élisabéthains." RLC, 14
(June), 333–37.
Defends Lee's argument (1904.2)--against Scott (1929.4)
--that Daniel was indebted to French sonneteers (particularly Du Bartas) for the epithet "care-charmer" in Delia
45. See 1935.2.

5   YATES, FRANCES A[MELIA]. John Florio: The Life of an Italian
in Shakespeare's England. Cambridge: Cambridge University
Press, 372 pp.
Discusses the friendship between Daniel and Florio;
suggests that Daniel was the author of "Phaeton to His
Friend Apollo," a commendatory poem in Second Fruits;
identifies the "Daniel" in Second Fruits with Daniel;
identifies the H. Samford referred to in the Defense of
Rhyme as Hugh Sanford, suggesting "that it must have been
Sanford's criticism of Daniel's poetry which Florio re-
sented so strongly" in the prefatory matter of World of
Words (passim).

1935

1   DANIEL, SAMUEL. The Vision of the Twelve Goddesses, in The
English Drama: An Anthology, 900–1642. Edited by Edd
Winfield Parks and Richmond Croom Beatty. New York:
W. W. Norton, pp. 562–73.
Provide annotated, modernized text based on 1897.1.

2   ESPINER, JANET G[IRVAN SCOTT]. "Les Sonnets élisabéthains."
RLC, 15 (January), 107–109.
Accepts Vaganay's suggestion (1934.4) that Daniel
probably borrowed the epithet "care-charmer" (Delia 45)
from Du Bartas but points out that this does not modify
her conclusion in 1929.4 that Daniel had put into harmonious English ancient ideas that he had found in the works
of foreign poets.

3   LITCHFIELD, FLORENCE LeDUC. "The Treatment of the Theme of
Mutability in the Literature of the English Renaissance:
A Study of the Problem of Change between 1558 and 1660."
Ph.D. dissertation, University of Minnesota. [Abstract in
University of Minnesota Summaries of Ph.D. Theses, 1
(1939), 164–68.]
Draws on Daniel in a wide-ranging analysis of the theme.

1936

1   CASTELLI, ALBERTO. "La Gerusalemme liberata" nella Inghilterra
    di Spenser. Pubblicazioni della Università Cattolica del
    Sacro Cuore, vol. 20. Milan: Vita e Pensiero, 142 pp.
        Traces influence of Tasso's poem on Daniel's works,
    especially Civil Wars (pp. 43-48).

2   COLERIDGE, SAMUEL TAYLOR. Coleridge's Miscellaneous Criti-
    cism. Edited by Thomas Middleton Raysor. Cambridge:
    Harvard University Press, 484 pp.
        Brings together Coleridge's comments on Daniel (many
    from marginalia in a copy of 1793.1 and from Lamb's copy
    of 1718.1) (pp. 235-40, passim).

3   DUNN, ESTHER CLOUDMAN. The Literature of Shakespeare's Eng-
    land. New York: Charles Scribner's Sons, 336 pp.
        Suggests that Rosamond "leaves us unmoved" because of
    the loss of taste for narrative punctuated by rhetorical
    speeches. Observes that the sonnets "crawl, weighted
    down with abstract words" and that "[t]o see a person of
    passion, real or imagined, beneath them is impossible"
    (pp. 50-53, 76-78).

4   FARNHAM, WILLARD. The Medieval Heritage of Elizabethan
    Tragedy. Berkeley: University of California Press,
    501 pp.
        In chapter 8 ("The Progeny of the Mirror," pp. 304-39),
    discusses the place of Rosamond in the tradition of the
    tragical complaint. Examines Daniel's balancing of fate
    and free will in the poem and its influence on later
    works (pp. 319-23).

5   GOTTLIEB, HANS JORDAN. "Robert Burton's Knowledge of English
    Poetry." Ph.D. dissertation, New York University. [Pub-
    lished abridgment: New York: Graduate School of New York
    University, 1937, 22 pp.]
        Discusses twelve passages from Daniel quoted in Anatomy
    of Melancholy. Points out that the "sententious quality"
    of Rosamond (which accounted for ten passages) "made it
    especially suitable for quotation" and that "[i]n Rosa-
    mond's moralistic recital of her relations with Henry II,
    Burton found ample support for his warnings against the
    tragic consequences to which heroical love may lead."

1936

6 MEYER, CATHARINE. "Elizabethan Gentlemen and the Publishing
    Trade: A Study in Literary Conventions." Ph.D. disser-
    tation, Radcliffe College. [Abstract in Radcliffe College
    Summaries of Theses, 1935-1938, pp. 72-76.]
        Discusses Daniel, particularly as he "looked back
    [during the reign of James I] to the golden age of poetry
    in Elizabeth's day."

7 SCHÜTZE, JOHANNES. "Daniels Cleopatra und Shakespeare."
    Englische Studien, 71: 58-72.
        Argues that in 1607 Daniel recast the earlier versions
    of Cleopatra and was not influenced by Antony and Cleo-
    patra. Suggests that Daniel, because of financial need,
    revised the play to make it more stage-worthy.

8 SHORT, RAYMOND W. "The Patronage of Poetry under James First."
    Ph.D. dissertation, Cornell University. [Separately pub-
    lished abstract: Ithaca: n.p., 1936, 6 pp.]
        Draws frequently on Daniel in examining patronage from
    Elizabeth I through Charles I.

9 THALER, ALWIN. "Shakspere, Daniel, and Everyman." PQ, 15
    (April), 217-18.
        Suggests influence of Rosamond on passages in Romeo and
    Juliet and Richard III.

1937

1 BROOKS, ALDEN. Will Shakspere: Factotum and Agent. New
    York: Round Table Press, 378 pp.
        Argues that Daniel wrote Rape of Lucrece, Romeo and
    Juliet, and some of Shakespeare's sonnets (passim).
    Incorporated in 1943.2.

2 CLARK, ELEANOR GRACE. Elizabethan Fustian: A Study in the
    Social and Political Backgrounds of the Drama, with Parti-
    cular Reference to Christopher Marlowe, Vol. I. New York:
    Oxford Press, 237 pp.
        Includes Philotas in examination of plays ostensibly
    related to Essex. Observes: "If he [Daniel] had intended
    an application to Essex . . . the tragedy of 1601 would
    have made either its stage presentation or its publi-
    cation a danger not to be risked during the Queen's life-
    time" (pp. 133-39).

3   ECCLES, MARK. "Samuel Daniel in France and Italy." SP, 34
    (April), 148-67.
        Analyzes Daniel's handwriting at various stages of his
    life and other evidence to argue that the two letters by
    "Samuell Daniell" to Walsingham (in the Public Record
    Office) are by Daniel. Transcribes the two letters as
    well as several other records in tracing his travels in
    France. Argues that Daniel was not Walsingham's secret
    agent. Establishes that he was probably in Italy in 1590-
    1591 with Dymoke and corrects several misconceptions about
    his travels there.

*4 KELLEY, TRACY R. "Studies in the Development of the Prosody
    of the Elizabethan Sonnet." Ph.D. dissertation, Univer-
    sity of California, Berkeley, 86 pp.

5   NICOLL, ALLARDYCE. Stuart Masques and the Renaissance Stage.
    London: G. Harrap, 224 pp.
        Draws frequently on Daniel's masques in an analysis of
    the staging of the Stuart masque (passim).

6   NUNGEZER, EDWIN. "Samuel Daniel." TLS (27 March), p. 240.
        Announces that he is preparing a complete edition.

7   TRAUB, WALTHER. Auffassung und Gestaltung der Cleopatra in
    der englischen Literatur. Ph.D. dissertation, University
    of Tübingen. Würzburg: Konrad Triltsch, 114 pp.
        Analyzes Daniel's characterization of Cleopatra and
    places it in the context of the treatments of her in Eng-
    lish literature from Chaucer through 1935 (pp. 11-18).

8   UHLAND, MAUDE [LEONA]. "A Study of Samuel Daniel." Ph.D.
    dissertation, Cornell University. [Abstract in Cornell
    University Abstracts of Theses . . . 1937 (Ithaca:
    Cornell University Press, 1938), pp. 40-42.]
        Places Daniel "against a background of Elizabethan and
    Jacobean England" and "portray[s] him as a gentleman-
    scholar in courtly circles, a patriot, a moralist, and a
    writer." Also examines his poetic theory and influence on
    Shakespeare. Concludes: "Daniel's poetry lacks the
    spontaneity and lyrical charm of that of his great con-
    temporaries, but he was a true leader and guide, promoting
    advancement and checking attendant extremes and extra-
    vagances."

1937

*9 WASSERMAN, EARL R[EEVES]. "The Elizabethan Revival: Its
    Background and Beginning." Ph.D. dissertation, Johns
    Hopkins University.
        Revised as 1947.10.

                            1938

1   BRAY, DENYS [DE SAUMAREZ]. Shakespeare's Sonnet-Sequence.
    London: Martin Secker, 258 pp.
        Revises 1927.2 as chapter 3 ("The Art-Form of the
    Elizabethan Sequence," pp. 42-72): analyzes Daniel's use
    of rhyme patterns ("line-link," "rhyme-word repetition,"
    and "rhyme-echo") in Delia.

2   BULLOUGH, GEOFFREY. "Bacon and the Defence of Learning,"
    in Seventeenth Century Studies Presented to Sir Herbert
    Grierson. Edited by J[ohn] Dover Wilson. Oxford:
    Clarendon Press, pp. 1-20.
        Discusses ways in which Musophilus anticipates Advance-
    ment of Learning in examining Renaissance attacks on and
    defenses of learning as background to Bacon's work.

3   HOTSON, LESLIE. "Marigold of the Poets." EDH, 17: 47-68.
        Examines the biographical importance of Daniel's part
    in the suit brought by the Earl of Lincoln against Edward
    Dymoke. Suggests that "the bee transormed into Musaeus"
    in Dymoke's Caltha Poetarum is Daniel.

4   JOHN, LISLE CECIL. The Elizabethan Sonnet Sequences:
    Studies in Conventional Conceits. Columbia University
    Studies in English and Comparative Literature, no. 133.
    New York: Columbia University Press, 288 pp. [Also sub-
    mitted as Ph.D. dissertation, Columbia University.]
        Draws frequently on Delia in analyzing conventional
    conceits and themes in Elizabethan sonnet sequences. Con-
    cludes that Daniel's "verse, which is pervaded by a gentle
    longing and mild unhappiness, often has genuine beauty,
    yet it is so correct, so restrained, so perfect a tribute
    of poet to patroness, that mediocrity is often the result"
    (passim).

5   NEWCOMB, EMILIE ALDEN. "The Countess of Pembroke's Circle."
    Ph.D. dissertation, University of Wisconsin. [Abstract
    in University of Wisconsin Summaries of Doctoral Disser-
    tations, 3 (1938), 298.]
        Discusses Daniel in examining the "interest of the
    members of the circle in politics"; notes that the plays

of Greville and Daniel "display an increasingly critical attitude toward kings."

6 NUNGEZER, EDWIN. "'Inedited Poems of Daniel.'" N&Q, 175 (10 December), 421.

Points out that the poems attributed to Daniel by Simeon (1856.1) are from Jonson's Underwood. Announces that he is "preparing a complete edition" of Daniel.

7 ROLLINS, HYDER EDWARD, ed. The Poems. New Variorum Edition of Shakespeare. Philadelphia: J. B. Lippincott, 685 pp.

In notes and appendix to Lucrece, gathers commentary on the influence of Rosamond on Shakespeare's poem (passim).

1939

1 BULLOUGH, GEOFFREY. "Introduction," in his edition of Poems and Dramas of Fulke Greville, First Lord Brooke. 2 volumes. Edinburgh: Oliver and Boyd, Vol. I, pp. 1-72; Vol. II, pp. 1-62.

Discusses Daniel's relationship with Greville and suggests that "Greville's influence on Daniel was more important than Daniel's on Greville." Analyzes relationship of Musophilus to Greville's works, particularly Of Human Learning, suggesting "that Daniel wrote his poem to counter some of [Greville's] . . . practical objections [against learning] as well as those of more worldly critics." Also discusses relationship of Cleopatra and Philotas to Greville's plays (passim).

2 GREG, W[ALTER] W[ILSON]. A Bibliography of the English Printed Drama to the Restoration. Vol. I. London: Oxford University Press for The Bibliographical Society, 529 pp., 63 plates.

Provides bibliographical description of the early editions of Cleopatra (pp. 216-19), Vision of the Twelve Goddesses (pp. 331-32), Philotas (pp. 349-50), Queen's Arcadia (pp. 354-55), Tethys' Festival (pp. 428-29), and Hymen's Triumph (p. 466). See 1957.3.

3 NUNGEZER, EDWIN. "The Use of the Contraction '$^{u}_{y}$' for 'thou.'" N&Q, 177 (2 September), 171-72.

Catalogues Daniel's use of the contraction--"something of a bibliographical curiosity"--in various editions of Delia and Cleopatra.

1939

4   SHORT, R[AYMOND] W. "Jonson's Sanguine Rival." RES, 15
    (July), 315-17.
        Argues against the usual identification of Daniel as
    the rival mentioned in Forest, Epistle 12; suggests Dray-
    ton instead. See 1939.5.

5   SIMPSON, PERCY. "'Jonson's Sanguine Rival.'" RES, 15
    (October), 464-65.
        In reply to 1939.4 argues for Daniel as the rival men-
    tioned in Forest, Epistle 12.

6   WILSON, JOHN DOVER. "Introduction," in his edition of Wil-
    liam Shakespeare's King Richard II. Cambridge: Cambridge
    University Press, pp. vii-lxxvi.
        Discusses influence of Civil Wars on the play.

7   WINTERS, YVOR. "The 16th Century Lyric in England: A Criti-
    cal and Historical Reinterpretation." Poetry, 53 (Feb-
    ruary), 258-72; 53 (March), 320-35; 54 (April), 35-51.
        In a major revaluation of sixteenth-century lyric
    poets, comments: "Of Samuel Daniel little need be
    said. . . . Like Sidney, he aims primarily at grace
    of expression; his tone is less exuberant than that of
    Sidney; his style is more consistently pure; his inspira-
    tion is less rich." Revised 1967.18; reprinted 1967.19.

1940

1   [JACKSON, WILLIAM ALEXANDER, ed.] The Carl H. Pforzheimer
    Library: English Literature, 1475-1700. Vol. I. New
    York: privately printed, 419 pp.
        Includes bibliographical descriptions of the following
    editions: STC 6236, 6237, 6239, 6247, 6253, 6260, 6261,
    6262, 11900, and 13161 (pp. 236-46).

2   MEOZZI, ANTÈRO. La Drammatica della Rinascita italiana in
    Europa, sec. XVI-XVII. Pisa: Nistri-Lischi, 221 pp.
        In chapter 2 ("La Drammatica italiana in Inghilterra,"
    pp. 75-129), discusses influence of Italian pastoral
    drama on Queen's Arcadia and Hymen's Triumph (pp. 117-19).

3   MUIR, KENNETH. "The Imagery of All for Love." PLPLS-LHS,
    5: 140-47.
        Examines Dryden's indebtedness (particularly for his
    imagery in Act V) to Cleopatra; suggests that "[i]t is not
    too much to say that the effectiveness of Act V depends
    very largely on echoes from Daniel's play."

1941

*4   ZOCCA, LOUIS RALPH. "Sixteenth Century Narrative Poetry in
        England." Ph.D. dissertation, Brown University, 141 pp.
        Published version 1950.11.

                              1941

1   BAMBAS, RUDOLPH CHARLES. "The Verb in Samuel Daniel's The
        Collection of the History of England." Ph.D. disserta-
        tion, Northwestern University, 123 pp. [Abstract in
        Northwestern University Summaries of Doctoral Disserta-
        tions, 9 (1941), 10-13.]
            Offers a detailed examination of verb forms, syntax,
        archaisms, periphrasis, voice, and mood in describing the
        "language usage" of Daniel. Compares his usage "and that
        of late modern English . . . in an effort to determine
        the modernity of Daniel's language." Concludes: "Daniel
        was remarkably in advance of the literary usage of his
        day in the trend towards later modern English idiom, but
        he retained a sufficient number of peculiarly Elizabethan
        constructions to render his language distinct from
        present-day English."

2   BATESON, F[REDERICK] W[ILSE], ed. The Cambridge Bibliography
        of English Literature, I: 600-1660. Cambridge: Cam-
        bridge University Press, 952 pp.
            Includes selective list of works by and about Daniel
        (contributed by H. J. Byrom) (pp. 422-23, passim). Re-
        vised 1974.18.

3   BORGESE, G. A. "The Dishonor of Honor: From Giovanni Mauro
        to Sir John Falstaff." RR, 32: 44-55.
            Suggests that "[i]t seems safe to assume that the curse
        on honor [by Falstaff, 1 Henry IV, V.i.127-41] is a para-
        phrase of Tasso's words transmitted to Shakespeare through
        the channel of Daniel's translation" of the Chorus from
        Act I of Aminta ("O Happy Golden Age").

*4   HUNT, JAMES CLAY. "The Beginnings of the Neo-Classic Move-
        ment in Elizabethan Poetry." Ph.D. dissertation, Johns
        Hopkins University, 438 pp.
            See 1941.5.

5   HUNT, [JAMES] CLAY. "The Elizabethan Background of Neo-
        Classic Polite Verse." ELH, 8 (December), 273-304.
            Includes Daniel's Epistles in a survey of Renaissance
        "familiar verse." Points out that Daniel's poems "are

1941

never chatty or really familiar, but they have the easy
versification and some of the discursive manner of familiar
verse, and sometimes the tone of friendly personal address."

6   YATES, FRANCES A[MELIA]. "The Emblematic Conceit in Giordano
Bruno's De gli eroici furori and in the Elizabethan Sonnet
Sequences." JWCI, 6: 101-21.
    Examines some of the "emblem-conceits" in Delia to show
their closeness to those in Eroici furori and to suggest
that Daniel was influenced by Bruno's work.

<u>1942</u>

1   MICHEL, LAURENCE A[NTHONY], JR. "An Edition of Samuel Daniel's Philotas with Introduction and Notes." Ph.D. dissertation, Fordham University, 301 pp. [Abstract in
Dissertations . . . Fordham University, 9 (1943), 22-26.]
    Provides critical edition, using 1623 edition as copy-
text. Discusses the relationship of the play to the
literary and political interests of the Pembroke circle,
its connection with the Essex affair, and its dramatic
weaknesses. Examines revisions and influence on Philip
Frowde's Philotas (1731). Published version 1949.3.

2   STIRLING, BRENTS. "Daniel's Philotas and the Essex Case."
MLQ, 3 (December), 583-94.
    Attempts "to draw from the play itself and from other
documents . . . an adequate sketch of the Philotas incident, together with its revelation of Daniel's character,
and . . . to provide and analyze evidence concerning
Daniel's seditious intent."

3   TANNENBAUM, SAMUEL A[ARON]. Samuel Daniel (A Concise Bibliography). Elizabethan Bibliographies, no. 25. New York:
Samuel A. Tannenbaum, 47 pp.
    Provides classified listing of works by and about
Daniel (673 entries). In "Foreword" points out that
"[d]espite his many merits Daniel is read today only by
drudges who have to prepare Master's theses and Doctoral
dissertations." Continued by 1962.4 and 1967.6; reprinted 1967.17.

1943

1   BERRINGER, RALPH W.   "Jonson's Cynthia's Revels and the War
     of the Theatres."   PQ, 22 (January), 1-22.
         Argues against identifying Daniel with Hedon.

2   BROOKS, ALDEN.   Will Shakspere and the Dyer's Hand.   New York:
     Charles Scribner's Sons, 724 pp.
         Incorporates 1937.1 in identifying Sir Edward Dyer as
     the author of Shakespeare's plays.   Argues that "Daniel,
     by his hand in Lucrece and . . . Romeo and Juliet, was, I
     believe, for many years supposed to have been the chief
     author of both these compositions."   Also discusses Dan-
     iel's influence on and composition of some of Shake-
     speare's sonnets (passim).

3   BURKE, SR. MARY RANSOM.   "The Tragedy of Cleopatra, Queen of
     Aegypt, by Thomas May: Edited with an Introduction."
     Ph.D. dissertation, Fordham University, 102 pp.   [Abstract
     in Fordham University Dissertations Accepted for Higher
     Degrees in the Graduate School of Arts and Sciences, 10
     (1943), 27-30.]
         Discusses influence of Cleopatra on May's play.

*4   CRANTZ, EDNA RASMUS.   "Mary Sidney Countess of Pembroke
     (1561-1621):   Das Bild einer Frau und ihrer literarischen
     Kreises im England der Renaissance."   Ph.D. dissertation,
     Humboldt University, Berlin, 213 pp.
         Manuscript dissertation; cited in Richard Mummendey,
     Language and Literature of the Anglo-Saxon Nations as
     Presented in German Doctoral Dissertations, 1885-1950:
     A Bibliography (Bonn: Bouvier; Charlottesville: Biblio-
     graphical Society of the University of Virginia, 1954),
     p. 82, item 1486.

5   PELLEGRINI, ANGELO M.   "Giordano Bruno on Translations."
     ELH, 10 (September), 193-207.
         Argues that Daniel was not "influenced materially" by
     Bruno's comments on translation and that N. W. mentions
     Bruno in his prefatory epistle to Worthy Tract not because
     of his influence but for the authority of his name as an
     aid in the "struggle against the enemies of translation."

6   TOBIN, JAMES E.   "A 1607 Concept of Comparative Literature."
     Comparative Literature News-Letter, 1 (May), 3-4.
         Discusses Daniel's comments on "intellectual isola-
     tionists" in Defense of Rhyme.

1944

1944

1   HIBERNICUS. "Daniell: Stray Notes on the Text." N&Q, 186
        (1 January), 6-8.
        Offers several emendations to various works as printed
        in 1885.1, 1885.2, 1885.3, 1896.2, and 1896.3.

*2   NEARING, HOMER. "English Historical Poetry, 1599-1641."
        Ph.D. dissertation, University of Pennsylvania, 314 pp.
        Published 1945.2.

3   ROLLINS, HYDER EDWARD, ed. The Sonnets. 2 volumes. New
        Variorum Edition of Shakespeare. Philadelphia: J. B.
        Lippincott, 424, 539 pp.
        In notes gathers commentary on parallels between Dan-
        iel's poems (especially Delia) and the Sonnets. In vari-
        ous appendices, provides overview of scholarship on Delia
        as one of Shakespeare's sources and on Daniel as the Rival
        Poet. Concludes that there is no convincing evidence for
        identifying Daniel as the Rival Poet (passim).

4   TILLYARD, E[USTACE] M[ANDEVILLE] W[ETENHALL]. Shakespeare's
        History Plays. London: Chatto & Windus, 344 pp.
        Examines the close "intellectual kinship" between Daniel
        in Civil Wars and Shakespeare in Richard II and Henry IV:
        discusses their "same conceptions of the universe and of
        history," their identical "political philosophy" (noting
        their differing emphases), and their closeness in choice
        of incidents but difference in treatment. Suggests that
        Daniel's epic treatment of English history stimulated
        Shakespeare to improve upon Daniel (pp. 237-42).

1945

1   BUSH, DOUGLAS. English Literature in the Earlier Seventeenth
        Century, 1600-1660. Oxford History of English Literature,
        vol V. Oxford: Clarendon Press, 629 pp.
        Provides critical overview of Daniel's seventeenth-
        century works, stressing his "sense of time" and view of
        man and life (pp. 91-94, passim). Revised edition 1962.2.

2   NEARING, HOMER, JR. English Historical Poetry, 1599-1641.
        Ph.D. dissertation, University of Pennsylvania, 1944.
        Philadelphia: n.p., 222 pp.
        In published version of 1944.2, gives a detailed analy-
        sis of Daniel's historical peotry in an overview of

Renaissance historical verse: provides critical estimate of each work, and examines sources, influence, purpose, and revisions (passim).

3   WILSON, F[RANK] P[ERCY]. Elizabethan and Jacobean. Oxford: Clarendon Press, 152 pp.
    Offers an appreciative estimate of Daniel, pointing out that he "had (for his age) so little power over image and lyrical incantation, [that he] needed to start with some solid body of observation and experience" (as in Civil Wars) (pp. 60-64).

4   WILSON, JOHN DOVER. "The Origins and Development of Shakespeare's Henry IV." Library, 4th ser., 26: 2-16.
    Examines Shakespeare's indebtedness to Civil Wars; suggests that "[a]bove all, perhaps, Daniel furnished his great disciple with his interpretation of the character of King Henry IV."

1946

1   CHARLTON, H[ENRY] B[UCKLEY]. The Senecan Tradition in Renaissance Tragedy. Manchester: Manchester University Press, 205 pp.
    Reissues sheets of "Introduction" to 1921.3 with added index.

2   LEISY, ERNEST E. "Sources of Thoreau's Borrowings in A Week." AL, 18 (March), 37-44.
    Identifies Thoreau's borrowings from Daniel.

1947

1   ATKINS, J[OHN] W[ILLIAM] H[EY]. English Literary Criticism: The Renascence. London: Methuen, 383 pp.
    In chapter 7 ("Critical Developments: Nashe, Harington, Daniel, Meres, Hall," pp. 179-215), considers Defense of Rhyme as "one of the great achievements in Elizabethan criticism" and analyzes Daniel's defense of rhyme, his examination "of the relation of ancient literature to the modern effort," and his conception of "the lines of true progress in creative literary methods." Also examines Musophilus as a work of literary theory (pp. 195-207).

1947

2   ELLIS, OLIVER C[OLIGNY] DE C[HAMPFLEUR]. Cleopatra in the
      Tide of Time. [London:] Williams and Norgate for the
      Poetry Lovers' Fellowship and the International Fellowship
      of Literature, 303 pp.
          Examines Daniel's depiction of Cleopatra in Letter from
      Octavia and Cleopatra. Discusses the play in examining
      the influence of "French Seneca" on Renaissance literature
      and suggests that it "achieves its great status because of
      a reversion to a purer form" of Senecan tragedy (pp. 99-
      109).

3   GRIERSON, HERBERT J[OHN] C[LIFFORD], and J[AMES] C[RUICK-
      SHANKS] SMITH. A Critical History of English Poetry.
      Revised edition. London: Chatto & Windus, 547 pp. [The
      first edition, not seen, was published in 1944.]
          In chapter 8 ("Elizabethan Poetry," pp. 79-89), offer
      a general critical appreciation of Daniel and Drayton,
      who "are the best, after Spenser, of all the non-dramatic
      poets, certainly the most copious and varied" (pp. 81-83,
      passim).

4   HELTZEL, VIRGIL B[ARNEY]. Fair Rosamond: A Study of the
      Development of a Literary Theme. Northwestern University
      Studies in the Humanities, no. 16. Evanston: Northwest-
      ern University Studies, 143 pp.
          Analyzes the place of Rosamond in the development of
      the Rosamond Clifford story; examines influences on the
      poem and traces its influence on subsequent works (passim).

5   JONES, JOSEPH. "Musophilus Revisited." School and Society,
      65 (8 February), 97-100.
          Invokes Daniel's poem in defense of a liberal education.

6   LAW, ROBERT ADGER. "Daniel's Rosamond and Shakespeare."
      University of Texas Studies in English, 26: 42-48.
          Analyzes influence of Rosamond on Lucrece: discusses
      similarities in phrasing, meter, and treatment of the two
      women. Concludes that "the two narrative poems, con-
      fessedly alike in occasional phrasing, are much more alike
      in form and in fundamental thought." Also traces influ-
      ence of Daniel's poem on Shakespeare's plays, particularly
      Romeo and Juliet.

7   McKISACK, MAY. "Samuel Daniel as Historian." RES, 23
      (July), 226-43.
          Examines History of England and Defense of Rhyme in
      assessing Daniel as "an historian manqué who found his
      vocation too late in life to develop his talents to the

full" and in showing that "it is the quality of his mind
rather than the depth of his reading that lends Daniel
distinction as an historian." Surveys his sources and
critical treatment of them, examines his sense of the
past (particularly the "originality of [his] . . . approach
to medieval history"), and illustrates his "shrewd judge-
ment of character and lucid analyses of historical situations."

8 STRATMAN, CARL JOSEPH. "Dramatic Performances at Oxford and
Cambridge, 1603-1642." Ph.D. dissertation, University of
Illinois, 416 pp. [Separately published abstract: Urbana: n.p., 9 pp.]
Points out that the "historical importance [of Queen's
Arcadia] . . . lies in the fact that it was the first play
to exhibit on the English stage the direct and unequivocal
influence of the Italian pastoral drama." Also discusses
satire in the work.

9 TUVE, ROSEMOND. Elizabethan and Metaphysical Imagery:
Renaissance Poetic and Twentieth-Century Critics. Chicago:
University of Chicago Press, 448 pp.
Draws frequently on Daniel (particularly Delia and
Musophilus) in analyzing characteristics of Elizabethan
imagery (passim).

10 WASSERMAN, EARL R[EEVES]. Elizabethan Poetry in the Eighteenth Century. 'ISLL, 32. Urbana: University of Illinois
Press, 291 pp.
In revision of 1937.9 discusses the eighteenth-century
attitude toward and reception of Daniel (passim).

1948

1 CALLANAN, PHILIP WRIGHT. "Samuel Daniel's Delia: A Critical
Edition." Ph.D. dissertation, Cornell University.
Provides critical edition with notes on "Daniel's
methods of composition and revision."

2 HELTZEL, VIRGIL B[ARNEY]. "Sir Thomas Egerton as Patron."
HLQ, 11 (February), 105-27.
Discusses Daniel's relationship with Egerton.

3 SHACKFORD, MARTHA HALE. "Samuel Daniel's Poetical Epistles,
Especially That to the Countess of Cumberland." SP, 45
(April), 180-95.

1949

Provides a critical appraisal of Daniel's epistles,
particularly those addressed to women. Discusses influences on them and the "decorum, a severe reserve, which
prevents us from learning anything about his own life";
places the poems in the context of his relationship with
the respective addressees. Gives particular attention to
"To the Countess of Cumberland": points out that "[t]he
restrained yet warm admiration expressed for the Countess
is quite objective" and discusses Daniel's use of building
imagery and his characterization of the Countess.

1949

1   ANON. "A Seventeenth-Century Play." TLS (30 December),
    p. 860.
        In review of 1949.3 comments on Daniel's diction and
    versification.

2   APPEL, LOUIS DAVID. "The Concept of Fame in Tudor and Stuart
    Literature." Ph.D. dissertation, Northwestern University,
    224 pp. [Abstract in Summaries of Doctoral Disserta-
    tions . . . Northwestern University, 17 (1950), 9-13.]
        Examines how Musophilus "stands virtually alone as a
    comparatively long poem devoted in great measure to [the]
    . . . all-pervasive theme" of "literature as the chief
    medium for the achievement of fame."

3   DANIEL, SAMUEL. The Tragedy of Philotas. Edited by Laurence
    [Anthony] Michel. YSE, vol. 110. New Haven: Yale Uni-
    versity Press, 195 pp.
        In revision of 1942.1 provides critical edition, using
    1623 edition as copy-text. In "Introduction" (pp. 1-94),
    discusses Daniel's attitude toward literature and his
    attempt to write for the "'better sort of men'"; Philotas
    as a reflection of the political and literary concerns of
    the Countess of Pembroke's circle; the play as "an omnium
    gatherum of Daniel's political opinions, conflicting as
    they are"; the role of the chorus and Daniel's attitude
    toward the common people; the influence of Garnier and the
    Mirror for Magistrates tradition on the work; parallels
    with Daniel's other writings; sources; bibliographical
    particulars of and relationships among editions; and Dan-
    iel's revisions. Devotes considerable attention to the
    close relationship between the play and the Essex affair:
    traces the inconsistencies in political thought and unity
    to the influence of the trial and execution of Essex on
    Acts IV and V, suggesting that the "original emphasis . . .

on the disruptive power of ambition and insubordination"
was altered to "the schemes and machinations of bureau-
cratic tyranny." In appendix I (pp. 162-74), examines
influence of Philotas on Philip Frowde's Philotas (1731).
See 1962.15; reprinted 1970.5. Reviewed in T[homas]
W[hitfield] Baldwin, JEGP, 48 (July 1949), 440; 1949.1;
1950.6; 1950.8; 1951.10.

<u>1950</u>

1   BROWN, DOROTHY ISABELLE. "Religion in the Non-Dramatic
    Poetry of the Reign of Queen Elizabeth, with the Exception
    of the Works of Spenser." Ph.D. dissertation, University
    of Colorado. [Abstract in University of Colorado Studies,
    General Ser., 28, no. 4 (1951), 115-17.
        Points out that Daniel's "philosophical poems . . .
    make a distinct and weighty contribution toward an under-
    standing of Elizabethan theological beliefs."

2   DANIEL, SAMUEL. Poems and "A Defence of Ryme." Edited by
    Arthur Colby Sprague. London: Routledge & Kegan Paul,
    254 pp.
        Reissue of 1930.2. Reviewed in 1951.1.

3   FARNHAM, WILLARD. Shakespeare's Tragic Frontier: The World
    of His Final Tragedies. Berkeley: University of Cali-
    fornia Press, 297 pp.
        Provides detailed analysis of correspondences between
    Cleopatra and Antony and Cleopatra in arguing that Shake-
    speare was influenced by the 1594 version of Daniel's
    play. Also examines influence of Letter from Octavia on
    Antony and Cleopatra. Analyzes Daniel's characterization
    of Cleopatra (especially his emphasis on her "royal
    pride") to illustrate that she is "a heroine with mixed
    motives" (pp. 156-75, passim).

4   HIMELICK, RAYMOND. "Samuel Daniel's Musophilus: Containing
    a General Defense of All Learning: Edited, with Introduc-
    tion and Notes." Ph.D. dissertation, Indiana University,
    284 pp.
        Provides critical edition, using 1623 edition as copy-
    text. In "Introduction" gives a critical overview of
    Daniel's life and works; examines the structure, sources
    and analogues, and revisions of Musophilus; provides a
    critical analysis of the poem; and gives a bibliographical
    analysis of the early editions. Revised 1965.7.

1950

5   HUTCHESON, W[ILLIAM] J. FRASER. Shakespeare's Other Anne.
      Glasgow: William McLellan, 128 pp.
         Identifies Delia as Anne Whately (passim).

6   JENKINS, HAROLD. Review of Laurence [Anthony] Michel, ed.,
      The Tragedy of Philotas. MLR, 45 (April), 243–44.
         In review of 1949.3 criticizes Michel's bibliographical
      analysis and choice of 1623 edition as copy-text; points
      out errors in collation and presentation of text. Con-
      cludes that the edition does not satisfy "the high stand-
      ards of modern textual scholarship."

7   MICHEL, LAURENCE [ANTHONY]. "'Sommers heate' Again." N&Q,
      195 (8 July), 292–93.
         Identifies "Being checkt with Sommers heate" (1601
      Civil Wars, book 4, stanza 10) as an allusion to Edward
      Somerset, Earl of Worcester. Queries how Mountjoy was
      "checkt" by Somerset.

8   SHAABER, M[ATTHIAS] A[DAM]. Review of Laurence [Anthony]
      Michel, ed., The Tragedy of Philotas. MLN, 65 (November),
      494–97.
         In review of 1949.3 criticizes Michel's choice of 1623
      edition as copy-text and some aspects of his bibliograph-
      ical analysis.

9   TOLBERT, JAMES McDUFFIE. "Shakespeare's Lucrece: A Study of
      Its Antecedents, Sources, and Composition." Ph.D. disserta-
      tion, University of Texas.
         Discusses Daniel in chapter 3, "The Relationship of
      Lucrece to Writings Other Than Versions of the Lucretia
      Legend."

10 WHALLEY, A[RTHUR] G[EORGE] C[UTHBERT]. "Samuel Taylor Col-
      eridge, Library Cormorant: The History of His Use of
      Books; With a Consideration of Purpose and Pattern in His
      Reading, and an Account of the Books He Owned, Annotated,
      and Borrowed." Ph.D. dissertation, University of London.
         Discusses Coleridge's marginalia on Daniel in copies
      of 1718.1, 1793.1 (both Folger and Victoria and Albert
      copies), and 1810.1.

11 ZOCCA, LOUIS R[ALPH]. Elizabethan Narrative Poetry. New
      Brunswick: Rutgers University Press, 318 pp.
         In revision of 1940.4 discusses Rosamond as a complaint
      poem and provides a critical estimate of the work (pp. 70–
      73).

<u>1951</u>

1   ANON.   "Neglected Poet." <u>TLS</u> (26 January), p. 54.
        In review of 1950.2 calls Daniel "one of the major
    Elizabethan poets who is still absurdly little known."
    Objects to some of Sprague's omissions and discusses
    Daniel's style.

2   DENNETT, DAYTON NIGEL.   "Samuel Daniel's <u>Tragedy of Cleopatra</u>:
    A Critical Edition." Ph.D. dissertation, Cornell Univer-
    sity, 184 pp.
        Provides critical edition with three introductory es-
    says: bibliographical (discusses the various editions of
    the play and their relationship); historical (examines
    sources and the relationship of <u>Cleopatra</u> to <u>Mirror for
    Magistrates</u> and <u>Antony and Cleopatra</u>); and critical
    (analyzes Daniel's diction, thought, style, and revisions).

3   GREER, C. A.   "Did Shakespeare Use Daniel's <u>Civile Warres</u>?"
    <u>N&Q</u>, 196 (3 February), 53-54.
        Argues that Shakespeare in his history plays was not
    indebted to Daniel's poem.

4   HANSON, L. W.   "The Shakespeare Collection in the Bodleian
    Library, Oxford." <u>ShS</u>, 4: 78-96.
        Transcribes the special dedication by Daniel in copy
    of <u>Works</u> presented to the Bodleian and notes presence
    of list of properties for <u>Queen's Arcadia</u> in the Univer-
    sity Archives.

5   HUNTER, G. K.   "The Marking of <u>Sententiae</u> in Elizabethan
    Printed Plays, Poems, and Romances." <u>Library</u>, 5th ser., 6
    (December), 171-88.
        Draws on Daniel's works in analyzing characteristics
    of gnomic pointing.

6   LEWIS, ARTHUR ORCUTT, JR.   "Emblem Books and English Drama:
    A Preliminary Survey, 1581-1600." Ph.D. dissertation,
    Pennsylvania State University, 338 pp. [Abstract in
    <u>Pennsylvania State University Abstracts</u>, 14: 334-36.]
        Includes <u>Worthy Tract</u> in a survey of English emblem
    books.

7   McMANAWAY, JAMES G[ILMER].   "Some Bibliographical Notes on
    Samuel Daniel's <u>Civil Wars</u>." <u>SB</u>, 4: 31-39.
        Suggests that 1595 title page with royal arms at top
    was cancelled and replaced by the one with "IHS"; argues

1951

that the edition with "fift" preceded that with "fyft";
identifies John Wolfe as the printer of the former and
suggests James Roberts as the printer of the latter and
the errata leaf; suggests that Waterson had the Roberts
edition printed when he "discovered that he had an insufficient quantity of The fift Booke to match the remainder
copies of The First Fowre Bookes."

8   SERONSY, CECIL C. "Studies in Samuel Daniel." Ph.D. dissertation, Harvard University.
      Examines "Daniel's life and contemporary reputation,
his art and thought, and his influence as a writer."
Gives particular attention to his relationship with patrons, to his revisions and their relationship to his
style, to an analysis of his style (especially diction,
versification, and imagery), and to his influence (particularly that of Rosamond on the poetry of the 1590s, of
Civil Wars on Richard II, and of his poetry generally on
Wordsworth and other nineteenth-century writers).

9   URE, PETER. "A Note on 'Opinion' in Daniel, Greville, and
Chapman." MLR, 46 (July & October), 331-38.
      Examines "the special pejorative meaning" of Daniel's
allegorical use of "Opinion" and its relationship with
his "Stoic and Calvinist emphasis on inward discipline and
virtue, to which Opinion is an exterior ill." Reprinted
1974.17.

10   ____. Review of Laurence [Anthony] Michel, ed., The Tragedy
of Philotas. RES, NS 2 (January), 72-73.
      In review of 1949.3 suggests that Daniel's ambiguity
toward Philotas should be considered in the light of the
ambiguity of his "main source" (Quintus Curtius) and concludes that "the case for political allegory [in the play
is] fairly water-tight."

1952

1   HIMELICK, RAYMOND. "Thoreau and Samuel Daniel." AL, 24
(May), 177-85.
      Examines how Thoreau, in A Week on the Concord and
Merrimack Rivers, ignored the context of passages he
borrowed from Daniel.

2   HOEPFNER, THEODORE C. "Daniel's Delia, Sonnet XL." Expl, 10
      (April), item 38.
          Explicates line 12: "rail"="garment"; "needle"="needle-
      work"; the antecedent of "which" is "veil."

3   REES, JOAN. "Samuel Daniel's Cleopatra and Two French Plays."
      MLR, 47 (January), 1-10.
          Examines Daniel's indebtedness to Garnier's Marc-Antoine
      and Jodelle's Cléopâtre captive to illustrate the unrecog-
      nized "distinct merits" of Cleopatra. Discusses how Daniel
      unifies the play by concentrating on Cleopatra, examines
      his emphasis on the "conflict between Cleopatra's instincts
      as a queen and her instincts as a mother," and analyzes
      his characterization of Cleopatra.

4   SERONSY, CECIL C. "Samuel Daniel and Milton." N&Q, 197
      (29 March), 135-36.
          Explores the possible influence of Daniel (especially
      in Civil Wars) on the style and content of Milton's works.
      (See editor's correction, 24 May, p. 239).

5   SMITH, HALLETT. Elizabethan Poetry: A Study in Conventions,
      Meaning, and Expression. Cambridge: Harvard University
      Press, 367 pp.
          Examines Rosamond as a pioneer in the development of
      the "new kind of complaint poem" and Delia as "an oppor-
      tunity for Daniel to achieve the expression of a gentle
      melancholy characteristic of him, to celebrate the lasting
      powers of verse against the ravages of time and barbarism,
      and to show that the themes and devices which had been
      used so much by the French and Italian sonneteers had as
      much grace and dignity in English as they had in other
      tongues" (pp. 103-108, 157-61, passim).

6   THAYER, CALVIN GRAHAM. "Verse and Virtue: A Study of Samuel
      Daniel's Poetry." Ph.D. dissertation, University of
      California, Berkeley.
          In a critical survey of Daniel's poetry, argues "that
      the combination of verse and virtue helped produce Dan-
      iel's characteristic poetry"--"that Daniel was a moral
      and didactic poet who believed that it was 'the function
      of a poem, to discourse,' and that because of the moral-
      ity . . . which he preached, he had to write in a certain
      way," a way "that largely precluded his writing with what
      we might call characteristic Elizabethan fire and passion."
      Devotes chapters to Delia, tragic works, political poems,
      and humanistic works.

1952

7   THOMSON, PATRICIA. "The Literature of Patronage, 1580-1630."
    EIC, 2 (July), 267-84.
        Contrasts Daniel, "who was literally at home in the
    system of patronage" but retained his individuality and
    preserved the "dignity" of his poetry, with Donne, whose
    "genius reaped nothing but harm from patronage." See
    1953.5.

                              1953

*1 ABOUL-ENEIN, A. M. "Cleopatra in French and English Drama
    from Yodelle to Shakespeare." Ph.D. dissertation, Trinity
    College, Dublin.

2   LEAVENWORTH, RUSSELL EDWIN. "Daniel's Cleopatra: A Critical
    Study." Ph.D. dissertation, University of Colorado,
    255 pp. [Abstract in University of Colorado Studies,
    General Ser., 29, no. 3 (1954), 26-27.]
        Analyzes style, traces sources (suggesting that Daniel
    probably was influenced by Machiavelli's Discourses), and
    examines influence of the play on other authors, especial-
    ly Shakespeare. Argues that the 1607 revision "was not an
    attempt to make Cleopatra more dramatic and was in no way
    influenced by Shakespeare." Examines the "unity . . . be-
    tween the narrative and philosophical functions of the
    poem" and argues that "[i]ts confident restraint and over-
    all artistic unity make Cleopatra the first thoroughly
    neo-classical poem in the English [l]anguage." Published
    1974.10.

3   LOWERS, JAMES K. Mirrors for Rebels: A Study of Polemical
    Literature Relating to the Northern Rebellion, 1569.
    UCPES, 6. Berkeley: University of California Press,
    138 pp.
        In chapter 6 ("The Doctrine in Nonpolemical Litera-
    ture," pp. 80-106), analyzes how in Civil Wars Daniel
    "consciously introduced orthodox Tudor political doctrine
    [especially arguments against civil disobedience] which,
    in large part, had been made familiar to Elizabethans by
    the polemists" who wrote about the Northern Rebellion
    (pp. 87-107).

4   REES, JOAN. "An Elizabethan Eyewitness of Antony and Cleo-
    patra?" ShS, 6: 91-93.
        Suggests that in the 1607 edition of Cleopatra the
    passage at I.11.238-64 (especially "She drawes him up in
    rowles of taffaty" and "Tug'd at the pulley") was

influenced by Daniel's viewing of a performance of <u>Antony and Cleopatra</u>. (Rees reconsiders this suggestion in 1964.11, pp. 109-11.) <u>See</u> 1953.11.

5   SAUNDERS, J[OHN] W[HITESIDE]. "Donne and Daniel." <u>EIC</u>, 3 (January), 109-14.
     In response to 1952.7 argues that Daniel and Donne cannot be compared as professional poets. Sees Daniel as a "pensioner," "an out-and-out professional, printing all he could, and . . . something of an expert in accommodating his work to the market . . . by means of gift folio editions and the like." Finds that because Daniel "was sheltered, . . . his poetry suffers."

6   SERONSY, CECIL C. "Coleridge Marginalia in Lamb's Copy of Daniel's <u>Poetical Works</u>." <u>HLB</u>, 7 (Winter), 105-12.
     Transcribes Coleridge's marginalia and some of Lamb's textual notations in the latter's copy of 1718.1.

7   _____. "Daniel's Manuscript <u>Civil Wars</u> with Some Previously Unpublished Stanzas." <u>JEGP</u>, 52 (April), 153-60.
     Examines differences between the manuscript (British Library Sloane 1,443) and 1595 edition to argue "that the MS unquestionably gives us the earliest version of <u>The Civil Wars</u>"; dates the manuscript 1594, or earlier; and transcribes six stanzas not previously published, suggesting that they were omitted because they "are noticeably sympathetic to Richard." <u>See</u> "Correction by Cecil C. Seronsy," October, p. 594.

8   _____. "Daniel's <u>Panegyrike</u> and the Earl of Hertford." <u>PQ</u>, 32 (July), 342-44.
     Finds that in 1605 or later Daniel had some copies of a leaf with the prose epistle to Hertford and "The Passion of a Distressed Man" printed for insertion in a few remaining copies of <u>Panegyric Congratulatory</u> (1603). Discusses Daniel's relations with Hertford and reasons for waiting to have the prose epistle printed.

9   _____. "Wordsworth's Annotations in Daniel's <u>Poetical Works</u>." <u>MLN</u>, 68 (June), 403-406.
     Transcribes Wordsworth's annotations in his copy of 1718.1.

10   URE, PETER. "Two Passages in Sylvester's Du Bartas and Their Bearing on Shakespeare's <u>Richard II</u>." <u>N&Q</u>, 198 (September), 374-77.

1953

Examines possible connection between Delia and Civil
Wars, and Sylvester's translation.

11 WALKER, ROY. "Antony and Cleopatra." TLS (29 May), p. 349.
    In commenting on 1953.4 suggests possibility of a con-
    nection between Daniel's "rowles of taffeta" and stage
    business in an 1898 production of Antony and Cleopatra.

1954

1 BUXTON, JOHN. Sir Philip Sidney and the English Renaissance.
   London: Macmillan; New York: St. Martin's Press, 296 pp.
   Discusses the Countess of Pembroke and the Countess of
   Bedford as Daniel's patronesses, his relationship with
   Spenser and Greville, and the influence of Sidney on his
   work (pp. 188-93, passim). (In the second edition [1964],
   makes no substantive changes in discussion of Daniel.)

2 CUTTS, JOHN P. "Jacobean Masque and Stage Music." M&L, 35
   (July), 185-200.
   Identifies songs from Daniel's masques in British
   Library Add. MS. 10,444.

3 _____. "Original Music to Browne's Inner Temple Masque, and
   Other Jacobean Masque Music." N&Q, NS 1 (May), 194-95.
   Identifies setting of "From the Temple to the Board"
   (Hymen's Triumph) and "Time, Cruel Time" (Delia; see
   1930.2, p. 177) in MS. 1,018, St. Michael's College Li-
   brary, Tenbury Wells.

4 LEWIS C[LIVE] S[TAPLES]. English Literature in the Sixteenth
   Century (Exluding Drama). Oxford History of English Literature, vol. III. Oxford: Clarendon Press, 704 pp.
   In classifying Daniel as "Golden," discusses Delia
   ("a masterpiece of phrasing and melody") in section on
   sonnet sequences and provides a critical overview of
   Daniel's other works to c. 1600. Concludes: "Though
   Daniel's poetry is often uninspired, sometimes obscure,
   and not seldom simply bad, he has two strong claims on
   our respect"--"he can at times achieve the same masculine
   and unrestrained majesty which we find in Wordsworth's
   greater sonnets" and he "is . . . a poet of ideas"
   (pp. 491-93, 526-31, passim). See 1962.2.

5 MILLER, EDWIN HAVILAND. "Samuel Daniel's Revisions in Delia."
   JEGP, 53 (January), 58-68.

Examines Daniel's excision of feminine rhymes, verbal
changes which led to "conventionalization of language and
of imagery and diminution of passion," and alterations in
scansion. Provides detailed analysis of Delia 27 to illustrate Daniel's process of revision. Concludes that
"he attempted to perfect his lines, in sterile academic
fashion, according to an evolving poetic theory rather
than to recapture imaginatively the original emotion."

6   POTTER, JAMES LAIN. "The Development of Sonnet-Patterns in
     the Sixteenth Century." Ph.D. dissertation, Harvard Uni-
     versity, 185 pp.
         Includes Delia in an examination of the "forms of the
     sonnet used by" Elizabethan poets.

7   TILLYARD, E[USTACE] M[ANDEVILLE] W[ETENHALL]. The English
     Epic and Its Background. London: Chatto & Windus,
     558 pp.
         Devotes section of chapter 11 ("The Chronicler-Poets,"
     pp. 320-37) to an examination of the epic qualities of
     Civil Wars. Characterizes Daniel as "the true successor
     of Hall" in expounding the Tudor myth, discusses the in-
     fluence of Lucan and Homer on the work, examines his in-
     tention to praise the Tudors, compares his political
     philosophy with Shakespeare's, and analyzes his "philosophy
     of history and his solemn concern with the motives of
     great political action" as "the two things that most give
     his poem an epic tinge" (pp. 322-37).

1955

1   BEAUCHAMP, VIRGINIA WALCOTT. "Dramatic Treatment of Antony
     and Cleopatra in the Sixteenth and Seventeenth Centuries:
     Variations in Dramatic Form upon a Single Theme." Ph.D.
     dissertation, University of Chicago.
         Includes Cleopatra (1594 and 1607) in an analysis of
     the "artistic and non-artistic causes which account for"
     the evolution of the depiction of Antony and Cleopatra
     from 1590 to 1678. Examines Daniel's "purpose, character-
     ization, and diction" and speculates that "[p]ossibly
     Shakespeare's Antony and Cleopatra . . . and more certain-
     ly the rise of the popular theatre suggested Daniel's
     revision of his play in 1607."

1955

2   BLACK, MATTHEW W[ILSON], ed. The Life and Death of King
      Richard the Second. New Variorum Edition of Shakespeare.
      Philadelphia: J. B. Lippincott, 687 pp.
         In notes and a portion of the appendix on sources,
      gathers commentary on Shakespeare's use of Civil Wars as
      a source (passim).

3   [COLERIDGE, SAMUEL TAYLOR.] Coleridge on the Seventeenth
      Century. Edited by Roberta Florence Brinkley. Durham:
      Duke University Press, 742 pp.
         Reprints Coleridge's comments on Daniel: includes ex-
      tracts from published works, letters, and marginalia
      (pp. 509-16).

4   DAVIE, DONALD. Articulate Energy: An Inquiry into the Syn-
      tax of English Poetry. London: Routledge & Kegan Paul,
      181 pp.
         In chapter 5 ("Syntax as Action in Sidney, Shakespeare,
      and Others," pp. 43-55), examines syntax in Delia 45
      (pp. 46-50).

5   HERRICK, MARVIN T[HEODORE]. Tragicomedy: Its Origin and
      Development in Italy, France, and England. ISLL, 39.
      Urbana: University of Illinois Press, 337 pp.
         Devotes section of chapter 5 ("Pastoral Tragicomedy,"
      pp. 125-71) to "Samuel Daniel's Pastoral Tragicomedies"
      (pp. 157-61). Focuses on Queen's Arcadia and Hymen's
      Triumph as "conscious imitations" of Tasso's Aminta and
      Guarini's Pastor fido. Points out that "Hymen's Triumph
      is more English than the Queen's Arcadia; that is, it is
      less an imitation of the Italian pastoral tragicomedy."
      Concludes that neither is a pure pastoral tragicomedy and
      that the "comic features . . . probably most appealed to
      [Daniel's] . . . English audience."

6   MICHEL, LAURENCE [ANTHONY], and CECIL C. SERONSY. "Shake-
      speare's History Plays and Daniel: An Assessment." SP,
      52 (October), 549-77.
         Attempt "a summary and critique of estimates of the
      Daniel-Shakespeare relationship on a factual basis, to
      get the record straight." Conclude that in the case of
      Richard II all the evidence "points to the priority of
      Daniel's" Civil Wars; that Shakespeare used Civil Wars
      as a source for Henry IV; that Daniel drew upon Richard II,
      Henry IV, and (possibly) Henry VI in revising Civil Wars;
      and that the relationship of the various versions of
      Cleopatra to Antony and Cleopatra is undecided. Incor-
      porated in 1958.4.

7   NØRGAARD, HOLGER. "The Bleeding Captain Scene in <u>Macbeth</u> and
    Daniel's <u>Cleopatra</u>." <u>RES</u>, NS 6 (October), 395-96.
        Finds the source of the "spent swimmers" simile
    (Macbeth, I.ii.8) in <u>Cleopatra</u>, scene 1.

8   ____. "Shakespeare and Daniel's <u>Letter from Octavia</u>." <u>N&Q</u>,
    NS 2 (February), 56-57.
        Points out Shakespeare's indebtedness to <u>Letter from
    Octavia</u> in <u>Antony and Cleopatra</u> (I.i.).

9   SELLS, A[RTHUR] LYTTON. <u>The Italian Influence in English
    Poetry from Chaucer to Southwell</u>. London: George Allen
    & Unwin, 346 pp.
        Discusses influence of Italian authors on <u>Delia</u>, point-
    ing out that "[t]he Italian colour of <u>Delia</u> can be seen
    not merley in the verses which . . . [Daniel] lifted direct
    from Tasso and others . . . , but in the general atmos-
    phere of his book" (pp. 233-36).

10 URE, PETER. "Two Elizabethan Poets: Samuel Daniel and Sir
    Walter Ralegh," in <u>The Age of Shakespeare</u>. Volume II of
    <u>A Guide to English Literature</u>. Edited by Boris Ford.
    Harmondsworth: Penguin, pp. 131-46.
        Noting that the work of the two "has in common . . .
    the tradition of Sidney's <u>Apology for Poetry</u> and of
    Renaissance poetic generally," analyzes "the two poets'
    evaluative handling of emotion" and their shaping of
    "each poem purposively with a care for conscious design
    and logical control." Draws on <u>Delia</u> and <u>Rosamond</u> for
    examples. <u>See</u> 1964.8.

                            <u>1956</u>

1   FALLS, CYRIL. "Penelope Rich and the Poets: Philip Sidney
    to John Ford." <u>EDH</u>, 28: 123-37.
        Discusses Daniel's references to Lady Rich and Charles
    Blount, her lover.

2   GOTTFRIED, RUDOLF B[RAND]. "The Authorship of <u>A Breviary of
    the History of England</u>." SP, 53 (April), 172-90.
        Argues that Daniel, not Ralegh, is the author. De-
    scribes the extant manuscripts and their relationship;
    establishes "that the <u>Breviary</u> is related to . . . [Dan-
    iel's] <u>History</u> of 1612, rather than to that of 1618, and
    that it preceded rather than followed the <u>History</u> of
    1612"; and examines several parallels between the <u>Breviary</u>
    and Daniel's works.

1956

3 _____. "Samuel Daniel's Method of Writing History." <u>Studies
   in the Renaissance</u>, 3: 157-74.
       Provides detailed analysis of Daniel's use of <u>L'Histoire
   et chronique de Normandie</u> in <u>History of England</u> to show
   how "he not only sews . . . [his sources] together, as he
   says, but . . . condenses, amalgamates, and interprets his
   material into a narrative which is characteristically his
   own."

4 HENTZ, ANN LOUISE. "The Verse Epistles of Samuel Daniel: A
   Critical Edition." Ph.D. dissertation, Ohio State University, 343 pp. [<u>DA</u>, 16 (1956), 2164.]
       Provides critical edition of <u>Letter from Octavia</u> (based
   on 1599 edition), <u>Epistles</u> (based on 1603 edition), and
   "To James Montague" (based on the manuscript). Examines
   influences on the poems and classifies them as rhetorical
   epistle, formal verse essay, or Horation epistle.

5 HIMELICK, RAYMOND. "Samuel Daniel, Montaigne, and Seneca."
   <u>N&Q</u>, NS 3 (February), 61-64.
       Examines influence of Montaigne and Seneca on Daniel's
   works, especially <u>Musophilus</u> and the verse epistles. Suggests that Montaigne's <u>Essays</u> "may have . . . stimulated
   Daniel's Senecanism."

6 JORGENSEN, PAUL A. <u>Shakespeare's Military World</u>. Berkeley:
   University of California Press, 357 pp.
       In chapter 6 ("The Soldier in Society: From Casque to
   Cushion," pp. 208-314), discusses the effect of the Essex
   affair and the influence of the literary tradition of the
   "unlucky soldier" on "the defensive tactics used by Philotas [and] . . . the severe judgment upon them" (pp. 273-76,
   passim).

7 LEVER, J[ULIUS] W[ALTER]. <u>The Elizabethan Love Sonnet</u>. London: Methuen, 292 pp.
       In chapter 6 ("The Late Elizabethan Sonnet," pp. 139-
   61), discusses the importance of <u>Delia</u> in the evolution of
   the Elizabethan sonnet. Examines Daniel's "main con-
   cern . . . with the pathos of youth and beauty as victims
   of time" and the narrowness of his subject matter; discusses "the fine sensibility and intuitive perception that
   mark Daniel's treatments of his themes"; and identifies
   his two major contributions to the development of the
   sonnet: his employment of metaphorical imagery "as a
   structural principle binding together a run of sonnets"
   and his revelation of "the latent potentialities of the"

English sonnet form. Contrasts Daniel with Drayton
(pp. 150-55, passim). (The discussion of Delia is unre-
vised in the second edition, 1966.)

8 URE, PETER. "Introduction," in his edition of William Shakespeare's King Richard II. Arden Shakespeare. Cambridge:
Harvard University Press, pp. xiii-lxxxiii.
    Discusses relationship between Civil Wars and Richard
II, suggesting that it is a "reasonable guess" that Shakespeare was indebted to Daniel (pp. xlii-xliv).

9 WILKES, G[ERALD] A[LFRED]. "Poetry of Moral Reflection at
the Turn of the Sixteenth Century." Ph.D. dissertation,
Merton College, Oxford University.
    Provides detailed analysis of Daniel as a "reflective
poet," particularly as he "shows how the needs of specu-
lation and theorising could be satisfied without any de-
parture from the established modes." Discusses Rosamond,
Cleopatra, Musophilus, Epistles, Civil Wars, and Philotas.

1957

1 BLISSETT, WILLIAM. "Samuel Daniel's Sense of the Past."
ES, 38, no. 2, 49-63.
    Analyzes Daniel's "historical imagination" or his
"'sense of the past'--of its opportunities and pitfalls,
its lessons for the present, its place in the continuity
of history"--in History of England, Civil Wars, Defense
of Rhyme, and Musophilus.

2 DICKEY, FRANKLIN M. Not Wisely but Too Well: Shakespeare's
Love Tragedies. San Marino: Huntington Library, 215 pp.
    Places Cleopatra in the context of other Renaissance
treatments of Antony and Cleopatra and analyzes the influence of Daniel's play--especially his "action and characterization"--on Shakespeare's. Also discusses the influence of Letter from Octavia on Antony and Cleopatra.
Examines Daniel's "conception of Cleopatra as noble vil-
lain" and suggests that he "attempts to justify the
destruction of Antony's and Cleopatra's empire by reference to the working out of a universal plan" (pp. 168-73,
passim).

3 GREG, W[ALTER] W[ILSON]. A Bibliography of the English
Printed Drama to the Restoration. Vol. III. London:
Oxford University Press for The Bibliographical Society,
633 pp., 11 plates.

1957

Provides bibliographical description of collections of
Daniel's works in which one or more of his plays appear
(pp. 1048-1055). See 1939.2.

4   HIMELICK, RAYMOND. "A Fig for Momus and Daniel's Musophilus."
    MLQ, 18 (September), 247-50.
        Suggests that Lodge's Fig for Momus, Eclogue 4 (a de-
    bate between the "scholar-poet and the man of action" ad-
    dressed to Daniel), contributed "by its inconclusiveness
    and superficiality, to . . . [Daniel's] desire to give
    literature the kind of apologia he believed that it de-
    served."

5   _____. "Montaigne and Daniel's 'To Sir Thomas Egerton.'"
    PQ, 36 (October), 500-504.
        Traces Daniel's indebtedness to Montaigne's "Of Experi-
    ence" (in Florio's translation).

6   MUIR, KENNETH. Shakespeare's Sources, I: Comedies and
    Tragedies. London: Methuen, 279 pp.
        Examines Shakespeare's indebtedness in Antony and Cleo-
    patra to one of the earlier versions of Cleopatra but
    finds the evidence for Daniel's use of Shakespeare's play
    in the 1607 revision inconclusive. Also comments briefly
    on the influence of Rosamond on Romeo and Juliet and the
    possible influence of Queen's Arcadia on Macbeth (pp. 30,
    167, 209-19).

7   MURPHY, WILLIAM M. "Thomas Watson's Hecatompathia [1582] and
    the Elizabethan Sonnet Sequence." JEGP, 56 (July), 418-
    28.
        Traces influence of Watson's sequence on Daniel's son-
    nets published with Astrophel and Stella and on Delia.

8   SCHANZER, ERNEST. "Daniel's Revision of His Cleopatra." RES,
    NS 8 (November), 375-81.
        Argues that Daniel was indebted to the Countess of
    Pembroke's Antonius rather than to Shakespeare's Antony
    and Cleopatra in his 1607 revision of Cleopatra. Suggests
    that Shakespeare was influenced by the 1607 version as
    well as the earlier one. See 1958.10.

9   SERONSY, CECIL C. "The Doctrine of Cyclical Recurrence and
    Some Related Ideas in the Works of Samuel Daniel." SP,
    54 (July), 387-407.
        "[S]ketch[es] the background and possible origins of
    Daniel's particular brand of cyclical theory [i.e., the
    "notion of alternating progress and decay"], . . .

presents[s] the precise nature of his ideas on recurrence
and the way in which he artistically utilizes these ideas,
and . . . show[s] the extent to which the cyclical theory
supports his attitude towards tragedy, fame, and literary
history." Gives particular attention to Cleopatra, Philotas, Civil Wars, Musophilus, and Defense of Rhyme.

10   ____. "Well-Languaged Daniel: A Reconsideration." MLR, 52
        (October), 481-97.
        Provides detailed analysis of diction, versification,
        and imagery in attempting to isolate the particular char-
        acteristics of Daniel's style. In examining diction,
        discusses vocabulary, Latinate diction, "the almost total
        absence of the common pun," rhetorical devices, and syn-
        tactic features; in examining versification, discusses
        rhyme patterns and transitions; and in examining imagery,
        discusses lack of variety, abstractness, and subjects.
        Concludes that all the qualities of Daniel's style "com-
        bine . . . to form a kind of dignified, graceful eloquence."

1958

1   ANON. Review of Laurence [Anthony] Michel, ed., The Civil
    Wars. SCN, 16 (Fall & Winter), 38-39.
        In review of 1958.4 comments on Daniel's revisions and
    suggests possible influence of Civil Wars on Dryden's
    Absalom and Achitophel.

2   BARROLL, J[OHN] LEEDS. "Enobarbus' Description of Cleopatra."
    University of Texas Studies in English, 37: 61-78.
        Draws on Cleopatra and Letter from Octavia in analyzing
    "the Renaissance attitudes towards Cleopatra." Defines
    two basic characterizations of Cleopatra: "the sinning
    and responsible woman with a soul [as in Cleopatra], or
    the fatal and unanalyzed kind of lure [a Voluptas figure]
    around which mythological connotations tended to hover
    constantly [as in Letter from Octavia]."

3   BLUDAU, DIETHILD. "Sonettstruktur bei Samuel Daniel."
    Shakespeare-Jahrbuch, 94: 63-89.
        Analyzes the structure and prosody of selected Delia
    sonnets to argue that the greatness of Daniel's poetry
    lies in his ability to integrate form and emotion and to
    reconcile intellect and time.

1958

4   DANIEL, SAMUEL. The Civil Wars. Edited by Laurence [Anthony]
     Michel. New Haven: Yale University Press, 376 pp.
          Provides critical edition, using 1609 edition as copy-
     text. In "Introduction" (pp 1-62), discusses sources,
     reprints many of Coleridge's comments on Daniel, and pro-
     vides a bibliographical analysis of the extant manuscript
     and editions. Analyzes influence of the 1595 edition on
     Shakespeare's Richard II and Henry IV, provides overview
     of the controversy over the nature of the direction of
     influence, and discusses influence of the two plays (along
     with Henry VI) on Daniel's 1609 revision. Analyzes the
     nature of the revisions in successive editions, especially
     those involving structure, attitude toward figures, and
     style; argues against the notion that "Daniel was only a
     tinkerer" in his revisions. Announces that this is the
     first volume of a projected complete edition. Incorporates
     1955.6. See 1958.5, 1959.1, 1959.5, 1959.7, 1959.10, and
     1964.1. Reviewed in Arthur Colby Sprague, MLN, 74 (March
     1959), 254-55; 1958.1; 1958.5; 1959.1; 1959.7; 1959.10;
     1906.3; 1964.1.

5   EVANS, G. BLAKEMORE. Review of Laurence [Anthony] Michel, ed.,
     The Civil Wars. JEGP, 57 (October), 808-10.
          In review of 1958.4 corrects Michel's identification of
     a "second impression" of the 1595 edition and criticizes
     his choice of the 1609 edition as copy-text. Offers cor-
     rections to notes and "Introduction."

6   LaBRANCHE, ANTHONY [SPAHR]. "Drayton's Historical Poetry:
     The Barons Warres." Ph.D. dissertation, Yale University.
          Examines influence of Civil Wars on Barons' Wars, ob-
     serving that Drayton's poem "is less well integrated and
     less thoughtful, but more vigorous, than Daniel's."

7   MORRIS, HELEN. Elizabethan Literature. Home University
     Library of Modern Knowledge, 233. London: Oxford Uni-
     versity Press, 249 pp.
          Offers appreciative estimate of Daniel, "that rare
     creature, an unemphatic Elizabethan." Characterizes his
     poetry, which "has an un-Elizabethan, almost Augustan
     calm," as "silver rather than golden poetry, but polished
     to a wonderful degree of brilliance" (pp. 37-38, 67-69,
     passim).

8   NORMAN, ARTHUR M. Z. "Daniel's The Tragedie of Cleopatra and
     Antony and Cleopatra." SQ, 9 (Winter), 11-18.
          Provides act-by-act analysis of "echoes and parallels"
     between Daniel's play (1623 edition) and Shakespeare's

to argue that <u>Cleopatra</u> "if considered as a possible secondary influence upon <u>Antony and Cleopatra</u> . . . provides
an explanation of Shakespeare's daring use of two climaxes
and of his conception of Cleopatra as the embodiment of a
love transcending worldly obligations."

9 REES, JOAN. "Samuel Daniel and the Earl of Hertford." <u>N&Q</u>,
   NS 5 (September), 408.
   Identifies Diana of <u>Queen's Arcadia</u> with the Countess
   of Hertford and suggests that "[t]he address to Diana" in
   the play (11. 2406-15) "sounds like a dedication of loyalty and labour to a new patron and the production of the
   play may have provided an opportunity for a public proc-
   lamation of a new allegiance. If this is so then the
   Hertford patronage probably dates from not long before
   August 1605."

10 _____. Untitled letter. <u>RES</u>, NS 9 (August), 294-95.
    In response to 1957.8 argues that the Countess of Pem-
    broke's <u>Antonius</u> was not Daniel's source for the descrip-
    tion of Antony being hoisted into the monument in the 1607
    <u>Cleopatra</u>.

11 TAYLOR, DICK, JR. "The Masque and the Lance: The Earl of
    Pembroke in Jacobean Court Entertainments." <u>TSE</u>, 8: 21-53.
    Discusses the feud between Daniel and Jonson over the
    nature of the masque, suggesting that Pembroke supported
    Jonson.

1959

1 ANON. "The Admirable Daniel." <u>TLS</u> (25 September), p. 547.
   In review of 1958.4 finds that "[t]he fascination of
   the poem lies . . . in following the mind of a contempla-
   tive humanist . . . brooding over the distresses of his
   country." Comments on Daniel's style and objects to
   Michel's cavalier treatment of Grosart (1885.2). Reply by
   Michel, 1959.5.

2 CAIN, THOMAS HENRY. "The Poem of Compliment in the English
   Renaissance." Ph.D. dissertation, University of Wisconsin, 333 pp. [<u>DA</u>, 20 (1959), 2285.]
   Discusses "Daniel's epistles of compliment," character-
   izing them as "familiar in tone" with "a strong paraenetic
   bent."

1959

3　GRIFFIN, ERNEST G.　"The Dramatic Chorus in English Literary
　　　Theory and Practice."　Ph.D. dissertation, Columbia Uni-
　　　versity, 228 pp.　[DA, 20 (1960), 3726-27.]
　　　　　Discusses Daniel in tracing "the history of the dramatic
　　　chorus in English literature."

4　LEISHMAN, J[AMES] B[LAIR].　"Variations on a Theme in Shake-
　　　speare's Sonnets," in Elizabethan and Jacobean Studies
　　　Presented to Frank Percy Wilson in Honour of His Seventieth
　　　Birthday.　Edited by Herbert Davis and Helen Gardner.　Ox-
　　　ford:　Clarendon Press, pp. 112-49.
　　　　　Analyzes Daniel's treatment of the theme of poetic im-
　　　mortality in six sonnets, comparing his treatment with
　　　that by Shakespeare.　Concludes that Daniel's sonnets
　　　"constitute the fullest and finest treatment of this topic
　　　in English poetry before Shakespeare, and, although their
　　　tone is so much fainter, their accent is not perhaps
　　　greatly different from Shakespeare's own."　Expanded
　　　1961.4.

5　MICHEL, LAURENCE [ANTHONY].　"Daniel's Civil Wars."　TLS
　　　(30 October), p. 632.
　　　　　Responds to reviewer's charge (1959.1) of cavalier
　　　treatment of Grosart (1885.2).

6　MILLER, EDWIN HAVILAND.　The Professional Writer in Elizabe-
　　　than England:　A Study of Nondramatic Literature.　Cam-
　　　bridge:　Harvard University Press, 298 pp.
　　　　　Draws frequently on Daniel's life and works in analyzing
　　　various aspects (e.g., audience, patronage, censorship)
　　　of the life of the Elizabethan professional writer
　　　(passim).

7　MUIR, KENNETH.　Review of Laurence [Anthony] Michel, ed.,
　　　The Civil Wars.　SQ, 10: 442-43.
　　　　　In review of 1958.4 points out several misprints in the
　　　text and problems in the textual notes.

8　NORMAN, ARTHUR M. Z.　"The Tragedie of Cleopatra and the Date
　　　of Antony and Cleopatra."　MLR, 54 (January), 1-9.
　　　　　Examines Daniel's revisions of Cleopatra and their re-
　　　lationship to Antony and Cleopatra to suggest that Shake-
　　　speare "consulted and echoed one of the 1594-1605 editions
　　　of Daniel's Cleopatra" and that Daniel was influenced by
　　　Antony and Cleopatra in his 1607 revision.

9   PARSONS, ROGER LOREN. "Renaissance and Baroque: Multiple
      Unity and Unified Unity in the Treatment of Verse, Orna-
      ment, and Structure." Ph.D. dissertation, University of
      Wisconsin, 516 pp. [DA, 19 (1959), 2958.]
          Discusses Daniel in examining how "in sixteenth-century
      poetry syntactical divisions tend to reinforce the divi-
      sions defined by the line and by rime."

10 REES, JOAN. Review of Laurence [Anthony] Michel, ed., The
      Civil Wars. MLR, 54 (October), 587–88.
          In review of 1958.4 points out several errors in the
      text and textual notes.

11 _____. "Wordsworth and Samuel Daniel." N&Q, NS 6 (January),
      26–27.
          Suggests that Wordsworth drew on Civil Wars (book 6,
      stanzas 35–36) in "the famous retrospective account of
      Godwinism in Book XI of The Prelude."

12 SCHAAR, CLAES. "A Textual Puzzle in Daniel's Delia." ES, 40:
      382–85.
          Suggests that the obscurity of line 12 of Delia 37 re-
      sults from Daniel using a line from a sonnet by Berardino
      Rota (Rime in morte) "mainly as a piece of embellishment
      without considering his own context very closely."

13 SERONSY, CECIL C. "Daniel and Wordsworth." SP, 56 (April),
      187–213.
          Provides detailed examination of the resemblances be-
      tween the two (particularly "in their recurring moods and
      patterns of speech") and Wordsworth's knowledge of and
      indebtedness to Daniel.

                            1960

1   BULLOUGH, GEOFFREY. "Introduction [to Richard II]," in his
      edition of Narrative and Dramatic Sources of Shakespeare.
      Vol. III. London: Routledge and Kegan Paul; New York:
      Columbia University Press, pp. 353–82.
          Examines influence of Civil Wars on Richard II, suggest-
      ing that "Shakespeare was influenced slightly" by the 1595
      edition and that "Daniel was certainly influenced by
      Richard II in revising his poem later." Characterizes the
      work as "a painstaking epic poem in which . . . [Daniel]
      tried to apply Lucan's methods to a British theme, but in
      a plain clear style which at times dropped into the prosy

1960

and at other times rose to a restrained eloquence."
Includes excerpts from 1595 edition of Civil Wars
(pp. 434-60).

2   BUXTON, JOHN. "On the Date of Syr P. S. His Astrophel and
    Stella. . . . Printed for Matthew Lownes." BLR, 6
    (August), 614-16.
        Establishes that Lownes's edition (Revised STC 22538),
    which includes some of Daniel's sonnets, derives from
    Newman's 1591 edition (Revised STC 22536) and suggests
    1597 or 1598 as the date of publication.

3   HILL, CHRISTOPHER. "Daniel Come to Historians' Judgment."
    EIC, 10 (April), 207-11.
        In review of 1958.4 discusses Daniel's revisions (the
    "main interest" of Civil Wars) and finds Daniel "rather
    a bore."

4   HUGHEY, RUTH, ed. The Arundel Harington Manuscript of Tudor
    Poetry. 2 volumes. Columbus: Ohio State University
    Press, 444, 537 pp.
        Transcribes "Octavia to Anthony," an early version of
    Letter from Octavia (I, 265-74). In notes (II, 368-83),
    points out that the manuscript "represents an earlier
    version, which was considerably revised for the first
    printing of the epistle in 1599." Collates the manuscript
    with printed editions and points out that the earlier
    version "is more personal, more intimate, with the empha-
    sis placed upon the sorrowing but essentially forgiving
    Octavia." Discusses the relationship "in theme and in
    tone" of Letter from Octavia to Cleopatra, the influence
    of Garnier on the epistle, and the possible connections
    between Letter from Octavia and Brandon's Virtuous
    Octavia.

5   MILES, JOSEPHINE. Renaissance, Eighteenth-Century, and Mod-
    ern Language in English Poetry: A Tabular View. Berkeley:
    University of California Press, 77 pp.
        Includes Delia and Rosamond in tabular analyses of
    adjectives, nouns, and verbs; mode; types of measures;
    and major adjectives, nouns, and verbs in order of inno-
    vation (passim).

6   MUIR, KENNETH. "Source Problems in the Histories." Shake-
    speare-Jahrbuch, 96: 47-63.
        Discusses Shakespeare's use of Civil Wars in Richard II.

7   ORR, DAVID. "The Influence of Learned Italian Drama of the
     Sixteenth Century on English Drama before 1623." Ph.D.
     dissertation, University of North Carolina, 290 pp. [DA,
     21 (1961), 2705.]
     See 1970.12 (published version).

8   PRINCE, F. T. "The Sonnet from Wyatt to Surrey," in Eliza-
     bethan Poetry. Edited by John Russell Brown and Bernard
     Harris. Stratford-upon-Avon Studies, 2. New York: St.
     Martin's Press, pp. 10-29.
          Discusses Delia (particularly sonnets 30-36) as the
     "inspiration" for "Shakespeare's laments on time and
     transcience, as well as his promise of poetic immortality"
     in the early sonnets of his sequence. Points out that
     Daniel "was the first to show . . . [the] peculiar possi-
     bilities both in melody and in movement of thought" of
     the English sonnet form.

9   REES, D. G. "Italian and Italianate Poetry," in Elizabethan
     Poetry. Edited by John Russell Brown and Bernard Harris.
     Stratford-upon-Avon Studies, 2. New York: St. Martin's
     Press, pp. 52-69.
          Discusses "Daniel's interest in and adaptation of
     Italian poetry," particularly in Delia. Concludes that
     Daniel "writes sonnets which, while not rivalling the
     best of Petrarch, give the reader, more than any other
     English sequence, that impression of refined, eloquent
     decorum, which is the essence of Petrarch's style."

10   REES, JOAN. "Shakespeare's Use of Daniel." MLR, 55 (Janu-
     ary), 79-82.
          Traces Shakespeare's use of Civil Wars in Julius Caesar
     and of Letter from Octavia in Antony and Cleopatra.

11   SCHAAR, CLAES. An Elizabethan Sonnet Problem: Shakespeare's
     "Sonnets," Daniel's Delia," and Their Literary Background.
     LSE, 28. Lund: C. W. K. Gleerup; Copenhagen: Ejnar
     Munksgaard, 190 pp.
          In examining the question of Daniel's influence on
     Shakespeare, provides detailed comparison of motifs,
     structure, imagery, use of ambiguity, rhetorical figures,
     syntax, meter, and parallel passages in Delia and Sonnets.
     (For each of the preceding, places Delia in the context
     of English and Continental traditions.) In the course of
     the discussion, offers a detailed overview of scholarship
     on the question of influence. Concludes that "no sub-
     stantial arguments can be brought forward in support of
     the claim that Daniel influenced Shakespeare, but some

1960

facts indicate the reverse, while isolated parallels are ambiguous." Suggests that Daniel was indebted to Shakespeare's sonnets in the revision of Delia. See 1962.13. Reviewed in William Blissett, ES, 42 (February 1961), 61; S. B. Liljegren, Archiv, 198 (1961), 116-17; Laurence [Anthony] Michel, JEGP, 60 (July 1961), 583-84; Patricia Thomson, MLR, 56 (January 1961), 101; 1962.3; and 1962.9.

12   _____. On the Motif of Death in 16th Century Sonnet Poetry. Scripta Minora, 1959-1960, 3. Lund: C. W. K. Gleerup, 34 pp.
        Draws frequently on Delia in analyzing the motif. Points out that Daniel is the only Elizabethan sonneteer to use "the representation of Death as a power who snatches away the veil of a human being" (Delia 37), "one of the commonest symbols of death" among the Italian sonneteers (passim).

13   SERONSY, CECIL C. "Daniel's Complaint of Rosamond: Origins and Influence of an Elizabethan Poem." Lock Haven Bulletin, 1st ser., no. 2, pp. 39-57.
        Traces the influence of Rosamond, "which was more influential in its own day than any other of . . . [Daniel's] works," on the complaint poem (especially Chute's Beauty Dishonored, Shakespeare's Lucrece, and several of Drayton's works). Examines the place of the poem in the development of the Rosamond legend and analyzes the influence of Sackville's "Induction" and Churchyard's Shore's Wife on Rosamond.

14   _____. "Shakespeare and Daniel: More Echoes." N&Q, NS 7 (September), 328-29.
        Suggests influence of Queen's Arcadia on Macbeth, Hamlet on Queen's Arcadia, and Twelfth Night and As You Like It on Hymen's Triumph. (In a note, the editor points out parallel between Troilus and Cressida and Musophilus.)

1961

*1   AUE, WILHELM. "Die Lebensanschauung Samuel Daniels." Ph.D. dissertation, University of Hamburg, 225 pp.
        Manuscript dissertation; cited in Hans Walter Gabler, English Renaissance Studies in German, 1945-1967: A Check-List of German, Austrian, and Swiss Academic Theses, Monographs, and Book Publications on English Language and Literature, c. 1500-1650, Schriftenreihe der Deutschen Shakespeare-Gesellschaft West, NS 11 (Heidelberg: Quelle & Meyer, 1971), p. 23, item 89.

2   BLUM, IRVING D.   "The Paradox of Money Imagery in English
    Renaissance Poetry."   Studies in the Renaissance, 8:
    144-54.
       Discusses Daniel among a group of poets "who express
    scorn for wealth, yet use it metaphorically to give
    luster to the things that they hold most dear."   Notes
    money imagery in Musophilus and Delia.

3   JOHNSTON, GEORGE BURKE.   "Camden, Shakespeare, and Young
    Henry Percy."   PMLA, 76 (June), 298.
       Suggests, in passing, that behind Daniel's "young
    Hotspur" (Civil Wars) is the description of Percy in Cam-
    den's Britannia, which is Shakespeare's source.   See
    1962.12 and George Burke Johnston, "Camden, Daniel, and
    Shakespeare, II," PMLA, 77 (September 1962), 511-12.

4   LEISHMAN, J[AMES] B[LAIR].   Themes and Variations in Shake-
    speare's Sonnets.   New York: Hillary House, 254 pp.
       In expanded version of 1959.4, analyzes Daniel's treat-
    ment of "the theme of poetic immortality" in seven son-
    nets: traces influences (especially that of Tasso) on the
    sonnets and compares Daniel's treatment of the theme with
    Shakespeare's.   Concludes that Daniel's sonnets "consti-
    tute the fullest and finest treatment of this topic [i.e.,
    poetic immortality] in English poetry before Shakespeare,
    and, although their tone is so much fainter, their accent
    is not perhaps greatly different from Shakespeare's own"
    (pp. 78-85, passim).

5   LEVÝ, JIRÍ.   "The Development of Rhyme-Scheme and of Syntactic
    Pattern in the English Renaissance Sonnet."   Acta Uni-
    versitatis Palackianae Olomucensis, Philologica, 4: 167-85.
       In an analysis of "the syntactic patterns and arrange-
    ment of ideas" in the sonnet, provides a table illustrat-
    ing the distribution of "clause-limits" in Delia (as
    printed in 1904.2).   Finds that Daniel averages 10.7
    clauses per sonnet.

6   REESE, M[AX] M[EREDITH].   "The Cease of Majesty":   A Study of
    Shakespeare's History Plays.   New York: St. Martin's
    Press, 360 pp.
       Draws frequently on Civil Wars for comparisons with
    Shakespeare's attitude toward and treatment of history
    (passim).

1962

1   BULLOUGH, GEOFFREY, ed. Narrative and Dramatic Sources of
    Shakespeare. Vol. I. London: Routledge and Kegan Paul;
    New York: Columbia University Press, 550 pp.
        In "Introduction" to 1 Henry IV, pp. 155-79; "Introduc-
    tion" to 2 Henry IV, pp. 249-67; and "Introduction" to
    Henry V, pp. 347-75, discusses Shakespeare's indebtedness
    to Civil Wars. Prints excerpts from 1595 edition (pp. 208-
    15, 282-86, 420-36).

2   BUSH, DOUGLAS. English Literature in the Earlier Seventeenth
    Century, 1600-1660. Second edition, revised. Oxford
    History of English Literature, vol. V. New York: Oxford
    University Press, 688 pp.
        Revises earlier discussion (1945.1), adding comments on
    Daniel's "philosophic sense of history" and on History of
    England. Answers Lewis's adverse judgment (1954.4) of
    Daniel's poetry by suggesting that "his grave ethical
    passion and his faith in the immortal life of culture,
    poetry, and the English tongue do kindle poetic fire" in
    some readers (pp. 92-95, 225-27, passim).

3   BUXTON, JOHN. Review of Claes Schaar, An Elizabethan Sonnet
    Problem: Shakespeare's "Sonnets," Daniel's "Delia," and
    Their Literary Background, SN, 33: 337-40.
        In favorable review of 1960.11, points out that Schaar's
    "assessment of the frequency of feminine endings in Delia
    is misleading" because he does not take into account
    Daniel's revisions.

4   CARSON, NORMAN MATTHEWS. "The Literary Reputation of Samuel
    Daniel." Ph.D. dissertation, Boston University, 387 pp.
    [DA, 23 (1962), 1683.]
        Traces Daniel's reputation and that of specific works
    from 1590s to mid-twentieth century. Also supplements
    1942.3. Finds that "Daniel is either praised for his
    felicitous use of the English language, for his sweet and
    grave manner, and for his moral judiciousness; or he is
    condemned for his inability to soar in his verse and for
    his unemotional evenness of tone."

5   DULS, LOUISA DESAUSSURE. "The Complex Picture of Richard II
    Inherited by Sixteenth-Century Writers from Fourteenth-
    and Fifteenth-Century Chronicle Sources." Ph.D. disserta-
    tion, University of North Carolina, 623 pp. [DA, 23
    (1963), 4675A.]
        See published version 1975.2.

*6 ENZENSBERGER, CHRISTIAN. Sonett und Poetik: Die Aussagen
    der elisabethanischen Sonettzyklen über das Dichten im
    Vergleich mit der zeitgenössischen Dichtungslehre. Ph.D.
    dissertation, University of Munich. Munich: n.p, 269 pp.
        Cited in Hans Walter Gabler, English Renaissance Stud-
    ies in German, 1945-1967: A Check-List of German, Austri-
    an, and Swiss Academic Theses, Monographs, and Book Pub-
    lications on English Language and Literature, c. 1500-
    1650. Schriftenreihe der Deutschen Shakespeare-
    Gesellschaft West, NS 11 (Heidelberg: Quelle & Meyer,
    1971), p. 12, item 9.

7 GRUNDY, JOAN. "Shakespeare's Sonnets and the Elizabethan
    Sonneteers." ShS, 15: 41-49.
        Draws frequently from Delia for contrasts in examining
    "Shakespeare's attitude to the accepted 'poetic' of the
    sonnet-sequence." Gives particular attention to Daniel's
    use "of the poem as 'monument.'"

8 HENTZ, ANN LOUISE. "A Senecan Source for Samuel Daniel's
    Verse Epistle to Southampton." N&Q, NS 9 (June), 208-209.
        Examines Daniel's close dependence on Seneca's On
    Providence in the poem.

9 HONIGMAN, E. A. J. Review of Claes Schaar, An Elizabethan
    Sonnet Problem: Shakespeare's "Sonnets," Daniel's "Delia,"
    and Their Literary Background. SQ, 13 (Summer), 351-53.
        In review of 1960.11 suggests the need to examine
    Delia and Rosamond as complementary, "thematically related"
    works.

10 LEVINE, JAY ARNOLD. "The Status of the Verse Epistle before
    Pope." SP, 59 (October), 658-84.
        Includes "To Sir Thomas Egerton" and "To Henry
    Wriothesley" in section surveying Renaissance verse
    epistles. Gives particular attention to Daniel's concern
    for two audiences.

11 LIEVSAY, JOHN LEON. "Italian favole boscarecce and Jacobean
    Stage Pastoralism," in Essays on Shakespeare and Eliza-
    bethan Drama in Honor of Hardin Craig. Edited by Richard
    Hosley. Columbia: University of Missouri Press, pp. 317-
    26.
        Discusses Daniel's use of the chorus in Queen's Arcadia
    and Hymen's Triumph.

1962

12   MICHEL, LAURENCE [ANTHONY]. "Camden, Daniel, and Shakespeare,
     I." PMLA, 77 (September), 510–11.
          In response to 1961.3 argues that Daniel's "young
     Hotspur" (Civil Wars) was Shakespeare's immediate source
     for making Hal and Hotspur contemporaries and that Camden
     in the 1610 edition of Britannia was indebted to Daniel
     for details of Hotspur. See also George Burke Johnston,
     "Camden, Daniel, and Shakespeare, II," pp. 511–12.

13   SCHAAR, CLAES. Elizabethan Sonnet Themes and the Dating of
     Shakespeare's "Sonnets." LSE, 32. Lund: C. W. K. Gleerup;
     Copenhagen: Ejnar Munksgaard, 199 pp.
          Amplifies earlier argument (1960.11) that Daniel, es-
     pecially in revising Delia, was influenced by Sonnets.
     Also argues that Daniel was influenced by Shakespeare in
     revising Rosamond. Provides detailed comparison of several
     sonnets by the two authors and discusses, in particular,
     Daniel's use of the immortality theme (pp. 23–73). Re-
     viewed in 1963.7 and 1964.9.

14   TALBERT, ERNEST WILLIAM. The Problem of Order: Elizabethan
     Political Commonplaces and an Example of Shakespeare's
     Art. Chapel Hill: University of North Carolina Press,
     256 pp.
          In chapter 5 ("Clinias or Dramatist?," pp. 121–45),
     finds that in Philotas, "a play of ideas," Daniel did not
     intend to mirror the Essex affair. Analyzes the play to
     argue that Daniel "was interested primarily in ideas con-
     ventionally related to the complexities of rule. When
     the play is so read, it can be seen that just as it dev-
     elops in accordance with academic precepts about structure,
     so it represents, in a variety of lights, ideas about con-
     duct in high place. That those ideas in their execution
     are ambiguous, and that the result can be equivocally
     interpreted, especially by a chorus of the vulgar, seems
     to be an important aspect of Daniel's purpose. Philotas
     seems to be poor artistry, indeed, only when one assumes
     that the events and the characters were to the author of
     primary importance" (pp. 130–45, passim).

15   WILKES, G[ERALD] A[LFRED]. "Daniel's Philotas and the Essex
     Case: A Reconsideration." MLQ, 23 (September), 233–42.
          Argues against Michel's assertion (1949.3) that the
     connection of the play to the Essex affair "is essential
     to the interpretation of the play," particularly to an
     understanding of the ambiguity of Philotas and the design
     of the play. Finds that "the equivocal features of Dan-
     iel's Philotas . . . are implanted in the historical
     sources he used."

1963

1 ADAMANY, RICHARD GEORGE. "Daniel's Debt to Foreign Litera-
tures and Delia Edited." Ph.D. dissertation, University
of Wisconsin, 231 pp. [DA, 23 (1963), 4350-51.]
   Provides critical edition, using 1601 edition as copy-
text. Examines Daniel's revisions, noting that "[t]he
alterations generally produce sonnets that are more concise and skillfully organized, whose tone is more dis-
ciplined and less hyperbolic; also by focusing his arguments and by using more appropriate diction, Daniel
creates a new clarity in his expression as well as a more
logical and clear development of thought." In introduction
examines Daniel's French and Italian sources; concludes
that "there is a good deal of originality in his verse and
that originality found in the tone, imagery, metaphor and
music of his lines distinguishes his sonnets from their
sources and allows them to be more individual and independ-
ent than early twentieth century criticism has allowed."

2 AHERN, MATTHEW JOSEPH. "The Roman History Play, 1585-1640:
A Study Indicating How Plays Dealing with Roman History
Reflect Changing Political and Social Attitudes in England
during This Period." Ph.D. dissertation, Tulane University, 311 pp. [DA, 24 (1964), 3319.]
   Provides "an analysis of all the extant non-Shake-
spearean Roman history plays . . . written between 1585
and 1640."

3 BUXTON, JOHN. Elizabethan Taste. London: Macmillan, 384 pp.
   Discusses Daniel's relationship with the Countess of
Bedford and with other poets under her patronage (pp. 333-
37).

4 DANIEL, SAMUEL. The Complete Works in Verse and Prose of
Samuel Daniel. 5 volumes. Edited by Alexander B[alloch]
Grosart. New York: Russell & Russell, 324, 339, 409,
357, 331 pp.
   Reprint of 1885.1, 1885.2, 1885.3, 1896.2, and 1896.3.

5 _____. Daniel's "The Tragedie of Cleopatra" nach dem Drucke
von 1611. Edited by M[ax] Lederer. Materialien zur Kunde
des Älteren Englischen Dramas, 31. Vaduz: Kraus Reprint,
115 pp.
   Reprint of 1911.1.

1963

6   NERI, NICOLETTA. "Il Pastor fido" in Inghilterra con il testo
     della traduzione secentesca di Sir Richard Fanshawe. Uni-
     versità di Torino, Pubblicazioni della Facoltà di Magis-
     tero, 21. Turin: G. Giappichelli, 246 pp.
          Discusses influence of Guarini's play on Queen's
     Arcadia (pp. 18-20).

7   PRINCE, F. T. Review of Claes Schaar, Elizabethan Sonnet
     Themes and the Dating of Shakespeare's "Sonnets." SN, 35:
     307-10.
          In review of 1962.13 questions validity of the basis
     of Schaar's argument that Shakespeare influenced Daniel.

8   REICHERT, JOHN FREDERICK. "Formal Logic and English Renais-
     sance Poetry." Ph.D. dissertation, Stanford University,
     233 pp. [DA, 24 (1963), 1174-75.]
          Draws on Delia in analyzing the influence of the study
     of logic on Renaissance poetry. Finds that Daniel "re-
     sorted always to the analogy, never to the deductive kinds
     of argument."

9   SCHANZER, ERNEST. The Problem Plays of Shakespeare: A Study
     of "Julius Caesar," "Measure for Measure," "Antony and
     Cleopatra." New York: Schocken Books, 206 pp.
          In chapter 3 ("Antony and Cleopatra," pp. 132-83),
     draws frequently on Cleopatra for comparison with Shake-
     speare's play. Examines the complex motives of Cleopatra
     which evoke a divided response--"repugnance" and "admira-
     tion"--in Daniel's reader and discusses Cleopatra as a
     tragedy (passim).

10 STROEMER, KARLA [MARIANNE]. Samuel Daniels Geschichtsauf-
     fassung. Ph.D. dissertation, University of Hamburg.
     Hamburg: n.p., 111 pp.
          Analyzes Daniel's conception of history in Civil Wars
     and History of England.

1964

1   BLISSETT, WILLIAM. Review of Laurence [Anthony] Michel, ed.,
     The Civil Wars. ES, 45 (February), 61-63.
          Offers corrections and additions to 1958.4.

2   BROADBENT, J[OHN] B[ARCLAY]. Poetic Love. London: Chatto &
     Windus, 320 pp.
          Compares Daniel and Constable with Spenser to show the
     latter's inferiority as a sonneteer, and discusses Daniel's

treatment of "carpe diem as an erotic ritual" in Delia
(pp. 72-77, 153-56).

3   BULLOUGH, GEOFFREY, ed. Narrative and Dramatic Sources of
      Shakespeare. Vol. V. London: Routledge and Kegan Paul;
      New York: Columbia University Press, 591 pp.
         In "Introduction" to Antony and Cleopatra, pp. 215-53,
      discusses influence of Cleopatra on Shakespeare's play and
      the influence of Antony and Cleopatra on Daniel's 1607
      revision. Also suggests possibility that Shakespeare was
      influenced by Letter from Octavia. Reprints 1599 text of
      Cleopatra (pp. 406-49).

4   CUTTS, JOHN P. "Pericles and The Vision of Diana." AN&Q, 3
      (October), 21-22.
         Corrects F. David Hoeniger's reference in his edition
      of Pericles (London: Methuen; Cambridge: Harvard Uni-
      versity Press, 1963) to the costume of Diana in Vision of
      the Twelve Goddesses.

5   GODSHALK, WILLIAM LEIGH. "Daniel's History." JEGP, 63
      (January), 45-57.
         Argues on stylistic grounds that Daniel wrote the
      Breviary and examines its relationship to the First Part
      of the History of England. Discusses Daniel's revisions
      (especially in structure) from Breviary through Collection
      of the History of England, his concern for "truth," and
      his use of sources (especially in the section on Edward
      II).

6   _____. "Samuel Daniel and Sir Peter Leigh." N&Q, NS 11
      (September), 333-34.
         Investigates the cancelling of leaf E4 in 1609 edition
      of Civil Wars (and the cancelling of the cancel in 1623
      Works). Suggests that the addition of the marginal note
      on the Leighs was the reason for the original cancel and
      examines possible motives behind the addition of the note.

7   GOLDMAN, LLOYD NATHANIEL. "Attitudes Toward the Mistress
      in Five Elizabethan Sonnet Sequences." Ph.D. disserta-
      tion, University of Illinois, 297 pp. [DA, 25 (1965),
      6590-91.]
         Analyzes attitude of Daniel toward Delia "by examining
      his attitude toward his conceits": finds that Daniel and
      Spenser "employ their sonnets as emblems, through
      which . . . [they] illustrate, rather than examine, the
      attitudes of their personae." Gives particular attention
      to the influence of the emblem tradition on Delia and

1964

Daniel's use of the "'eye-conceits.'" Concludes that in
Delia, "Daniel was examining love as an ideal state that
cannot be attained."

8   GROVE, ROBIN. "Ralegh's Courteous Art." Melbourne Critical
     Review, 7: 104-13.
         In arguing against Ure's evaluation of Ralegh (1955.10),
     provides an analysis of Delia 42 to argue that the poem
     manifests "insecurity of tone" and that "[t]he quality of
     emotion satisfied in this sonnet could, despite the neat-
     ness and occasional sharpness of effect, fairly be called
     sentimental."

9   NOWOTTNY, WINIFRED. Review of Claes Schaar, Elizabethan
     Sonnet Themes and the Dating of Shakespeare's "Sonnets."
     RES, NS 15 (November), 423-29.
         In review of 1962.13 takes exception to several of
     Schaar's conclusions about the relationship of Delia and
     Rosamond to Shakespeare's sonnets.

10   ORUCH, JACK BERNARD. "Topography in the Prose and Poetry
     of the English Renaissance." Ph.D. dissertation, Indiana
     University, 303 pp. [DA, 25 (1964), 2966.]
         Discusses Daniel's treatment of Stonehenge in Musophilus
     as an example of the subordination of "topography to a
     larger purpose."

11   REES, JOAN. Samuel Daniel: A Critical and Biographical
     Study. Liverpool English Texts and Studies. Liverpool:
     Liverpool University Press, 198 pp.
         Offers "as complete an account as possible of . . .
     [Daniel's] life and work, so that his importance in lit-
     erary history and his qualities as a writer can be recog-
     nised and assessed on the basis of more information than
     has hitherto been available." Traces "the development of
     his mind and art through the chronological study of his
     works." Provides critical estimate of each of Daniel's
     major works: emphasizes his "serious and contemplative
     mind" and his ability to enter into "imaginative sympathy"
     with his characters. Suggests that "[b]eauty of sound and
     image, occasional bursts of strong feeling, and a notable
     psychological subtlety, combine to make Delia one of the
     finest and most pleasing of the Elizabethan sonnet se-
     quences"; that Cleopatra is a unified work and should be
     read as an attempt to refine English drama along the lines
     of Sidney's Defense; that the masque form was particularly
     uncongenial to Daniel; and that Civil Wars includes sev-
     eral references to the Essex affair. Concludes that "it

is . . . [Daniel's] gift of language and also and especially the range and the intelligence of his sensitivity
and responsiveness, the very fact of the ambivalence of
his attitudes which make him 'something' among poets,
'though' as he well knew, 'not the best.'" Reviewed in
William Blissett, ES, 51 (December 1970), 558-59; Werner
von Koppenfels, Anglia, 85 (1967), 221-23; Russell E[dwin]
Leavenworth, ELN, 4 (June 1967), 290-91; Laurence [Anthony]
Michel, Renaissance News, 18 (Summer 1965), 161-63;
Michel Poirer, EA, 18 (October-December 1965), 414; Jean
Robertson, RES, NS 16 (November 1965), 418-19; Cecil C.
Seronsy, JEGP, 64 (October 1965), 718-22; Patricia Thom-
son, MLR, 61 (January 1966), 103-104; 1965.1; and 1965.9.

12 ROSE, REMINGTON EDWARD, II. "Julius Caesar and the Late
    Roman Republic in the Literature of the Late 16th Century,
    with Especial Reference to Shakespeare's Julius Caesar."
    Ph.D. dissertation, Princeton University, 378 pp. [DA, 25
    (1964), 3558.]
        Draws on Cleopatra in analyzing the Elizabethan con-
    ception of Caesar and Caesarian Rome.

13 STIRLING, BRENTS. "Cleopatra's Scene with Seleucus: Plu-
    tarch, Daniel, and Shakespeare." SQ, 15 (Spring), 299-311.
        In examining question of Cleopatra's collusion with
    Seleucus in Shakespeare's play, uses Cleopatra "[a]s an
    example of what Shakespeare strives not to do with Cleo-
    patra, Seleucus, and Caesar." Points out that Daniel
    presented the action as Cleopatra's final act in her at-
    tempt to deceive Caesar. Reprinted 1964.14.

14 _____. "Cleopatra's Scene with Seleucus: Plutarch, Daniel,
    and Shakespeare," in Shakespeare 400: Essays by American
    Scholars on the Anniversary of the Poet's Birth. Edited
    by James G[ilmer] McManaway. New York: Holt, Rinehart,
    and Winston, pp. 299-311.
        Reprints 1964.13.

                            1965

1   ANON. "Daniel to Judgment." TLS (14 January), p. 28.
        In review of 1964.11 suggests that "the reason why . . .
    [Daniel] fell short of the best was the self-distrust
    which he recognized in himself."

107

1965

2   APPELBE, JANE LUND. "An Inquiry into the Rehabilitation of
    Certain Seventeenth-Century Poets, 1800-1832." Ph.D.
    dissertation, University of Toronto. [DA, 27 (1966),
    1777-78A.]
        Discusses the revival of interest in Daniel.

3   BARKER, J. R. "A Pendant to Drummond of Hawthornden's Con-
    versations." RES, NS 16 (August), 284-88.
        Points out that Drummond's marginalia in his copy of
    Jonson's Works (1616) establishes that Daniel, not Dray-
    ton, was the "better verser" of Forest, Epistle 12 (11.
    68-70).

4   BRAND, C[HARLES] P[ETER]. Torquato Tasso: A Study of the
    Poet and of His Contribution to English Literature. Cam-
    bridge: Cambridge University Press, 356 pp.
        Discusses influence of Gerusalemme liberata on Civil
    Wars, of Aminta on Queen's Arcadia and Hymen's Triumph,
    and of Rime on Delia (pp. 246-47, 281-83, 295-96).

5   CHANG, JOSEPH S. M. J. "Machiavellianism in Daniel's The
    Civil Wars." TSE, 14: 5-16.
        Analyzes how Daniel, while "clearly committed to the
    ideal of order, . . . seems to have Machiavelli's ethical
    neutrality," especially "in his analysis of the leading
    figures of The Civil Wars." Offers several parallels
    with The Prince to show that "[i]n his analysis of
    statesmen . . . Daniel . . . is a Machiavellian." Con-
    cludes: "Although didactic in intent, The Civil Wars
    addresses itself to a wider problem than that found in
    de casibus literature, the fall of kings. Its subject
    is the distemperature of the world, it is concerned with
    the erosion of society's fundamental principles."

6   DANIEL, SAMUEL. Poems and "A Defence of Ryme." Edited by
    Arthur Colby Sprague. Chicago: University of Chicago
    Press (Phoenix Books), 256 pp.
        Reprint of 1930.2.

7   _____. Samuel Daniel's "Musophilus: Containing a General De-
    fense of All Learning." Edited by Raymond Himelick. West
    Lafayette, Ind.: Purdue University Studies, 106 pp.
        In revision of 1950.4 provides critical edition, using
    1623 edition as copy-text. In introduction (pp. 9-59),
    provides overview of Daniel's life and works, examines
    Musophilus in the context of concerns of Renaissance
    criticism, analyzes Daniel's defense of "the life of

intellect and study," traces sources, examines revisions, and analyzes Daniel's style. Also provides bibliographical description of editions (pp. 99-100). See 1966.9. Reviewed in 1966.3 and 1966.9.

8 DAVISON, PETER H. "Richard and Hal--'Effeminate' Princes." N&Q, NS 12 (March), 94-95.
    Suggests possible influence of Daniel's characterization of Richard II (Civil Wars, book I, stanza 70) on Shakespeare's characterization of Hal in Richard II.

9 GOTTFRIED, RUDOLF [BRAND]. Review of Joan Rees, Samuel Daniel: A Critical and Biographical Study. MP, 63 (November), 159-60.
    In review of 1964.11 praises Rees's treatment of Daniel's literary development (except for the prose works), but questions her handling of some of the biographical material, especially her dating of Daniel's "first connection with the Pembroke circle."

10 HOBSBAUM, PHILIP. "Elizabethan Poetry." PoetryR, 56: 80-97.
    Argues that "it is high time that we ceased to see the [late Elizabethan] period as that of Sidney, Spenser, Daniel and Drayton; rather its key figures are Chapman, Jonson, Marston, Donne, Raleigh and Greville--together with the great translators, Stanyhurst, Golding and Harington." Characterizes Daniel and Drayton as "dull sticks that sometimes rub up against a few sparks of poetry."

11 JOHNSON, MARSUE McFADDIN. "The Well-Rimed Daniel: An Examination of Delia and A Defence of Ryme." Ph.D. dissertation, University of Arkansas, 224 pp. [DA, 26 (1966), 4661.]
    Analyzes Daniel's "recurrent use of themes and conceits" to achieve structural unity in Delia; also examines "keyword reference, word repetition, whole- and half-line repetition and the consequent use of rhyme as a structural device." Studies Defense of Rhyme "as a culmination of Renaissance critical development and as a summation statement of Daniel's own poetic practice as seen in Delia." Includes as appendices a photographic reproduction of 1601 edition of Delia, "Table of Conceits giving the larger themes of Cruel Fair and Plaintive Heart," and "Rhyme-Word Index to Delia."

1965

12 SERONSY, CECIL C. "An Autograph Letter by Swinburne on
    Daniel and Drummond of Hawthornden." N&Q, NS 12 (August),
    303-304.
        Prints unpublished letter in which Swinburne comments
    "on the relative merits of Samuel Daniel and William Drum-
    mond as poets": Swinburne refers to Daniel's "gentle
    genius" and to Drummond as an "artificial & untuneful
    rhetorician."

13 _____. "The Case for Daniel's Letter to Egerton Reopened."
    HLQ, 29 (November), 79-82.
        Argues for the authenticity of the letter.

14 STÜRZL, ERWIN [ANTON]. Der Zeitbegriff in der elisabethan-
    ischen Literatur: The Lackey of Eternity. WBEP, 69.
    Vienna: Wilhelm Braumüller, 536 pp.
        Draws frequently on Daniel's works in a wide-ranging
    analysis of the concept of time in Elizabethan literature
    (passim).

15 THOMSON, PATRICIA. "Sonnet 15 of Samuel Daniel's Delia: A
    Petrarchan Imitation." CL, 17 (Spring), 151-57.
        Identifies Rime 224 as Daniel's primary source and
    examines his modifications, comparing them with Desportes's.
    Reprinted 1974.16.

1966

1   CURTIS, JARED R. "William Wordsworth and English Poetry of
    the Sixteenth and Seventeenth Centuries." Cornell Li-
    brary Journal, no. 1, pp. 28-39.
        Includes Daniel in an overview of Wordsworth's reading
    during 1800-1802; traces a number of references to Daniel
    in Wordsworth's works and manuscripts.

2   DANIEL, SAMUEL. "A Defence of Ryme," in Samuel Daniel, "A De-
    fence of Ryme"; Thomas Campion, "Observations in the Art of
    English Poesie." Edited by G[eorge] B[agshawe] Harrison.
    Elizabethan and Jacobean Quartos, 14. New York: Barnes
    and Noble, pp. 1-46.
        Reprint of 1925.2.

3   DAVIS, WALTER R[ICHARDSON]. Review of Raymond Himelick, ed.,
    Samuel Daniel's "Musophilus: Containing a General Defense
    of All Learning." SCN, 24 (Summer), 27-28.
        In review of 1965.7 discusses Daniel's style, noting
    that in the poem he "created . . . a conversational style
    seldom equalled for its combination of clear discourse and
    sensuous appeal."

4   HARLOW, C. G. "Shakespeare, Nashe, and the Ostrich Crux in
     1 Henry IV." SQ, 17 (Spring), 171-74.
          Establishes that Nashe used Worthy Tract as his source
     for the description of Surrey's horse in Unfortunate
     Traveller.

5   HUMPHREYS, A[RTHUR] R[ALEIGH]. "Introduction," in his edi-
     tion of William Shakespeare's The Second Part of King
     Henry IV. Arden Shakespeare. London: Methuen; Cambridge:
     Harvard University Press, pp. xi-xci.
          Devotes section to the influence of 1595 Civil Wars,
     which "is rather on tone and attitude than on facts," on
     2 Henry IV. Discusses how Daniel "deeply affects the way
     Shakespeare treats Henry's culpability" and influences
     Shakespeare's handling of the death of Henry. Contrasts
     Daniel's Henry, who momentarily decides to give up the
     crown, with Shakespeare's, who tenaciously holds to his
     power (pp. xxxiii-xxxiv).

6   JUEL-JENSEN, BENT. "Contemporary Collectors XLIII." BC, 15
     (Summer), 152-74.
          Includes a brief description of his Daniel collection.

7   MEAGHER, JOHN C. Method and Meaning in Jonson's Masques.
     Notre Dame: University of Notre Dame Press, 224 pp.
          Discusses Vision of the Twelve Goddesses as background
     for understanding Jonson's masques. Examines Daniel's
     conception of the nature of the masque (and his disagree-
     ment with Jonson). Suggests that the reason for the sec-
     ond edition of Vision of the Twelve Goddesses was Daniel's
     wish "to defend himself publicly against criticisms of
     carelessness and inaccuracy" in the work--criticisms
     brought about by a change in audience expectations of the
     masque (pp. 11-22, passim).

8   PAPAJEWSKI, HELMUT. "An Lucanus Sit Poeta." DVLG, 40,
     no. 4, 485-508.
          Draws frequently on Daniel in examining the question in
     English literary criticism of whether Lucan was a poet or
     historian. Examines blurring of poetry and history in
     Daniel.

9   REES, JOAN. Review of Raymond Himelick, ed., Samuel Daniel's
     Musophilus: Containing a General Defense of All Learning.
     Renaissance News, 19 (Summer), 153-54.
          In review of 1965.7 discusses the need to place Muso-
     philus "in relation to Daniel's whole work" and corrects
     several notes.

1966

10   SAMPSON, SISTER HELEN LUCY, S.U.S.C. "A Critical Edition of
      Samuel Daniel's The Tragedie of Cleopatra." Ph.D. dis-
      sertation, St. Louis University, 338 pp. [DA, 27 (1967),
      3017A.]
          Provides critical edition. In introduction discusses
      sources and influences, the relationship of the 1607 ver-
      sion to Antony and Cleopatra, previous scholarship, and
      revisions.

11   SERONSY, CECIL [C.], and ROBERT KRUEGER. "A Manuscript of
      Daniel's Civil Wars, Book III." SP, 63 (April), 157-62.
          Describe manuscript (part of Harleian MS. 7,332),
      which represents "the earliest extant text of Book III,"
      discuss its relationship with the text of the published
      versions, and provide a list of "material textual differ-
      ences from" the 1595 edition.

12   SPENCER, THEODORE. "Two Classic Elizabethans: Samuel Daniel
      and Sir John Davies," in Theodore Spencer: Selected
      Essays. Edited by Alan C. Purves. New Brunswick: Rut-
      gers University Press, pp. 100-22. [Written in 1948].
          Provides critical overview of Daniel's works (with
      particular attention to Musophilus) in discussing him as
      "a classicist in terms of English literature as a whole."
      Points out that "at its best Daniel's poetry is musical,
      serious, convincing" and that he "is unsurpassed among
      the Elizabethans in the kind of poetry which is withdrawn
      from its emotional object and contemplates it reflectively
      from a distance." Compares Daniel and Davies, concluding
      that "the two poets share, in spite of their human and
      poetic differences, . . . the same kind of vocabulary and
      the same poetic aim."

                              1967

1   BALDWIN, ANNE WILFONG. "Thomas Berthelet and Tudor Propa-
     ganda." Ph.D. dissertation, University of Illinois,
     482 pp. [DA, 28 (1968), 5005-5006A.]
         Discusses Civil Wars in analyzing the possible influ-
     ence in later Renaissance literature of Henrican propa-
     ganda about "the nature of kingship." Points out that in
     "Civil Wars, Daniel, coping with the usurpation of kings,
     develops a political concept of complete obedience to
     established authority in order to prevent war."

2   DANIEL, SAMUEL. The Vision of the Twelve Goddesses, edited
       by Joan Rees, in A Book of Masques: In Honour of Allardyce
       Nicoll. Cambridge: Cambridge University Press, pp. 18–42.
          Provides modernized critical edition, using 1604 edition
       as copy-text. In "Introduction" (pp. 19–23), discusses
       Vision of the Twelve Goddesses as a "serious allegory of
       state." Examines Daniel's work in the context of the
       Jacobean masque, pointing out that the "visual representa-
       tion of ideas" was "the only possibility of the masque
       form which . . . [Daniel] cares to exploit."

3   DREWRY, CECELIA HODGES. "Samuel Daniel's Tragedy of Philotas:
       The Use of Contradiction and Paradox as Methods of Comment
       upon the Essex Affair and upon the Responsibilities of
       Monarchs." Ph.D. dissertation, Northwestern University,
       192 pp. [DA, 28 (1967), 2365A.]
          Analyzes Daniel's "use of familiar proverbs in para-
       doxical fashion, . . . use of recurrent images in a con-
       tradictory manner, and . . . reenforcement of the ambigu-
       ities of the play through several other types of contra-
       diction." Concludes "that Daniel uses paradox and
       familiar proverbs, in Philotas, in a fashion that can be
       construed as comment upon Essex' predicament and upon the
       responsibilities of monarchs" and that this "dramatic
       method" helps to unify the play.

4   DUNN, CATHERINE MARY. "A Survey of the Experiments in
       Quantitative Verse in the English Renaissance." Ph.D.
       dissertation, University of California, Los Angeles,
       355 pp. [DA, 28 (1967), 193A.]
          Discusses Daniel's treatment of quantitative verse in
       Defense of Rhyme.

5   GARDNER, THOMAS. "'A Parodie! A Parodie!': Conjectures on
       the Jonson-Daniel Feud," in Lebende Antike: Symposion
       für Rudolf Suhnel. Edited by Horst Meller and Hans-
       Joachim Zimmermann. Berlin: Erich Schmidt, pp. 197–206.
          Discusses reasons for the conflict between Daniel and
       Jonson, examines differences in their respective theories
       of the masque, and analyzes Tethys' Festival (particularly
       the song "Are they shadows that we see?") as a parody of
       Jonson's theory and "a not too veiled attack upon the"
       poet himself. Speculates that "some influential person
       in the court"--likely Queen Anne herself--exerted consid-
       erable influence on Daniel's attack and thus caused Jonson
       to mute his reply.

1967

6　GUFFEY, GEORGE ROBERT. "Samuel Daniel, 1942-1965," in his
　　Elizabethan Bibliographies Supplements, VII: Samuel
　　Daniel, 1942-1965; Michael Drayton, 1941-1965; Sir Philip
　　Sidney, 1941-1965. London: Nether Press, 13-21.
　　　　Continues 1942.3; provides chronological list of 115
　　works published 1942-1965.

7　HEBERT, C. A. "Belinda and Rosamond." CEA, 30 (November),
　　10.
　　　　Suggests influence of Rosamond (11. 85-91, 540-47) on
　　Rape of the Lock (11. 149-60).

8　LAMBRECHTS, G[UY]. "Sur deux prétendues sources de Richard
　　II." EA, 20 (April-June), 118-39.
　　　　Examines parallels to argue that Daniel probably used
　　Richard II as a source for Civil Wars (1595 and 1609).

9　LEVY, F[RED] J[ACOB]. Tudor Historical Thought. San Marino:
　　Huntington Library, 317 pp.
　　　　In chapter 7 ("Politic History," pp. 237-85), points
　　out that in his historical works Daniel was interested in
　　"the relation of men to the manifestations of political
　　power." Gives particular attention to History of England--
　　the originality of the work, Daniel's intention to teach
　　"political behavior," and the political philosophy under-
　　lying the work (pp. 273-79, passim).

10　LOGAN, GEORGE MEREDITH. "Lucan in England: The Influence of
　　the Pharsalia on English Letters from the Beginnings
　　through the Sixteenth Century." Ph.D. dissertation,
　　Harvard University.
　　　　Examines influence of Pharsalia on Civil Wars.

11　MAXWELL, J[AMES] C[LOUTTS]. "'Rebel powers': Shakespeare
　　and Daniel." N&Q, NS 14 (April), 139.
　　　　Suggests influence of Cleopatra (1594, 1. 1595) on a
　　phrase in Shakespeare's Sonnet 146.

12　MUIR, KENNETH. Introduction to Elizabethan Literature. New
　　York: Random House, 213 pp.
　　　　In chapter 4 ("Two Professional Poets," pp. 64-83),
　　provides a general critical overview of Daniel's works.
　　Observes that even with all his faults, he should not be
　　dismissed "as a minor poet of little interest" (pp. 64-
　　74).

13   PRESCOTT, ANNE LAKE. "The Reception of Marot, Ronsard, and
        Du Bartas in Renaissance England." Ph.D. dissertation,
        Columbia University, 245 pp. [DA, 28 (1967), 1406-1407A.]
            See published version, 1978.7.

14   ROBBINS, ROSSELL HOPE. "A Late-Sixteenth-Century Chaucer
        Allusion (Douce MS. 290)." ChauR, 2: 135-37.
            Points out allusion to Chaucer resembling that in
        Musophilus.

15   SERONSY, CECIL [C.]. Samuel Daniel. TEAS, 49. New York:
        Twayne, 198 pp.
            Attempts "to present an account of Daniel's life and
        work in the successive stages of his career . . . [,] to
        provide a critical examination of his significant writ-
        ings, . . . [and] to assess his mind and art." Discusses--
        when appropriate--sources and background, revisions, char-
        acteristics, and influence of each work. In final chapter
        appraises Daniel as poet and thinker through an analysis
        of his diction, versification, imagery, and "his pervasive
        sense of history." Although Daniel "tended to give up
        metaphor for abstraction, occasional audacity for discreet
        caution, vigor and color for sober fact," suggests that
        his career defies categorization by period because "[h]e
        seems to rally and return from time to time to the tender
        lyricism of his earliest verse." Includes annotated
        selected bibliography. Reviewed in William Leigh Godshalk,
        RenQ, 21 (1968), 490-91.

16   SHEAVYN, PHOEBE. The Literary Profession in the Elizabethan
        Age. Second edition, revised by J[ohn] W[hiteside]
        Saunders. Manchester: Manchester University Press; New
        York: Barnes & Noble, 258 pp.
            In revision of 1909.7 draws frequently on Daniel in an
        analysis of various aspects of the profession of letters
        (passim).

17   TANNENBAUM, SAMUEL A[ARON]. Samuel Daniel, in Samuel A[aron]
        Tannenbaum and Dorothy R[osenzweig] Tannenbaum, Eliza-
        bethan Bibliographies. Vol. II. Port Washington, N.Y.:
        Kennikat Press, 47 pp. [Separately paginated.]
            Reprint of 1942.3.

18   WINTERS, YVOR. "Aspects of the Short Poem in the English ·
        Renaissance," in his Forms of Discovery: Critical & His-
        torical Essays on the Forms of the Short Poem in English.
        Chicago: Alan Swallow, pp. 1-120.
            In revision of 1939.7 offers no substantive changes in
        estimate of Daniel.

1967

19 _____ . "The 16th Century Lyric in England: A Critical and
Historical Reinterpretation," in Elizabethan Poetry:
Modern Essays in Criticism. Edited by Paul J. Alpers.
New York: Oxford University Press, pp. 93-125.
    Reprints 1939.7.

1968

1 BUTRICK, LYLE HOWARD. "The Queenes Arcadia by Samuel Daniel:
Edited, with Introduction and Notes." Ph.D. dissertation,
State University of New York at Buffalo, 355 pp. [DA,
29 (1968), 1863A.]
    Provides critical edition, using 1606 edition as copy-
text. In introduction examines the play "as a court
satire [representing "the University invaded and corrupted
by the royal court"], probably directed at the Royal visit
to Oxford in 1605," during which the play was performed.
Examines Daniel's use of Montaigne, and suggests that the
importance of the influence of Italian pastoral drama
"has been considerably exaggerated."

2 DANIEL, SAMUEL. The Complaint of Rosamond, in Elizabethan
Verse Romances. Edited by M[ax] M[eredith] Reese. Routledge English Texts. London: Routledge & Kegan Paul,
pp. 25-57.
    Provides modernized, annotated reprint. In "Introduc-
tion" (pp. 1-23), discusses Rosamond in an overview of the
Elizabethan Ovidian erotic poem. Examines briefly the
influence of Mirror for Magistrates on the poem and its
place among the treatments of the Rosamond Clifford story.
Finds "[t]he emotional situation . . . confusing" and
suggests that the poem is "a suasio to Delia."

3 _____ . The Complaint of Rosamond, in Elizabethan Narrative
Verse. Edited by Nigel Alexander. Stratford-upon-Avon
Library, 3. Cambridge: Harvard University Press,
pp. 215-36.
    Provides annotated reprint of Rosamond (1592). In
"Introduction" (pp. 1-26), discusses Rosamond in an over-
view of Elizabethan narrative verse.

4 DOBRÉE, BONAMY. "Cleopatra and 'That Criticall Warr,'" in
Twentieth Century Interpretations of "All for Love": A
Collection of Critical Essays. Edited by Bruce King.
TCI. Englewood Cliffs, N.J.: Prentice-Hall, pp. 19-31.
    Reprints "slightly abridged" version of 1928.1.

5   GOLDMAN, LLOYD [NATHANIEL]. "Samuel Daniel's Delia and the
    Emblem Tradition." JEGP, 57 (January), 49-63.
        In arguing that Delia is a "sequence of verbalized
    emblems," analyzes Daniel's adaptation of the character-
    istics of emblem and impresa (as defined in Worthy Tract)
    to the sonnet, suggests several parallels between specific
    sonnets and emblems, examines how he incorporates aspects
    of the emblem into his adaptations of foreign sources,
    and points out that he took most of his devices from
    classical literature in order to help render his verse
    timeless.

6   GÜNTHER, PETER. "Shakespeares Antony and Cleopatra: Wandel
    und Gestaltung eines Stoffes." SJH, 1968: 94-108.
        Discusses influence of Cleopatra on Antony and Cleo-
    patra.

7   HARDIN, RICHARD F[RANCIS]. "Convention and Design in Dray-
    ton's Heroicall Epistles." PMLA, 83 (March), 35-41.
        Discusses influence of Rosamond on Drayton's England's
    Heroical Epistles.

8   HOWARTH, R[OBERT] G[UY]. "The Model-Source of John Webster's
    A Monumental Columne." ESA, 11: 127-34.
        Discusses Webster's use of Funeral Poem upon the Death
    of the Earl of Devonshire as the model for his poem.
    Also points out Webster's indebtedness to "To Henry Howard"
    in a commendatory poem in William Barksted's Mirrha.

9   JACK, RONALD D. S. "Imitation in the Scottish Sonnet." CL,
    20 (Fall), 313-28.
        Points out influence of Delia on William Fowler's
    Tartantula of Love and William Alexander's Aurora.

10 KAU, JOSEPH LEONG CHOO. "Art That Conceals Art: Samuel
    Daniel's Delia." Ph.D. dissertation, Tufts University,
    249 pp. [DAI, 31 (1970), 1762A.]
        Examines rhythm, persona, and the "seemingly unsubstan-
    tial imagery" in Delia to show how "Daniel's consummate
    poetic art which renders his sonnets polished and 'easy,'
    hs sprezzatura del verso, conceals the very art that con-
    ceived the poetry."

11 LEIMBERG, INGE. Shakespeares "Romeo und Julia": Von der
    Sonettdichtung zur Liebestragödie. Beihefte zur Poetica,
    4. Munich: Wilhelm Fink, 214 pp.
        Discusses importance of Daniel's use of the Icarus myth
    in Delia and examines determination and individual respon-
    sibility in Rosamond (pp. 100-15, passim).

1968

12 SPRIET, PIERRE. <u>Samuel Daniel (1563-1619): Sa vie--son oeuvre</u>. Études Anglaises, 29. Paris: Didier, 647 pp.
    In part 1 provides detailed biography: places works in the context of Daniel's life and times, examines his various friendships and his relationships with patrons, and analyzes various influences on his thought. In part 2 provides detailed analysis of Daniel's works under the headings: Daniel and lyric poetry, the theater, Daniel and history, and Daniel and literature. For most works examines revisions, sources, form, influence, and literary merit. Concludes with an analysis of Daniel's versification and style. Reviewed in Joan Grundy, <u>RES</u>, NS 20 (August 1969), 335-38; 1970.15.

13 WILLIAMSON, C. F. "The Design of Daniel's <u>Delia</u>." <u>RES</u>, NS 19: 251-60.
    Analyzes how Daniel "first establishes the theme of unhappy love, and then weaves about it new and contrasting motifs, each one enriching the harmony and tone colour," to argue that he "produce[d] a highly wrought and subtly textured whole." Examines movement from the "relationship with Delia . . . seen only as a cause of suffering" to the recognition of the relationship "as the opportunity for achieving distinction as a poet." Observes, also, that the change in the relationship occurs "after sonnet XXXII, which divides the sequence, perhaps not accidentally, in proportions approximating to those of the octave and sestet of a sonnet."

<u>1969</u>

1   BONI, JOHN MICHAEL. "Two Epics of English History: Samuel Daniel's <u>Civile Wars</u> and Michael Drayton's <u>Barons Wars</u>." Ph.D. dissertation, University of Denver, 214 pp. [<u>DAI</u>, 30 (1970), 4398A.]
    Analyzes the "grave weaknesses" of the poems in terms of the "three traditions from which . . . [they] spring: sixteenth century English history writing, <u>The Mirror for Magistrates</u>, and the epic tradition."

2   DANIEL, SAMUEL. <u>"Delia" with "The Complaint of Rosamond,"</u> <u>1592</u>. Menston: Scolar Press, n.p.
    Facsimile reprint of 1592 edition.

3   _____. <u>A "Panegyrike" with "A Defence of Ryme" [1603]</u>. Menston: Scolar Press, n.p.
    Facsimile reprint of 1603 edition.

4   DONOW, HERBERT S. "Concordance and Stylistic Analysis of Six
      Elizabethan Sonnet Sequences." CHum, 3 (March), 205-208.
        Describes "stylistic tests" on data in and the making
      of 1969.5.

5   _____. A Concordance to the Sonnet Sequences of Daniel,
      Drayton, Shakespeare, Sidney, and Spenser. Carbondale:
      Southern Illinois University Press; London: Feffer &
      Simons, 784 pp.
        Includes Delia (from 1885.1) in a computer-generated
      "single merged index." Provides word-frequency list for
      Delia in appendix (pp. 722-28). In "Preface" (pp. vi-xi),
      suggests applications of the concordance to stylistic
      studies. See 1969.4.

6   MITCHELL, DENNIS S. "Samuel Daniel's Sonnets To Delia--A
      Critical Edition." Ph.D. dissertation, Princeton Univer-
      sity, 207 pp. [DAI, 31 (1970), 1235A.]
        Provides critical edition. In introduction discusses
      place of Delia in the development of the sonnet, "the
      organization of the sequence," "the nature and purpose of
      Daniel's revisions," the printing history of the work, and
      bibliographical details of early editions.

7   MUIR, KENNETH. "Elizabeth I, Jodelle, and Cleopatra." RenD,
      NS 2: 197-206.
        Discusses the "ambivalence" of Daniel, Jodelle, and
      Shakespeare toward Cleopatra.

8   PATTON, JON FRANKLIN. "Essays in the Elizabethan She-Trage-
      dies or Female-Complaints." Ph.D. dissertation, Ohio
      University, 155 pp. [DAI, 30 (1969), 1534A.]
        Includes essay on Rosamond in arguing that "the She-
      tragedies consitute a separate genre from the De Casibus
      poems of the Mirror for Magistrates." Discusses Daniel's
      poem to show "how the genre could be embellished by a
      serious artist interested in the theme of love."

1970

*1 AKAGAWA, YUTAKA. "Renaissance no Sonnets [Sonnets in the
      Renaissance]." Ronso (Meijigakuin Daigaku), no. 164
      (October), pp. 17-116.
        Cited in [Kazuyoshi Enozawa and Sister Miyo Takano,]
      "The 1970 Bibliography," RenB, 5 (1978), 19, item 7.

1970

2   CHANG, JOSEPH S. M. J. "Julius Caesar in the Light of Renaissance Historiography." JEGP, 69 (January), 63-71.
      Discusses Daniel (Civil Wars) as one of "the new
historians [who] found in the past a complex web of
causes and pressures, the sum of which reduced the signi-
ficance of individual initiative," and who fostered ethical
neutrality, refusing to impose a pattern on historical
events where none existed.

3   CLARK, IRA. "Samuel Daniel's Complaint of Rosamond." RenQ,
23 (Summer), 152-62.
      Analyzes Daniel's exploitation in the casket passage
of "the tradition of moral allegorization of classical
myth" and its relation to the unity of the poem. Gives
particular attention to Daniel's modification of the Io
myth, which "provides the structural center of 'Rosamond.'"
Concludes: "Daniel has alluded to moralizations of Amy-
mone, Pasiphae, Danae, and Atalanta to underscore the
fact that he is retelling through Rosamond the Io myth
about the self-transforming fall of a prostitute, in which
she herself signifies the moral outcome by serving as a
bestial emblem of her lost humanity which cannot be re-
deemed even by royal pardon."

4   DANIEL, SAMUEL. Delia, in Elizabethan Sonnet Sequences.
Edited by Herbert Grabes. English Texts, 3. Tübingen:
Max Niemeyer, pp. 65-87.
      Reprints 1592 edition.

5   _____. The Tragedy of Philotas. Edited by Laurence [Anthony]
Michel. [Hamden, Conn.:] Archon Books, 199 pp.
      Reprints 1949.3, adding "Preface to the 1970 Edition"
(pp. v-xi) and "Addenda & Corrigenda" (pp. 178-81), which
includes some additional textual notes. In preface reconsiders choice of copy-text, reviews controversy over
the relationship between Philotas and the Essex affair,
and modifies some of his original "views on Daniel's
artistry as a poet-dramatist" by suggesting that the in-
effective relationship between theme and structure, not
the connection with the Essex case, causes the play to be
"'poorer as a piece of art.'"

6   ESPLIN, ROSS STOLWORTHY. "The Emerging Legend of Sir Philip
Sidney, 1586-1652." Ph.D. dissertation, University of
Utah, 336 pp. [DAI, 31 (1970), 2341A.]
      Discusses Daniel in section on the "Sidney school"
headed by the Countess of Pembroke.

7   FREEMAN, ARTHUR. "An Epistle for Two." Library, 5th ser.,
      25 (September), 226-36.
        Describes manuscript in his collection of "To the
      Countess of Cumberland" which Daniel had retitled and
      adapted to Elizabeth Hatton. Transcribes the manuscript,
      providing textual notes on variants from the published
      texts; dates it 1598 or earlier; and discusses the revi-
      sions, some of which can be attributed to the change of
      addressee. Considers problem of preferred version. Finds
      that the poem "is no portrait at all, as the very ambi-
      guity of address displays, but a meditation, spiritually
      sincere or not, but quite adequately convincing, formed
      tenuously into an Epistle to whichever recipient served
      the author's interests best." See 1971.15 and 1973.7.

8   KAU, JOSEPH [LEONG CHOO]. "Daniel's Delia and the Imprese of
   ⸤ Bishop Paolo Giovio: Some Iconological Influences."
      JWCI, 33: 325-28.
        Traces influence of Giovio's Dialogo dell'imprese
      militari et amorose on Delia. Finds that "Daniel's debt
      [is] to imprese which stress wit and simple thoughts like
      love rather than to emblemi which emphasize plain state-
      ment and sententiae."

9   _____. "Samuel Daniel and the Renaissance Impresa-Makers:
      Sources for the First English Collection of Imprese."
      HLB, 18 (April), 183-204.
        Identifies Lodovico Domenichi's Ragionamento and Gabri-
      ele Simeoni's Imprese heroiche et morali as Daniel's
      sources for "A Discourse of Imprese" appended to Worthy
      Tract. Shows that Daniel worked from French translations
      and suggests that he also translated Giovio's treatise
      from a French version.

10 KELLY, HENRY ANSGAR. Divine Providence in the England of
      Shakespeare's Histories. Cambridge: Harvard University
      Press, 356 pp.
        Devotes chapter 8 ("Daniel's Civil Wars," pp. 183-202)
      to a detailed analysis of the providential patterns in
      the manuscript version and 1595, 1601, and 1609 editions
      of Civil Wars. Concludes: "[I]n the books written after
      1595, there is no return to or elaboration of the large
      providential designs of the 1595 version. In that first
      version, in addition to the possible suggestion that the
      wars were a necessary prelude to the Tudor union, . . .
      [Daniel] indicated that they were meant to rein in pre-
      sumption, and that they were part of God's plague for sin,
      a punishment that began with his sending the child-ruler

1970

Richard II. In 1609 this latter reason was changed, and
Richard was considered as a plague that God sent because
of his intention to transfer the royal line or to bring
defeat to the nation. And later on, the wars are explained
simply as a sharing in the pain that God in his providence
requires all men to suffer. The importance of these ex-
planations is magnified, however, by lifting them out of
context in this way; for in the actual development of the
civil wars, regarded as a whole, these concepts do not
seem to have been controlling influences on Daniel's
thought. They do not even appear to be organically related to the remarks he makes concerning the providential
establishment of Henry IV's regime. If he had gone on to
finish the Civil Wars as he had first projected it, he
might have made the divine dimension of the work more
consistent; but it is evident that any such consistency
would have been an afterthought, and not the result either
of a long-standing tradition or personal conviction."

11   LaBRANCHE, ANTHONY [SPAHR]. "Imitation: Getting in Touch."
      MLQ, 31 (September), 308-29.
          Analyzes Daniel's "careful imitation [in Delia] of a
      balance between involvement and distance" from Desportes
      in examining the modern sense of the sixteenth-century
      attitude toward imitation.

12   ORR, DAVID. Italian Renaissance Drama in England before
      1625: The Influence of "Erudita" Tragedy, Comedy, and
      Pastoral on Elizabethan and Jacobean Drama. UNCSCL, 49.
      Chapel Hill: University of North Carolina Press, 151 pp.
          In revision of 1960.7 discusses the influence of Ital-
      ian pastoral drama--particularly that of Tasso and
      Guarini--on Queen's Arcadia and Hymen's Triumph. Points
      out that the latter play is less closely imitative
      (pp. 85-90, passim).

13   PALMER, D[AVID] J[OHN]. "The Verse Epistle," in Metaphysical
      Poetry. Edited by D[avid] J[ohn] Palmer and Malcolm
      Bradbury. Stratford-upon-Avon Studies, 11. New York:
      St. Martin's Press, pp. 72-99.
          Includes a general discussion of Daniel's verse
      epistles (stressing his "stoic sententiousness") in an
      overview of the Renaissance verse epistle.

14   PATTERSON, ANNABEL M. Hermogenes and the Renaissance: Seven
      Ideas of Style. Princeton: Princeton University Press,
      256 pp.

Analyzes influence of Hermogenes' Seven Ideas of Style on Civil Wars (Gravity), Delia (Verity), and Musophilus (Speed). Gives particular attention to Civil Wars, concluding that the work "provide[s] internal evidence of considerable strength that . . . [Daniel] was influenced by the Hermogenic rhetoric of Ideas in his concept of epic style, and that he deliberately combined as many of these Ideas as he could within the framework of a basically 'grave' poem" (pp. 145-48, 172-73, 193-98, 202-203).

15   REES, JOAN. "Samuel Daniel." EA, 23 (October-December), 399-401.
      In a generally favorable review of 1968.12, discusses problems resulting from Spriet's two-part division and comments on Daniel's "verbal imagination."

16   RICE, JULIAN C. "The Allegorical Dolabella." CLAJ, 13 (June), 402-407.
      Contrasts the complexity of Daniel's Dolabella (Cleopatra) with Shakespeare's "symbolic or perhaps . . . allegorical" character. Notes that Daniel "takes . . . pains . . . to insure his psychological probability."

17   SAUNDERS, J[OHN] W[HITESIDE]. "The Social Situation of Seventeenth-Century Poetry," in Metaphysical Poetry. Edited by D[avid] J[ohn] Palmer and Malcolm Bradbury. Stratford-upon-Avon Studies, 11. New York: St. Martin's Press, pp. 236-76.
      Discusses Daniel's discontent--noting its similarity to Drayton's--with the literary climate in a survey of the "social context" of poetry, 1600-1660.

18   SIDNEY, PHILIP. "Astrophel and Stella," 1591. Menston: Scolar Press, 102 pp.
      Facsimile reprint of 1591 edition which includes 28 sonnets by Daniel.

19   STRZETELSKI, JERZY. The English Sonnet: Syntax and Style. Zeszyty Naukowe Uniwersytetu Jagiellońskiego, 213: Prace Jezykoznawcze, 27. Kraków: Nakładem Uniwersytetu Jagiellońskiego, 149 pp.
      Includes Delia in investigating "what describable formal syntactic features of the sonnets differentiate the style of the English sonneteers from one another." Anlyzes syntactic structures in selected sonnets, concluding that "the obvious syntactical simplicity accounts largely for the conspicuous overall simplicity of Daniel's

poetry." In the development of the sonnet, finds that "Daniel represents a step towards a more balanced syntax, which is to reach its perfection in Shakespeare" (pp. 97-100, passim).

20 ZACHARIAS, PETER JAMES. "An Analysis of the Motif of Death and Revival in the Tragicomedies of Shakespeare, Daniel, and Fletcher." Ph.D. dissertation, Michigan State University, 331 pp. [DAI, 31 (1971), 6028-29A.]
Examines Daniel's use of the motif in Queen's Arcadia and Hymen's Triumph "to reveal the social and moral evils in his society."

1971

1 BAZERMAN, CHARLES. "Verse Occasioned by the Death of Queen Elizabeth I and the Accession of King James I." Ph.D. dissertation, Brandeis University, 118 pp. [DAI, 32 (1971), 2674A.]
Includes Panegyric Congratulatory in a survey of verse on the topics.

2 BEITH-HALAHMI, ESTHER YAËL. "Angell Fayre of Strumpet Lewd: The Theme of Jane Shore's Disgrace in Ten Sixteenth Century Works." Ph.D. dissertation, Boston University, 444 pp. [DAI, 32 (1971), 2050A.]
See 1974.4 (published version).

3 BROWER, REUBEN A[RTHUR]. Hero & Saint: Shakespeare and the Graeco-Roman Heroic Tradition. Oxford: Clarendon Press, 436 pp.
In chapter 8 ("Heroic Tragedy, Heroic Love: Antony and Cleopatra," pp. 317-53), observes that "[a]lthough a number of parallels between Shakespeare and Daniel have been pointed out, they hardly add up to a conception or an attitude that Shakespeare 'took over' from The Tragedy of Cleopatra. A more likely explanation is that certain sorts of heroic diction would be used in any Elizabethan version of the 'fall' of Antony and Cleopatra" (pp. 346-48). Excerpted 1977.1.

4 CRAUN, EDWIN DAVID. "The DeCasibus Complaint in Elizabethan England, 1559-1593." Ph.D. dissertation, Princeton University, 354 pp. [DAI, 32 (1972), 6420-21A.]
Devotes chapter to Rosamond: places the work in its historical context, discusses its relationship with Delia, and examines Daniel's "use of rhetoric and . . . allegorized mythological tales."

5   CREIGH, GEOFFREY. "Samuel Daniel's Masque The Vision of the
    Twelve Goddesses." E&S, NS 24: 22-35.
        In arguing that Daniel's masque "warrants greater re-
    spect than it has been paid," shows that "a highly devel-
    oped theory of the nature of masque executed with consid-
    erable skill" underlies the work. Analyzes Daniel's
    theory of the masque--particularly its emblematic nature--
    and its relationship to "his general aesthetic views";
    examines structure of Vision of the Twelve Goddesses; and
    analyzes Daniel's Platonic purpose, particularly in his
    "self-conscious manipulation of overlapping layers of
    reality."

6   DAY, W. G. "The Athenian Society: Poets' Reputations,
    1692-1710." N&Q, NS 18 (September), 329.
        Notes that Daniel and Drayton were among "recommended
    authors" in "An Essay upon All Sorts of Learning, Written
    by the Athenian Society" (1692); when the essay was re-
    printed in 1710, Drayton's name was dropped.

7   DUNCAN-JONES, KATHERINE. "Two Elizabethan Versions of
    Giovio's Treatise on Imprese." ES, 52 (April), 118-23.
        Establishes that "To the Friendly Reader" (Worthy
    Tract) is "a mosaic of quotations from [Girolamo] Ruscel-
    li's Discorse" and that the supplementary chapter is "a
    translation of about two thirds of the Ragionamento by
    Domenichi . . . and of three devices by Symeoni"--all of
    which were published in various editions of Giovio's work.
    Observes that "it is difficult to resist the inference
    that Daniel sought to mislead the reader into thinking
    [the supplementary chapter] . . . a genuine collection of
    its own" and that the Worthy Tract "must at the time have
    lain in the large debatable land between acknowledged
    translation and wilful plagiary."

8   FERGUSON, ARTHUR B. "The Historical Thought of Samuel Dan-
    iel: A Study in Renaissance Ambivalence." JHI, 32
    (April-June), 185-202.
        Studies Daniel (Civil Wars, History of England, Defense
    of Rhyme, and Musophilus) as an example of the Renaissance
    ambivalence which "arose from the attempt to apply to the
    contemplation of society and its history two quite differ-
    ent modes of thought in the sincere hope of reconciling
    temporal process and an absolute nature, relativity and
    universality."

1971

9   KOPPENFELS, WERNER VON. "Two Notes on Imprese in Elizabethan
Literature: Daniel's Additions to The Worthy Tract of
Paulus Iovius; Sidney's Arcadia and the Tournament Scene
in The Unfortunate Traveller." RenQ, 24 (Spring), 13–25.
     Identifies Dialogue des d'armes et d'amours (Lyon,
1561), a French translation of Giovio, Domenichi, and
Simeoni, as Daniel's source for his supplementary chapter
in Worthy Tract. (Notes that in translating Giovio's
work Daniel used an Italian text for only about two-fifths
of the work, and turned to a French text for the remainder.) Discusses Daniel's stylistic embellishments of his
sources and points out instances of Nashe's borrowing from
Worthy Tract.

10   LAVIN, J. A. "The First Two Printers of Sidney's Astrophil
and Stella." Library, 5th ser., 26 (September), 249–55.
     Identifies John Charlewood as the printer of the first
quarto of 1591, which included twenty-eight of Daniel's
sonnets.

11   LOGAN, GEORGE M[EREDITH]. "Daniel's Civil Wars and Lucan's
Pharsalia." SEL, 11 (Winter), 53–68.
     Provides detailed account of Daniel's indebtedness
to Lucan.

12   MAXWELL, J[AMES] C[LOUTTS]. "'Enjealous': An Antedating."
N&Q, 18 (August), 286.
     Points out that Daniel's use of the word in Philotas
(1607 edition, 1. 23) antedates the first recorded use
in the Oxford English Dictionary.

13   RAHM, LINDA KATHRYN. "The Poet-Lover and Shakespeare's Sonnets." Ph.D. dissertation, Cornell University, 229 pp.
[DAI, 32 (1971), 451A.]
     Examines Daniel's use of the "immortalization theme"
in Delia in analyzing "the use of the poet-lover persona
in English Renaissance poetry." Finds that in Delia
"the speaker's awareness of the permanence of the poetic
image in relation to the evanescence of human life and
experience directs us toward an interpretation of the
sequence as a study of the devlopment of a poet's mind."

14   REES, JOAN. Fulke Greville, Lord Brooke, 1554–1628: A
Critical Biography. Berkeley: University of California
Press, 252 pp.
     Examines Greville's influence on Daniel's conception of
poetry. Compares Daniel's "To Sir Thomas Egerton" with
Greville's Of Monarchy; discusses Greville's Letter to a

Honorable Lady as "a companion piece" to *Letter from Octavia*, the relation of Greville's poem to "To the Countess of Cumberland," and the relationship of *Letter from Octavia* to *Mustapha* (pp. 125-29, 175-78, 200-206).

15   SHAPIRO, I. A.   "The Hatton Manuscript."   *Library*, 5th ser., 26 (March), 63-64.
    In commenting on 1970.7 argues that the adaptation of "To the Countess of Cumberland" to Elizabeth Hatton "should be dated in or after the second half of 1617" and suggests that the fair copy for the manuscript was the 1603 version.   *See* 1973.7.

1972

1   DeWITT, SUSAN VERA.   "Ben Jonson and the English Verse Letter."   Ph.D. dissertation, University of Washington, 272 pp.   [*DAI*, 33 (1973), 6868A.]
    Discusses Daniel's verse epistles, noting that although he "writes formally to patrons, rather than to friends, he convinces the reader that his moral perspective is important to him and to the receiver, and that it is thought through in the poem."

2   HARNER, JAMES LOWELL.   "Jane Shore: A Biography of a Theme in Renaissance Literature."   Ph.D. dissertation, University of Illinois, 177 pp.   [*DAI*, 33 (1972), 274A.]
    Examines the influence of Churchyard's *Shore's Wife* on *Rosamond*, the place of Daniel's poem in the development of the female complaint, and its influence on Churchyard's revision of *Shore's Wife* and on Anthony Chute's *Beauty Dishonored*.

3   MARTIN, PHILIP.   *Shakespeare's Sonnets: Self, Love, and Art*. Cambridge: Cambridge University Press, 179 pp.
    In chapter 4 ("The Sonnet and the Sonneteers," pp. 100-21), finds that "*Delia* . . . is marked by a greater ease, a more fluid musicality [than *Astrophel and Stella*]; whatever its limitations, it does sing, and often memorably."   Concludes that Daniel's poetry is "intellectually . . . feeble," that it lacks passion, and that "[m]elody is its aim, and banality, sometimes, its end" (pp. 113-15, passim).

1972

4   ROWSE, A[LFRED] L[ESLIE].   The Elizabethan Renaissance: The
    Cultural Achievement.   New York: Charles Scribner's Sons,
    428 pp.
        Provides appreciative estimate of Daniel as poet and
    historian (pp. 65-67, 320-21).

                            1973

1   BARTON, ANNE.   "Nature's piece 'gainst fancy":   The Divided
    Catastrophe in "Antony and Cleopatra":   An Inaugural Lecture.
    [London]:   Bedford College, University of London, 20 pp.
        In discussing influence of Cleopatra on Antony and
    Cleopatra, suggests that Shakespeare's "reading of Daniel's
    play impelled him towards the one use, in all his trage-
    dies, of the divided catastrophe" (pp. 9-11).

2   BJORK, GARY FLOYD.   "The Renaissance Mirror for Fair Ladies:
    Samuel Daniel's Complaint of Rosamond and the Tradition of
    the Feminine Complaint."   Ph.D. dissertation, University of
    California, Irvine, 232 pp.   [DAI, 34 (1974), 7698A.]
        Places Rosamond in development of the genre.   Examines
    influences on Daniel's poem, his intent in it, and the
    influence of Rosamond on later complaints.

3   BRERETON, JOHN C.   "Heroic Praise: Dryden and the State
    Panegyric."   Ph.D. dissertation, Rutgers University, 199
    pp.   [DAI, 34 (1973), 306A.]
        Includes discussion of Daniel in the first part, "a
    brief history of the seventeenth-century state panegyric."

4   COLE, HOWARD C.   A Quest of Inquirie: Some Contexts of Tudor
    Literature.   Indianapolis: Pegasus (Bobbs-Merrill),
    596 pp.
        Examines the "moral and patriotic concerns" of Defense
    of Rhyme and places it in the context of Renaissance criti-
    cal treatises.   Discusses Daniel's work as a reply to
    Campion, suggesting that their "quarrel over the limita-
    tions of artifice and proportion is best explained simply
    in terms of their different responses to the claims of
    the classics" (passim).

5   CROFT, P. J.   "Samuel Daniel," in his edition of Autograph
    Poetry in the English Language: Facsimiles of Original
    Manuscripts from the Fourteenth to the Twentieth Century.
    Vol. I.   London: Cassell, entry 21.

Provides facsimile and transcription of "The Song of
the First Chorus" (Hymen's Triumph) from Edinburgh University Library MS. De. 3. 69.

6 DANIEL, SAMUEL. Tethys' Festival, in Stephen Orgel and Roy
    Strong, Inigo Jones: The Theatre of the Stuart Court,
    Including the Complete Designs for Productions at Court
    for the Most Part in the Collection of the Duke of Devon-
    shire Together with Their Texts and Historical Documenta-
    tion. Vol. I. London: Sotheby Parke Bernet; Berkeley:
    University of California Press, pp. 191-201.
        Provides modernized reprint of 1610 edition together
    with notes on historical documents concerned with the play
    and annotated reproductions of Jones's designs for costumes.

7 FREEMAN, ARTHUR, and I. A. SHAPIRO. "The Hatton Manuscript."
    Library, 5th ser., 28 (December), 333-37.
        In exchange over 1970.7 and 1971.15 each restates,
    clarifies, and expands his arguments on the date and nature
    of the text of the manuscript of "To the Countess of Cum-
    berland" adapted to Elizabeth Hatton.

8 GRABES, HERBERT. Speculum, Mirror und Looking-Glass: Kon-
    tinuität und Originalität der Spiegelmetapher in den
    Buchtiteln des Mittelalters und der englischen Literatur
    des 13. bis 17. Jahrhunderts. Buchreihe der Anglia,
    Zeitschrift für Englische Philologie, 16. Tübingen: Max
    Niemeyer, 425 pp.
        Draws frequently on Daniel for examples in a detailed
    analysis of the appearance of the looking-glass metaphor
    in Renaissance literature (passim).

9 MAURER, MARGARET ANN. "The Verse Letter in the English
    Renaissance." Ph.D. dissertation, Cornell University,
    296 pp. [DAI, 34 (1974), 7196-97A.]
        Includes Daniel in a study of the "characteristics of
    the genre of the familiar verse epistle and its value as
    a means of studying the concept of decorum as it applies
    to Renaissance occasional poetry." In discussing the
    Horatian tradition, finds that "Daniel's epistles . . .
    exemplify the moral concerns of the Horatian epistle, but
    they do not appear to be sensitive to the personal quality
    that distinguishes his model."

10 MELCHIORI, GIORGIO. L'uomo e il potere: Indagine sulle
    strutture profonde dei "Sonetti" de Shakespeare. Einaudi
    Paperbacks, 42. Turin: Giulio Einaudi, 248 pp.

1973

Includes <u>Delia</u> in tabular analyses of words most frequently used, pronouns, and frequency of terms related to
love in five Elizabethan sonnet sequences (Drayton, Sidney,
Spenser, and Shakespeare). Compares Daniel's usage with
that of the others (passim). Revised 1976.7.

11   SIMMONS, J[OSEPH] L[ARRY]. Shakespeare's Pagan World: The
     Roman Tragedies. Charlottesville: University Press of
     Virginia, 214 pp.
         Examines "Daniel's dramatic and moral view of Cleopatra's
     suicide" and its influence on Shakespeare (pp. 127-31).

                              1974

1   ADLER, THOMAS P. "An Echo of Daniel in Tennyson's 'Ulysses.'"
     Tennyson Research Bulletin, 2, no. 3: 128-30.
         Suggests possibility that Tennyson used "Ulysses and
     the Siren" as a source. Notes contrast in character of
     Ulysses in the two poems.

2   ATTRIDGE, DEREK. Well-Weighed Syllables: Elizabethan Verse
     in Classical Metres. Cambridge: Cambridge University
     Press, 266 pp.
         In "Epilogue" (pp. 228-36), examines how "Daniel . . .
     in the course of his Defence of Ryme succeeds in denying
     nearly every principle on which the humanist attempt to
     match classical verse had been based," pointing out that
     his attack on "quantitative experiments . . . and the
     taste for 'artificiality' in art" are the result of "a
     general dissatisfaction with humanist ideals" (pp. 232-
     34).

3   BEALL, JULIANNE. "Didactic Techniques in Baldwin's Mirror
     for Magistrates and Other Sixteenth-Century Poems of the
     Fall Tradition." Ph.D. dissertation, University of Cali-
     fornia, Los Angeles, 319 pp. [DAI, 35 (1975), 5387A.]
         Analyzes how Rosamond "is like a Mirror poem in that
     its tragic-figure narrator, even though she speaks in a
     manner appropriate to her flawed character, reliably con-
     veys [an] authorial message."

4   BEITH-HALAHMI, ESTHER YAËL. Angell Fayre or Strumpet Lewd:
     Jane Shore as an Example of Erring Beauty in 16th Century
     Literature. 2 volumes. ElizS, 26-27. Salzburg: Institut
     für Englische Sprache und Literatur, Universität Salzburg,
     367 pp.
         In published version (unrevised) of 1971.2, compares
     Daniel's handling of the Rosamond story with various

Elizabethan treatments of the Shore legend; discusses influence of Rosamond on several of the works (passim).

5   BERTHOLD, MARY HAINES. "The Meaning and Function of the
     'Speaking Picture': Description of Pictures in English
     Narrative Poetry, 1590-1606." Ph.D. dissertation, Uni-
     versity of Wisconsin, Madison, 398 pp. [DAI, 35 (1975),
     7859A.]
         Examines how "Daniel and Drayton use pictures as moral
     exempla which express and universalize the fate of
     Rosamond."

6   HILD, HAROLD NORBERT. "'The Speaking Picture of the Mind':
     The Poetic Style of Samuel Daniel." Ph.D. dissertation,
     Loyola University of Chicago, 140 pp. [DAI, 35 (1974),
     2224-25A.]
         Analyzes Delia and Rosamond "to note the interaction
     of imagery, diction, and syntax as parts of that rhetorical
     organization which Daniel deems appropriate to each type
     of poem; and to disclose how Daniel modified, refined, and
     enlarged each type of poem to embody the consistent mind
     of his poetic speaker."

7   HULSE, SHIRLEY CLARK, III. "Myth and Narrative in Elizabethan
     Poetry." Ph.D. dissertation, Claremont Graduate School,
     255 pp. [DAI, 35 (1975), 5408-5409A.]
         In an analysis of mythological and historical narrative
     poems, discusses how "Daniel mediates between his alle-
     giance to chronicle, to epic, and to the mythic shape of
     his material by interweaving his Complaint of Rosamond
     with analogues between his Medieval heroine and Io, Danaë,
     and Eve to create a panoply of sensuous decay."

8   KAU, JOSEPH [LEONG CHOO]. "Delia's Gentle Lover and the
     Eternizing Conceit in Elizabethan Sonnets." Anglia, 92,
     nos. 3-4, 334-48.
         Analyzes Daniel's "innovative use of the eternizing
     conceit and the character of his gentle lover" to show how
     he refined "the Petrarchan sonnet tradition." Points out
     that Daniel's "innovation appears conventional because of
     the gentlemanly character of the lover and because of his
     own unaffected ease and good taste in handling the
     [eternizing] conceit."

9   LaBRANCHE, ANTHONY [SPAHR]. "Samuel Daniel: A Voice of
     Thoughtfulness," in The Rhetoric of Renaissance Poetry:

1974

From Wyatt to Milton. Edited by Thomas O. Sloan and Raymond B. Waddington. Berkeley: University of California
Press, pp. 123-39.
   Reacting to the tendency to characterize much of Daniel's poetry as honest or "eloquent, but not really poetic
or poetically engaging," analyzes Daniel's rhetorical
strategies for creating a speaking voice (particularly in
his epistles). Demonstrates that much of Daniel's "rhetoric is directed to specific representations of the
speaker's stance, balance, and manner of discourse, rather
than to isolated vivid turns and 'effective' argumenta-
tion." Shows "that Daniel's rhetoric is not really ora-
torical in purpose and tone, but it is a rhetoric of
thoughtfulness, creating a poetry that presents habits of
mind through certain rhetorical signals, a mind given . . .
to tracing cause and effect, analogy, recapitulation and
the like." Suggests that "a thought process . . . [is]
the basic activity of his poetry--the poetic imitation
of an argument rather than the argument itself" and that
"Daniel's sense of organization . . . may owe something
to Montaigne's loose, discursive intimate essay style."

10   LEAVENWORTH, RUSSELL E[DWIN]. Daniel's "Cleopatra": A Critical Study. ElizS, 3. Salzburg: Institut für Englische
Sprache und Literatur, Universität Salzburg, 137 pp.
   In published version of 1953.2, examines the intellectual and literary background of the play, "narrative
quality," "the advances which Daniel made in poetic technique in the course of writing Cleopatra," "philosophic
content," sources (particularly Plutarch and Machiavelli),
revisions, influence (especially on Shakespeare and Dryden), and scholarship on the work. Places Cleopatra in
the context of Daniel's career, suggesting that it "represents the transition in Daniel's art from poetry which
arises out of images to poetry which arises out of ideas."
Argues that "Daniel did not revise Cleopatra as a result
of seeing Shakespeare's version" and that Shakespeare's
"debt to Daniel . . . [is] much larger than anyone has so
far seen fit to recognize."

11   LEVER, J[ULIUS] W[ALTER], ed. Sonnets of the English Renaissance. Athlone Renaissance Library. London: Athlone
Press, 202 pp.
   Provides annotated selection from Delia. In "Introduction" (pp. 1-30), briefly discusses the distinctive qualities of Daniel's sonnets.

12 MARCHESANI, JOSEPH JOHN, JR. "The Revisions of Michael Dray-
     ton's Four Legends." Ph.D. dissertation, University of
     Rochester, 340 pp. [DAI, 36 (1975), 905A.]
          Examines influence of Rosamond on the structure of
     Drayton's Matilda.

13 MORRISON, MARY. "Some Aspects of the Treatment of the Theme
     of Antony and Cleopatra in Tragedies of the Sixteenth
     Century." JES, 4 (June), 113-25.
          Includes Cleopatra in a comparative analysis of nine
     sixteenth-century plays on Antony and Cleopatra.

14 SHAWCROSS, JOHN T. "The Poet as Orator: One Phase of His
     Judicial Pose," in The Rhetoric of Renaissance Poetry:
     From Wyatt to Milton. Edited by Thomas O. Sloan and Ray-
     mond B. Waddington. Berkeley: University of California
     Press, pp. 5-36.
          Analyzes Delia 11 as an example of the "employment of
     the forensic mode . . . through the rhetorical technique
     of distributio-recapitulatio." Argues that "Daniel is
     concerned in the poem (and the sequence) with achievement
     in writing" and invites the reader to judge his "poetic
     abilities."

15 SINNOTT, AIDAN JOHN BARRY. "Stuart Politics and the Court
     Masque." Ph.D. dissertation, University of North Carolina
     at Chapel Hill, 190 pp. [DAI, 35 (1974), 3771A.]
          Contrasts Daniel's theory of and practice in the masque
     with Jonson's and places Daniel's works "in their social
     settings, as celebrations of great national moments, sup-
     porting Stuart views of national and international policy."

16 THOMSON, PATRICIA. "Sonnet 15 of Samuel Daniel's Delia: A
     Petrarchan Imitation," in Übersetzung und Nachahmung im
     europäischen Petrarkismus: Studien und Texte. Edited by
     Luzius Keller. SAVL, 7. Stuttgart: J. B. Metzler,
     pp. 210-17.
          Reprints 1965.15.

17 URE, PETER. "A Note on 'Opinion' in Daniel, Greville, and
     Chapman," in Elizabethan and Jacobean Drama: Critical
     Essays by Peter Ure. Edited by J[ames] C[loutts] Maxwell.
     English Texts and Studies. New York: Barnes & Noble,
     pp. 209-20.
          Reprints 1951.9.

1974

18 WATSON, GEORGE, ed. The New Cambridge Bibliography of Eng-
    lish Literature, I: 600–1660. Cambridge: Cambridge Uni-
    versity Press, 56 pp., 2476 columns.
        Revises selective lists of works by and about Daniel in
    1941.2. William A. Ringler compiled the section on Daniel
    as a poet and Norman J. Endicott, the one on Daniel as
    historian (columns 1061–65, 2235–37, passim).

19 WILLIAMSON, MARILYN L. Infinite Variety: Antony and Cleo-
    patra in Renaissance Drama and Earlier Tradition. Mystic,
    Conn.: Lawrence Verry, 262 pp.
        Places Cleopatra in the tradition of literary treatments
    of Cleopatra. Analyzes the play, "the last and greatest
    of the Senecan tragedies on the theme," as a Senecan
    tragedy; examines Daniel's focus on and isolation of Cleo-
    patra, use of chorus, and employment of the motif of
    Cleopatra's concern for her children to achieve unity;
    and traces the thematic development in the play. Discusses
    revisions in 1607 edition, an "artistically inferior"
    version. In Appendix A ("Daniel's Cleopatra, Brandon's
    Octavia, and Antony and Cleopatra," pp. 238–44), argues
    that Cleopatra influenced Shakespeare on the level of the
    scene, an aspect of influence previously ignored (pp. 134–
    52, 222–36, 238–41, passim).

20 WILSON, KATHARINE M[ARGARET]. Shakespeare's Sugared Sonnets.
    New York: Barnes & Noble, 382 pp.
        Points out several parallels between Delia and Sonnets
    to argue that Daniel influenced Shakespeare and that
    Shakespeare, at times, parodied Daniel. Also comments on
    Sir John Davies's parody of Delia in Gulling Sonnets
    (passim).

1975

1   CHRISTOPHER, ROBERT J. "The Emergence of Story: The Rela-
    tionship of Fiction and History in English Historical
    Poetry, 1559–1621." Ph.D. dissertation, University of
    California, Berkeley, 299 pp. [DAI, 37 (1976), 2891A.]
        Examines Rosamond, Civil Wars, and History of England
    in analyzing "the gradual movement [during 1590–1620] of
    story from an historical category to a literary one." Dis-
    cusses how "Daniel radically altered the style and his-
    torical emphasis of the legend poem" in Rosamond; analyzes
    revisions to show how "Daniel began the Civil Wars as a
    Tudor apologist, [but] . . . ended as the analytic

political historian"; observes that in History of England "Daniel carefully excluded historical fictions from his narrative and argued that history could only be determined through judicious documentation."

2 DULS, LOUISA DESAUSSURE. Richard II in the Chronicles. SEngL, 79. The Hague: Mouton, 274 pp.
     In revision of 1962.5 discusses depiction of Richard II in Civil Wars (pp. 199-202).

3 KAU, JOSEPH [LEONG CHOO]. "Daniel's Influence on an Image in Pericles and Sonnet 73: An Impresa of Destruction." SQ, 26 (Winter), 51-53.
     Argues that the description of "an impresa with a down-turned torch" in Worthy Tract is the source of a similar image in Pericles and Sonnet 73.

4 LEIDIG, HEINZ-DIETER. Das Historiengedicht in der englischen Literaturtheorie: Die Rezeption von Lucans "Pharsalia" von der Renaissance bis zum Ausgang des achtzehnten Jahrhunderts. Europäische Hochschulschriften, 26. Bern: Herbert Lang; Frankfurt: Peter Lang, 200 pp.
     Examines influence of Pharsalia on Daniel's treatment of history in Civil Wars (pp. 78-86, passim).

5 LOVE, JOHN MICHAEL. "'To varietie inclin'd': A Study of Michael Drayton's Idea." Ph.D. dissertation, University of North Carolina at Chapel Hill, 158 pp. [DAI, 36 (1975), 3732-33A.]
     Discusses Drayton's "slavish imitation" of Delia in Idea's Mirror.

6 PATRICK, J[OHN] MAX. "The Cleopatra Theme in World Literature up to 1700," in The Undoing of Babel: Watson Kirkconnell, the Man and His Work. Edited by J[ames] R[ussell] C[onway] Perkin. Toronto: McClelland and Stewart, pp. 64-76.
     Includes brief discussion of the place of Cleopatra in the early treatment of the story. Points out that Daniel "reacted against . . . [the Countess of Pembroke's] meanness to Cleopatra" in Antonius and that "he began to recognize the dramatic possibilities of the tension themes that were developed later."

7 PERCY, LeROY PRATT, JR. "Shakespeare's Lucrece and Its Literary Traditions." Ph.D. dissertation, University of Virginia, 158 pp. [DAI, 36 (1975), 2853A.]
     Uses Rosamond in "analyzing the differences between Lucrece and its forerunners."

1975

8   PRIMEAU, RONALD. "Daniel and the <u>Mirror</u> Tradition: Dramatic
    Irony in <u>The Complaint of Rosamond</u>." <u>SEL</u>, 15 (Winter),
    21-36.
        Analyzes Daniel's modifications of the <u>Mirror</u> tradition
    to illustrate the dramatic irony in <u>Rosamond</u> (also comments
    on irony in several of his other poems). Argues that "the
    'moral' of Daniel's poem issues more from the mimetic
    representation of character and situation than the homil-
    etic presentation of a lesson"; "that Rosamond is not a
    repentant heroine but a self-centered, fame-seeking hedon-
    ist who uses her pretended repentance in an attempt to
    free herself from the guilt resulting from her treatment of
    the king; that Daniel uses his characterization of Henry
    to throw into relief and comment on the shallowness of
    his Rosamond; that Rosamond's selfishness is in fact a
    target of satire in the poem; and, finally, that the
    variety of plot devices and strands of irony in the poem
    create a consistent satire on conventional moralizing and
    transform the complaint genre into a comment on the ill
    effects of adhering to a distorted or hypocritical reli-
    gious outlook."

1976

1   ARDINGER, BARBARA R. "Cleopatra on Stage: An Examination of
    the <u>Persona</u> of the Queen in English Drama, 1592-1898."
    Ph.D. dissertation, Southern Illinois University, 290 pp.
    [<u>DAI</u>, 37 (1976), 3634A.]
        Discusses <u>Cleopatra</u>.

2   FINK, LILA RUTH. "Time's Trans-Shifting: Classical Conven-
    tions of Time in Renaissance Lyric Poetry." Ph.D. disser-
    tation, University of Southern California. [<u>DAI</u>, 36
    (1976), 7407-7408A.]
        Analyzes how "Daniel, in <u>Delia</u>, uses <u>carpe diem</u>,
    <u>carpe-florem</u> and <u>eternization through poetry</u> to create
    both a structural frame for the cycle and a thematic
    focus, converting a Petrarchan love story into a statement
    about time's dominion on earth."

3   GIOVIO, PAOLO. "<u>The Worthy Tract of Paulus Iovius</u>" (1585)
    <u>Translated by Samuel Daniel; Together with Giovio's</u>
    "<u>Dialogo dell'imprese militari et amorose</u>." Introduction
    by Norman K. Farmer, Jr. Delmar, N.Y.: Scholar's Facsi-
    miles & Reprints, n.p.

Provides facsimile reprint of 1585 edition. In "Intro-
duction" (pp. v-ix), discusses generally the "role [of
Daniel's translation] in the expansion and growth of
Renaissance European culture."

4   HULSE, S[HIRLEY] CLARK. "Elizabethan Minor Epic: Toward a
       Definition of Genre." SP, 73 (July), 302-19.
       Draws frequently on Rosamond in analyzing the character-
     istics of various "overlapping families" of poems which
     make up the genre. Concludes: "The genre of minor epic,
     like any uncanonical genre, must remain loosely defined,
     embracing a number of subgroupings with different bases."

5   LAMB, MARY ELLEN. "The Countess of Pembroke's Patronage."
       Ph.D. dissertation, Columbia University, 288 pp. [DAI,
       37 (1977), 6501-6502A.]
       Discusses the Countess's patronage of Daniel.

6   LOGAN, GEORGE M[EREDITH]. "Lucan--Daniel--Shakespeare: New
       Light on the Relation between The Civil Wars and Richard
       II." ShakS, 9: 121-40.
       Examines Daniel's borrowings from Pharsalia as a basis
     for arguing that Shakespeare used 1595 Civil Wars as a
     source for Richard II.

7   MELCHIORI, GIORGIO. Shakespeare's Dramatic Meditations:
       An Experiment in Criticism. Oxford: Clarendon Press,
       218 pp.
       In revision of 1973.10 includes Delia in a comparative
     statistical analysis of word-frequency, personal pronominal
     forms, and frequencies of connotative words in five Eliza-
     bethan sonnet sequences (Drayton, Sidney, Spenser, and
     Shakespeare). Points out that in Drayton's and Daniel's
     sonnets, data from word-frequency analysis "confirm their
     relative linguistic and lexical poverty, their greater
     monotony; their faithful following of convention is
     demonstrated also by the fact that they show no outstand-
     ing variations from the norm" (passim).

8   PLATZER, RONALD M. "Causation and Character in Samuel Dan-
       iel's The Civil Wars." Ph.D. dissertation, Columbia
       University, 158 pp. [DAI, 37 (1977), 6509A.]
       Analyzes reasons behind Daniel's subordination of
     character and celebration of heroic deeds to a "concern
     for the effect of men's actions on the stability of Eng-
     land" in Civil Wars and History of England. Finds that
     although he attempts "to explain events in terms of human

actions, Daniel understands that the flow of events must be
seen as a manifestation of a just, divine plan." Contrasts
Shakespeare's "treatment of key political figures" with
Daniel's, and contrasts Drayton's interest in the heroic
in Barons' Wars and Mortimeriados with Daniel's focus on
"the effects of men's deeds on the nation" in Civil Wars.

1977

1 BROWER, REUBEN A[RTHUR]. "Antony and Cleopatra: The Heroic
 Context," in Twentieth Century Interpretations of "Antony
 and Cleopatra": A Collection of Critical Essays. Edited
 by Mark [Allen] Rose. TCI. Englewood Cliffs, N.J.:
 Prentice-Hall, pp. 30-37.
  Reprints chapter of 1971.3 in which Brower discusses
 Cleopatra.

2 DANIEL, SAMUEL. Delia, in Elizabethan Sonnets. Edited by
 Maurice Evans. London: Dent; Totowa, N.J.: Rowman and
 Littlefield, pp. 62-86.
  Provides annotated reprint of 1594 edition. In "Intro-
 duction" (pp. vii-xxxi), provides a brief critical estimate
 of Delia.

3 DOYLE, CHARLES CLAY. "The Loneliness of Icarus: Ovid,
 Brueghel, and the Later Poets." Classical Outlook, 54
 (March), 73-74.
  Notes similarity of Daniel's handling of the Icarus
 myth in Delia 27 to Brueghel's in Landscape with the Fall
 of Icarus. Does not argue that Brueghel influenced Daniel,
 but points out "that both . . . made the same alteration
 in Ovid's account, alike perceiving in the fall of Icarus
 the terror of loneliness and isolation."

4 GILES, MARY DOOLEY. "The Elizabethan Sonnet Sequence: Seg-
 mented Form in Its Earliest Appearances, Astrophil and
 Stella, Hekatompathia, and Delia." Ph.D. dissertation,
 University of Virginia, 261 pp. [DAI, 39 (1978), 872-73A.]
  In arguing that "[p]eriodic analogy, a common feature
 of Renaissance music, best describes the structural principle . . . in the Elizabethan sequence," finds that
 "periodic analogy [in Delia] depends . . . primarily on
 theme" and that Daniel organizes his sequence around "four
 core groups of sonnets."

5   GILL, R. B.   "Moral History and Daniel's The Civil Wars."
    JEGP, 76 (July), 334-45.
        In arguing that "The Civil Wars . . . exemplifies the
    tendency of providential history conceived in terms of
    moral law to become a closed system of second causes and
    effects analogous to natural law," analyzes Daniel's view
    of the cyclical nature of history, his reasons for "ex-
    plain[ing] particular actions in other than providential
    terms," his conception of moral law, and his concern with
    "recurrent moral patterns."

6   GODSHALK, WILLIAM L[EIGH].   "Samuel Daniel," in The New Intel-
    lectuals: A Survey and Bibliography of Recent Studies in
    English Renaissance Drama.   Edited by Terence P. Logan and
    Denzell S. Smith.   Lincoln: University of Nebraska Press,
    pp. 281-301.
        Provides overview in essay form of scholarship c. 1923-
    1973.   Comments that "Daniel is not generally thought of
    as a dramatist"; notes that the masques and pastoral plays
    have been neglected while the "tragedies have received
    most of the critical attention devoted to his drama."

7   MAURER, MARGARET [ANN].   "Samuel Daniel's Poetical Epistles,
    Especially Those to Sir Thomas Egerton and Lucy, Countess
    of Bedford."   SP, 74 (October), 418-44.
        Provides detailed analysis of Daniel's "poetic of
    occasional poetry," particularly his use of an emblematic
    method which "admits his ulterior motives without compro-
    mising his expressed ones" in the epistles.   Discusses
    "his practice in the court masque" as "an analogue to his
    method in the epistles."

8   SHAPIRO, MICHAEL.   Children of the Revels: The Boy Companies
    of Shakespeare's Time and Their Plays.   New York: Columbia
    University Press, 331 pp.
        Discusses problems resulting from the production of
    Philotas and draws on Daniel's work in examining the
    characteristics of the plays performed by the companies
    (passim).

9   STAMNITZ, SUSANNE.   "Prettie Tales of Wolues and Sheepe":
    Tragicomik, Pastorale und Satire im Drama der englischen
    und italienischen Renaissance, 1550-1640.   AF, 125.
    Heidelberg: Carl Winter, 255 pp.
        Draws frequently on Hymen's Triumph and Queen's Arcadia
    for examples (passim).

1977

10   SZENCZI, MIKLÓS. "Romantic Qualities in English Renaissance
      Criticism?" HSE, 11 (December), 51-56.
          Argues contra Smith (1904.4) that Defense of Rhyme does
      not represent a move toward romantic principles of criti-
      cism. Finds that the "main motive" for Daniel's "defence
      of medieval English literature was . . . patriotic pride
      in his country's past."

                            1978

1   ALTMAN, JOEL B. The Tudor Play of Mind: Rhetorical Inquiry
      and the Development of Elizabethan Drama. Berkeley:
      University of California Press, 416 pp.
          Examines how Cleopatra "seem[s] designed to forge a
      complex response to its protagonist" through Daniel's
      "prismatic approach to his subject matter," with each act
      giving "a different glimpse of Cleopatra." Concludes that
      Daniel attempted "to create a complex·character, not sim-
      ply discrete vignettes" and that "[t]he multiple views of
      Cleopatra are intended to qualify her case in our eyes and
      evoke tragic understanding" (pp. 288-92).

2   JACKSON, MacD. P. "The Printer of the First Quarto of Astro-
      phil and Stella (1591)." SB, 31: 201-203.
          Identifies John Charlewood as the printer of the sur-
      reptitious edition, which included some of Daniel's
      sonnets. Provides bibliographical analysis of the edition.

3   KOPPEL, CATHERINE CONSTANTINO. "'Of Poets and Poesy': The
      English Verse Epistle, 1595-1640." Ph.D. dissertation,
      University of Rochester, 285 pp. [DAI, 39 (1978), 2292-
      93A.]
          Draws frequently on Daniel in an attempt to define the
      genre and trace its evolution. Examines, in particular,
      the relationship between Daniel's verse epistles and his
      poetic theories.

4   MUIR, KENNETH. The Sources of Shakespeare's Plays. New
      Haven: Yale University Press, 328 pp.
          Discusses Shakespeare's indebtedness to Rosamond in
      Romeo and Juliet; to Civil Wars in Richard II, King John,
      1 and 2 Henry IV, and Henry V; to Queen's Arcadia in Mac-
      beth; and to Cleopatra and Letter from Octavia in Antony
      and Cleopatra (passim).

5   MURCHISON, MARGARET LYNNE.   "A Study of the Imagery in Samuel
    Daniel's Delia." Ph.D. dissertation, University of
    Mississippi, 298 pp. [DAI, 39 (1978), 1597A.]
        Provides detailed analysis of the types and character-
    istics of Daniel's imagery. Discusses, in particular,
    the subjects of his imagery, its "non-sensory appeal,"
    and its abstractness.

6   NEELY, CAROL THOMAS.   "The Structure of English Renaissance
    Sonnet Sequences." ELH, 45 (Fall), 359-89.
        Draws frequently on Delia in arguing that English Ren-
    aissance sonnet sequences share "a characteristic overall
    structure," one adopted with modifications from Petrarch
    and Dante. Analyzes the generation of the sequences
    (pointing out "that fragmentary composition over a long
    period of time is compatible with a deliberately ordered
    structure"), characteristics of the beginnings (noting the
    importance of "the metaphor of breeding"), strategies of
    development, the two-part division, and characteristics
    of the endings (giving particular attention to Delia as
    representative of a type wherein "detachment from conflicts
    is achieved by a shift to forms of poetry other than
    sonnets").

7   PRESCOTT, ANNE LAKE.   French Poets and the English Renais-
    sance: Studies in Fame and Transformation. New Haven:
    Yale University Press, 304 pp.
        In published version of 1967.13, discusses Du Bellay's
    influence on Delia and (possibly) Defense of Rhyme, and
    Desportes's influence on Delia (pp. 58-60, 146-48, passim).

8   ROSS, DONALD, JR.   "Stylistics and the Testing of Literary
    Hypotheses." Poetics, 7 (December), 389-416.
        Includes tabular analyses of various stylistic elements
    of selected Delia sonnets in comparing stylistic features
    of Keats, Coleridge, Wordsworth, and Blake with those of
    Elizabethan sonnets.

1979

1   GIOVIO, PAOLO.   The Worthy Tract of Jovius, translated by
    Samuel Daniel, in "Dialogo dell'imprese," Paolo Giovio;
    "Imprese heroiche et morali," Gabriello Simeoni; "Ragiona-
    mento," Lodovico Domenichi; "The Worthy Tract of Jovius,"
    Samuel Daniel. The Philosophy of Images, 6. Edited by
    Stephen Orgel. New York: Garland, n.p.
        Provides facsimile reprint of 1585 edition.

1979

2   HELGERSON, RICHARD. "The Elizabethan Laureate: Self-
          Presentation and the Literary System." <u>ELH</u>, 46 (Summer),
          193-220.
              Draws frequently on Daniel in analyzing the evolution
          of the laureate (as distinct from amateur and professional)
          poet and the techniques of "literary self-presentation"
          and "self-definition" accompanying the creation of the
          role.

3   HULSE, S[HIRLEY] CLARK. "Samuel Daniel: The Poet as Liter-
          ary Historian." <u>SEL</u>, 19 (Winter), 55-69.
              Examines "Daniel's evolving sense of literary history"
          and its effect as "a shaping force in Daniel's . . .
          development from Petrarchan to plain stylist." Analyzes
          how his "deepening disenchantment with the 'modern' move-
          ment in letters . . . and . . . his increasing sense of
          isolation from a corrupt culture" result in Daniel's
          development of an "idiosyncratic plain style which reaches
          its maturity between 1595 and 1603." Finds that "[t]he
          evolution of Daniel's historical technique from <u>Rosamond</u>
          to the completion of the <u>Civil Wars</u> is a continuous inter-
          action between the demands of history and poetic form."

4   RØSTVIG, MAREN-SOFIE. "A Frame of Words: On the Craftsman-
          ship of Samuel Daniel." <u>ES</u>, 60 (April), 122-37.
              Analyzes "the close collaboration between thematic and
          verbal patterns" in <u>Rosamond</u>, "To the Reader," "To the
          Countess of Cumberland," and "To Anne Clifford" to show
          that Daniel "used a technique of verbal repetition where
          the repetition of a nexus of identical rhymewords is the
          most striking method of achieving the desired linking be-
          tween parts."

5   WILSON, CHRISTOPHER S. "<u>Astrophil and Stella</u>: A Tangled
          Editorial Web." <u>Library</u>, 6th ser., 1 (December), 336-46.
              Suggests possibility that Daniel was involved in the
          preparation of Newman's 1591 edition of <u>Astrophel and
          Stella</u>, which included some of Daniel's sonnets. Also
          discusses the importance of his dedicatory epistle in
          <u>Delia</u> (1592) to his relationship with the Countess of
          Pembroke.

Michael Drayton

Major Works

1591   Harmony of the Church

1593   Shepherd's Garland

        Gaveston

1594   Idea's Mirror

        Matilda

1595   Endymion and Phoebe

1596   Mortimeriados

        Robert

1597   England's Heroical Epistles

1599   Idea

1600   Oldcastle

1603   Barons' Wars

        To the Majesty of King James

1604   Owl

        Paean Triumphal

        Moses

1606   Odes

        Man in the Moon

        Eclogues

1607   Cromwell

1612   Polyolbion, Part I

1622   Polyolbion, Part II

1627   Battle of Agincourt

        Nymphidia

        Margaret

        Quest of Cynthia

        Sirena

        Moon-Calf

        Elegies

1630   Muses' Elysium

        Noah's Flood

        David and Goliath

Annotated Bibliography

1684

1 WINSTANLEY, WILLIAM. "The Life of Mr. Michael Drayton," in
his Englands Worthies: The Lives of the Most Eminent
Persons from Constantine the Great to This Presant Time.
[London:] Obadiak Blagrave, pp. 340-41.
Offers brief biography and critical appraisal.

1687

1 WINSTANLEY, WILLIAM. "Mr. Michael Drayton," in his The Lives
of the Most Famous English Poets. London: Samuel Manship,
pp. 105-108.
Provides a brief biographical and critical notice,
concluding: "He was a Poet of a pious temper, his Con-
science having always the command of his Fancy; very
temperate in his Life, slow of speech, and inoffensive in
company."

1703

1 OLDMIXON, JOHN. Amores Britannici: Epistles Historical and
Gallant, in English Heroic Verse: From Several of the
Most Illustrious Personages of Their Times. London:
John Nutt.
Rewrites, without acknowledging Drayton's authorship,
England's Heroical Epistles in a manner more acceptable to
Augustan taste.

1709

1 [DRAYTON, MICHAEL, ANTHONY MUNDAY, RICHARD HATHAWAY, and
ROBERT WILSON]. The History of Sir John Oldcastle, in
The Works of Mr. William Shakespear. Vol. VI. Edited by
Nicholas Rowe. London: Jacob Tonson, pp. 3115-82.
Provides reprint of unidentified edition.

1737

1   DRAYTON, MICHAEL. <u>England's Heroical Epistles, Written in</u>
<u>Imitation of the Stile and Manner of Ovid's Epistles</u>.
London: J. Hazard, L. Gilliver, J. Clarke, and R. Dodsley,
288 pp.
     Provides text based on one of the seventeenth-century
editions of <u>Poems</u>.

1748

1   DRAYTON, MICHAEL. <u>The Works of Michael Drayton, Esq</u>. [Edit-
ed by Charles Coffey?] London: R. Dodsley, J. Jolliffe,
and W. Reeve, 412 pp.
     Provides "modernized" texts of <u>Battle of Agincourt</u>,
<u>Barons' Wars</u>, <u>England's Heroical Epistles</u>, <u>Margaret</u>,
<u>Nymphidia</u>, <u>Moon-Calf</u>, <u>Robert</u>, <u>Matilda</u>, <u>Gaveston</u>, <u>Cromwell</u>,
<u>Quest of Cynthia</u>, <u>Sirena</u>, <u>Polyolbion</u>, <u>Elegies</u>, and <u>Idea</u>.
In "An Historical Essay on the Life and Writings of Michael
Drayton, Esq." (pp. 3-12), provides a chronological overview of Drayton's life and writings, with particular emphasis on his style. Suggests a rivalry between Drayton
and Daniel over preferment at court. Attributes Drayton's
lack of success to the spirit of the age: "That he did
not thrive, arose from no great Singularity in that Age
in which he flourished; for the Men of Interest were not
then remarkably great or good, that is to say, they were
not either proper Judges of Merit, or real Friends to Virtue." After Oldys (1750.1) pointed out omissions, an
<u>Appendix</u> was issued c. 1752 (1752.1).

1750

1   [OLDYS, WILLIAM]. "Michael Drayton," in <u>Biographia Britan-</u>
<u>nica; or, The Lives of the Most Eminent Persons Who Have</u>
<u>Flourished in Great Britain and Ireland</u>. Vol. III. Lon-
don: W. Innys et al., pp. 1744-49.
     Provides overview of Drayton's life and a general
critical estimate of his works. In particular discusses
poems omitted from 1748.1. <u>See</u> 1752.1.

1751

1   DRAYTON, MICHAEL. <u>The History of Queen Mab; or, The Court of</u>
<u>Fairy: Being the Story upon Which the Entertainment of</u>
<u>Queen Mab, now Exhibiting at Drury-Lane, Is Founded</u>.
London: M. Cooper, 25 pp.

Reprints <u>Nymphidia</u> from 1748.1. (There was another
edition in 1751 which included a reprint of "An Historical
Essay on the Life and Writings of Michael Drayton, Esq."
from 1748.1.)

1752

1 DRAYTON, MICHAEL. <u>Appendix to "The Works of Michael Drayton."</u>
   N.p.: n.p., 92 pp.
       Provides "modernized" reprints of <u>Owl</u>, <u>Man in the Moon</u>,
   <u>Odes</u>, <u>Pastorals</u>, <u>Muses' Elysium</u>, <u>Noah's Flood</u>, <u>Moses</u>, and
   <u>David and Goliath</u>. This was issued after Oldys (1750.1)
   pointed out omissions in 1748.1.

1753

1 ANON. Review of <u>The Works of Michael Drayton, Esq.</u> <u>Monthly</u>
   <u>Review; or, Literary Journal</u>, 1st ser., 9 (September), 187.
       In review of 1753.3 points out omissions in 1748.1 and
   observes: "It must doubtless afford a sensible pleasure
   to every lover of <u>English</u> poetry, to see so great a regard
   paid by the present age . . . to the works of this worthy
   bard."

2 CIBBER, [THEOPHILUS]. "Michael Drayton," in his <u>The Lives of</u>
   <u>the Poets of Great Britain and Ireland to the</u> <u>Time of Dean</u>
   <u>Swift</u>. Vol. I. London: R. Griffiths, pp. 212-19.
       Provides overview of life and major works. Concludes
   that Drayton's "genius seems to have been of the second
   rate, much beneath Spencer and Sidney, Shakespear and
   Johnson, but highly removed above the ordinary run of
   versifyers."

3 DRAYTON, MICHAEL. <u>The Works of Michael Drayton, Esq.</u> 4 volumes. London: W. Reeve, 1649 pp.
       Reprints 1748.1 and 1752.1. Reviewed in 1753.1.

1758

1 ANON. "The Poetical Scale." <u>Literary Magazine; or, Univer-</u>
   <u>sal Review</u>, 3 (January), 6-8.
       Rates twenty-nine poets from Chaucer through Hughes on
   a scale of 20: gives Drayton 10 in Genius, 11 in Judgment,
   16 in Learning, and 13 in Versification.

1780

1 [DRAYTON, MICHAEL, ANTHONY MUNDAY, RICHARD HATHAWAY, and ROBERT WILSON]. Sir John Oldcastle, Part I, in Supplement to the Edition of Shakspeare's Plays Published in 1778 by Samuel Johnson and George Steevens. Vol. II. Edited by Edmond Malone. London: C. Bathurst et al., pp. 265-370.
Provides annotated text based on 1600 edition.

1786

1 O., C. T. "On Michael Drayton." European Magazine, 10 (September), 153-55; (November), 361-62.
Argues that Drayton has been unustly neglected and points out several parallels between Drayton and Milton to illustrate the influence of the former on Paradise Lost.

2 W., T. H. "Michael Drayton Defended." Gentleman's Magazine, 56 (December), 1059-60.
Comments on versification in defending Drayton against Warburton's characterization of him as "a very ordinary poet" (Preface to Shakespeare).

1787

1 HEADLEY, HENRY, ed. Select Beauties of Ancient English Poetry: With Remarks. 2 volumes. London: T. Cadell, 215, 200 pp.
Includes an appreciative "Biographical Sketch" of Drayton, who he thinks merits a better contemporary reputation. Comments on his style and finds the satiric works to be Drayton's least effective ones (I, 1-lii). Provides several annotated extracts arranged under various headings, for example, "Pathetic Pieces," "Descriptive Pieces" (passim). See 1851.1. (For the importance of Headley's collection, see Earl R[eeves] Wasserman, "Henry Headley and the Elizabethan Revival," SP, 36 [July 1939], 491-502.)

1788

1 ANON. "Biographical Sketches of English Poets: Michael Drayton." Town and Country Magazine; or, Universal Repository of Knowledge, Instruction, and Entertainment, 20 (December), 557-58.

Offers a general appreciative discussion of Drayton,
noting in particular the value of Polyolbion to the anti-
quary. Comments on Drayton's style, observing: "In a
most pedantic aera he was unaffected, and seldom exhibits
his learning at the expence of his judgment."

2   DRAYTON, MICHAEL. England's Heroical Epistles. [Edited by
James Hurdis?] London: J. Johnson, 344 pp.
Provides modernized, annotated text. In "Preface"
(pp. v-vii), gives a brief biographical sketch.

1793

1   DRAYTON, MICHAEL. "The Poetical Works of Michael Drayton,
Esq.," in The Works of the British Poets, with Prefaces,
Biographical and Critical. Vol. III. Edited by Robert
Anderson. London: John & Arthur Arch et al., pp. i-vi,
1-670.
Provides modernized reprints of Battle of Agincourt,
Barons' Wars, England's Heroical Epistles, Nymphidia,
Moon-Calf, Margaret, Robert, Matilda, Gaveston, Cromwell,
Quest of Cynthia, Sirena, Polyolbion, Elegies, Idea, Owl,
Man in the Moon, Odes, Pastorals, Muses' Elysium, Noah's
Flood, Moses, and David and Goliath. In "The Life of
Drayton" (pp. i-vi), provides a sketchy overview of his
life and works, and discusses his critical reputation.
(The general title page for the volume is dated 1795; the
title page for the Drayton section is dated 1793.)

1795

1   [WALDRON, FRANCIS GODOLPHIN]. "Michael Drayton," in his The
Biographical Mirrour: Comprising a Series of Ancient and
Modern English Portraits of Eminent and Distinguished
Persons, from Original Pictures and Drawings. Vol. I.
London: S. and E. Harding, pp. 102-11.
Provides overview of Drayton's life and works (with
extracts). Numbers him among the "first-rate deceased
Poets" and suggests that "it is in the Pastoral and Fairy
stiles of writing that Drayton eminently excels . . .
every other English poet." Includes engraving based on
the Dulwich College portrait.

1800

1   C. "Drayton and Dryden." European Magazine, 38 (December), 416.
Notes parallel between Drayton's description of the effect of David's music on Saul (David and Goliath) and Dryden's description of the effect of Jubal's music on his "brethren" in "A Song for St. Cecilia's Day."

2   PHILLIPS, EDWARD. Theatrum Poetarum Anglicanorum: Containing the Names and Characters of All the English Poets from the Reign of Henry III. to the Close of the Reign of Queen Elizabeth. Revised by S[amuel] E[gerton] Brydges. Canterbury: J. White, 422 pp.
Enlarges the brief entry in 1675 edition with extracts from various sources and a list of works. Observes that "Drayton's taste was less correct, and his ear less harmonious than Daniel's--but his genius was more poetical, though it seems to have fitted him only for the didactic, and not for the bolder walks of Poetry" (pp. 262-71).

1806

1   ANON. "Warburton and Drayton." The Monthly Anthology and Boston Review, 3: 64-65.
Defends Drayton against Warburton, "the hierophant of England" who "allude[d] obscurely to" him in Preface to Shakespeare. Points out that Drayton "had an eye, that looked carefully and curiously on nature, and a mind, that did not despise learning."

1810

1   DRAYTON, MICHAEL. "The Poems of Michael Drayton," in The Works of the English Poets, from Chaucer to Cowper. Vol. IV. Edited by Alexander Chalmers. London: J. Johnson et al., pp. vii-xx, 1-498.
Provides modernized reprint of much of the poetry. In "The Life of Michael Drayton" (pp. ix-xiii), surveys his life, works, and critical reputation.

2   [DRAYTON, MICHAEL, ANTHONY MUNDAY, RICHARD HATHAWAY, and ROBERT WILSON.] Sir John Oldcastle, in The Ancient British Drama. Vol. I. London: William Miller, pp. 318-49.
Provides annotated, modernized text.

1813

1   ANON. "Drayton." General Repository and Review, 4 (July),
    74-79.
        Describes Nymphidia as "the poem in which Drayton dis-
    played the greatest efforts of his imagination, and sport-
    iveness of his fancy" and provides synopsis of the work.

1814

1   DRAYTON, MICHAEL. Nymphidia: The Court of Fairy. Edited by
    [Samuel] Egerton Brydges. Kent: Johnson and Warwick at
    the Private Press of Lee Priory, 76 pp.
        Reprints 1619 edition; also includes "To Henry Rey-
    nolds," "To Sir Henry Goodere," and Idea 53. In "Adver-
    tisement" (pp. 1-12), suggests that Nymphidia "probably
    retains more charms for modern readers of poetry than any
    of . . . [Drayton's] other productions" and identifies his
    major weakness as the inability to be selective in details
    in his poems.

1815

1   BRYDGES, [SAMUEL] EGERTON. "Sonnet by Michael Drayton," in
    his Restituta; or, Titles, Extracts, and Characters of Old
    Books in English Literature, Revived. Vol. II. London:
    Longman, Hurst, Rees, Orme, and Brown, p. 104.
        Reprints "To Sir David Murray," prefixed to Murray's
    Sophonisba and "uncollected by . . . [Drayton's] Editors."
    On p. 111 reprints "To John Davies" from Davies of Here-
    ford's Holy Rood.

2   DRAYTON, MICHAEL. How the Lord Cromwell Exalted from Meane
    Estate, Was after by the Enuie of the Bishop of Winches-
    ter . . . Brought to Vntimely End, in Mirror for Magis-
    trates. Vol. II, part III. Edited by Joseph Haslewood.
    London: Lackington, Allen; and Longman, Hurst, Rees,
    Orme, and Brown, pp. 502-39.
        Provides reprint from 1610 edition of Mirror, collated
    with the text in Poems (1637).

Michael Drayton

1817

1 DRAKE, NATHAN. Shakspeare and His Times: Including the Bio-
      graphy of the Poet; Criticisms on His Genius and Writings;
      a New Chronology of His Plays; a Disquisition on the Ob-
      ject of His Sonnets; and a History of the Manners, Customs,
      and Amusements, Superstitions, Poetry, and Elegant Litera-
      ture of His Age. 2 volumes. London: T. Cadell and W.
      Davies, 747, 683 pp.
         Offers a brief critical estimate of Drayton's major
      works, suggesting that "[i]t is chiefly as a pastoral poet
      that Drayton will live in the memory of his countrymen"
      (I, 615-17, passim).

1819

1 CAMPBELL, THOMAS, ed. Specimens of the British Poets: With
      Biographical and Critical Notices, and An Essay on English
      Poetry. Vol. III. London: John Murray, 432 pp.
         Includes generous modernized selection from Drayton's
      poetry. In prefatory note provides a brief biography and
      critical estimate, observing that his "language . . . is
      free and perspicuous" and that he is at his best in short
      lyrics (pp. 1-57). In "Essay on English Poetry" (I, 3-
      271), comments briefly on Drayton, classifying him and
      Daniel as "pre-eminent in the second poetical class of
      their age" (pp. 165-67).

2 DRAYTON, MICHAEL. "Select Poems of Michael Drayton with a
      Life of the Author," in The Works of the British Poets:
      With Lives of the Authors. Vol. II. Edited by Ezekiel
      Sanford. Philadelphia: Mitchell, Ames, and White,
      pp. 321-91.
         Provides modernized reprints of Nymphidia and Moon-Calf.
      In "Life of Drayton" (pp. 323-26), offers a brief critical
      appreciation; concludes by agreeing with Headley's esti-
      mate (1787.1) of Drayton's merits.

1823

1 HOOD, EU. "Fly Leaves, No. XIV." Gentleman's Magazine, 93
      (August), 109-11.
         Quotes "To John Savage" and commendatory sonnet to
      Politeuphuia, pointing out that neither is reprinted in
      modern editions.

1827

1   H[OOD, EU.?]. Untitled letter on <u>Polyolbion</u>. <u>Gentleman's</u>
<u>Magazine</u>, 97 (April), 302-304.
    Calls <u>Polyolbion</u> "perhaps one of the most singular
performances the ingenuity of a poet ever devised" but
recognizes it cannot "become popular, or be read with
pleasure as a <u>poem</u>" because of the "minuteness and continuity of detail."

1828

1   DRAYTON, MICHAEL. <u>Paean Triumphal</u>, in John Nichols, <u>The</u>
<u>Progresses, Processions, and Magnificent Festivities of</u>
<u>King James the First</u>. Vol. I. London: J. B. Nichols,
pp. 402-407.
    Provides annotated reprint.

1829

1   P., W. "Drayton as a Dramatic Poet." <u>Gentleman's Magazine</u>,
99 (August), 108-10.
    Cites <u>Idea</u> 47 as "evidence and proof of [Drayton] . . .
having written for the stage, and written successfully."
Suggests that he witheld his plays from publication out of
fear of comparison with "the higher order of authors in the
dramatic line." Also cites "To Henry Reynolds" as evidence of Drayton's "very sound judgment as a critic."

1831

1   DRAYTON, MICHAEL. "Michael Drayton," in <u>Select Works of the</u>
<u>British Poets, from Chaucer to Jonson, with Biographical</u>
<u>Sketches</u>. Edited by Robert Southey. London: Longman,
Rees, Orme, Brown, and Green, pp. 596-685.
    Provides modernized texts of <u>Nymphidia</u> and <u>Polyolbion</u>.

1834

1   BRYDGES, [SAMUEL] EGERTON. "Michael Drayton," in his <u>Imagi-</u>
<u>native Biography</u>. Vol. II. London: Saunders and Otley,
pp. 237-50.
    Presents little biographical material; instead, uses
Drayton as an occasion for an essay on the relationship
of genius and fame to poverty. Comments briefly on

1834

Nymphidia, which "retains more charms for modern readers . . . than any of his other productions."

2   SOUTHEY, ROBERT. The Doctor &c. Vol. II. London: Longman,
     Rees, Orme, Brown, Green, and Longman, 379 pp.
         In chapter 36 (pp. 32-36), discusses Polyolbion, ob-
     serving that "notwithstanding its common-place personifi-
     cations and its inartificial transitions" it "is neverthe-
     less a work much to be valued." Provides a brief critical
     appraisal of Drayton as a poet.

                            1836

1   [DRAYTON, MICHAEL, ANTHONY MUNDAY, RICHARD HATHAWAY, and ROB-
     ERT WILSON]. Sir John Oldcastle: Ein historisches
     Schauspiel von Shakspear, in Vier Schauspiele von Shak-
     speare. Translated by [Johann] Ludwig Tieck. Stuttgart:
     Gotta'schen, pp. 163-276.
         Provides German translation.

                            1837

1   COLLIER, J[OHN] PAYNE. A Catalogue, Bibliographical and
     Critical, of Early English Literature; Forming a Portion of
     the Library at Bridgewater House, the Property of the Rt.
     Hon. Lord Francis Egerton, M.P. London: Thomas Rodd,
     370 pp. [Bridgewater Catalogue.]
         Describes four editions of Drayton's works (STC 7190,
     7204, 7211, and 7222) with notes, bibliographical and
     appreciative (pp. 108-10). Incorporated in 1866.1; see
     1862.1.

                            1839

1   BELL, ROBERT. "Michael Drayton, 1563-1631: With Notices of
     His Contemporaries," in his Lives of the Most Eminent
     Literary and Scientific Men of Great Britain, I: English
     Poets. London: Longman, Orme, Brown, Green, & Longman,
     and John Taylor, pp. 1-37.
         In an overview of Drayton's life and a critical discus-
     sion of his major works, observes that "[t]he Poly-olbion
     [sic] must be considered as the chief production of this
     estimable man and true poet." Discusses Drayton's rela-
     tionships with his contemporaries: in comparing him to
     Daniel, concludes that the latter "had more tenderness
     and elegance, and Drayton more strength and variety."

1840

1 [DRAYTON, MICHAEL, ANTHONY MUNDAY, RICHARD HATHAWAY, and ROB-
    ERT WILSON. Sir John Oldcastle, in Nachträge zu Shak-
    speare's Werken von Schlegel und Tieck. Vol. I. Trans-
    lated by Ernst Ortlepp. Stuttgart: L. F. Rieger, pp. 261-
    372.
        Provides German translation.

2 _____. Sir John Oldcastle, in Supplemente zu allen Ausgaben
    Shakespeare's sämmtlicher Schauspiele. Vol. I. Trans-
    lated by Heinrich Döring. Erfurt: Hennings und Hopf,
    103 pp. [Separately paginated.]
        Provides German translation.

1841

1 D'ISRAELI, I[SAAC]. "Drayton," in his Amenities of Litera-
    ture, Consisting of Sketches and Characters of English
    Literature. Vol. III. London: Edward Moxon, 135-43.
        Focuses on Polyolbion, providing an overview of con-
    tents, defects, and contemporary reception. Praises
    Nymphidia but conludes: "Drayton was a poet of volume,
    but his genius was peculiar; from an unhappy facility in
    composition, in reaching excellence he too often declined
    into mediocrity."

1843

1 DRAYTON, MICHAEL. The Harmony of the Church. Edited by
    Alexander Dyce. Percy Society, vol. 7. London: T.
    Richards for The Percy Society, 77 pp. [Separately
    paginated.]
        Reprints 1591 edition. Reprinted 1965.4.

1845

1 CRAIK, GEORGE L[ILLIE]. Sketches of the History of Litera-
    ture and Learning in England with Specimens of the Princi-
    pal Writers, Series Second: From the Accession of Eliza-
    beth to the Revolution of 1688. Vol. III. London:
    Charles Knight, 228 pp.
        Offers a general critical estimate of Drayton, whom he
    sees as superior to Daniel. Suggests that "[t]he genius

of Drayton is neither very imaginative nor very pathetic;
but he is an agreeable and weighty writer, with a spark-
ling, if not very warm, fancy." Praises Polyolbion as "a
very remarkable work for the varied learning it displays,
as well as for its poetic merits" (pp. 149-55).

2   DRAYTON, MICHAEL. "Drayton's Nymphidia," in Illustrations of
    the Fairy Mythology of "A Midsummer Night's Dream." Edited
    by James Orchard Halliwell. London: Shakespeare Society,
    pp. 195-218.
        Provides annotated, modernized text.

1849

1   ANON. "Notes from Fly Leaves, No. II: Dr. Farmer on Dray-
    ton's Works." N&Q, 1 (10 November), 28-29.
        Transcribes Farmer's bibliographical notes in a copy of
    Poems (1619). See 1849.2.

2   M., I. H. "Notes in Answer to Minor Queries: Countess of
    Pembroke's Letter--Drayton's Poems--A Flemish Account--
    Bishop Burnet." N&Q, 1 (22 December), 119-20.
        Adds Idea's Mirror to list of works in 1849.1.

3   S[INGER], S. W. "Drayton's Poems." N&Q, 1 (8 December),
    82-83.
        Transcribes Farmer's marginalia in a copy of Poems
    (1610) and offers miscellaneous bibliographical notes on
    various editions of Drayton's works.

1850

1   COLLIER, J[OHN] PAYNE. "Michael Drayton and His Idea's
    Mirror." Gentleman's Magazine, 189 (September), 262-65.
        On the basis of an allusion in Nathaniel Baxter's Sir
    Philip Sidney's Ourania, suggests that in 1587 Drayton
    wrote a poem, now lost, on the death of Sidney. Describes
    the "unique" 1594 edition of Idea's Mirror and speculates
    about reasons ("youthful passion" and irregularity of
    verse and sonnet form) for not reprinting several of the
    sonnets.

2   _____. "Michael Drayton and Thomas Lodge." Gentleman's
    Magazine, 189 (August), 132-34.

Supplements 1850.3 by discussing an allusion to Endymion and Phoebe in Lodge's Fig for Momus, suggesting that "the unfavourable reception of . . . [Drayton's poem] by certain parties, and their 'railing and detraction,' subsequently led to" his suppression of the work. Reprinted 1889.2.

3   ____. "An Unknown Poem by Michael Drayton." Gentleman's Magazine, 189 (July), 31-36.

Describes Endymion and Phoebe and dates its publication as 1594 or early 1595. Suggests that a poor reception caused Drayton never to reprint the poem. Prints several extracts and discusses allusions to Spenser and Lodge. See 1850.2; reprinted 1889.2.

4   DRAYTON, MICHAEL, ANTHONY MUNDAY, RICHARD HATHAWAY, and ROBERT WILSON. First Part of Sir John Oldcastle, in The Doubtful Plays of Shakspere. Edited by Henry Tyrrell. London: John Tallis, pp. 128-67.

Provides annotated, modernized text. In introductory note discusses the historical Oldcastle and the authors' "sympathy with the reformers." Finds that the "merit" of the play lies in its "comic power."

1851

1   COLERIDGE, HARTLEY. "Drayton," in his Essays and Marginalia. Vol. II. Edited by Derwent Coleridge. London: Edward Moxon, pp. 3-4.

Reacting to Headley's assertions that Drayton wrote "no masques" and rarely used allegory (1787.1), asks "What is the Polyolbion but an allegory?" and briefly traces Drayton's career as a dramatist. Includes some of Samuel Taylor Coleridge's annotations in a copy of 1793.1.

1852

1   [DRAYTON, MICHAEL, ANTHONY MUNDAY, RICHARD HATHAWAY, and ROBERT WILSON]. First Part of Sir John Oldcastle, in The Supplementary Works of William Shakspeare, Comprising His Poems and Doubtful Plays. Edited by William Hazlitt. London: George Routledge, pp. 105-64.

Provides annotated text.

1854

1   ANON. "Drayton's Polyolbion." Retrospective Review, 2 (February), 105-16.
   Gives synopsis of first eighteen songs.

2   HAZLITT, WILLIAM. "Michael Drayton," in his Johnson's Lives of the British Poets Completed. Vol. I. London: Nathaniel Cooke, pp. 180-82.
   Provides biographical sketch with a list of works.

1855

1   [DRAYTON, MICHAEL, ANTHONY MUNDAY, RICHARD HATHAWAY, and ROBERT WILSON]. Sir John Oldcastle, in A Supplement to the Plays of William Shakespeare. Edited by William Gilmore Simms. Auburn, N.Y.: Alden and Beardsley: New York: J. C. Derby, pp. 87-115.
   Provides annotated, modernized text. In "Introduction to Sir John Oldcastle" (pp. 87-89), discusses the question of authorship and characterizes the play as "a performance of very considerable merit."

1856

1   DRAYTON, MICHAEL. Poems by Michael Drayton from the Earliest and Rarest Editions, or from Unique Copies. Edited by J[ohn] Payne Collier. London: J. B. Nichols for the Roxburghe Club, 531 pp.
   Provides annotated reprints of Harmony of the Church (1591), Shepherd's Garland (1593), Idea's Mirror (1594), Endymion and Phoebe (1595), Mortimeriados (1596), Poems Lyric and Pastoral (1606), and Idea (1599 and 1619). In "Introduction" (pp. i-li), gives an overview of Drayton's life along with critical estimates of and bibliographical particulars about his works.

1857

1   CORNEY, BOLTON. "Michael Drayton." N&Q, 15 (7 March), 183.
   Identifies Drayton as author of prefatory sonnet in Politeuphuia.

2 _____ "Munday, Drayton, and Chettle." N&Q, 15 (4 April),
261.
   Identifies Drayton as author of "Of the Work and Translation," a prefatory poem in Munday's Primaleon (1596).

3 LAING, DAVID. "A Brief Account of the Hawthornden Manuscripts
in the Possession of the Society of Antiquaries of Scot-
land: With Extracts Containing Several Unpublished Letters
and Poems of William Drummond of Hawthornden." Archaeologia
Scotica: or, Transactions of the Society of Antiquaries of
Scotland, 4: 57-116.
   Prints four letters to Drayton and one to the Earl of
Stirling on Drayton's death (pp. 90-91, 93-94).

1858

1 LOWNDES, WILLIAM THOMAS. The Bibliographer's Manual of Eng-
lish Literature. Vol. II, part III. Revised by Henry
G[eorge] Bohn. London: Henry G. Bohn, pp. i-iv, 577-850.
   Lists, with bibliographical notes, several editions of
Drayton's works (pp. 671-73). See 1862.1 and 1862.2.

1859

1 RIMBAULT, EDWARD F. "Michael Drayton's Poems, Lyrick and
Pastorall." N&Q, 20 (23 July), 75.
   In response to earlier query (19 [4 June 1859], 457),
provides bibliographical information about the edition.
Notes that perfect copies "are of the greatest rarity."

1862

1 COLLIER, J[OHN] PAYNE. "Drayton's Endymion and Phoebe."
N&Q, 26 (15 November), 394.
   Corrects Hazlitt's location of a copy (1862.2) and gives
background information on his description of Drayton editions in 1837.1. See 29 November, p. 435, for Hazlitt's
reply.

2 HAZLITT, W[ILLIAM] CAREW. "Lowndes's Bibliographer's Manual:
Notes on the New Edition, No. VII." N&Q, 26 (8 November),
362-64.
   Offers additions and corrections to Drayton entries in
1858.1. See Collier's correction (1862.1) and Hazlitt's
response, 29 November, p. 435.

1865

1   [HITCHCOCK, ETHAN ALLAN]. Spenser's Poem, Entitled "Colin
    Clouts Come Home Againe," Explained; with Remarks upon the
    "Amoretti" Sonnets, and Also upon a Few of the Minor Poems
    of Other Early English Poets. New York: James Miller,
    306 pp.
        In chapter 6 ("Drayton," pp. 139-54), explicates several
    sonnets from Idea "[t]o show the metaphysical [i.e.,
    "Hermetic," actually religious] character of Drayton's
    studies." Concludes: "The acute reader . . . can hardly
    fail to see that most of the Sonnets of the [Elizabethan]
    period . . . are poetic studies into the mysteries of
    nature."

1866

1   COLLIER, J[OHN] PAYNE. A Bibliographical and Critical Account
    of the Rarest Books in the English Language. Vol. I.
    New York: D. G. Francis, 335 pp.
        Incorporates and revises material from 1837.1, adding
    entries on STC 7192 and 7202.

2   [THOMS, WILLIAM J.]. "Drayton and Shakespeare." N&Q, 33
    (23 June), 512.
        In response to query by D., gives 1627 as the date of
    first publication of Nymphidia.

1867

1   COLLIER, J[OHN] PAYNE. "Thomas Lord Cromwell, a Singer and
    Comedian." N&Q, 35 (26 January), 74.
        Comments on and queries passages in Cromwell where
    Drayton describes Cromwell as a singer and comedian in
    his youth.

2   HAZLITT, W[ILLIAM] CAREW. Hand-Book to the Popular, Poetical,
    and Dramatic Literature of Great Britain, from the Inven-
    tion of Printing to the Restoration. London: John Rus-
    sell Smith, 716 pp.
        Provides bibliographical description of and notes on
    several editions of Drayton's works (pp. 164-67). For
    additions and corrections see 1876.3, 1887.3, and 1903.7.

1868

1   WHIPPLE, E[DWIN] P[ERCY]. "Minor Elizabethan Poets." Atlan-
tic Monthly, 22 (July), 26-35.
Includes brief estimate of Drayton, calling him "more
powerful . . . than Daniel" and noting that "[t]he defect
of his mind was not the lack of materials, but the lack of
taste to select, and imagination to fuse, his materials."
Reprinted 1869.1.

1869

1   WHIPPLE, EDWIN P[ERCY]. "Minor Elizabethan Poets," in his The
Literature of the Age of Elizabeth. Boston: Fields,
Osgood, pp. 221-49.
Reprints 1868.1.

1870

1   DANIEL, SAMUEL, and MICHAEL DRAYTON. Early Poems of Daniel
and Drayton. Edited by J[ohn] Payne Collier. London:
privately printed, n.p.
Provides type facsimiles of Shepherd's Garland (1593)
and Endymion and Phoebe (1595). Apparently made up from
copies of 1870.2 and 1870.3.

2   DRAYTON, MICHAEL. Endimion and Phoebe. Ideas Latmvs. Edited
by J[ohn] P[ayne] C[ollier]. N.p.: n.p., n.p.
Provides type facsimile of 1595 edition. In "Introduction" (pp. i-ii), speculates about reasons for Drayton's
suppression of the poem. See 1870.1.

3   _____. Idea, the Shepheards Garland. [Edited by John Payne
Collier. London: n.p.,] 76 pp.
Provides "typographical fac-simile" of 1593 edition.
In "Introduction" comments briefly on bibliographical and
biographical particulars. See 1870.1.

4   G., W. "Drayton and Wordsworth." N&Q, 41 (14 May), 464-65.
Suggests influence of Polyolbion (Song 13) on Wordsworth's "To Joanna."

1872

1 HOOPER, RICHARD. "The Metre of Tennyson's In Memoriam."
   N&Q, 46 (26 October), 338.
       Points out influence ("It almost seems a plagiarism of
   thought") of "Ballad of Agincourt" on the meter and "idea"
   of "The Charge of the Light Brigade." Also notes Pope's
   indebtedness in Essay on Criticism to "To Henry Reynolds."
   See H. A. B., "The Metre of Tennyson's 'Charge of the Six
   Hundred,'" 16 November, p. 390, and 1872.2.

2 OAKLEY, J. H. I. "Tennyson's 'Charge of the Six Hundred.'"
   N&Q, 46 (14 December), 479.
       Rejects Hooper's suggestion of plagiarism (1872.1),
   noting that because "Drayton's ode is well known" Tennyson
   might have "intended" that the similarity be "very notice-
   able."

1873

1 BROWNE, C. ELLIOT. "The Earliest Mention of Shakspeare."
   N&Q, 47 (10 May), 378-79.
       Rejects the identification of Drayton with "Watson's
   heir" in Polimanteia.

*2 DRAYTON, MICHAEL. "Nymphidia:" Dem englischen des Michael
   Drayton Nachgedichtet. Translated by Wilhelmine
   Wickenburg-Almásy and Albrecht Wickenburg. Heidelberg.
       Cited in British Museum General Catalogue of Printed
   Books to 1955: Compact Edition, XXVII, 10.

3 HOOPER, RICHARD. "Alexander Gill, Milton's Tutor, and Drayton's Polyolbion." N&Q, 47 (10 May), 381.
       Discusses Gill's supposed gift of a copy of Polyolbion
   to Trinity College Library; points out that the copy was
   presented by Nathaniel Gill.

4 MASSON, DAVID. Drummond of Hawthornden: The Story of His
   Life and Writings. London: Macmillan, 506 pp.
       Traces the friendship between Drayton and Drummond, and
   prints letters between the two (pp. 78-85, 112-14, 181-85).

5 NICHOLSON, BRINSLEY. "Jottings in By-Ways, I: Drayton and
   Sir Philip Sidney." N&Q, 48 (6 December), 442-43.
       Suggests that Eclogue 4 (Shepherd's Garland) is the
   poem on Sidney's death alluded to by Baxter in his Sir
   Philip Sidney's Ourania. Notes several echoes of the
   Eclogue in Baxter's verse.

1874

1   DRAYTON, MICHAEL. "Nymphidia oder der Feenhot." Translated
    by H[hermann] Freih[err] von Friesen. Shakespeare-Jahrbuch,
    9: 107-26.
        Provides German translation of Nymphidia (with brief
    introduction.

2   MINTO, WILLIAM. Characteristics of English Poets from Chaucer
    to Shirley. Edinburgh: William Blackwood and Sons, 495 pp.
        In a general critical appreciation of Drayton, notes
    that Aetion in Spenser's Colin Clout may refer to him, that
    rather than having "any special call to poetry beyond the
    contagion of circumstances . . . ambition made his verses,"
    and that his sonnets are primarily interesting for "their
    illustrative bearing on the sonnets of Shakespeare"
    (pp. 268-74).

1876

1   DRAYTON, MICHAEL. The Complete Works of Michael Drayton.
    3 volumes. Edited by Richard Hooper. Library of Old
    Authors. London: John Russell Smith, 281, 292, 310 pp.
        Includes modernized reprints of 1622 edition of Polyol-
    bion and 1591 edition of Harmony of the Church. In "Intro-
    duction" (I, ix-xxiv), offers a general critical overview--
    drawing frequently on published criticism--of Drayton,
    "one of the greatest poets of the Elizabethan or any pe-
    riod." (The edition was never completed.) Reviewed in
    Anon., "Drayton's Complete Works," Spectator, 12 February
    1876, pp. 214-15; 1876.2.

2   GROSART, ALEXANDER B[ALLOCH]. Review of Richard Hooper,
    ed., The Complete Works of Michael Drayton. Vols. I-III.
    Academy, 9 (19 February), 163-64.
        In review of 1876.1 takes issue with Hooper's assertion
    that Drayton is "undoubtedly one of the greatest poets of
    the Elizabethan or any period," questioning whether he
    "can be truthfully described as [even] a great poet." Also
    argues that the evaluation of Drayton in Citizen of the
    World was not Goldsmith's own.

3   HAZLITT, W[ILLIAM] CAREW. Collections and Notes, 1867-1876.
    London: Reeves and Turner, 510 pp.
        Provides corrections and additions to 1867.2 (pp. 133-
    34). See 1887.3 and 1903.7 for further additions and cor-
    rections.

1876

4   LEGIS, R. H.   "Identification of Michael Drayton with the
    Rival Poet of Shakspeare's Sonnets." N&Q, 54 (26 August),
    163-64.
        Argues that Drayton was the Rival Poet and Polyolbion,
    the work Shakespeare was envious of. See 1877.2.

                            1877

1   CORSER, THOMAS. Collectanea Anglo-Poetica: or, A Biblio-
    graphical and Descriptive Catalogue of a Portion of a
    Collection of Early English Poetry, with Occasional Ex-
    tracts and Remarks Biographical and Critical. Part VI.
    Chetham Society, vol. 100. [Manchester:] Chetham Society,
    pp. 251-310.
        Assigns Drayton to "the foremost rank of what may be
    termed the second class of our poetical writers of the
    sixteenth and seventeenth centuries." Provides extensive
    notes on several early editions of Drayton's works: the
    annotations frequently include description of content,
    auction record of copies, locations, collation, extracts,
    variant readings, references to scholarship, and critical
    estimate. Includes the following editions: STC 7190,
    7198, 7200, 7203, 7208, 7209, 7210, 7211(?), 7216, 7217,
    7218, 7220, 7221, 7224, 7225, 7228, and 7231, as well as
    1748 Works.

2   LEGIS, R. H.   "Shakspeariana: Sonnet LXXXVI." N&Q, 55
    (31 March), 244-45.
        Finds allusion to Polyolbion in the sonnet. See 1876.4.

3   NEWTON, ALFRED, A. SMYTHE PALMER, AND A. B. "Birds Named in
    Drayton's Polyolbion." N&Q, 55 (6 January), 12-13.
        In responses to query by John Pickford (54 [23 December
    1876], 513), provide present-day names of several birds
    mentioned in Polyolbion.

                            1879

1   DESHLER, CHARLES D. Afternoons with the Poets. New York:
    Harper & Brothers, 320 pp.
        In a general critical estimate of Drayton, finds his
    sonnets inferior to Daniel's (pp. 104-108).

2   PALGRAVE, FRANCIS T[URNER]. <u>Landscape in Poetry from Homer to</u>
     <u>Tennyson</u>. London: Macmillan, 314 pp.
          In chapter 12 ("Landscape Poetry under the Stuart Kings,"
     pp. 145-65), discusses <u>Polyolbion</u>; points out that Drayton
     has "a truly affectionate interest in each natural feature
     of his country" but objects to his overuse of personifica-
     tion (pp. 146-48).

3   ROBINSON, A. MARY F. "Michael Drayton." [<u>Dublin</u>] <u>University</u>
     <u>Magazine</u>, 4 (July), 56-65.
          Provides critical overview of Drayton's "melancholy"
     life and works, emphasizing his lyrics. Identifies "play-
     fulness and irritability" as the qualities which give his
     lyrics their "charm." Suggests that "charm of character
     must unconsciously have done a great deal to widen Dray-
     ton's influence among his fellow poets, and to build up a
     renown for which we should find it hard to account on
     purely critical grounds."

                              1880

1   NOBLE, JAMES ASHCROFT. "The Sonnet in England." <u>Contemporary</u>
     <u>Review</u>, 38 (September), 446-71.
          In a survey of the sonnet from Wyatt through Rossetti,
     singles out <u>Idea</u> 61 as one of the very few memorable son-
     nets by Elizabethan and Jacobean poets. Revised 1893.4.

2   SAINTSBURY, G[EORGE EDWARD BATEMAN]. "Michael Drayton," in
     <u>The English Poets: Selections with Critical Introductions</u>
     <u>by Various Writers</u>. Vol. I. Edited by Thomas Humphry
     Ward. London: Macmillan, pp. 526-28.
          Examines magnitude and variety of Drayton's output,
     observing "that if he had written less and concentrated
     his efforts, the average merit of his work would have been
     higher." Offers brief critical estimates of several of
     Drayton's poems.

                              1883

1   ANON. Review of A[rthur] H[enry] Bullen, ed., <u>Selections</u>
     <u>from the Poems of Michael Drayton</u>. <u>Athenaeum</u>, no. 2894
     (14 April), pp. 470-71.
          In review of 1883.3 offers a general appreciation of
     Drayton, noting, for example, that "no one who reads
     Drayton can fail to admire the energy which sustains his

verse, the purity which animates it, the brightness of
fancy and the felicity of expression which give life and
colour to his pages." See 1883.4.

2   DRAYTON, MICHAEL. Idea, in An English Garner: Ingatherings
    from Our History and Literature. Vol. VI. Edited by
    Edward Arber. Birmingham: E. Arber, pp. 289-322.
        Provides modernized reprint of 1619 edition. Reprinted
    1904.2.

3   _____. Selections from the Poems of Michael Drayton. Edited
    by A[rthur] H[enry] Bullen. Chilworth: Unwin Brothers,
    223 pp.
        Provides annotated selection of poems and extracts from
    longer works. In "Introduction" (pp. ix-xxiii), gives an
    overview of Drayton's life and career, with a brief criti-
    cal estimate of each work. Reviewed in 1883.1; 1884.2.

4   ORMSBY, JOHN. "Drayton and Surrey." Athenaeum, no. 2895
    (21 April), p. 506.
        In response to comment in 1883.1, cites Comte de
    Puymaigre's Précurseurs de Don Quichotte to show that
    "Drayton is not the only authority [in England's Heroical
    Epistles] for the story" of Surrey travelling to Italy to
    defend Geraldine's beauty.

                            1884

1   ANON. "The Folk-Lore of Drayton." Folklore Journal, 2: 111-
    20, 142-51, 225-35, 266-77, 357-69; 3 (1885), 69-90, 134-
    55.
        Provides detailed analysis of the folklore background
    of Drayton's references to plants, springs, minerals,
    animals, portents, witchcraft and the supernatural, astrol-
    ogy, local traditions, proverbs, and fairies.

2   ANON. "Mr. Bullen's Selections from Drayton." Spectator, 57
    (22 March), 386-88.
        In review of 1883.3 offers an appreciative estimate of
    Drayton's poetry; observes that Polyolbion "is more re-
    markable for its length and the careful labour expended
    upon it" than for its poetic qualities, that "Ballad of
    Agincourt" "is one of the finest war lyrics we possess,"
    and that of the poems in England's Heroical Epistles
    "there are few . . . that may not still be read with
    pleasure."

3   HALL, A. "A Literary Craze." N&Q, 70 (12 July), 21-22;
    (26 July), 61-62; (9 August), 101-102; (6 September),
    181-82.
        Finds several references to Drayton in Shakespeare's
    sonnets.

1887

1   DRAYTON, MICHAEL. "The Barons' Wars," "Nymphidia," and Other
    Poems. Edited by Henry Morley
    brary, 47. London: George Routledge and Sons, 288 pp.
        Provides modernized texts of Barons' Wars and Nymphidia
    along with selected poems and extracts.

2   [DRAYTON, MICHAEL, ANTHONY MUNDAY, RICHARD HATHAWAY, and ROB-
    ERT WILSON]. The First Part of Sir John Oldcastle, in The
    Doubtful Plays of William Shakespeare. Edited by William
    Hazlitt. London: George Routledge and Sons, pp. 105-64.
        Provides annotated, modernized text.

3   HAZLITT, W[ILLIAM] CAREW. Third and Final Series of Biblio-
    graphical Collections and Notes on Early English Litera-
    ture, 1474-1700. London: Bernard Quaritch, 327 pp.
        Provides additions and correction to 1867.2 and 1876.3
    (pp. 67-68). See 1903.7 for further additions and cor-
    rections.

4   SAINTSBURY, GEORGE [EDWARD BATEMAN]. A History of Elizabethan
    Literature. London: Macmillan, 485 pp.
        In an appreciative overview of Drayton's works, ob-
    serves: "[I]f ever there was a poet who could write, and
    write, perhaps beautifully, certainly well, about any
    conceivable broomstick in almost any conceivable manner,
    that poet was Drayton." Finds "it most difficult to be-
    lieve" that Idea 61 is Drayton's; implies it is by
    Shakespeare (pp. 139-44, passim). See 1891.2.

1888

1   B[ULLEN], A[RTHUR] H[ENRY]. "Michael Drayton," in The Dic-
    tionary of National Biography. Vol. XVI. Edited by
    Leslie Stephen. New York: Macmillan; London: Smith,
    Elder, pp. 8-13.
        Provides biography along with critical estimates of
    several works.

2   DRAYTON, MICHAEL. Poems: By Michael Draiton, Esquire. 2
    parts. Publications of the Spenser Society, nos. 45-46.
    Manchester: Spenser Society, 504 pp.
        Reprints 1605 edition. Reprinted 1967.6.

3   GREENSTREET, JAMES. "The Whitefriars Theatre in the Time of
    Shakspere." Transactions of the New Shakspere Society,
    1887-1892, pp. 269-84.
        Transcribes documents in the Chancery suit of George
    Androwes v. Martin Slater; includes the agreement among
    the Whitefriars' stockholders (including Drayton). (The
    paper was read 9 November 1888.)

1889

1   A BOOKHUNTER. "Drayton's Polyolbion." Bookworm, 2: 209-13.
        Gives a general overview of publishing history and
    contents. Observes that reading the poem "is too tremen-
    dous and unprofitable a task to be undertaken even by a
    very earnest student at the present day."

2   COLLIER, J[OHN] PAYNE. "An Unknown Poem by Michael Drayton"
    and "Michael Drayton and Thomas Lodge," in Bibliographical
    Notes: A Classified Collection of the Chief Contents of
    "The Gentleman's Magazine" from 1731-1868. Edited by
    George Laurence Gomme. Gentleman's Magazine Library.
    London: Elliot Stock, pp. 75-82, 82-85.
        Reprints 1850.3 and 1850.2.

3   DRAYTON, MICHAEL. The Poly-Olbion: A Chorographical De-
    scription of Great Britain. 3 parts. Publications of the
    Spenser Society, NS, nos. 1-3. Manchester: Spenser Soci-
    ety, 507 pp.
        Reprints 1622 edition. (Parts 2 and 3 were published
    in 1890.) Reprinted 1970.6.

4   FLEAY, FREDERICK GARD, ed. The Land of Shakespeare: A Series
    of Thirty-One Etchings from Original Drawings Specially
    Made for the Work by John MacPherson. London: John
    Bumpus, n.p.
        In "To the Reader" (pp. vii-ix), comments on the schol-
    arly neglect of the relationship between Drayton and
    Shakespeare, especially in terms of the similarity of their
    work; observes: "[T]he mind of Drayton was cast into a
    mould so similar to Shakespeare's, that we shall be quite
    safe in taking his work as representing, not indeed what

Shakespeare would have written on any subject, but certainly somewhat blurred copies . . . of the finished works . . . as the master-hand might have left them." In notes to the various etchings, frequently discusses associations of a place with Drayton and draws frequently on his works (especially Polyolbion) for illustration. In commenting on Number 23, a distant view of Coventry, identifies Idea as Anne Goodere.

5 ROGERS, SHOWELL. "A Contemporary of Shakespeare's." Shakespeariana, 6 (December), 519-27.
    Offers a general biographical sketch and critical estimate of Polyolbion. Concludes that "Drayton had a fatal facility of writing, which caused his pen to outrun his imagination and become diffuse and labored," that his "chief power lay in the presentation of ideas of a descriptive and cataloguing kind," and that his "real poetic gift . . . lay in lyrical rather than in heroic verse." (Report of a lecture by Rogers.)

1890

1 A BOOKHUNTER. "Drayton's Polyolbion." Bookmart, 7 (May), 548-50.
    Classifies Polyolbion as an example of Montaigne's "low and moderate sort of poetry" and traces the publishing history of the poem.

2 TYLER, THOMAS. "Introduction," in his edition of Shakespeare's Sonnets. London: David Nutt, pp. 1-154.
    Examines parallels between Sonnets and Idea (1599) to argue that Drayton was indebted to Shakespeare (pp. 38-43).

1891

1 ANON. "Notes." The Builder, 61 (12 September), 201-202.
    Identifies No. 185 Fleet Street as Drayton's residence and includes a drawing of Nos. 184-85, which are to be torn down.

2 D., J. "Michael Drayton versus His Critic." Spectator, 66 (2 May), 625.
    Finds Saintsbury's praise of "Ballad of Agincourt" (1891.6) inconsistent with his doubt about Drayton's authorship of Idea 61 (1887.4). Observes: "If Drayton's poetical inspiration enabled him to write the most

splendid war-song in the language, might it not have
enabled him in another happy moment to write the loveliest
of all love-sonnets?"

3   DRAYTON, MICHAEL. Poemes, Lyrick and Pastorall. Publications of the Spenser Society, NS, no. 4. Manchester:
Spenser Society, 122 pp.
    Reprints 1606(?) edition. Reprinted 1967.5.

4   ETTLINGER, JOSEF. Christian Hofmann von Hofmanswaldau: Ein
Beitrag zur Literaturgeschichte des siebzehnten Jahrhun-
derts. Halle: Max Niemeyer, 130 pp.
    Suggests that England's Heroicall Epistles influenced
Hofmann von Hofmannswaldau's Heldenbriefe (pp. 58-61).

5   FLEAY, FREDERICK GARD. "Michael Drayton" and "William Shake-
speare," in his A Biographical Chronicle of the English
Drama, 1559-1642. 2 volumes. London: Reeves and Turner,
I, 137-61; II, 176-232.
    In entry on Drayton provides a chronological overview
of his life, a section on "Connexion of 'The Heroicall
Epistles' with Other Poems and Plays," and a list of works,
of plays attributed to him, and of his pastoral names.
Offers conjectures about several of Drayton's pastoral
names (especially Olcon, whom he identifies as Sir John
Davies), examines his career as a dramatist (attributes
several plays to him), and examines revisions of various
works (particularly deletions of allusions to individuals).
In examining Shakespeare's sonnets discusses the possibility that Drayton is the Rival Poet and notes several
parallels between the sonnets of the two to argue that
Shakespeare took Idea's Mirror (actually Idea since he
quotes from the 1619 edition) "as a model." Concludes
that "hardly a stanza of Drayton has been left unused by
Shakespeare" (pp. 219-20, 226-32). See 1899.4, 1900.1,
1903.11, 1904.5, and 1956.7.

6   SAINTSBURY, GEORGE [EDWARD BATEMAN]. "English War-Songs."
Macmillan's Magazine, 64 (May), 26-36.
    Offers appreciative estimate of "Ballad of Agincourt"
in an overview of the subject. See 1891.2.

1892

1   CHOATE, ISAAC BASSETT. Wells of English. Boston: Roberts
Brothers, 310 pp.

In chapter 20 ("Michael Drayton, 1563-1645," pp. 151-58), offers a general critical estimate of Drayton as a lyric poet and discusses his patriotism as it is reflected in the subject matter of his works.

2 DRAYTON, MICHAEL. The Mvses Elizivm. Publications of the Spenser Society, NS, no. 5. Manchester: Spenser Society, 215 pp.
Reprints 1630 edition. Reprinted 1970.5.

3 HANSEN, ADOLF. "Engelske Sonetter indtil Milton." Tilskueren (February), pp. 195-222.
Discusses Drayton in an overview of the development of the sonnet from Wyatt through Milton. Translates four sonnets from Idea.

4 SACHS, R. "Die Shakespeare zugeschriebenen zweifelhaften Stücke." Shakespeare-Jahrbuch, 27: 135-99.
Includes section on Oldcastle.

1893

1 ANON. Catalogue of Original and Early Editions of Some of the Poetical and Prose Works of English Writers from Langland to Wither. New York: Grolier Club, 254 pp.
Provides annotated bibliographical descriptions of STC 7189, 7190, 7203, 7208, 7210, 7211, 7216, 7219, 7220, 7222, 7224, 7226, 7227, 7228, 7229, and 7231 (pp. 65-74).

2 DRAYTON, MICHAEL. The Battaile of Agincourt. Edited by Richard Garnett. London: Charles Whittingham, Chiswick Press, 144 pp.
Provides annotated reprint of 1627 edition (includes "Ballad of Agincourt"). In "Introduction" (pp. vii-xxiii), gives a critical survey of Drayton's career, pointing out "that Drayton's genius was naturally not so much epical as lyrical and descriptive." Treats Battle of Agincourt as an epic and criticizes Drayton for "over-faithful adherence . . . to the method of the chronicler." Compares the poem to Shakespeare's Henry V. Reviewed in 1895.2.

3 MORLEY, HENRY. English Writers, X: Shakespeare and His Time: Under Elizabeth. London: Cassell, 523 pp.
Traces career of Drayton, giving brief critical estimate and summary of major works (to c. 1603). Provides synopsis of Barons' Wars and compares it to Daniel's Civil Wars (pp. 209-11, 314-22). See 1895.3.

1893

4 NOBLE, J[AMES] ASHCROFT. "The Sonnet in England," in his <u>The
   Sonnet in England & Other Essays</u>. London: Elkin Mathews
   and John Lane, pp. 1-63.
        In revision of 1880.1 makes no substantive changes in
   discussion of Drayton.

1894

1 DRAYTON, MICHAEL, ANTHONY MUNDAY, RICHARD HATHAWAY, and ROB-
   ERT WILSON. <u>The First Part of Sir John Oldcastle</u>. Edited
   by A[rthur] F[rederic] Hopkinson. Shakespeare's Doubtful
   Plays. London: M. E. Sims, 121 pp.
        Provides modernized reprint of 1600 edition. In "In-
   troduction" (pp. i-xx), traces background of composition,
   and publishing and stage history. Attempts to distinguish
   the share of each collaborator; discusses characterization
   and the "religious aspect." "Introduction" revised 1900.2.

2 GOSSE, EDMUND [WILLIAM]. <u>The Jacobean Poets</u>. University
   Extension Manuals. London: John Murray, 234 pp.
        In chapter 5 ("Campion--Drayton--Drummond--Sir John
   Beaumont," pp. 89-115), discusses Drayton as a poet who,
   though overrated during the past two-hundred years, "is
   nevertheless a poet of considerable originality and merit,
   whose greatest enemy has been his want of measure." Provides a brief critical estimate of his post-1603 works,
   and concludes: "[I]n spite of . . . egotism, Drayton is
   a writer who commands our respect. He is manly and direct,
   and his virile style has the charm of what is well-
   performed in an easy and straightforward manner. . . .
   His variety, his ambition, his excellent versification
   claim our respect and admiration; but Drayton's weak point
   is that he fails to interest his reader" (pp. 93-101).

1895

1 ELTON, OLIVER. <u>An Introduction to Michael Drayton</u>. Manchester: Spenser Society, 96 pp.
        Provides chronological overview of Drayton's life and
   works, with discussion of his style, sources, and patrons.
   Includes bibliography and seven appendices (on revisions,
   identification of names, conjectural family tree, and
   "Verses the Night before He Died"). Substantially revised
   and expanded as 1905.3. See 1903.11. Reviewed in Anon.,
   "An Introduction to Michael Drayton," <u>Saturday Review</u>, 80
   (17 August 1895), 210-11.

1897

2   LE GALLIENNE, RICHARD. "Michael Drayton: The Battaile of
    Agincourt," in his Retrospective Reviews: A Literary Log,
    II: 1893-1895. London: John Lane; New York: Dodd, Mead,
    pp. 50-56.
        In review of 1893.2 discusses the "many faults of con-
    struction" and patriotism in Battle of Agincourt. Pro-
    vides a critical estimate of Drayton, finding "[l]yrical
    sweetness, fertility of invention, [and] richness of de-
    scriptive power . . . [his] most characteristic qualities."

3   MORLEY, HENRY, and W[ILLIAM] HALL GRIFFIN. English Writers,
    XI: Shakespeare and His Time: Under James I. London:
    Cassell, 484 pp.
        Continue overview of career from 1893.3. Provide
    bibliography (pp. 317-22, 373-75).

4   WINDSCHEID, KATHARINA. Die englische Hirtendichtung von
    1579-1625: Ein Beitrag zur Geschichte der englischen
    Hirtendightung [sic]. Halle: Max Niemeyer, 122 pp.
        Includes Shepherd's Garland in survey of the pastoral
    eclogue; examines, in particular, the influence of Spen-
    ser's Shepherd's Calendar on Drayton (pp. 14-22).

                            1896

1   BOUCHIER, JONATHAN. "Drayton: Birds." N&Q, 94 (29 August),
    176.
        In response to Bouchier's query, editor identifies
    three birds in Polyolbion (Song 13).

2   DRAYTON, MICHAEL. "Nimphidia" and "The Muses Elizium."
        Edited by John Gray. London: Hacon & Ricketts, 137 pp.
        Provides reprints "from the earliest editions."

3   _____. Odes, in An English Garner: Ingatherings from Our
    History and Literature. Vol. VIII. Edited by Edward
    Arber. Westminster: Archibald Constable, pp. 528-63.
        Provides modernized reprint of 1619 edition (and of
    1606 for those not reprinted in 1619). Reprinted 1903.3.

                            1897

1   ANON. "Academy Portraits, XV: Michael Drayton." Academy,
    51 (20 February), 235.

1897

In a brief overview of Drayton's career, points out the
variety of his works and calls him "England's ideal
laureate" (because of his patriotism) and a "gentleman."
Includes tipped-in plate of portrait.

2   ANON. "A Collection of Mss." Academy, 52 (17 July), 43-44.
        In review of W. Hale White, ed., A Description of the
     Wordsworth and Coleridge Mss. in the Possession of Mr. T.
     Norton Longman (London: Longmans, 1897), points out
     Wordsworth's indebtedness to Nymphidia, Polyolbion, Muses'
     Elysium, and Barons' Wars.

3   DRAYTON, MICHAEL. Idea, in Elizabethan Sonnet-Cycles. Vol.
     III. Edited by Martha Foote Crow. London: Kegan Paul,
     Trench, Trübner, pp. 3-72.
        Provides modernized reprint of 1619 edition. In intro-
     ductory note (pp. 3-8), calls Drayton's life the "picture
     of the ideal poet," discusses his relationship with Anne
     Goodere, and offers a brief critical estimate of his
     sonnets.

4   RUCKDESCHEL, [JOHANN] ALBERT. Die Quellen des Dramas "The
     Downfall & the Death of Robert, Earle of Huntington,
     Otherwise Called Robin Hood." Ph.D. dissertation,
     Friedrich-Alexanders Universität, Erlangen. Erlangen:
     Fr. Junge, 76 pp.
        Discusses Munday's use of Matilda and England's Heroical
     Epistles (King John-Matilda) as sources (pp. 52-58).

*5   SMALL, ROSCOE ADDISON. "The Stage-Quarrel between Ben Jonson
     and the So-Called Poetasters." Ph.D. dissertation,
     Harvard University.
        Published as 1899.4.

                                1898

1   ANON. "Anthologies in Little, I: Michael Drayton." Academy,
     53 (19 February), 203-204.
        Offers a general appreciative estimate of Drayton:
     characterizes him as "a real poet, a man of rich temper
     and strenuous ardours" and suggests that "[t]he crowning
     feature of his work is surely its inexhaustible variety."

2   HANNAY, DAVID. The Later Renaissance. Periods of European
     Literature, 6. Edinburgh: William Blackwood and Sons,
     395 pp.

Provides an appreciative overview of Drayton's work,
stressing both its quantity and quality (pp. 215-19).

3   SPENCER, VIRGINIA EVILINE. Alliteration in Spenser's Poetry:
    Discussed and Compared with the Alliteration as Employed
    by Drayton and Daniel. 2 parts. Ph.D. dissertation,
    University of Zurich. N.p.: n.p., 96, 48 pp.
        Gives a classified, tabular comparison of the use of
    alliteration by the three poets. Concludes that "Drayton
    employs alliteration profusely in many of his poems, but
    not with a masterful touch. . . . We find in his poetry
    but little trace of that finer feeling for music, which
    alone can guide in a good use of alliteration."

4   WYNDHAM, GEORGE. "Notes: Sonnets," in his edition of The
    Poems of Shakespeare. London: Methuen, pp. 242-335.
        Notes several parallels between Drayton's works and
    Sonnets. Concludes that he would choose Drayton "[i]f
    compelled to select one of Shakespeare's contemporaries
    for the Rival Poet" (pp. 255-59).

1899

1   ANON. "Daniel and Drayton." Academy, 56 (19 August), 175-76.
        In review of 1899.3 characterizes Drayton as "one of
    the most masculine and individual among our minor poets"
    and discusses his style and use of a variety of meters.
    Finds that he is "a clumsy workman," especially as evi-
    denced by his "awkward" and "crabbed" ellipses.

2   BEECHING, H[ENRY] C[HARLES]. "The Sonnets of Michael Dray-
    ton." Literature, NS, no. 31 (11 August), pp. 107-109.
        Argues that in his sonnets "Drayton copied from Shake-
    speare, and not Shakespeare from Drayton." Traces the
    successive influence of Daniel, Sidney, and Shakespeare
    on Drayton's stylistic revisions. Reprinted 1904.1.

3   DANIEL, SAMUEL, and MICHAEL DRAYTON. A Selection from the
    Poetry of Samuel Daniel & Michael Drayton. Edited by
    H[enry] C[harles] Beeching. London: J. M. Dent, 219 pp.
        Provides annotated, modernized selection (pp. 57-185).
    In "Introduction" (pp. ix-xxi), compares the careers and
    works of the two poets. Reviewed in Anon., Athenaeum,
    no. 3751 (16 September 1899), pp. 379-80; 1899.1.

1899

4   SMALL, ROSCOE ADDISON. The Stage-Quarrel between Ben Jonson
     and the So-Called Poetasters. Forschungen zur Englischen
     Sprache und Litteratur, vol. 1. Breslau: M. & H. Marcus,
     214 pp.
         In published version of 1897.5, argues contra Fleay
     (1891.5) that Drayton took no part in the quarrel and re-
     futes his theory that "Daniel and Drayton had a violent
     quarrel with regard to the patronage of Lucy, Countess of
     Bedford" (pp. 195-97, passim).

1900

1   CHURCHILL, GEORGE B[OSWORTH]. Richard the Third up to Shake-
     speare. Palaestra, 10. Berlin: Mayer & Müller, 564 pp.
         Argues against Fleay's identification (1891.5) of an
     allusion to England's Heroical Epistles in True Tragedy of
     Richard the Third (scene 10). Discusses date of composi-
     tion of England's Heroical Epistles and comments on ref-
     erences therein to Richard III and Jane Shore (pp. 439-
     41, 534-39).

2   HOPKINSON, A[RTHUR] F[REDERIC]. "An Essay on the Merry Devil
     of Edmonton" and "An Essay on Sir John Oldcastle," in his
     Essays on Shakespeare's Doubtful Plays. London: M. E.
     Sims, 30, 25 pp. [Separately paginated.]
         Finds the evidence insufficient to support a claim for
     Drayton as author of Merry Devil of Edmonton (pp. 10-13).
     (Revised 1914.2.) In a somewhat revised version of "In-
     troduction" to 1894.1, makes no substantive changes in
     discussion of Drayton.

3   LIEBAU, GUSTAV. König Eduard III. von England und die Gräfin
     von Salisbury: Dargestellt in ihren Beziehungen nach
     Geschichte, Sage und Dichtung, unter eingehender Berücks-
     ichtigung des pseudo-shakespeare'schen Schauspiels "The
     Raigne of King Edward the Third." AF, 13. Berlin: Emil
     Felber, 213 pp.
         Discusses Drayton's treatment, derived from Painter, of
     the Edward III-Countess of Salisbury story in England's
     Heroical Epistles (pp. 131-34).

1902

1   MOULTON, CHARLES WELLS. "Michael Drayton," in his edition of
     The Library of Literary Criticism of English and American
     Authors, I: 680-1638. Buffalo: Moulton, pp. 701-709.
         Prints extracts from criticism, 16th-19th centuries.

2   PROBST, ALBERT. Samuel Daniel's "Civil Wars between the Two
     Houses of Lancaster and York" und Michael Drayton's
     "Barons' Wars": Eine Quellenstudie. Ph.D. dissertation,
     Kaiser-Wilhelms-Universität. Strasbourg: M. DuMont-
     Schauberg, 134 pp.
          Provides a general overview of Drayton's sources (par-
     ticularly the chronicles, Mirror for Magistrates, and
     Marlowe's Edward II) and examines his metaphoric language
     in Barons' Wars, comparing it with Spenser's in Faerie
     Queene.

3   SCHELLING, FELIX E[MMANUEL]. The English Chronicle Play: A
     Study in the Popular Historical Literature Environing
     Shakespeare. New York: Macmillan; London: Macmillan,
     322 pp.
          Discusses relationship of Oldcastle to Henry IV and, in
     passing, the relationship of several of Drayton's histori-
     cal poems to dramas on similar subjects (passim).

                              1903

1   COURTHOPE, W[ILLIAM] J[OHN]. A History of English Poetry,
     III: The Intellectual Conflict of the Seventeenth Cen-
     tury; Decadent Influence of the Feudal Monarch; Growth of
     the National Genius. London: Macmillan, 565 pp.
          In chapter 3 ("Spenser's Successors," pp. 27-53), gives
     a chronological overview of Drayton's life and works.
     Argues that Idea was originally the Countess of Bedford
     and that Drayton transferred the name to Anne Goodere
     after being slighted by his former patroness. Finds that
     Drayton "lacked . . . loftiness and resolution of artistic
     purpose": "Instead of leading the taste of his day, he
     sought to follow it, and to make his art an instrument of
     his own promotion" (pp. 27-46). See 1905.3 and 1907.4.

2   CURRY, JOHN T. "Drayton's Poly-Olbion." N&Q, 108 (8 August),
     102-103.
          Calculates that Polyolbion contains approximately
     16,620 lines (about 17,000 if the arguments are included),
     not 30,000 as is generally supposed. See 1903.6.

3   DRAYTON, MICHAEL. Odes, in Some Longer Elizabethan Poems.
     Edited by A[rthur] H[enry] Bullen. An English Garner.
     Westminster: Archibald Constable, pp. 405-41.

Reprints <u>Odes</u> from 1896.3. In "Introduction"
(pp. vii-xxiv), asserts that the <u>Odes</u> "contain some of
[Drayton's] . . . best writing" but points out that
"some . . . are so ineptly harsh that one has to grope
for the writer's meaning."

4 EICHOFF, THEODOR. <u>Unser Shakespeare: Beiträge zu einer</u>
<u>wissenschaftlichen Shakespeare-Kritik</u>. Vol. II. Halle:
Max Niemeyer, 189 pp.
In part II, chapter 4 ("Die satirischen Sonette von
Michael Drayton," pp. 152-76), examines Drayton's satire,
especially of the conventions of love poetry, in his
sonnets.

5 ERSKINE, JOHN. <u>The Elizabethan Lyric: A Study</u>. Columbia
University Studies in English, vol. 2. New York: Mac-
millan, 362 pp. [Also submitted as Ph.D. dissertation,
Columbia University.]
In a "chronological survey of the English lyric in
Elizabeth's time," offers brief critical estimates of
<u>Idea's Mirror</u>, <u>Harmony of the Church</u>, <u>Shepherd's Garland</u>,
and "Ballad of Agincourt." Calls Drayton, "next to Spen-
ser, . . . the prominent lyrist of" the 1590s (passim).

6 FRY, J. F. "Drayton's <u>Poly-Olbion</u>." <u>N&Q</u>, 108 (12 September),
214.
In reply to 1903.2 points out that the total number of
lines (including arguments) in <u>Polyolbion</u> is 14,718.

7 HAZLITT, W[ILLIAM] CAREW. <u>Bibliographical Collections and</u>
<u>Notes on Early English Literature Made during the Years</u>
<u>1893-1903</u>. London: Bernard Quaritch, 450 pp.
Provides addition to 1867.2, 1876.3, and 1887.3 (p. 114).

8 MAIBERGER, MAX. <u>Studien über den Einfluss frankreichs auf</u>
<u>die elisabethanische Literatur, erster Teil: Die Lyrik in</u>
<u>der zweiten Hälfte des XVI. Jahrhunderts</u>. Ph.D. disser-
tation, Ludwig-Maximilians-Universität, Munich. Frankfurt:
Knauer, 55 pp.
Discusses <u>Idea's Mirror</u> in an overview of French influence on Elizabethan sonnets (pp. 42-43, passim).

9 OEHNIGER, LUDWIG. <u>Die Verbreitung der Königssagen der "His-</u>
<u>toria Regum Britanniae" von Geoffrey of Monmouth in der</u>
<u>poetischen elisabethanischen Literatur</u>. Ph.D. disserta-
tion, Ludwigs-Maximilians-Universität, Munich. Kitzingen:
Meschett & Hissiger, 126 pp.
Outlines Drayton's use of <u>Historia</u> as a source in the
first ten songs of <u>Polyolbion</u> (pp. 117-18).

10 OWEN, DANIEL E[DWARD]. Relations of the Elizabethan Sonnet
    Sequences to Earlier English Verse, Especially That of
    Chaucer. Ph.D. dissertation, University of Pennsylvania.
    Philadelphia: Chilton Printing Co., 34 pp.
        Draws on Idea in analyzing resemblances in conceits and
    in subject matter and its treatment between Elizabethan
    sonnets and Middle English love poetry (passim).

11 WHITAKER, LEMUEL. "Michael Drayton as a Dramatist." PMLA,
    18 (July), 378-411. [Also submitted as Ph.D. dissertation,
    University of Pennsylvania, 1902.]
        In an overview of Drayton's career as a dramatist, dis-
    cusses his earnings, collaborators, patrons, other literary
    activity during his association with the theater, and
    affinities with Spenser. Argues against several of the
    theories of Fleay (1891.5) and Elton (1895.1), particularly
    that poverty caused Drayton to write for the stage. Sug-
    gests instead that "environment" and "the constitution of
    his mind" led him to drama. Also examines reasons for his
    failure to publish his plays, noting that Drayton, as a
    Spenserian, was unsuited for drama and would hardly want
    to preserve work "which would not enhance his reputation
    as an author." Includes table of Drayton's plays in
    Henslowe's Diary.

                              1904

1   BEECHING, H[ENRY] C[HARLES]. "A Note on the Sonnets of
    Michael Drayton," in his edition of The Sonnets of Shake-
    speare. Athenaeum Press Series. Boston: Ginn, pp. 132-
    39.
        Reprints 1899.2.

2   DRAYTON, MICHAEL. Idea, in Elizabethan Sonnets: Newly Ar-
    ranged and Indexed. Vol. II. [Edited by Edward Arber.]
    Introduction by Sidney Lee. An English Garner. Westmin-
    ster: Archibald Constable, pp. 179-212.
        Reprints 1883.2. In "Introduction" (I, ix-cx) devoted
    to "illustrat[ing] the close dependence of the Elizabethan
    sonnet on foreign models," traces Drayton's debt to for-
    eign authors, particularly Pontoux.

3   GREG, WALTER W[ILSON], ed. Henslowe's Diary. 2 volumes.
    London: A. H. Bullen, 292, 416 pp.
        Provides annotated transcription of the Diary, which
    includes several entries for payments to Drayton for
    plays (passim).

1904

4   STOTSENBURG, JOHN H[AWLEY]. An Impartial Study of the Shake-
    speare Title. Louisville: John P. Morton, 542 pp.
        In chapter 11 ("Daniel's Letter to Egerton Does Not
    Refer to Shaksper," pp. 108–15), argues that Daniel refers
    to Drayton as "the author of plays now daily presented."
    In chapter 27 ("Michael Drayton Considered [as Shake-
    speare]," pp. 324–47), provides overview of Drayton's
    career as a basis for the later identification of Drayton
    as author of portions of several of Shakespeare's plays.
    Aruges that Drayton "had a principal part in" the compo-
    sition of Richard II and attributes his loss of royal
    favor to James's knowledge of his collaboration. Suggests
    that Drayton "was married, probably in Dublin, to Mary
    Martin" (passim).

5   WHITAKER, LEMUEL. "The Sonnets of Michael Drayton." MP, 1
    (April), 563–67.
        Classifies Idea as a sonnet sequence "dictated by
    friendship or by mere conventionality" and argues that
    Drayton was not in love with Anne Goodere. Refutes
    Fleay's argument (1891.5) that Shakespeare in his sonnets
    was closely dependent on Drayton.

                              1905

1   BAESKE, WILHELM. Oldcastle-Falstaff in der englischen
    Literatur bis zu Shakespeare. Palaestra, 50. Berlin:
    Mayer & Müller, 125 pp.
        Examines depiction of Oldcastle in Oldcastle as part
    of an analysis of the treatment of the character in his-
    tory and literature (pp. 106–15).

2   DRAYTON, MICHAEL. Poems of Michael Drayton. Newnes' Pocket
    Classics. London: George Newnes; New York: Charles
    Scribner's Sons, 264 pp. Prints modernized selections.

3   ELTON, OLIVER. Michael Drayton: A Critical Study. London:
    Archibald Constable, 232 pp.
        In revision of 1895.1 includes much new information
    which had come to light since 1895. Traces Drayton's life
    and career, providing a detailed critical assessment of
    each work. Shows that Idea is Anne Goodere and not the
    Countess of Bedford and argues against identifying Selena
    with the latter. Shows that Drayton did not shift his
    attention capriciously from Anne to the Countess, thus
    disproving Courthope's accusation against his behavior
    (1903.1). Offers a balanced assessment of Drayton's

strengths and weaknesses as a poet, suggesting that he was
at his best in his lyrics and that "his most insuperable
flaw, apart from his bluntness, . . . is that want of clear
and right grammar." Includes bibliography of editions and
index to the sonnets in their various editions (Appendix A).
Reprinted 1966.3. Reviewed in Anon., "An Elizabeth Poet,"
Academy, 69 (30 September 1905), 1001-1002; 1906.1.

4   MOORMAN, FREDERIC W[ILLIAM]. The Interpretation of Nature in
      English Poetry from "Beowulf" to Shakespeare. QFSK, 95.
      Strassburg: Karl J. Trübner, 258 pp.
         Examines Drayton's depiction of "country scenery" in
      his poems, observing that "he had a true appreciation for
      the scenery of the English midlands" (pp. 191-96).

1906

1   BRADLEY, W. A. "Revival of an Elizabethan Poet." Dial
      (1 July), pp. 10-11.
         In review of 1905.3 points out that Drayton "was in all
      respects a representative Elizabethan . . . indicating best
      of all . . . the general level of cultivation and the gen-
      eral aims and tendencies of the age in letters."

2   CARTER, C. H. "Nymphidia, The Rape of the Lock, and The
      Culprit Fay." MLN, 21 (November), 216-19.
         Suggests influence of Nymphidia on Pope's poem and
      Joseph Drake's Culprit Fay.

3   DRAYTON, MICHAEL. Nymphidia; or, The Court of Faery. Photo-
      gravure and Colour Series. London: George Routledge;
      New York: E. P. Dutton, 100 pp.
         Provides modernized, illustrated te.t.

4   GREG, WALTER W[ILSON]. Pastoral Poetry & Pastoral Drama: A
      Literary Inquiry, with Special Reference to the Pre-
      Restoration Stage in England. London: A. H. Bullen,
      476 pp.
         In chapter 2 ("Pastoral Poetry in England," pp. 68-154),
      devotes section to Drayton, "the greatest poet who was
      content to follow immediately in Spenser's footsteps."
      Examines Shepherd's Garland as an imitation of Shepherd's
      Calendar and Muses' Elysium as an example of "the freer
      and more spontaneous vein traceable in many English pas-
      toralists from Henryson onwards." Contrasts Muses' Elysi-
      um with Shepherd's Calendar, representative of "the more
      orthodox tradition" in pastoral (pp. 103-10, passim).

1906

5   POLLARD, ALFRED W[ILLIAM]. "A Literary Causerie: Shakespeare
in the Remainder Market." Academy, 70 (2 June), 528-29.
       Describes a set of Pavier quartos (including Oldcastle),
suggesting that they were "remaindered" because of "the
news of the forthcoming folio of 1623." Revised and incorporated in 1909.4.

6   PRIDEAUX, W. F. "'Quam nihil ad genium, Papiniane, tuum!.'"
N&Q, 113 (10 February), 116.
       In reply to 1906.7 suggests that Coleridge's immediate
source was the reprint of Polyolbion in 1793.1.

7   T., W. "'Quam nihil ad genium, Papiniane, tuum!.'" N&Q, 113
(13 January), 27.
       In response to query by William Knight ("Lyrical Bal-
lads: Motto," 112 [28 October 1905], 350), identifies
Selden's "From the Author of the Illustrations" (Polyolbion) as Coleridge's source. See 1906.6. (For a similar
query see J. Bass Mullinger, "Wordsworth: 'Quam nihil ad
genium, Papiniane, tuum!,'" N&Q, 124 [21 October 1911],
325; and J. E. Sandys's comment, 30 December, p. 531.)

1907

1   DRAYTON, MICHAEL, ANTHONY MUNDAY, RICHARD HATHAWAY, and ROB-
ERT WILSON. The First Part of Sir John Oldcastle: A Historical Drama. Edited by John Robertson Macarthur. Ph.D.
dissertation, University of Chicago, 1903. Chicago:
Scott, Foresman, 157 pp.
       Provides annotated reprint of 1619 edition, collated
with the 1600 edition. In "Introduction" (pp. 7-64),
discusses the relationship between the two editions,
traces the historical background of Oldcastle, examines
the genesis of the play and its relationship to Shakespeare's Henry plays and Peele's Edward I, and offers a
critical evaluation of the work. Conjectures that Drayton
was responsible for the scenes including Welsh or Irish
dialect.

2   DRAYTON, MICHAEL. Minor Poems of Michael Drayton. Edited
by Cyril Brett. Oxford: Clarendon Press, 283 pp.
       Provides unannotated (but for a few textual notes)
selection of Drayton's lyrics. In "Introduction" (pp. v-
xxiv), gives an overview of Drayton's life and development,
with a brief critical estimate of most of his poems.
Comments on style and prosody, and defends Polyolbion as a

work "easy and pleasant to read," containing "many things
truly poetical." Concludes with a summary of Drayton's
strengths and weaknesses.

3   ELLERSHAW, HENRY. "Drayton." Modern Language Teaching, 3
    (March), 33-40.
        In arguing that Drayton does not deserve his current
    neglect, provides an appreciative critical survey of his
    poetry to illustrate its "encyclopaedic . . . range" and
    characteristics of style.

4   GREG, W[ALTER] W[ILSON]. Drayton's Sonnets." MLR, 2 (Janu-
    ary), 164-65.
        Queries Courthope's authority for the three variants
    "from the accepted text" in his transcription of Idea 61
    (1903.1). (These are the variants which support Court-
    hope's theory that the sonnet is addressed to the Countess
    of Bedford.)

5   NEUBNER, ALFRED. Missachtete Shakespeare-Dramen: Eine
    literarhistorische-kritische Untersuchung. Neue Shake-
    speare-Bühne, 3. Berlin: Otto Elsner, 209 pp.
        In chapter 4 ("Sir John Oldcastle," pp. 33-40), pro-
    vides an overview of the composition and publication of
    the play, the historical Oldcastle, and the relationship
    of the work to Shakespeare's Henry plays.

6   STOPES, CHARLOTTE CARMICHAEL. Shakespeare's Warwickshire
    Contemporaries. Revised edition. Stratford-upon-Avon:
    Shakespeare Head Press, 283 pp.
        Devotes chapter 13 (pp. 187-209) to a chronological
    survey of Drayton's life and works; concentrates on his
    relations with other authors and his patrons. Argues that
    Idea is Anne Goodere and "that Drayton was possessed by a
    faithful though hopeless love for" her. (The chapter on
    Drayton was included for the first time in this edition.)

1908

1   BRYAN, J[OHN THOMAS] INGRAM. The Feeling for Nature in Eng-
    lish Pastoral Poetry. Ph.D. dissertation, University of
    Pennsylvania, 1907. Tokyo: Kyo-Bun-Kwan, 108 pp.
        In chapter 7 ("Minor Elizabethan Pastoralists," pp. 53-
    63), includes an appreciative discussion of pastoral ele-
    ments in Drayton's poetry.

1908

2 [COLERIDGE, SAMUEL TAYLOR]. Coleridge's Literary Criticism.
Edited by J[ohn] W[illiam] Mackail. London: Henry Frowde,
286 pp.
Reprints passages on Drayton from Coleridge's writings
(passim).

3 CRAWFORD, CHARLES. "Englands Parnassus, 1600." N&Q, 118
(2 May), 341-43; (23 May), 401-403; 119 (4 July), 4-6;
(1 August), 84-85; (5 September), 182-83; (3 October),
262-63; (7 November), 362-63; (5 December), 444-45; 120
(2 January 1909), 4-5; (13 February), 123-24; (13 March),
204-205; (10 April), 283-85; (15 May), 383-84; (5 June),
443-45; (26 June), 502-503.
Identifies several passages from Drayton's works, cor-
recting and supplementing Collier's edition (London, 1867).

4 DANIEL, SAMUEL, and MICHAEL DRAYTON. Daniel's "Delia" and
Drayton's "Idea." Edited by Arundell [James Kennedy]
Esdaile. King's Classics. London: Chatto and Windus,
219 pp.
Reprints 1619 edition of Idea (pp. 67-141) and provides
"Bibliography of the Early Editions" (pp. 145-50). In
"Introduction" (pp. ix-xlii), examines the sincerity of
feeling in Idea.

5 DRAYTON, MICHAEL. Nymphidia, in The Sources and Analogues of
"A Midsummer-Night's Dream." Compiled by Frank Sidgwick.
Shakespeare Classics, 9. New York: Duffield; London:
Chatto & Windus, pp. 158-87.
Provides modernized, annotated text.

6 _____. Nymphidia: The Court of Fairy. Stratford-on-Avon:
Shakespeare Head Press, 35 pp.
Provides modernized reprint of unidentified edition.

7 [DRAYTON, MICHAEL, ANTHONY MUNDAY, RICHARD HATHAWAY, and ROB-
ERT WILSON]. The Life of Sir John Oldcastle, 1600.
Edited by Percy Simpson. Malone Society Reprints, 83.
[London:] Malone Society Reprints, n.p.
Provides reprint of 1600 edition. In introductory note
(pp. v-xvi), discusses bibliographical matters and print-
ing history; provides list of variants in the two seven-
teenth-century editions.

8 DRAYTON, MICHAEL, ANTHONY MUNDAY, RICHARD HATHAWAY, and ROB-
ERT WILSON. Sir John Oldcastle, in The Shakespeare
Apocrypha: Being a Collection of Fourteen Plays Which

Have Been Ascribed to Shakespeare. Edited by C[harles]
F[rederick] Tucker Brooke. Oxford: Clarendon Press,
pp. 127-64.
Provides critical edition based (apparently) on the
first quarto, 1600. In "Introduction" (pp. vi-lvi),
discusses Oldcastle as a reply to Shakespeare's Henry
plays and asserts that there is "no adequate reason to
accept . . . Drayton . . . as the author" of The Merry
Devil of Edmonton.

9 GREG, W[ALTER] W[ILSON]. "On Certain False Dates in Shake-
spearian Quartos." Library, 2d ser., 9 (April), 113-31.
Shows through an analysis of paper and typographical
evidence that the supposed 1600 edition of Oldcastle
(Revised STC 18796) was actually printed in 1619.

10 KOEPPEL, E[MIL]. "Eine Spur des Orosius des Königs Alfred in
Michael Drayton's Polyolbion." Anglia Beiblatt, 19
(November), 332-33.
Points out influence of Alfred's translation of Oro-
sius's Historiae adversum Paganos (through the version
in Hakluyt's Principal Navigations) on Polyolbion, Song 19.

11 LEE, SIDNEY. "The Elizabethan Sonnet," in The Cambridge History of English Literature, III: Renascence and Reforma-
tion. Edited by A[dolphus] W[illiam] Ward and A[lfred]
R[ayney] Waller. Cambridge: Cambridge University Press,
pp. 247-72.
Discusses Drayton's successive revisions of Idea as "a
microcosm of the whole sonneteering movement" and examines
his sources.

12 SAINTSBURY, GEORGE [EDWARD BATEMAN]. A History of English
Prosody from the Twelfth Century to the Present Day, II:
From Shakespeare to Crabbe. London: Macmillan; New York:
Macmillan, 593 pp.
Examines Drayton's importance in the development of
English prosody (particularly the couplet) and assesses the
variety of his metrical experiments (pp. 97-104, passim).

13 UPHAM, ALFRED HORATIO. The French Influence in English Literature from the Accession of Elizabeth to the Restoration.
Columbia University Studies in Comparative Literature.
New York: Columbia University Press, 570 pp. [Also submitted as Ph.D. dissertation, Columbia University.]
Discusses influence of Du Bartas and Sylvester on Moses
and Noah's Flood (pp. 193-97, passim).

1909

1   B., C. C. "Drayton on Valentine's Day." N&Q, 119 (13 March),
    218.
        In response to query by Geo[rge] Drayton (27 February,
    p. 170), notes Drayton's reference to Valentine's Day in
    "To His Valentine." See 1909.2.

2   BAYNE, THOMAS. "Drayton on Valentine's Day." N&Q, 119
    (27 March), 257.
        Suggests that Drayton wrote "make" in line 3 of "To His
    Valentine," not "mate" as printed in 1896.3. See C. C. B.,
    13 March, p. 218. (The "mate" was the result of a print-
    er's error in N&Q; see C. C. B., 1 May, p. 358).

3   CHILD, HAROLD H[ANNYNGTON]. "Michael Drayton," in The Cam-
    bridge History of English Literature, IV: Prose and
    Poetry, Sir Thomas North to Michael Drayton. Edited by
    A[dolphus] W[illiam] Ward and A[lfred] R[ayney] Waller.
    Cambridge: Cambridge University Press, pp. 168-96.
        Provides a chronological overview of Drayton's career
    with critical estimates of most of his works. Discusses
    Drayton as "a map or mirror of his age." Concludes: "In
    the long period which his work covered, the many subjects
    and styles it embraced, the beauty of its results and its
    value as a kind of epitome of an important era, there are
    few more interesting figures in English literature than
    Michael Drayton."

4   POLLARD, ALFRED W[ILLIAM]. Shakespeare Folios and Quartos:
    A Study in the Bibliography of Shakespeare's Plays,
    1594-1685. London: Methuen, 188 pp.
        In chapter 4 ("The Quartos of 1619," pp. 81-107), shows
    that the 1600 Thomas Pavier quarto of Oldcastle (Revised
    STC 18796) was actually printed by William Jaggard in
    1619. See 1906.5.

5   SHEAVYN, PHOEBE. The Literary Profession in the Elizabethan
    Age. Publications of the University of Manchester, Eng-
    lish Series, 1. Manchester: Manchester University Press,
    234 pp.
        Draws frequently on Drayton in analyzing various aspects
    of the profession of letters (passim). Revised 1967.14.

1910

1 ANON. "Avon Club. Mr. A. H. Bullen on 'Michael Drayton.'"
Stratford-upon-Avon Herald, 23 December.
Prints liberal extract from Bullen's paper (published
as 1924.2) and summary of the ensuing discussion, which
included appreciative estimates of various poems and comments on Drayton's influence on Shakespeare.

2 C[OOPER], L[ANE]. "On Wordsworth's 'To Joanna.'" Academy,
78 (29 January), 108-10.
Discusses the possible influence of Polyolbion (Song 30,
11. 145-64) on Wordsworth's poem; also suggests passage in
Aeschylus's Agamemnon as the "ultimate literary model" for
Drayton's lines. Offers supplementary information in
"Lamb on Wordsworth's 'To Joanna,'" N&Q, 127 (22 March
1913), 223-24.

3 CORY, HERBERT E[LLSWORTH]. "The Golden Age of the Spenserian
Pastoral." PMLA, 25, no. 2, 241-67. [Also submitted as
part of "The Influence of Spenser on English Poetry,"
Ph.D. dissertation, Harvard University.]
Examines influence of Shepherd's Calendar on Shepherd's
Garland (and its revisions). Observes that Drayton brought
to the formal eclogue "an English yeoman's temperament and
something of Chaucer's sly sense of humour" and comments
on Drayton's influence on later pastoral works.

4 HOWARD, CLAUD. "The Dramatic Monologue: Its Origin and
Development." SP, 4: 31-88.
Discusses the place of Idea 61 in the development of
the form.

5 LEE, SIDNEY. The French Renaissance in England: An Account
of the Literary Relations of England and France in the
Sixteenth Century. New York: Charles Scribner's Sons,
518 pp.
Examines Drayton's debt to French writers (passim).

6 McKERROW, R[ONALD] B[RUNLEES]. "The Supposed Calling-In of
Drayton's Harmony of the Church, 1591." Library, 3rd
ser., 1 (October), 348-50.
Demonstrates that Harmony of the Church was not sup-
pressed as was popularly supposed. Identifies the work
referred to in the Stationers' records as An Harmony of the
Confessions of the Faith of the Christian and Reformed
Churches. Reprinted 1974.12.

1910

7   SCHELLING, FELIX E[MMANUEL]. <u>English Literature during the</u>
     <u>Lifetime of Shakespeare</u>. New York: Henry Holt, 501 pp.
         Provides general critical overview of Drayton, particu-
     larly as a lyric and historical poet (passim). (The dis-
     cussion of Drayton is essentially the same in the revised
     edition [New York: Henry Holt, 1927].)

8   THOMAS, EDWARD. <u>Feminine Influence on the Poets</u>. London:
     Martin Secker, 360 pp.
         In chapter 5 ("Passion and Poetry," pp. 91–119), treats
     <u>Idea</u> as autobiography and argues that the sonnets fail
     because of Drayton's "too great deliberation of his atti-
     tude" and inability "to make poetry straight out of ex-
     perience." Finds superior Drayton's poems "which either
     profess to express another's love or deal artificially
     with his own" (pp. 100–104).

                              1911

1   BÖHME, TRAUGOTT. <u>Spensers literarisches Nachleben bis zu</u>
     <u>Shelley</u>. Palaestra, 93. Berlin: Mayer & Müller, 359 pp.
         Examines influence of Spenser on the form, style, and
     content of Drayton's poetry (passim).

2   [DRAYTON, MICHAEL, ANTHONY MUNDAY, RICHARD HATHAWAY, and ROB-
     ERT WILSON]. "Sir John Oldcastle": "Written by William
     Shakespeare," 1600. Edited by John S[tephen] Farmer.
     Tudor Facsimile Texts. [Amersham, England:] Tudor
     Facsimile Texts, n.p.
         Provides facsimile reprint of 1600 edition. Reprinted
     1970.7.

3   FORSYTHE, R[OBERT] S[TANLEY]. "Certain Sources of <u>Sir John</u>
     <u>Oldcastle</u>." <u>MLN</u>, 26 (April), 104–107.
         Traces influence of <u>1</u> and <u>2 Henry IV</u>, <u>Henry V</u>, and <u>1</u>,
     <u>2</u>, and <u>3 Henry VI</u> on <u>Oldcastle</u>.

4   LEGOUIS, ÉMILE [HYACINTHE]. "Michael Drayton." <u>Revue des</u>
     <u>Cours et Conférences</u>, 2d ser., 19 (30 March), 118–26;
     (13 April), 231–39.
         Groups Drayton's works as "fantaisistes, allegoriques,
     patriotiques et guerrières," providing a brief critical
     discussion of each type. Devotes second portion to <u>Poly-</u>
     <u>olbion</u>, observing that Drayton's command over form is
     better than over content.

                              190

1912

1 DELATTRE, FLORIS. English Fairy Poetry from the Origins to
   the Seventeenth Century. London: Henry Frowde; Paris:
   Henri Didier, 235 pp.
      Examines Nymphidia in analyzing "the slow but obvious
   decay of fairy poetry" from 1627 to 1648. Discusses the
   poem as a burlesque and concludes that it "is an elegant
   trifle, in which, obviously, the fairy theme serves as a
   mere pretext for a display of patient and strenuous work-
   manship." Also comments on Drayton's depiction of fairies
   in other poems (pp. 148-55).

2 DIXON, W[ILLIAM] MACNEILE. English Epic and Heroic Poetry.
   London: J. M. Dent; New York: E. P. Dutton, 351 pp.
      Argues that Drayton fails as a heroic poet because of
   his "discontinuous" style (pp. 180-88, passim).

3 HALL, HENRY MARION. Idylls of Fishermen: A History of the
   Literary Species. Columbia University Studies in Comparative Literature. New York: Columbia University Press,
   228 pp. [Also submitted as Ph.D. dissertation, Columbia
   University.]
      Discusses lyricism in the Sixth Nymphal of Muses' Elysi-
   um, comparing the poem to Phineas Fletcher's Piscatory
   Eclogues. Points out that Drayton's handling of piscatory
   elements "forms a marked contrast with the thin pretense
   of activities" in earlier eclogues (pp. 143-48, passim).
   (The discussion of Drayton is unchanged in the revised
   edition, 1914.)

4 REED, EDWARD BLISS. English Lyrical Poetry: From Its Origins
   to the Present Time. New Haven: Yale University Press;
   London: Oxford University Press, 626 pp.
      In a history of the lyric, offers a general critical
   estimate of Idea (with particular emphasis on style) and
   of several of Drayton's other poems (pp. 162-64, 186-88).

1913

1 CLAASSEN, WILHELM. Michael Drayton's "England's Heroical
   Epistles": Eine Quellenstudie. Ph.D. dissertation,
   Kaiser-Wilhelms-Universität, Strassburg im Elsass.
   Borna-Leipzig: Robert Noske, 78 pp.
      Provides an epistle-by-epistle examination of sources
   and a classified analysis of similes in the work.

1913

2 DRAYTON, MICHAEL, ANTHONY MUNDAY, RICHARD HATHAWAY, and ROB-
   ERT WILSON. Sir John Oldcastle: Den gode Lord Cobham,
   første del, in Den lystige Djaevel: Tre pseudo-
   shakespeareske Skuespil. Translated by A[xel] Halling.
   Copenhagen: Glydendal, pp. 5-109.
       Provides Danish translation of Oldcastle.

3 PETERSEN, OTTOMAR. "Pseudoshakespearesche Dramen." Anglia,
   37: 424-62.
       Discusses Oldcastle in a general overview of the subject.

                              1914

1 EAGLE, R[ODERICK LEWIS]. "The Rival Poet." Baconiana, 3rd
   ser., 12 (October), 227-30.
       Argues that Drayton is the Rival Poet and suggests
   several parallels between Idea and Sonnets. Incorporated
   in 1916.2.

2 HOPKINSON, A[RTHUR] F[REDERIC]. "Introduction," in his edition of The Merry Devil of Edmonton. London: M. E. Sims,
   pp. i-xxxvi.
       In revision of "An Essay on the Merry Devil of Edmon-
   ton" (see 1900.2), still finds the evidence insufficient
   to assign the play to Drayton.

3 POOLE, CHARLES HENRY. "Michael Drayton," in his edition of
   Warwickshire Poets. The Poets of the Shires. London:
   N. Ling, pp. 76-87.
       In a sketchy and frequently inaccurate overview of
   Drayton's career, comments on the influence of Warwick-
   shire on his poetry. Includes selections from his works.

4 ROBERTSON, JOHN MACKINNON. Elizabethan Literature. Home
   University Library of Modern Knowledge, 89. New York:
   Henry Holt; London: Williams and Norgate, 256 pp.
       In chapter 7 ("Poetry after Spenser," pp. 140-75),
   provides a general critical discussion of Drayton, finding
   "that his occasional prose has rather more distinction
   than the bulk of his abundant yet laboured verse"
   (pp. 155-59).

5 TATLOCK, JOHN S[TRONG] P[ERRY]. "Origin of the Closed Couplet
   in English." Nation, 98 (9 April), 390.
       Discusses place of England's Heroical Epistles in the
   development of the couplet.

1915

1   ALBRIGHT, EVELYN MAY. "Eating a Citation." MLN, 30 (Novem-
    ber), 201-206.
       Examines possible sources for the eating of the cita-
    tion and seal in Oldcastle; notes several literary and
    historical parallels, particularly with a thirteenth-
    century court case.

2   KAUN, ERNST. Konventionelles in den elisabethanischen Son-
    etten mit Berücksichtigung der französischen und italien-
    ischen Quellen. Ph.D. dissertation, Universityt of Greifs-
    wald, 1914. Greifswald: Hans Adler, 122 pp.
       Includes several examples from Idea in a classification
    of conventional elements in Elizabethan sonnets. Arranges
    passages under the following heads (which are then subdi-
    vided): praise of mistress's beauty, poet's assertion of
    his love, mistress's refusal of love, psychological condi-
    tion of the unrequited lover, poet's attempt to extricate
    himself from the relationship, poet's censure of his
    mistress, and parting (passim).

3   NUMERATZKY, WILLY. Michael Draytons Belesenheit und lit-
    erarische Kritik. Ph.D. dissertation, Friedrich-Wilhelms-
    Universität, Berlin. Berlin: Mayer & Müller, 98 pp.
       Discusses Drayton's life and career, provides classified
    list of works ostensibly read by him (including references
    to the respective work or author in Drayton's poems), and
    analyzes principles of his literary criticism (with parti-
    cular attention to his comments on critics, the nature of
    poetry, and style).

4   SMITH, ROBERT METCALF. Froissart and the English Chronicle
    Play. Columbia University Studies in English and Compara-
    tive Literature. New York: Columbia University Press,
    179 pp. [Also submitted as Ph.D. dissertation, Columbia
    University.]
       In chapter 9 ("Daniel's Civil Wars and Shakespeare's
    Richard II," pp. 143-57), finds that Drayton used Richard
    II as a source in Richard II-Queen Isabel epistles in
    England's Heroical Epistles (pp. 154-57).

1916

1   ALDEN, RAYMOND MACDONALD, ed. The Sonnets of Shakespeare:
    From the Quarto of 1609 with Variorum Readings and Com-
    mentary. Boston: Houghton, Mifflin, 562 pp.

1916

Provides overview of scholarship on identification of
Drayton as the Rival Poet ("There are possible grounds for
his claim") and on the influence of Drayton's sonnets on
Shakespeare's (discounts Drayton's influence because the
parallels involve commonplace conceits and themes). In
the variorum notes cites parallels between Drayton's poems
and Sonnets (passim).

2   EAGLE, R[ODERICK] L[EWIS]. New Light on the Enigmas of
Shakespeare's Sonnets. London: John Long, 95 pp.
    Incorporates, with minor changes, 1914.1 (pp. 42–48).

3   LONG, EDGAR. "Notes from the English Seminar, I: Drayton's
'Eighth Nymphal.'" SP, 13 (July), 180–83.
    Examines combination of pastoral and fairy worlds in
Muses' Elysium, Eighth Nymphal, and the place of Drayton's
poem in the tradition of the combination.

4   MADDEN, D[ODGSON] H[AMILTON]. Shakespeare and His Fellows:
An Attempt to Decipher the Man and His Nature. London:
Smith, Elder, 245 pp.
    Discusses Drayton's moral character as the basis for
his close association with Shakespeare (pp. 109–13).

5   WIETFELD, ALBERT. Die Bildersprache in Shakespeare's Sonetten.
SzEP, 54. Halle: Max Niemeyer, 144 pp.
    Draws frequently on Idea for parallels in analyzing
Shakespeare's metaphoric language (passim).

1917

1   ADAMS, JOSEPH QUINCY. Shakespearean Playhouses: A History
of English Theatres from the Beginnings to the Restoration.
Boston: Houghton, Mifflin, 489 pp.
    Discusses Drayton's association with the Whitefriars
playhouse and the Children of His Majesty's Revels. Calls
him "[t]he chief spirit in the organization of the new
playhouse" at Whitefriars (pp. 311–17).

2   COLVIN, SIDNEY. John Keats: His Life and Poetry; His Friends,
Critics, and After-Fame. New York: Charles Scribner's
Sons, 618 pp.
    Discusses influence of Man in the Moon (and possibly
Endymion and Phoebe) on Endymion (pp. 168–71, passim).

3   CROSLAND, T[HOMAS] W[ILLIAM] H[ODGSON]. The English Sonnet.
    London: Martin Secker, 276 pp.
         Argues that Drayton's "position . . . among the earlier
    sonneteers is very nearly paramount." Characterizes his
    traits as a sonnet writer, especially the "quality of
    rugged, forthright force" which sets him apart from most
    of his contemporary sonneteers. Compares him with Shake-
    speare, observing that "[i]n some regards certain of his
    sonnets are greater even than Shakespeare's." Singles out
    Idea 61 for special praise (pp. 158-75).

                            1918

1   ADAMS, JOSEPH QUINCY. "Michael Drayton's 'To the Virginia
    Voyage.'" MLN, 33 (November), 405-408.
         Analyzes Drayton's indebtedness to "Hakluyt's First
    Voyage to Virginia as printed in his Principal Naviga-
    tions." See 1957.1.

2   SHAFER, ROBERT. The English Ode to 1660: An Essay in Lit-
    erary History. Ph.D. dissertation, Princeton University,
    1916. Princeton: Princeton University Press, 173 pp.
         Examines Drayton's conception of the ode (he "had a
    fairly correct idea of the nature of the true ode"), in-
    fluences on his Odes, and the combination of classical and
    native elements in them. Concludes that although none of
    his poems is a true ode, "his performance rises far above
    that of any of his predecessors, and marks the real begin-
    ning of the ode as a separable lyric 'kind' in our poetry"
    (pp. 82-91).

                            1920

1   C., A. R. "Drayton's Battle of Agincourt." Athenaeum,
    no. 4697 (7 May), p. 617.
         Suggests that the lines should be scanned "two 'beats'
    in the line, no matter whether they come on important or
    unimportant, 'accented' or 'unaccented,' words."

2   GUINEY, L. I. "Elizabethan Guesses." N&Q, 138 (February),
    32-33.
         Identifies allusion to Drayton in Samuel Sheppard's
    A Mausolean Lament, 1651. See 1920.4.

1920

3   HEWLETT, MAURICE. "Polyolbion," in his In a Green Shade: A
     Country Commentary. London: G. Bell and Sons, pp. 45-49.
        Discusses Drayton's anthropomorphic representation of
     rivers; finds that his "weakness is that he can conceive
     of no other relation than a sex-relation, and in so de-
     scribing the relations of every river in England, he very
     naturally becomes tedious."

4   L., G. G. "Elizabethan Guesses." N&Q, 138 (17 April), 137.
        Offers additional evidence to support Guiney's identi-
     fication (1920.2) of an allusion to Drayton in Sheppard's
     A Mausolean Lament.

5   SCHAUBERT, ELSE VON. Draytons Anteil an "Heinrich VI," 2.
     u. 3. Teil. Neue Anglistische Arbeiten, no. 4. Cöthen:
     Otto Schulze, 235 pp.
        Provides detailed analysis of characteristics of Dray-
     ton's style and of parallel passages between his works and
     2 and 3 Henry VI to argue that he wrote portions of the
     plays. See 1921.5, 1922.3, 1922.11, 1923.8, and 1926.4.
     Reviewed in H. Jantzen, Zeitschrift für Französischen und
     Englischen Unterricht, 21 (1922), 138-39; 1921.5; 1922.3.

                              1921

1   ANON. "Nimphidia Reprinted." TLS (7 July), p. 433.
        In review of 1921.4 provides appreciative essay touch-
     ing on "the gentle and humorous imagery," "versification,"
     and the poem "as a tribute to pastoral England." Calls
     Nymphidia "one of the most delightful vanities ever
     penned."

2   BROADUS, EDMUND KEMPER. The Laureateship: A Study of the
     Office of Poet Laureate in England with Some Account of
     the Poets. Oxford: Clarendon Press, 247 pp.
        In chapter 4 ("Spenser, Drayton, and Daniel as Tradi-
     tional Poets Laureate," pp. 33-39), examines tradition
     that Drayton was poet laureate. Notes that although there
     is no evidence of an official appointment "there are few
     court poets of the late Elizabethan period whose careers
     would seem to have furnished more occasion for it."

*3   CAWLEY, ROBERT RALSTON. "The Influence of the Voyages in
     Non-Dramatic English Literature between 1550 and 1650."
     Ph.D. dissertation, Harvard University.
        See 1923.1.

4 DRAYTON, MICHAEL. Nimphidia, the Court of Fayrie. Edited by
   H[erbert] F[rancis] B[rett] Brett-Smith. Stratford-upon-
   Avon: Shakespeare Head Press; Oxford: Basil Blackwell,
   34 pp.
       Provides slightly modernized reprint of 1627 edition.
   Reviewed in 1921.1.

5 KELLER, WOLFGANG. Review of Else von Schaubert, Draytons
   Anteil an "Heinrich VI," 2. u. 3. Teil. Shakespeare-
   Jahrbuch, 57: 97-100.
       In review of 1920.5 questions several of Schaubert's
   arguments for Drayton's authorship. See 1922.11 and
   1923.8.

1922

1 BARTLETT, HENRIETTA C[OLLINS]. Mr. William Shakespeare:
   Original and Early Editions of His Quartos and Folios,
   His Source Books, and Those Containing Contemporary No-
   tices. New Haven: Yale University Press; London: Oxford
   University Press, 247 pp.
       Includes several notes on references in sixteenth- and
   seventeenth-century books to Drayton and provides biblio-
   graphical description of Oldcastle (both editions),
   Idea's Mirror (1594), and Matilda (1594) (passim).

2 [BLUNDEN, EDMUND]. "The Happy Island." TLS (17 August),
   pp. 525-26.
       Offers appreciative estimate of Polyolbion, especially
   the many "fluent poetical passages." Discusses its relationship with Drayton's other poems and the difficulties
   in reading caused by the scope, alexandrines, and over-
   abundance of personification. Reprinted 1932.3.

3 CHARLTON, H[ENRY] B[UCKLEY]. Review of Else von Schaubert,
   Draytons Anteil an "Heinrich VI," 2. u. 3. Teil. MLR, 17
   (July), 301-303.
       Criticizes Schaubert's methodology and conclusions in
   1920.5.

4 DRAYTON, MICHAEL. The Qvest of Cynthia. London: Medici
   Society, 26 pp.
       Reprints unidentified edition.

*5 FAULKNER, E. "Michael Drayton." Poetry, 5 (February), 49-55.
       Cited in 1941.10.

1922

*6   FINNEY, CLAUDE LEE. "Shakespeare and Keats." Ph.D. disser-
tation, Harvard University.
     Discusses Drayton's influence on Keats.

7   HARRIS, M. DORMER. "Michael Drayton." N&Q, 143 (19 August),
147.
     Reports discovery of a deed from 1541/2 "which may con-
tain a reference to one of . . . [Drayton's] kin," a
Christopher Drayton. Asks for information on Drayton's
parentage. See reply by Edward Bensly (2 September),
p. 196; and 1922.12.

8   HILLEBRAND, HAROLD NEWCOMB. "The Children of the King's
Revels at Whitefriars." JEGP, 21: 318-34.
     Discusses Drayton's association with Whitefriars, cor-
recting some errors about his role in the syndicate. Incorporated in 1926.7.

*9   IDEN, OTTO. "Das persönliche Geschlecht unpersönlicher
Substantiva (einschliesslich der Tiernamen) bie Michael
Drayton." Ph.D. dissertation, University of Kiel.
     Cited in 1922 MHRA Annual Bibliography, item 310.

10   ROBERTSON, J[OHN] M[ACKINNON]. The Shakespeare Canon. London: George Routledge & Sons; New York: E. P. Dutton,
221 pp.
     Suggests "the possible presence of Drayton in the pre-
Shakespearean form of the first part of" Julius Caesar
(pp. 126-34).

11   SCHAUBERT, ELSE VON. "Zu der Frage nach Draytons Anteil an
Shakespeares Heinrich VI." Englische Studien, 56: 463-75.
     Responds to 1921.5, reinforcing her argument in 1920.5
for Drayton's part-authorship of 2 and 3 Henry VI. See
1923.8.

12   W., M. E. "Michael Drayton." N&Q, 143 (9 September), 213-
14.
     In reply to 1922.7 asserts that Drayton was a relative
of the Gooderes and that "he was still at Polesworth in
1584-85." See 1928.3.

1923

1   CAWLEY, ROBERT RALSTON. "Drayton and the Voyagers." PMLA,
38 (September), 530-56.

Provides detailed examination of Drayton's use of
Hakluyt's Principal Navigations as the source of Polyolbion, Song 19, 11. 156-394. Shows that Drayton relied on
Hakluyt's summaries and marginal notes, sometimes following "them so slavishly that his passages became notable
examples of the art of casting prose into verse."

2 CHAMBERS, E[DMUND] K[ERCHEVER]. The Elizabethan Stage. Vol.
III. Oxford: Clarendon Press, 524 pp.
Provides biographical sketch, bibliographical and historical notes on Oldcastle, and a list of lost or doubtful
plays (pp. 306-308). (Also identifies Drayton as author
of song about Agincourt in 1 Edward IV [IV, 307].)

3 GOSSE, EDMUND [WILLIAM]. "The Court of Faery," in his More
Books on the Table. New York: Charles Scribner's Sons,
pp. 45-53.
In discussion of Nymphidia classifies "Drayton . . .
among the artisans rather than among the artists of
poetry." Finds "a deliberate attack" upon Shakespeare in
lines 17-20 of Nymphidia, which he calls "a poem of fancy,
not of imagination." Compares Midsummer Night's Dream
with Drayton's poem; concludes that Nymphidia "is a work
of abiding merit, eminent in its place and time if we
refrain from comparing it too closely with" Shakespeare's
play. (Reprint of one of his Sunday Times columns.)

4 HEBEL, J[OHN] WILLIAM. "The Surreptitious Edition of Michael
Drayton's Peirs Gaueston." Library, 4th ser., 4 (September), 151-55.
Examines revisions in 1595(?) edition of Gaveston,
suggesting that the text was set from "a manuscript which
Drayton was in process of revising for a new edition."
Also suggests that the edition was published by Nicholas
Ling and John Busby, Drayton's publishers, in response to
the popularity of the poem and that the edition "can only
be called 'surreptitious' in that Drayton knew nothing of
it before it was published and that he evidently was not
present to read the proof."

5 HILLYER, ROBERT. "The Drayton Sonnets." Freeman, 6 (31 January), 488-89.
Reacting to overemphasis on source hunting and to the
usual focus on Idea 61, examines several of Drayton's
other "distinctive" sonnets to argue that "the sonnets to
'Idea' are the most varied, the liveliest, perhaps the
greatest, of all the sonnets of that age except those of
Shakespeare."

1923

6   HOOKES, NICHOLAS. <u>Amanda, a Sacrifice to an Unknown Goddesse;</u>
     <u>or, a Free-Will Offering of a Loving Heart to a Sweet-</u>
     <u>Heart</u>. London: Elkin Mathews, 219 pp.
          Reprints 1653 edition, which includes Hookes's Latin
     translation of the Henry II-Rosamond epistles from <u>Eng-</u>
     <u>land's Heroical Epistles</u> (pp. 164-91).

7   JENKINS, RAYMOND. "Drayton's Relation to the School of Donne,
     as Revealed in the <u>Shepheards Sirena</u>." <u>PMLA</u>, 38 (Septem-
     ber), 557-87. [Also submitted as Ph.D. dissertation, Yale
     University, 1921.]
          Interprets <u>Sirena</u> as Drayton's allegorical defense of
     the Spenserians against the school of Donne. Identifies
     Drayton with Dorilus, the shepherds with the Spenserian
     poets, Donne with Olcon, and the swineherds with Donne's
     followers; suggests that Sirena is not only Drayton's muse
     but also represents the Mermaid Tavern Club. Also identi-
     fies Selena with the Countess of Bedford and Donne with
     Cerberon in Eighth Eclogue of <u>Eclogues</u> (1606). Examines
     Drayton's relationship with Donne and his attitude toward
     the court wits. <u>See</u> 1924.7 and 1927.4.

8   KELLER, WOLFGANG. "Noch einmal Drayton's angebliche Mitar-
     beit an <u>Heinrich VI</u>: Eine Erwiderung." <u>Englische Studien</u>,
     57: 141-45.
          Responds to 1922.11 .

*9   NEWDIGATE, B[ERNARD HENRY]. "Michael Drayton and Some of His
     Friends." <u>Shakespeare Club, Stratford-upon-Avon, Summary</u>
     <u>of Papers, 1923-1924</u>.
          Cited in E[dward] L[indsay] C[arson] Mullins, <u>A Guide</u>
     <u>to the Historical and Archaeological Publications of Soci-</u>
     <u>eties in England and Wales, 1901-1933</u> (London: Athlone
     Press, 1968), p. 362, item 4948b.

10   WYLD, HENRY CECIL [KENNEDY]. <u>Studies in English Rhymes from</u>
     <u>Surrey to Pope: A Chapter in the History of English</u>.
     London: John Murray, 154 pp.
          Draws frequently on Drayton for examples in analyzing
     the characteristics (e.g., vowel quality and quantity,
     consonants) of rhymes (passim).

1924

1   BENSLY, EDWARD. "Poem by Drayton: The Willy." <u>N&Q</u>, 147
     (1 November), 323.

In response to query by W. S. (18 October, p. 282), identifies "Willy" (Idea 32) as "the Wylye, or Wiley, in Wiltshire." G. A. Gibbs offers a similar identification (p. 323).

2   BULLEN, A[RTHUR] H[ENRY]. "Michael Drayton," in his Eliza-
    bethans. New York: E. P. Dutton, pp. 3-23.
        Attempts to show that Drayton does not deserve his lack
    of reputation among "moderns" by providing an appreciative
    chronological overview of his life and works to illustrate
    that he was "one of the choicest spirits of the Elizabethan
    Age." See 1910.1.

3   DRAYTON, MICHAEL. Nimphidia: The Court of Fayrie. Edited by
    J[ohn] C[ollings] Squire. Shakespeare Head Quartos.
    Stratford-upon-Avon: Basil Blackwell for the Shakespeare ·
    Head Press, 38 pp.
        Reprints 1627 edition. In introductory note (pp. 5-6),
    characterizes Nymphidia as "one of the most charming
    pieces of English fairy poetry" and comments on Drayton's
    humor. Reviewed in Anon., "Some Reprints," TLS (5 March
    1925), p. 152.

4   FINNEY, CLAUDE L[EE]. "Drayton's Endimion and Phoebe and
    Keats's Endymion." PMLA, 39 (December), 805-13.
        Discusses influence of Endymion and Phoebe on Keats's
    poem, particularly its structure. See 1929.1

5   FORBIS, JOHN F. The Shakespearean Enigma and an Elizabethan
    Mania. New York: American Library Service, 348 pp.
        Discusses Idea in arguing that Drayton, Daniel, Sidney,
    Shakespeare, and a host of other sonneteers were actually
    writing about the intoxicating effects of wine. Deter-
    mines that Drayton's drinking "was probably intermittent":
    "The greater mass of his work was done in soberness, while
    his sonnets, most of them, were the product of his sober-
    ing times." Identifies other poems (especially Sirena) as
    "wine-songs" (pp. 302-10, passim).

6   HAINES, C. R. "Shakespeare Allusions." TLS (5 June), p. 356.
        Points out allusions to Daniel and (possibly) Drayton in
    Sylvester's translation of Du Bartas (Divine Weeks, Second
    Week).

7   HEBEL, J[OHN] WILLIAM. "Drayton's Sirena." PMLA, 39 (Decem-
    ber), 814-36.
        In response to 1923.7 suggests alternative interpreta-
    tion of Sirena: identifies Selena, Cerberon, and Olcon of

1924

Eighth Eclogue (Eclogues) as Countess of Bedford, John
Florio, and Daniel, respectively; traces history of the
relationship between Drayton and Countess of Bedford; suggests Olcon, the swineherds, and the shepherds of Sirena
represent, respectively, Jonson, the Tribe of Ben, and the
Spenserians; and identifies Sirena as Anne Goodere. See
1927.4.

8 _____. "Nicholas Ling and Englands Helicon." Library, 4th
ser., 5 (September), 153-60.
In arguing that Ling was the editor of England's Helicon, points out that, as Drayton's publisher, he would
have had access to Drayton's manuscripts from which passages in the miscellany were set. Notes some variants between passages in England's Helicon and editions of
Drayton's works.

9 HUGHES, WILLIAM JOHN. Wales and the Welsh in English Litera-
ture from Shakespeare to Scott. Wrexham: Hughes and Son;
London: Simpkin, Marshall, Hamilton, Kent, 215 pp.
Discusses the description of Wales in Polyolbion and
compares Drayton's poem with Churchyard's Worthiness of
Wales (pp. 22-25, passim).

10 LEGOUIS, É[MILE HYACINTHE], and L[OUIS] CAZAMIAN. Histoire
de la littérature anglaise. Paris: Hachette, 1340 pp.
In book 4, chapter 3 ("La Poésie de 1590 à 1625,"
pp. 286-333), Legouis provides an overview of Drayton's
strengths and weaknesses as a poet. Emphasizes style and
prosody in his comments (pp. 291-97, passim). Translated
1927.5.

11 PIERCE, FREDERICK E. "Blake and Seventeenth Century Authors."
MLN, 39 (March), 150-53.
Suggests influence of Polyolbion on geographical names
in Jerusalem.

12 WELLS, HENRY W[ILLIS]. Poetic Imagery Illustrated from
Elizabethan Literature. Columbia University Studies in
English and Comparative Literature. New York: Columbia
University Press, 239 pp. [Also submitted as Ph.D. disser-
tation, Columbia University.]
Draws frequently on Drayton's poetry in analyzing types
of images (decorative, sunken, violent, radical, intensive,
expansive, and exuberant) (passim).

1925

1 CAWLEY, ROBERT RALSTON. "Drayton's Use of Welsh History." SP,
22 (April), 234-55.
Traces Drayton's indebtedness to Humphrey Llwyd and
David Powel, A History of Cambria, in Polyolbion, Song 9,
11. 177-436: also notes Drayton's use of Polydore Vergil's
English History.

2 COLERIDGE, STEPHEN. Quiet Hours in Poets' Corner. London:
Mills & Boon, 131 pp.
In chapter 17 ("Drayton and Granville Sharp," pp. 109-
14), gives a brief description of the monument to Drayton,
"whom [sic] it is safe to say is now a forgotten poet,
though the name of his chief poem, 'Polyolbion,' recalls
something faintly reminiscent to the minds of some of us."

3 DRAYTON, MICHAEL. Endimion & Phoebe, Ideas Latmus. Edited by
J[ohn] William Hebel. Oxford: Basil Blackwell for the
Shakespeare Head Press, 70 pp.
Reprints 1595 edition. In "Introduction" (pp. vii-
xviii), discusses publishing history, place in the development of mythological love poems, sources, and influence.
See 1925.6, 1925.7, 1925.8, 1925.9, and 1925.10. Reviewed
in Anon., "Print and Pictures," TLS (26 November 1925),
p. 793; Émile [Hyacinthe] Legouis, Revue Anglo-Américaine,
3 (August 1926), 542-43; 1925.8.

4 _____. The Quest of Cynthia. Chelsea: Swan Press, 13 pp.
Reprints unidentified edition.

5 GREG, W[ALTER] W[ILSON], ed. English Literary Autographs,
1550-1650: Part I--Dramatists. [London:] Oxford University Press, n.p.
Reproduces, with transcriptions, three examples of
Drayton's handwriting in plate VIII.

6 LUCAS, F[RANK] L[AURENCE]. "Drayton's Endymion and Phoebe."
New Statesman, 25 (1 August), 447.
Responds to 1925.9 by defending some of his earlier
(1925.8) assertions of errors and problems in 1925.3 and
by noting some additional problem passages resulting from
the "slavish reproduction" of an early edition. See
1925.7 and 1925.10.

1925

7 _____. "Drayton's Endimion and Phoebe." New Statesman, 25
   (15 August), 500.
       Responds to 1925.10 by reasserting his original posi-
   tion (1925.8) that 1925.3 is not a good edition because of
   the editorial policy. See 1925.6 and 1925.9.

8 _____. "Michael Drayton." New Statesman, 25 (11 July),
   368-69.
       In a review of 1925.3 offers a general critical apprecia-
   tion of Drayton's poetry. Calls Endymion and Phoebe a
   "poor" work: it "has neither passion nor pity; it has no
   story, only a thin thread on which to string . . . coloured
   beads of word-painting." Objects strongly to Hebel's editorial policy, noting "errors" and problems caused by re-
   producing the original spelling and punctuation. Reprinted
   1926.10. See 1925.6, 1925.7, 1925.9, and 1925.10.

9 NEWDIGATE, B[ERNARD] H[ENRY]. "Drayton's Endimion and Phoebe."
   New Statesman, 25 (25 July), 419.
       In response to 1925.8 defends editorial policy in
   1925.3, arguing against errors and problems noted by Lucas.
   See 1925.6, 1925.7, and 1925.10.

10 _____. "Drayton's Endimion and Phoebe." New Statesman, 25
   (8 August), 472.
       Responds to 1925.6 by explaining the new "problem"
   passages in 1925.3 and defending the literal reprinting
   of early works. See 1925.7, 1925.8, and 1925.9.

11 WHITE, NEWPORT B. "Keats and Drayton." TLS (2 April),
   p. 240.
       Reports copy of 1595 edition of Endymion and Phoebe and
   1596 edition of Mortimeriados in Marsh's Library, Dublin.
   See B[ernard] H[enry] Newdigate, "Keats and Drayton,"
   9 April, p. 253; Anon., "Print and Pictures," 26 November,
   p. 793; and R[obert] H[ope] Case, "Endymion and Phoebe,"
   10 December, p. 862.

1926

1 BAINTON, EDGAR L[ESLIE]. The Virginian Voyage: Unison Song.
   Musical Times, 1004. London: Novello, 4 pp.
       Provides musical setting for Drayton's "To the Virginian
   Voyage."

2   CAWLEY, R[OBERT] R[ALSTON]. "'Make rope's in such a scarre.'"
    PQ, 5 (April), 183-84.
        Points out Drayton's marginal definition of "scarr" as
    "rock" in Polyolbion, Song 27, 1. 326, in explaining mean-
    ing of the term in All's Well That Ends Well.

3   DRAYTON, MICHAEL. "The Ballad of Agincourt" and "Ode to the
    Virginian Voyage." [Edited by Bernard Henry Newdigate.]
    Oxford: Basil Blackwell for the Shakespeare Head Press,
    32 pp.
        Provides reprints from 1619 Poems. In "Introduction"
    (pp. ix-xvi), traces publication histories and places the
    poems in the context of Drayton's career. Reviewed in
    Émile [Hyacinthe] Legouis, Revue Anglo-Américaine, 3
    (August 1926), 542-43.

4   GOURVITCH, I. "Drayton and Henry VI." N&Q, 151 (18 Septem-
    ber), 201-204; (25 September), 219-21; (2 October), 239-41;
    (9 October), 256-58.
        Provides detailed examination of Schaubert's arguments
    (1920.5) for Drayton's authorship of portions of Henry VI.
    Concludes that "no portion . . . was written by Drayton"
    but that he "borrowed freely from" the plays.

5   GRAY, ARTHUR. A Chapter in the Early Life of Shakespeare:
    Polesworth in Arden. Cambridge: Cambridge University
    Press, 133 pp.
        Devotes section 17 ("Michael Drayton," pp. 83-88) to a
    general discussion of Drayton's association with Polesworth
    and of the extent of his acquaintance with Shakespeare
    (passim).

6   HEBEL, J[OHN] WILLIAM. "Drayton and Shakespeare." MLN, 41
    (April), 248-50.
        Traces influence of Venus and Adonis and of Marlowe's
    Hero and Leander (in manuscript) on Gaveston.

7   HILLEBRAND, HAROLD NEWCOMB. The Child Actors: A Chapter in
    Elizabethan Stage History. ISLL, vol. 11, nos. 1-2.
    Urbana: University of Illinois, 355 pp.
        Revises 1922.8 as chapter 9 ("The King's Revels at
    Whitefriars," pp. 220-36), but makes no substantive
    changes in discussion of Drayton.

8   HULL, VERNAM EDWARD NUNNEMACHER. "The English and Welsh
    Topographical Sources of Drayton's Polyolbion, with Special
    Reference to Camden's Britannia and Saxton's Atlas."
    Ph.D. dissertation, Harvard University. [Abstract in
    Harvard University Summaries of Theses, 2 (1930), 177-79.]

1926

> Provides detailed analysis of Polyolbion to demonstrate
> that Drayton "derived nine-tenths of the topography" from
> Camden and Saxton. Also shows that, contrary to assertions
> of earlier scholars, Drayton "does not seem to have known
> Speed's maps [in his Theatre of the Empire of Great
> Britain] or Leland's Itinerary, and even Warner's Albions
> England at best could only have served as a model."

9   JENKINS, RAYMOND. "The Source of Drayton's Battaile of Agin-
>   court." PMLA, 41 (June), 280–93.
>   Concludes that Speed's History of Great Britain and
>   either Holinshed's Chronicles or Halle's Union were Dray-
>   ton's principal sources. Also suggests that he drew on
>   Shakespeare's Henry V.

10 LUCAS, F[RANK] L[AURENCE]. "Michael Drayton," in his Authors
>   Dead & Living. New York: Macmillan, pp. 46–53.
>   Reprints 1925.8, omitting the final paragraph.

11 POLLARD, A[LFRED] W[ILLIAM], and G[ILBERT] R[ICHARD] REDGRAVE,
>   comps. A Short-Title Catalogue of Books Printed in England,
>   Scotland, & Ireland and of English Books Printed Abroad,
>   1475–1640. London: The Bibliographical Society, 625 pp.
>   Provide list of extant editions (with locations) of
>   Drayton's works (pp. 160–61). (New edition in progress.)
>   See 1954.4.

12 SCHAUBERT, E[LSE] V[ON]. "Zur Geschichte der Black-Letter
>   Broadside Ballad." Anglia, 50: 1–61.
>   Argues that the source of A Courtly New Ballad of the
>   Princely Wooing of the Fair Maid of London by King Edward
>   and the two parts of The Woeful Lamentation of Mrs. Jane
>   Shore is England's Heroical Epistles.

13 SCOTT, JANET G[IRVAN]. "The Names of the Heroines of Eliza-
>   bethan Sonnet-Sequences." RES, 2 (April), 159–62.
>   Suggests that Drayton's use of Idea was the result of
>   the general influence of Platonism on love poetry and finds
>   only a "slender possibility" that he took the name from
>   Pontoux's L'Idée.

14 SHANNON, GEORGE POPE. "The Heroic Couplet in the Sixteenth
>   and Early Seventeenth Centuries, with Special Reference to
>   the Influence of Ovid and the Latin Elegiac Distich."
>   Ph.D. dissertation, Stanford University. [Abstract in
>   Stanford University Abstracts of Dissertations, 2 (1927),
>   127–34.]
>   Discusses Drayton in examining the "'classical'" coup-
>   let, 1590–1610.

15   SNEATH, GEORGE MARK. "The Influence of the English Literary
      Critics of the Sixteenth Century on English Verse from
      1590 to 1599." Ph.D. dissertation, Boston University.
         Discusses influence of earlier criticism on Drayton's
      poetry.

16   TAYLOR, HILDA [BIDDELL]. "Topographical Poetry in England
      during the Renaissance." Ph.D. dissertation, University
      of Chicago. [Abstract in University of Chicago Abstracts
      of Theses, Humanistic Ser., 5 (1929), 493-97.]
         Discusses Polyolbion in examining the influences
      (Classical, Medieval and Renaissance Latin works, and
      English pageants and masques) on and analyzing the charac-
      teristics of topographical poetry during the Renaissance.

17   TRENEER, ANNE. The Sea in English Literature from "Beowulf"
      to Donne. Liverpool: University Press of Liverpool;
      London: Hodder and Stoughton, 317 pp.
         Discusses Drayton's references to the sea, by which he
      "was not . . . much moved." Points out that he was at his
      best in his lyrics (pp. 225-30).

1927

1   AUBIN, ROBERT ARNOLD. "The Topographical Poem." Ph.D. dis-
      sertation, Harvard University. [Abstract in Harvard Uni-
      versity Summaries of Theses, 1927, pp. 143-45.]
         Examines Polyolbion as an example of a "region-poem"
      in tracing "the origin and development of the topographical
      poem." Published version 1936.2.

2   DRAYTON, MICHAEL. Michael Drayton: A Selection of Shorter
      Poems. Edited by G[eorge] D[ouglas] H[oward] Cole and
      M[argaret] I[sabel] Cole. Ormond Poets, no. 5. London:
      Noel Douglas, 61 pp.
         Print modernized selection.

3   HASSELKUSS, HERMANN KARL. Der Petrarkismus in der Sprache
      der englischen Sonettdichter der Renaissance. Ph.D. dis-
      sertation, Westfälischen Wilhelms-Universität, Münster.
      [Barmen: Montanus und Ehrenstein,] 249 pp.
         Includes Drayton's sonnets in analyzing influences on,
      stylistic traits of, and thematic concerns in Elizabethan
      sonnets. Comments briefly on parallels between the son-
      nets of Drayton and Pontoux (pp. 63-65, passim).

1927

4   JENKINS, RAYMOND. "Drayton's <u>Sirena</u> Again." <u>PMLA</u>, 42 (March),
     129-39.
          Responds to 1924.7 by arguing against Hebel's identifi-
     cation of Olcon with Jonson, the swineherds with the Tribe
     of Ben, and Sirena with Anne Goodere; also finds that
     Hebel "exaggerates the evidence of unfriendliness" between
     Drayton and Jonson. <u>See</u> 1923.7.

5   LEGOUIS, ÉMILE [HYACINTHE], and LOUIS CAZAMIAN. <u>A History of</u>
     <u>English Literature, I: The Middle Ages & the Renascence</u>
     <u>(650-1660)</u>. Translated by Helen Douglas Irvine. New York:
     Macmillan, 399 pp. [Volume I is by Legouis.]
          Translation of 1924.10; <u>see</u> pp. 190-94, passim.

6   POTTER, GEORGE REUBEN. "Milton's Early Poems, the School of
     Donne, and the Elizabethan Sonneteers." <u>PQ</u>, 6 (October),
     396-400.
          Notes parallel between <u>Idea</u> 16 and "On the Death of a
     Fair Infant" in arguing that the influence of the Eliza-
     bethan sonneteers on Milton's conceits is "considerably
     greater . . . than is usually assumed."

1928

1   GENOUY, HECTOR. <u>L'Élément pastoral dans la poésie narrative</u>
     <u>et le drame en Angleterre, de 1579 à 1640</u>. Paris: Henri
     Didier, 448 pp.
          Calls Drayton the most important pastoral poet between
     Spenser and Browne, and provides an extended analysis of
     <u>Shepherd's Garland</u>. Examines revisions in the work, struc-
     ture, and Drayton's realism, nationalism, and style.
     Groups poems into those treating love, great persons, and
     national or rustic topics. Provides detailed analysis of
     similarities to <u>Shepherd's Calendar</u> to illustrate Spenser's
     influence as well as Drayton's originality (pp. 121-59).

2   GERRARD, ERNEST A[LLEN]. <u>Elizabethan Drama and Dramatists,</u>
     <u>1583-1603</u>. Oxford: Oxford University Press, 398 pp.
          In part 1, chapter 12 ("The Revision of <u>Richard II</u>,"
     pp. 54-55), suggests that Drayton was the author of the
     "additions to the First Quarto." In part 2, chapter 10
     ("Michael Drayton," pp. 256-69), finds a "strong Protes-
     tant bias," a "characteristic worship of form," a penchant
     for end-stopped lines, and a lack of "tonal sensitiveness"
     which frequently resulted in "bastard rhymes" in Drayton's
     works. Using these characteristics, attributes to him

portions of Oldcastle; 1, 2, and 3 Henry VI; Peele's
Edward I; Marlowe's Massacre at Paris (verse portions);
and Hamlet (Drayton "assisted Shakespeare in the revision").
Also assigns him the whole of Edward II (apparently on the
basis of Meres's allusion to Drayton's "great Gaveston")
and Edward III. Concludes that "Drayton was an upright,
plodding, puritanical formalist who could be depended upon
to turn out average verse in regular installments."

3   G[OURVITCH], I. "Drayton and Polesworth." N&Q, 154 (2 June),
     388.
          Requests M. E. W.'s source for his assertion that Drayton
     was at Polesworth in 1584-1585 (1922.12). See response by
     H. Askew, 23 June, p. 447.

4   GOURVITCH, I. "Drayton's Debt to Geoffrey of Monmouth." RES,
     4 (October), 394-403.
          Finds that in Polyolbion "Drayton's indebtedness to the
     Historia was . . . twofold: both directly and indirect-
     ly . . . it provided him with a mass of material bearing
     upon the early history of his country, as well as addi-
     tional or corroborative detail for the legends with which
     he adorned his songs."

5   _____. "The Welsh Element in the Polyolbion." RES, 4
     (January), 69-77.
          Traces Drayton's sources for Songs 4-10. Provides a
     detailed analysis of his use of Llwyd's History of Cambria
     in Song 9.

*6   TURNER, JULIA CELESTE. "Anthony Mundy: A Study in the Eliza-
     bethan Profession of Letters." Ph.D. dissertation, Uni-
     versity of California, Berkeley.
          Published as 1928.7.

7   TURNER, [JULIA] CELESTE. Anthony Mundy: An Elizabethan Man
     of Letters. University of California Publications in
     English, vol. 2, no. 1. Berkeley: University of Califor-
     nia Press, 244 pp.
          In published version of 1928.6, discusses Drayton's
     collaboration with Munday on various plays (passim).

1929

1   BUSH, DOUGLAS. "Some Notes on Keats." PQ, 8 (July), 313-15.
          Questions one of the parallels between Endymion and
     Phoebe and Endymion noted by Finney (1924.4).

1929

*2 DRAYTON, MICHAEL. <u>Roundelay between Two Shepherds</u>. Haarlem.
   Juel-Jensen (1955.4) reports that only two copies are
   known, both in private collections.

3 HÄFELE, KARL. <u>Die Godivasage und ihre Behandlung in der</u>
   <u>Literatur: Mit einem Überblick über die Darstellungen</u>
   <u>der Sage in der bildenden Kunst</u>. AF, vol. 66. Heidelberg:
   Carl Winter, 326 pp. [Also submitted as Ph.D. dissertation, University of Heidelberg, 1928.]
    Discusses Drayton's depiction of Lady Godiva in <u>Polyol-</u>
   <u>bion</u> in examining literary treatments of the story (pp. 74-
   77).

4 LOWELL, AMY. <u>John Keats</u>. 2 volumes. Boston: Houghton,
   Mifflin, 649, 662 pp.
    Provides detailed analysis of Keats's indebtedness to
   <u>Endymion and Phoebe</u> and <u>Man in the Moon</u> in <u>Endymion</u>; discusses how Keats might have seen a copy of <u>Endymion and</u>
   <u>Phoebe</u>. Also comments on the influence of other Drayton
   poems on Keats (I, 320-39, passim).

5 OLIPHANT, E[RNEST] H[ENRY] C[LARK], ed. <u>Shakespeare and His</u>
   <u>Fellow Dramatists: A Selection of Plays Illustrating the</u>
   <u>Glories of the Golden Age of English Drama</u>. Vol. I. New
   York: Prentice-Hall.
    In "Notes on the Dramatists," suggests that <u>Merry Devil</u>
   <u>of Edmonton</u> "is the work of some established dramatist . . . , and there is no one who 'fills the bill'
   better than Drayton" (pp. 43-44).

6 PEARSON, LU EMILY HESS. "The Love Conventions of the English
   Sonnet: A Study of the Elizabethan Protest against Pet-
   rarchism." Ph.D. dissertation, Stanford University.
   [Abstract in <u>Stanford University Abstracts of Disserta-</u>
   <u>tions</u>, 5 (1929-1930), 50-57.]
    Notes that "[i]n Drayton, one finds a variety of moods,
   but the later sonnets reflect his disgust over man's dis-
   regard of the best instincts of his nature." Published
   version 1933.8.

7 SCOTT, JANET G[IRVAN]. <u>Les Sonnets élisabéthains: Les</u>
   <u>Sources et l'apport personnel</u>. Bibliothèque de la Revue
   de Littérature Comparée, 60. Paris: Honoré Champion,
   344 pp.
    In chapter 10 ("Michael Drayton," pp. 143-57), dis-
   cusses style, form, and themes of <u>Idea's Mirror</u> and <u>Idea</u>
   (1619). Notes that in his sonnets Drayton does not rely

directly on a single source; instead, in recalling other poems, he transforms his sources into original sonnets. Suggests that determining the direction of influence between Shakespeare and Drayton is impossible (pp. 254-56). Concludes that Idea is full of variety and written in a crisp and lively style but is frequently spoiled by Drayton's questionable or poorly developed artistic sense. In "Appendice" lists themes and analogues of sonnets in Idea (pp. 317-19).

1930

1   BENNETT, R. E. "The Parson of Wrotham in Sir John Oldcastle." MLN, 45 (March), 142-44.
     Suggests Fabyan's Chronicle as the source for the name of Sir John, Parson of Wrotham.

2   DICKSON, J. M. "William Trevell and the Whitefriars Theatre." RES, 6 (July), 309-12.
     Discusses Bill of the Trevill v. Methold suit in the Court of Requests (concerns the King's Revels syndicate, in which Drayton was a holder). See 1930.3.

3   DOWLING, MARGARET. "Further Notes on William Trevell." RES, 6 (October), 443-46.
     Corrects and supplements 1930.2, pointing out that the suit involves the complaint of one group of creditors against another. Cites other documents in the case.

4   EAGLE, RODERICK [LEWIS]. Shakespeare: New Views for Old. London: Cecil Palmer, 179 pp.
     In chapter 4 ("The 'Rival Poet,'" pp. 59-72), argues that Drayton is the Rival Poet.

*5   GOURVITCH, I. "The Life and Work of Drayton with Particular Reference to the Polyolbion and Its Sources." Ph.D. dissertation, King's College, University of London.
     See 1928.4, 1928.5, and 1930.6.

6   _____. "A Note on Drayton and Philemon Holland." MLR, 25 (July), 332-36.
     Identifies Holland's translation as the edition of Camden's Britannia that Drayton used as a source in Polyolbion; argues that Drayton had access to the translation in manuscript. See 1931.2.

1930

7   HÖHNA, HEINRICH. <u>Der Physiologus in der elisabethanischen</u>
    <u>Literatur</u>. Ph.D. dissertation, Friedrich-Alexander-
    Universität, Erlangen. Erlangen: Höfer & Limmert, 96 pp.
        Catalogues and suggests sources for selected natural
    history references in Drayton's works (pp. 32-37), passim).

8   LATHAM, MINOR WHITE. <u>The Elizabethan Fairies: The Fairies</u>
    <u>of Folklore and the Fairies of Shakespeare</u>. Columbia
    University Studies in English and Comparative Literature.
    New York: Columbia University Press, 323 pp. [Also sub-
    mitted as Ph.D. dissertation, Columbia University.]
        Discusses the fairies of <u>Nymphidia</u> and <u>Muses' Elysium</u> as
    the descendants of the fairies of <u>Midsummer Night's Dream</u>
    (pp. 202-207).

9   STEVENSON, HAZEL ALLISON. "Herbal Lore as Reflected in the
    Works of the Major Elizabethans." Ph.D. dissertation,
    University of North Carolina. [Abstract in <u>University of</u>
    <u>North Carolina Record</u>, no. 276 (1931), pp. 41-42.]
        Examines Drayton's herbal lore.

10 WHITE, HAROLD OGDEN. "Plagiarism and Imitation in English
    Literature, 1558-1625." Ph.D. dissertation, Harvard Uni-
    versity. [Abstract in <u>Harvard University Summaries of</u>
    <u>Theses, 1930</u>, pp. 218-21.]
        Discusses Drayton in examining "the attitude of English
    writers . . . toward imitation and originality." Pub-
    lished as 1935.10.

                                1931

1   ANON. "Michael Drayton." <u>TLS</u> (17 December), p. 1022.
        In review of 1931.4 points out that because of his re-
    visions and "because his poetry directly and indirectly
    reveals his own and his age's conception of what poetry is
    and of what a poet is" Drayton must be studied in a com-
    plete edition. Discusses his dedication to poetry and his
    prosody, and suggests that the pace of change in England
    will make readers more favorably disposed than ever before
    toward <u>Polyolbion</u>.

2   CONSTABLE, KATHLEEN [MARY]. "Drayton and the Holland Family."
    <u>MLR</u>, 26 (April), 174-76.
        Supports Gourvitch's argument (1930.6) that Drayton saw
    Holland's translation of <u>Britannia</u> in manuscript by dis-
    cussing Drayton's connection with Abraham Holland, Phile-
    mon's son.

*3   DRAYTON, MICHAEL.   Drayton, Campion, & Jonson: Selected
       Poems.   Edited by George Beaumont.   Kings' Treasuries of
       Literature.   London: J. M. Dent & Sons, 250 pp.
           Cited in British Museum General Catalogue of Printed
       Books to 1955:   Compact Edition, II, 682.

4   _____.   The Works of Michael Drayton.   Vol. I.   Edited by
       J[ohn] William Hebel.   Oxford: Basil Blackwell for the
       Shakespeare Head Press, 519 pp.
           Includes: Harmony of the Church (1591), Shepherd's
       Garland (1593), Idea's Mirror (1594), Endymion and Phoebe
       (1595), Gaveston (1593), Matilda (1594), Robert (1596),
       Mortimeriados (1596), Oldcastle (1600), Majesty of King
       James (1603), Paean Triumphal (1604), sonnets not printed
       in Idea's Mirror or Idea (1619), odes from Poems Lyric
       and Pastoral not reprinted in 1619, and uncollected poems.
       In "Preface" (pp. v–ix), discusses need for a complete
       edition and plan of the work.   For introductions and
       explanatory and textual notes see 1941.4.   See also
       1936.17.   Reprinted 1961.2.   Reviewed in K[athleen] M[ary]
       Constable, "A Complete Drayton," Week-End Review, 5
       (6 February 1932), 178; A. E., Library Association Record,
       3rd ser., 2 (1932), 134; Oliver Elton, RES, 8 (October
       1932), 475–77; Frank A. Patterson, JEGP, 34 (1935), 127–
       30; V[ictoria Mary] Sackville-West, "Michael Drayton,"
       Spectator, 148 (20 February 1932), 255; C[harles] J[asper]
       Sisson, MLR, 37 (July 1942), 372–76; 1931.1; 1941.2;
       1941.9.

5   LODGE, JOHN.   "Drayton's Polyolbion."   TLS (24 December),
       p. 1041.
           Argues that "the title was derived from the topographi-
       cal poem of the late Greek writer Dionysius Periegetes."
       See 1932.13.

6   THALER, ALWIN.   "Sir Thomas Browne and the Elizabethans."
       SP, 28 (January), 87–117.
           Discusses Browne's knowledge and appreciation of
       Drayton.

1932

1   AIKEN, PAULINE.   The Influence of the Latin Elegists on Eng-
       lish Lyric Poetry, 1600–1650, with Particular Reference
       to the Works of Robert Herrick.   University of Maine
       Studies, 2d ser., 22.   [Maine Bulletin, 34, no. 6.]
       Orono: University Press, 115 pp.

Notes that although Drayton "wrote in the conventions of courtly and Platonic love, rather than in the Latin erotic strain . . . some traces of elegiac influence may be found." Suggests several parallels between the poetry of Drayton and that of Latin elegists, particularly Propertius and Ovid (pp. 28–31).

2   ANON. "The Shakespeare Head Drayton." TLS (8 September), p. 621.
    In review of 1932.6 and 1932.7, comments on Drayton's revisions and discusses the place of various poems in his development as a poet.

3   BLUNDEN, EDMUND. "The Happy Island," in his Votive Tablets: Studies Chiefly Appreciative of English Authors and Books. New York: Harper and Bros., pp. 36–46.
    Reprints 1922.2.

4   BRINKLEY, ROBERTA FLORENCE. Arthurian Legend in the Seventeenth Century. Johns Hopkins Monographs in Literary History, 3. Baltimore: Johns Hopkins University Press, 240 pp.
    Discusses Arthurian material in Polyolbion and Selden's commentary; points out that Drayton favored the "British matter" and Selden the Saxon (pp. 66–72, passim).

5   BUSH, DOUGLAS. Mythology and the Renaissance Tradition in English Poetry. Minneapolis: University of Minnesota Press; London: Oxford University Press, 370 pp.
    In chapter 8 ("Drayton: Giles and Phineas Fletcher: William Browne," pp. 156–76), examines mythological elements in Endymion and Phoebe. Discusses Drayton's Platonism, comments on the similarity of the poem to Du Bartas's Uranie, and traces the influence of Marlowe, Shakespeare, and Spenser on the work. Compares Endymion and Phoebe to other mythological poems, concluding that "Drayton showed originality chiefly in abandoning half-realistic eroticism for idealistic symbolism." Comments briefly on mythological elements in Drayton's other works (pp. 156–65, passim). Revised edition 1963.1.

6   DRAYTON, MICHAEL. The Works of Michael Drayton. Vol. II. Edited by J[ohn] William Hebel. Oxford: Basil Blackwell for the Shakespeare Head Press, 600 pp.
    Reprints 1619 edition of Poems (Barons' Wars, England's Heroical Epistles, Idea, Odes, Robert, Matilda, Gaveston, Cromwell, Owl, Pastorals, and Man in the Moon). In

"Preface" (pp. v-viii), points out that "[i]t is by the
text of 1619 that Drayton evidently wished his early poems
to be finally judged." In support of his assertion that
because of the limited choices of anthologists "the merit
of the rest of the volume . . . has been unjustly obscured
by the excellence of the popular favourites," shows that
the "general assumption" that in Idea "there is a single
masterpiece [Idea 61] . . . and that the other sonnets
give no hint of the poetic qualities which produced the one
success" is erroneous. See 1941.4 for introductions and
textual and explanatory notes. Reprinted 1961.2. Reviewed
in A. E., Library Association Record, 3rd ser., 3 (1933),
63; Oliver Elton, RES, 8 (October 1932), 475-77; Frank A.
Patterson, JEGP, 34 (1935), 127-30; C[harles] J[asper]
Sisson, MLR, 37 (July 1942), 372-76; 1932.2; 1932.12;
1941.2; 1941.9.

7 _____. The Works of Michael Drayton. Vol. III. Edited by
J[ohn] William Hebel. Oxford: Basil Blackwell for the
Shakespeare Head Press, 447 pp.
    Reprints Battle of Agincourt, 1627 (Battle of Agincourt,
Margaret, Nymphidia, Quest of Cynthia, Sirena, Moon-Calf,
Elegies) and Muses' Elysium, 1630 (Muses' Elysium, Noah's
Flood, Moses, David and Goliath). In "Preface" (pp. v-vi),
points out that Drayton "was among the first to write in
the Caroline manner" and comments on his pessimism about
the current age. See 1941.4 for introduction and textual
and explanatory notes. Reprinted 1961.2. Reviewed in
A. E., Library Association Record, 3rd ser., 3 (1933), 63;
Oliver Elton, RES, 9 (October 1933), 478-79; Frank A.
Patterson, JEGP, 34 (1935), 127-30; C[harles] J[asper]
Sisson, MLR, 37 (July 1942), 372-76; 1932.2; 1941.2;
1941.9.

8 GREENLAW, EDWIN [ALMIRON]. Studies in Spenser's Historical
Allegory. [Edited by Ray Heffner.] Johns Hopkins Monographs in Literary History, 2. Baltimore: Johns Hopkins
University Press; London: Oxford University Press,
230 pp.
    In chapter 1 ("The Battle of the Books," pp. 1-58),
examines in Polyolbion Drayton's "exaltation of the Britons
as against the Saxons, . . . vindication of the legend [of
Arthur] against the attacks of Polydore and his school,
and . . . celebration of the Tudor house in the same terms
as those employed by Spenser" (pp. 30-37).

1932

9   MAIR, MARY. "Michael Drayton: His Third Centenary." <u>Poetry</u>
<u>Review</u>, 23 (February), 33-36.
Provides general appreciation, singling out <u>Nymphidia</u>
and <u>Idea</u> 61 for special praise.

10 NEWDIGATE, B[ERNARD] H[ENRY]. "Michael Drayton, 'Poett Law-
reatt.'" <u>Spectator</u>, 148 (27 February), 289.
In response to Sackville-West's query (in review; <u>see</u>
1931.4) why Drayton called himself poet laureate (in the
title to "Verses the Night before He Died"), points out
that "[t]here is no evidence that Drayton ever so described
himself," that is, he was not responsible for the "title."

11 NOYES, RUSSELL. "The Influence and Reputation of Michael
Drayton." Ph.D. dissertation, Harvard University. [Ab-
stract in <u>Harvard University Summaries of Theses, 1932</u>,
pp. 268-70.]
Provides detailed examination of critical opinion on
Drayton from the sixteenth through early twentieth centuries. Traces fluctuations in his reputation and analyzes
his influence on later writers. In part 2 offers a "collection of allusions to Drayton from 1591 to 1742." Published version 1935.4.

12 SACKVILLE-WEST V[ICTORIA MARY]. "Michael Drayton." <u>Specta-</u>
<u>tor</u>, 149 (6 August), 186-87.
In review of 1932.6 finds that the mixture of pedantry
and poetry makes it difficult, "with the best will in the
world, to read through Drayton's collected works."

13 SOUTHERN, A. C. "Drayton's <u>Polyolbion</u>." <u>TLS</u> (7 January),
p. 12.
In response to 1931.5 suggests John Leslie's <u>A Treatise</u>
<u>Concerning the Defence of the Honor of Mary Queen of Scot-</u>
<u>land</u> (1571) as the source of the Albion/Olbion pun, "which
seems to have been well enough known in Drayton's day."

14 WALLER, ROSS D. "'Dunghill': 'Peasant': 'Slave.'" <u>TLS</u>
(17 November), p. 859.
Notes parallel between <u>Gaveston</u> (11. 995-96) and <u>Ham-</u>
<u>let</u> (II.ii.534 and the variants in the first and second
quartos).

15 WATSON, H[AROLD] F[RANCIS]. "A Note on <u>Othello</u>." <u>PQ</u>, 11
(October), 400-402.
Suggests Cassio was modelled on Drayton.

1933

1   ANON. "Drayton's England." TLS (31 August), p. 573.
    In review of 1933.4 discusses relationships between the
    maps and text of Polyolbion.

2   BALL, LEWIS F[RANKLIN]. "Studies in the Structure of the
    Minor English Renaissance Epics." Ph.D. dissertation,
    Johns Hopkins University.
    Discusses "Drayton's general theory of poetry," Eng-
    land's Heroical Epistles, Mortimeriados, Barons' Wars,
    Polyolbion, Battle of Agincourt, Margaret, and various
    legends. See 1934.1, which was also published separately
    as a "Summary" of the dissertation (Baltimore: n.p., 1934).

3   CONSTABLE, KATHLEEN M[ARY]. "The Rival Poet and the Youth of
    the Sonnets." TLS (9 November), p. 774.
    In response to 1933.6 suggests identification of Minerva
    (Idea's Mirror 51) and Pandora (Shepherd's Garland, Sixth
    Eclogue) with the Countess of Pembroke; Dorus and Pamela
    (Idea's Mirror 51) with the characters from Arcadia, noting
    also that "Dorus may be one of Drayton's names for Sidney";
    Meredian (Idea's Mirror 51) with a rival poet, perhaps
    Daniel. See 1933.7.

4   DRAYTON, MICHAEL. The Works of Michael Drayton. Vol. IV.
    Edited by J[ohn] William Hebel. Oxford: Basil Blackwell
    for the Shakespeare Head Press, 621 pp.
    Reprints Polyolbion from 1622 edition. In "Preface"
    (pp. v-x), questions the legend that the poem is "little
    read although widely known by name," discusses ways the
    work "may be read," and traces its composition and publi-
    cation. See 1941.4 for introduction, textual and explana-
    tory notes, and index. Reprinted 1961.2. Reviewed in
    Oliver Elton, RES, 9 (October 1933), 478-79; Frank A. Pat-
    terson, JEGP, 34 (1935), 127-30; C[harles] J[asper] Sisson,
    MLR, 37 (July 1942), 372-76; 1933.1; 1941.2; 1941.9.

5   LAGARDE-QUOST, P. H. J. "Étude comparative de trois sonnets."
    French Quarterly, 13: 143-50.
    Compares Idea 8 with sonnets by Petrarch and Ronsard on
    a similar subject. Examines, in particular, Drayton's
    rhymes and language; suggests that some of his imagery was
    influenced by Francesco Berni.

1933

6   NEEDHAM, FRANCIS. "The Rival Poet." TLS (12 October), p. 691.
        Argues that Drayton is the Rival Poet on the basis of
    the relationship between opening stanzas of Gaveston
    (1594) and Sonnet 86. Identifies Dorus (Gaveston, 1.
    1729, and Idea's Mirror 51) as Anthony Cooke and Meredian
    (Gaveston, 1. 1736) and Meridianis (Idea's Mirror 51) as
    Anne Goodere. See 1933.3 and 1933.7.

7   NEWDIGATE, B[ERNARD] H[ENRY]. "The Rival Poet and the Youth
        of the Sonnets." TLS (9 November), p. 774.
        Notes additional relationship between Gaveston (11.
    1717-18) and Sonnet 86 in support of Needham's identi ica-
    tion of Drayton as the Rival Poet (1933.6). Also examines
    possibility that Sir Walter Aston, one of Drayton's
    patron's, is the Youth of the Sonnets, and discusses possi-
    ble interpretation of Drayton's dedicatory poem to Aston
    in Poems (1605). Suggests identifications in Idea's Mir-
    ror 51: Meridianis, John Soowthern; Dorus and Pamela, the
    characters in Arcadia. See 1933.3 and, for additions and
    corrections, B[ernard] H[enry] Newdigate, 16 November,
    p. 795; and Charles Strachey, 16 November, p. 795.

8   PEARSON, LU EMILY [HESS]. Elizabethan Love Conventions.
        Berkeley: University of California Press, 375 pp.
        In revision of 1929.6 examines "the changing moods" in
    the revisions of Idea. Suggests that Drayton was "working
    toward the principle . . . whereby the sonnet was to be
    used, not for portraying personal emotion, but for trans-
    muting personal experience into poetry." Concludes that
    Drayton "is most interesting because of his baffling
    changes of mood, and for the undercurrent of honesty which
    runs through his most rebellious sonnets" (pp. 188-201).

9   REILLY, JOSEPH J. "Foothills of Parnassus." Catholic World,
        137 (June), 281-90.
        Includes Drayton, represented by Idea 61, in survey of
    minor poets who produced one truly great poem.

10 SIBLEY, GERTRUDE MARIAN. The Lost Plays and Masques, 1500-
        1642. CSE, vol. 19. Ithaca: Cornell University Press,
        219 pp.
        Includes listings for non-extant plays in which Drayton
    was a collaborator (passim).

1934

1 BALL, LEWIS F[RANKLIN]. "The Background of the Minor English
Renaissance Epics." ELH, 1 (April), 63–89. [Also published separately (Baltimore: n.p., 1934) as a "Summary"
of 1933.2.]
    Argues that Polyolbion "should be regarded as . . .
[an epic] on the basis of classical and Renaissance theory
and practice, and that . . . [it was] actually considered
as such by the Elizabethans." Analyzes Drayton's use of
various epic conventions and concludes: "Landscape and
history conjoin to produce an epic which answered to the
spirit that in France had demanded 'un long poëme Fran-
çoys,' to the Italian belief that the epic was all-embracing,
and to the English desire for a national background no less
noble than that of Troy and Rome and to her conviction that
her present rulers incarnated the ancient tradition."

2 MEOZZI, ANTÈRO. Il Petrarchismo europeo (secolo XVI). Volume
II of his Azione e diffusione della letteratura italiana in
Europa (secolo XV–XVII). Pisa: Vallerini, 436 pp.
    Traces French and Italian influence on Idea and dis-
cusses the curious concordia discors between Platonism and
misogynic antipetrarchism in the sonnets (pp. 237–40).

3 MERTEN, MARIA. Michael Draytons "Poly-Olbion" im Rahmen der
englischen Renaissance. Ph.D. dissertation, Westfälischen
Wilhelms-Universität, Münster, 1933. Oranienburg: Imma-
culatahaus, 86 pp.
    Discusses Drayton's conception of the poet and his vo-
cation, the influence of Spenser and of Sidney's Arcadia
on Polyolbion, Drayton's sources for geography and history,
and his use of Hakluyt. Provides brief estimate of Drayton
as a poet.

1935

1 LITCHFIELD, FLORENCE LeDUC. "The Treatment of the Theme of
Mutability in the Literature of the English Renaissance:
A Study of the Problem of Change between 1558 and 1660."
Ph.D. dissertation, University of Minnesota. [Abstract in
University of Minnesota Summaries of Ph.D. Theses, 1
(1939), 164–68.]
    Draws on Drayton in a wide-ranging analysis of the theme.

1935

2   N[EWDIGATE], B[ERNARD] H[ENRY]. "The Blazons of the Shires in
        Drayton's Poly-Olbion." N&Q, 169 (30 November), 387-88.
            Requests sources for the passage in Song 23.

3   _____. "The Catalogue of Ships in Drayton's Battaile of Agin-
        court, 1627." N&Q, 169 (5 October), 242-43.
            Request sources for catalogue of ships (11. 369-464).

4   NOYES, RUSSELL. Drayton's Literary Vogue since 1631. Indiana
        University Studies, vol. 22, no. 107. Bloomington:
        Indiana University, 23 pp.
            In revision of 1932.11 traces fluctuations in Drayton's
        critical and popular reputation from 1631 to c. 1850.
        Examines popularity and influence (especially on nineteenth-
        century writers) of several works (particularly England's
        Heroical Epistles, Polyolbion, and "Ballad of Agincourt").

5   SHARPE, ROBERT BOIES. The Real War of the Theaters: Shake-
        speare's Fellows in Rivalry with the Admiral's Men, 1594-
        1603: Repertories, Devices, and Types. Modern Language
        Association of America Monograph Series, 5. New York:
        Modern Language Association of America, 286 pp.
            Discusses place of Oldcastle in the rivalry and examines
        the contemporary significance and topography of the play
        (pp. 144-47, passim).

6   T., K. "Shakespeare and Agincourt: Drayton's 'Dauphin.'"
        N&Q, 169 (9 November), 336-37.
            In response to H. W. Crundell ("Shakespeare and Agin-
        court," 26 October, p. 295), explains that "Drayton's
        'confusion' of Sir Guiscard Dauphin and the Dauphin of
        Auvergne in his 'Battaile of Agincourt' . . . is due to
        his use of Speed's 'Historie.'"

7   TILLOTSON, KATHLEEN [MARY]. "Spenser's 'Aetion.'" TLS (7
        February), p. 76.
            Responds to Arthur Gray's identification (24 January,
        p. 48) of Aetion (Colin Clout) with Marlowe by reviewing
        evidence for identifying Drayton with Aetion.

8   WALLERSTEIN, RUTH [COONS]. "The Development of the Rhetoric
        and Metre of the Heroic Couplet, Especially in 1625-1645."
        PMLA, 50 (March), 166-209.
            Provides detailed analysis of meter and rhetoric in
        couplets of England's Heroical Epistles (Rosamond to Henry
        II and Isabel to Mortimer).

9   WEITZMANN, FRANCIS WHITE. "Notes on the Elizabethan Elegie."
     PMLA, 50 (June), 435-43.
          Draws frequently on Drayton's Elegies in examining "the
     variety of meanings . . . attached to" elegy by Elizabethan
     authors.

10   WHITE, HAROLD OGDEN. Plagiarism and Imitation during the
     English Renaissance: A Study in Critical Distinctions.
     Harvard Studies in English, 12. Cambridge: Harvard Uni-
     versity Press, 221 pp.
          In revision of 1930.10 discusses Drayton's comments on
     correct and incorrect imitation in his works (pp. 148-50).

                              1936

1   ATKINS, SIDNEY H. "Who was 'Labeo?'" TLS (4 July), p. 564.
          Argues for identification of Drayton with Hall's Labeo
     (Virgidemiae, book 6). See J. Denham Parsons, 11 July,
     p. 580; A. G. H. Dent, 18 July, p. 600; Sidney H. Atkins,
     25 July, p. 616.

2   AUBIN, ROBERT ARNOLD. Topographical Poetry in XVIII-Century
     England. Modern Language Association of America Revolving
     Fund Series, 6. New York: Modern Language Association of
     America, 431 pp.
          In revision of 1927.1 characterizes Polyolbion as "a
     museum of topics proper to topographical poetry of all
     ages and especially of those wearisome features of nature
     poetry that resulted from an aping of the classics: per-
     sonification, excessive reference to pagan divinities,
     otiose epithets, generic nouns, Homeric similes, and the
     Nature-and-Art logomachy." Throughout the work, offers
     comparisons with Polyolbion and comments on its influence
     on eighteenth- and nineteenth-century topographical poems
     (passim).

3   BENSLY, EDWARD, and L. R. M. STRACHAN. "Sources Wanted."
     N&Q, 170 (13 June), 429-30.
          Supply sources in Ovid for passages in Shepherd's Gar-
     land (in response to query by N., 30 May, p. 390).

4   BONTOUX, GERMAINE. La Chanson en Angleterre au temps
     d'Élisabeth. Oxford: Oxford University Press, 717 pp.
          Comments briefly on the "musicalité du talent poétique"
     of Drayton and provides short critical appraisals of his
     songs "Near to the Silver Trent" (Sirena) and "Upon a Bank

                              221

1936

with Roses Set about" (<u>Pastorals</u>, Second Eclogue). Transcribes John Ward's setting of the latter (pp. 253-58).

5   BOYD, EVA PHILLIPS. "Trailing Michael Drayton: A Summer Idyl
for Dryasdusts." <u>SR</u>, 44 (July), 303-19.
     Provides appreciative essay on Drayton's life and works
occasioned by a visit to places associated with the poet.

6   CASTELLI, ALBERTO. <u>"La Gerusalemme liberata" nella Inghilterra di Spenser</u>. Pubblicazioni della Università Cattolica
del Sacro Cuore, vol. 20. Milan: Vita e Pensiero, 142 pp.
     Traces influence of Tasso's poem on Drayton's works,
especially <u>Robert</u> (pp. 48-53).

7   COLERIDGE, SAMUEL TAYLOR. <u>Coleridge's Miscellaneous Criti-
cism</u>. Edited by Thomas Middleton Raysor. Cambridge:
Harvard University Press, 484 pp.
     Gathers Coleridge's appreciative comments (some from
marginalia) on Drayton (passim).

8   CURRIER, FRANCIS MORTON. "Native and Foreign Influences in
the Works of Hofmanswaldau." Ph.D. dissertation, Harvard
University. [Abstract in <u>Harvard University Summaries of
Theses, 1936</u>, pp. 365-68.]
     Examines influence of <u>England's Heroical Epistles</u> on
Hofmannswaldau's <u>Heldenbriefe</u>.

9   DUNN, ESTHER CLOUDMAN. <u>The Literature of Shakespeare's Eng-
land</u>. New York: Charles Scribner's Sons, 336 pp.
     Traces evolution "from convention to stark realism" in
revisions of <u>Idea</u> and finds that "<u>Polyolbion</u> is a griev-
ously neglected book" (pp. 90-92, 95-96).

10 FARNHAM, WILLARD. <u>The Medieval Heritage of Elizabethan Trag-
edy</u>. Berkeley: University of California Press, 501 pp.
     In chapter 8 ("The Progeny of the <u>Mirror</u>," pp. 304-39),
discusses place of <u>Matilda</u>, <u>Gaveston</u>, and <u>Robert</u> in the
tradition of the tragical complaint. Characterizes <u>Matilda</u>
"as out-and-out sentimental melodrama" and the two others
as "more than ordinarily competent pieces of poetry"
(pp. 322-24, 327-29).

11 FINNEY, CLAUDE LEE. <u>The Evolution of Keats's Poetry</u>. 2 volumes. Cambridge: Harvard University Press, 824 pp.
     Analyzes Keats's indebtedness to <u>Endymion and Phoebe</u>
and <u>Man in the Moon</u> in <u>Endymion</u>; also discusses influence
of other Drayton works on Keats (pp. 247-55, passim).

12 GLEISSNER, FRIEDRICH. "Die Eklogendichtung von Barclay bis
    Pope in ihrer Abhängigkeit von greichischen, lateinischen,
    und heimischen Vorbildern." Ph.D. dissertation, Univer-
    sity of Vienna, 138 pp.
       In an eclogue-by-eclogue analysis of Shepherd's Garland,
    discusses motifs, prosody, influence, and, in particular,
    sources (especially Barnabe Googe and Spenser) (pp. 32-52).

13 GOTTLIEB, HANS JORDAN. "Robert Burton's Knowledge of English
    Poetry." Ph.D. dissertation, New York University. [Pub-
    lished abridgment: New York: Graduate School of New York
    University, 1937, 22 pp.]
       Discusses Burton's sources for and uses of seven quota-
    tions from Drayton's works in Anatomy of Melancholy.
    Points out that England's Heroical Epistles (the source
    for five passages) afforded "vivid illustrations of the
    effects of heroical love upon the hearts and minds of
    notable personages in English history."

14 HASKELL, GLENN PERCIVAL. "Drayton's Secondary Modes: A
    Critical Study." Ph.D. dissertation, University of Illi-
    nois. [Published abstract: Urbana: n.p., 1936, 9 pp.]
       Provides critical analysis of Drayton's "religious
    verse, . . . legends in the Mirror manner, . . . satires,
    and . . . Elegies." Finds that "[i]n these, his selection
    of subject and form and his manner of treatment show him
    to be the experimenter who is trying to raise the standards
    of English poetry by following established models and by
    handling his themes in an elevated and learned manner."
    Concludes that the works "were a deliberate experiment in
    the practical application of Drayton's critical theories,
    and that these theories . . . had a tendency to lead him
    to uncongenial modes, like the scriptural paraphrase and
    the legend, or to urge him into misdirected efforts to
    elevate his tone out of all proportion to the mode or the
    theme, as in the satires and elegies."

15 MEYER, CATHARINE. "Elizabethan Gentlemen and the Publishing
    Trade: A Study in Literary Conventions." Ph.D. disser-
    tation, Radcliffe College. [Abstract in Radcliffe College
    Summaries of Theses, 1935-1938, pp. 72-76.]
       Discusses Drayton, particularly as he "looked back
    [during the reign of James I] to the golden age of poetry
    in Elizabeth's day."

1936

16　SHORT, RAYMOND W. "The Patronage of Poetry under James First."
　　Ph.D. dissertation, Cornell University. [Separately pub-
　　lished abstract: Ithaca: n.p., 1936, 6 pp.]
　　　Draws frequently on Drayton's works, particularly his
　　"dedications and complimentary poems," in examining
　　patronage from Elizabeth I through Charles I.

17　TILLOTSON, KATHLEEN [MARY]. "Another Collier Forgery." <u>TLS</u>
　　(11 July), p. 576.
　　　Argues that the signature of the Earl of Essex and
　　manuscript notes in the British Library copy of <u>Shepherd's
　　Garland</u> were written by Collier. Notes that two of Col-
　　lier's fabrications were introduced into the text in
　　1931.4. Also discusses variant states and manuscript cor-
　　rections--which might have been done in the printing-
　　house--in other copies.

18　WATKINS, W[ALTER] B[ARKER] C[RITZ]. <u>Johnson and English
　　Poetry before 1660</u>. Princeton Studies in English, 13.
　　Princeton: Princeton University Press, 129 pp.
　　　Discusses Johnson's knowledge of and fondness for
　　Drayton's works. In "Appendix" (pp. 85-110), identifies
　　sources for Drayton quotations in the <u>Dictionary</u> (passim).

1937

1　ALLEN, DON CAMERON. "The Relation of Drayton's <u>Noah's Flood</u>
　　to the Ordinary Learning of the Early Seventeenth Century."
　　<u>MLN</u>, 52 (February), 106-11.
　　　Traces analogues to Drayton's "embellishments" of the
　　"Vulgate account of the deluge" "not for the purpose of
　　indicating ultimate sources, but with the intention of
　　showing that this material was probably . . . 'middle
　　class learning.'" Suggests that "[t]o the modern reader
　　of this poem these deviations from the Biblical account
　　seem very erudite, but to the reader of Drayton's age
　　they were probably not only well known details but ex-
　　pected ones." <u>See</u> 1938.5.

2　HOLMES, URBAN T[IGNER]. "Chaucer's Tydif: 'A Small Bird.'"
　　<u>PQ</u>, 16 (January), 65-67.
　　　Identifies Drayton's "tydie" (<u>Polyolbion</u>, Song 13, 1.
　　79) as the same bird as Chaucer's "tydif," "a bird of
　　prey" connected "with the <u>tyto</u> . . . or <u>noctua</u> of the
　　ancient world." <u>See</u> 1938.7.

*3   KELLEY, TRACY R. "Studies in the Development of the Prosody
       of the Elizabethan Sonnet." Ph.D. dissertation, University
       of California, Berkeley, 86 pp.

*4   KUTEK, MARGARETHE. "Ovids Heroides und die englischen
       Heroidenbriefe von der Renaissance bis Pope." Ph.D. dis-
       sertation, University of Vienna.
            Cited in Gernot U. Gabel and Gisela R. Gabel, Disserta-
       tions in English and American Literature: Theses Accepted
       by Austrian, French, and Swiss Universities, 1875-1970
       (Hamburg: Gernot Gabel, 1977), p. 21, item 257.

5   LOANE, GEORGE G. "A Poetical Picnic." TLS (4 December),
       p. 928.
            Supplements 1937.11 by pointing out that Charles Lamb
       identified St. Dunstan's Well, the location "of a 'poeti-
       cal picnic' taken by" Wither, Browne, Drayton, et al.
       (Browne, A Shepherd's Pipe, Second Eclogue), as the Devil
       Tavern by St. Dunstan's. See 1937.6.

6   NEWDIGATE, B[ERNARD] H[ENRY]. "The Devil and Saint Dunstan's."
       TLS (11 December), p. 947.
            Supplements 1937.5 by noting Drayton's reference to
       "the Club in the Apollo Room" in "Sacrifice to Apollo";
       also finds "that Drayton's Ode inspired some of the 'Leges
       Convivales.'"

7   N[EWDIGATE], B[ERNARD] H[ENRY]. "The Knot and King Canute."
       N&Q, 173 (27 November), 389.
            Requests identification of Drayton's source for Polyol-
       bion, Song 25, 11. 341-44.

8   NEWDIGATE, B[ERNARD] H[ENRY]. "Michael Drayton and His Idea."
       Dublin Review, 200: 79-92.
            Traces Drayton's love for and devotion to Anne Goodere
       throughout his poems, especially Idea's Mirror, Idea, and
       Shepherd's Garland.

9   [TILLOTSON, GEOFFREY]. "Elizabethan Decoration: Patterns
       in Art and Passion." TLS (3 July), p. 485.
            Uses passage from Endymion and Phoebe (11. 35-54) to
       illustrate how Elizabethans saw "external nature in terms
       of art." Reprinted 1942.4.

10   TILLOTSON, KATHLEEN [MARY]. "Drayton and Chettle." TLS
       (14 August), p. 592.
            Points out unrecorded allusion to Drayton's Majesty of
       King James in John Fenton's King James His Welcome to
       London, 1603.

1937

11 _____. "Drayton, Browne, and Wither." TLS (27 November),
p. 911.
    Points out allusions to Browne and Wither in Sirena
(11. 348-83) and identifies Olcon with James I. See
1937.5.

12 _____. "The Language of Drayton's Shepheards Garland." RES,
13 (July), 272-81.
    Examines the influence of Spenser (and, to a lesser
extent, Chaucer) on Drayton's linguistic experiments in
Shepherd's Garland. Discusses his use of "archaic inflex-
ions and forms," dialect, and "'Spenserian' elements."
Comments briefly on his revision of the work.

*13 WASSERMAN, EARL R[EEVES]. "The Elizabethan Revival: Its
Background and Beginning." Ph.D. dissertation, Johns
Hopkins University.
    Published version 1947.6.

14 WILLIAMS, FRANKLIN B[URLEIGH], JR. "A Sonnet by Drayton?"
TLS, (11 December), p. 947.
    Suggests that "Of the Author," a commendatory sonnet in
John Weever's Faunus and Melliflora, is by Drayton.

1938

1 ALLEN, DON CAMERON. "Drayton's Lapidaries." MLN, 53
(February), 93-95.
    Identifies Drayton's sources among medieval lapidaries
(especially Boodt's Gemmarum et Lapidum Historia) for the
list of stones in Muses' Elysium, Ninth Nymphal, "the most
extended section on the influence of jewels in Elizabethan
literature."

2 BRAY, DENYS [DE SAUMAREZ]. Shakespeare's Sonnet-Sequence.
London: Martin Secker, 258 pp.
    In chapter 3 ("The Art-Form of the Elizabethan Sequence,"
pp. 42-72), analyzes Drayton's use of "rhyme-echo" in Idea.
(The chapter is a revision of "The Art Form of the Elizabethan Sonnet Sequence and Shakespeare's Sonnets" [Shake-
speare-Jahrbuch, 63 (1927), 159-82], which includes only
a brief mention of Drayton.) See 1950.2.

3 HIBERNICUS. "British Precious Stones." N&Q, 174 (9 April),
265.
    Identifies precious stones in Polyolbion (Song 4) in
response to query by B[ernard] H[enry] N[ewdigate], 19
March, pp. 205-206.

4   JOHN, LISLE CECIL. The Elizabethan Sonnet Sequences: Studies
     in Conventional Conceits. Columbia University Studies in
     English and Comparative Literature, no. 133. New York:
     Columbia University Press, 288 pp. [Also submitted as
     Ph.D. dissertation, Columbia University.]
         Draws frequently on Idea's Mirror and Idea in analyzing
     conventional conceits and themes in Elizabethan sonnet
     sequences. Concludes that Drayton's "sonnets often come
     off badly when placed side by side with those of his fel-
     low craftsmen, for his quest for originality led him to
     unjustifiable hyperbole" (passim).

5   TILLOTSON, KATHLEEN [MARY]. "Drayton's Noah's Flood." MLN,
     53 (April), 277.
         Adds to Allen's list of analogues and sources (1937.1).

6   _____. "The Source of An Excellent New Ballad, Shewing the
     Petigree of . . . King Iames." RES, 14 (April), 173-75.
         Identifies Majesty of King James as the anonymous
     writer's source for Revised STC 14423.

7   WILSON F[RANK] P[ERCY]. "The Tidy." PQ, 17 (April), 216-18.
         Argues against Holmes's identification of Drayton's
     "tydie" as the brown owl (1937.2) but does not offer an
     alternative.

                              1939

1   CRUNDELL, H. W. "Drayton and Edward III." N&Q, 176 (15
     April), 258-60.
         Points out parallels between Drayton's works and the
     play in arguing that Edward III was "an early work of
     Drayton's." Also finds his hand in Edward IV and Warning
     for Fair Women. See 1939.9 and Crundell, 20 May, pp. 356-
     57.

2   EAGLES [i.e., EAGLE], R[ODERICK] L[EWIS]. "The Date and
     Authorship of the MS. Play 'Sir Thomas More.'" N&Q, 177
     (29 July), 78.
         Suggests Drayton as one of the authors (hand D). See
     H. W. Crundell, 12 August, pp. 120-21, who finds the
     identification unconvincing.

3   GREG, W[ALTER] W[ILSON]. A Bibliography of the English
     Printed Drama to the Restoration. Vol. I. London:
     Oxford University Press for The Bibliographical Society,
     529 pp., 63 plates.

1939

Provides bibliographical description of the early editions of Oldcastle (pp. 271-72).

4   OSENBURG, FREDERIC CHARLES. "The Ideas of the Golden Age and the Decay of the World in the English Renaissance." Ph.D. dissertation, University of Illinois. [Published abstract: Urbana: n.p., 1939, 17 pp.]
         Discusses Drayton's depiction of the Golden Age (he stressed simplicity) and of the decay of the world.

5   ST. CLAIR, F[OSTER] Y[ORK]. "Drayton's First Revision of His Sonnets." SP, 36 (January), 40-59.
         Provides detailed analysis of Drayton's revisions in 1599 Idea--the "marked tendency to view the world through the eyes of a dramatist rather than through those of a lyric poet"; corrections of "many of the worst cases of obscurity, faulty syntax, and roughness in metre"; omission of many sonnets "containing badly overworked Petrarchan conceits"; change in "attitude towards love"; prevalence of satire--to show him modifying the Petrarchan mode of Idea's Mirror. Discusses the influence of Sidney, Donne, and (possibly) Shakespeare on the revisions.

6   SHORT, R[AYMOND] W. "Jonson's Sanguine Rival." RES, 15 (July), 315-17.
         Argues that Drayton is the rival mentioned in Forest, Epistle 12. See 1939.8.

7   SIMPSON, PERCY. "Ben Jonson and the Devil Tavern." MLR, 34 (July), 367-73.
         Comments on the relationship of "Sacrifice to Apollo" to Jonson's Leges Convivales.

8   _____. "'Jonson's Sanguine Rival.'" RES, 15 (October), 464-65.
         In reply to 1939.6 argues that Daniel rather than Drayton is the rival mentioned in Forest, Epistle 12.

9   TILLOTSON, KATHLEEN [MARY]. "Drayton and Edward III." N&Q, 176 (6 May), 318-19.
         In reply to 1939.1 argues against Drayton's authorship; explains the parallels cited by Crundell as the result of Drayton knowing the play. See Crundell's reply, 20 May, pp. 356-57.

10   _____. "Drayton and Richard II: 1597-1600." RES, 15 (April), 172-79.

Examines changes in 1600 version of Richard II-Queen
Isabel epistles (England's Heroical Epistles) to suggest
that Drayton revised the poems because of Queen Elizabeth's
"touchiness . . . on the subject of Richard II and the
consequent troubles of Sir John Hayward in 1599-1600 over
his" Henry IV.

11   _____. "Michael Drayton as 'Historian' in the Legend of
      Cromwell." MLR, 34 (April), 186-200.
          In "attempt[ing] to define Drayton's attitude and
      purpose in his poem," examines his use of sources, the
      originality of "his historical perspective and general
      commentary," his bias, his "general pity for vicissitudo
      rerum and the ruins of time," and the inconsistency of his
      views. Notes, in particular, how Cromwell "expresses an
      attitude to the reign of Henry VIII for which in 1607 there
      was little precedent, an attitude which marks a turning
      away from the lines laid down (and followed by later writ-
      ers) in Hall's Chronicle."

12   WATSON, SARA RUTH. "'Moly' in Drayton and Milton." N&Q, 176
      (8 April), 244.
          Suggests that Milton was indebted to Drayton's refer-
      ences to Moly in Endymion and Phoebe and Muses' Elysium,
      Fifth Nymphal.

13   WINTERS, YVOR. "The 16th Century Lyric in England: A Criti-
      cal and Historical Reinterpretation." Poetry, 53 (Febru-
      ary), 258-72; (March), 320-35; 54 (April), 35-51.
          In a major revaluation of the sixteenth-century lyric,
      discusses how Drayton's sonnets exhibit "the Petrarchist
      tendency in conflict with the earlier tendency," a "forth-
      rightness" as represented by Gascoigne. In comparing
      Drayton with Sidney, finds that "Drayton has greater
      toughness and directness . . . [but] less subtlety of
      perception and of subject than has Sidney at his best and
      is a less considerable poet." Revised 1967.17; reprinted
      1967.18.

                              1940

1   [JACKSON, WILLIAM ALEXANDER, ed.]. The Carl H. Pforzheimer
      Library: English Literature, 1475-1700. Vol. I. New
      York: privately printed, 419 pp.
          Includes bibliographical description of several edi-
      tions of Drayton's works: STC 7189, 7190, 7195, 7204,
      7210, 7213 ("three entirely distinct settings"), 7222,
      7228, and 7230 (pp. 290-304).

Michael Drayton

2   JONAS, LEAH. The Divine Science: The Aesthetic of Some
     Representative Seventeenth-Century English Poets. Colum-
     bia University Studies in English and Comparative Litera-
     ture, 151. New York: Columbia University Press, 304 pp.
     [Also submitted as Ph.D. dissertation, Columbia Univer-
     sity.]
         In chapter 3 ("Michael Drayton," pp. 47-79), studies
     Drayton's theory of poetry as it is revealed in his works.
     Analyzes the relationship of his endeavors in various
     poetic types (especially the historical poem) to his
     theory of poetry and his evolution as a poet. Examines
     Polyolbion, "his great commemorative masterpiece" and "the
     categorical imperative of his poetic career," as a Renais-
     sance epic. Concludes: "The true function of the English
     poet, as he conceived it, was to preserve the record of
     national greatness past and thereby stimulate greatness in
     the present and the future. He proposed to make virtue
     lovely by awarding to slighted merit the compensation of
     eternal fame, and he hoped to make his country glorious by
     immortalizing her history and even her geography. Although
     he delighted in minor verse and wrote it successfully,
     poetry was to Drayton not a toy nor a mere personal endow-
     ment, but at its highest a great instrument for social and
     national education" (passim).

3   SHARP, ROBERT LATHROP. From Donne to Dryden: The Revolt
     against Metaphysical Poetry. Chapel Hill: University of
     North Carolina Press, 235 pp.
         In chapter 4 ("The Protest of the Poets," pp. 93-120,
     discusses Drayton's relationship to and attitude toward
     metaphysical verse (pp. 94-98).

4   SHORT, R[AYMOND] W. "Ben Jonson in Drayton's Poems." RES,
     16 (April), 149-58.
         In identifying Selena with the Countess of Bedford and
     Cerberon with Jonson, discusses the Countess's patronage
     of Drayton (suggesting possible reasons for his loss of
     it) and argues "that Drayton's relationship with Jonson
     generally has been misunderstood: they were not friends
     but enemies." See 1940.5 and 1940.7.

5   SIMPSON, PERCY. "'Ben Jonson in Drayton's Poems,' I." RES,
     16 (July), 303-305.
         In reply to 1940.4 offers several corrections; finds
     that Short's conjectures are guesswork and a travesty of
     literary history. See 1940.7.

6 TILLOTSON, GEOFFREY. "Contemporary Praise of Polyolbion."
   RES, 16 (April), 181-83.
   Transcribes manuscript poem by John Bladen (in St.
   John's College, Cambridge, copy of 1622 Polyolbion),
   praising the poem.

7 TILLOTSON, KATHLEEN [MARY]. "'Ben Jonson in Drayton's Poems,'
   II." RES, 16 (July), 305-306.
   Offers several corrections to 1940.4 and argues that
   Cerberon is not necessarily a poet. See 1940.5.

8 _____. "Drayton and the Gooderes." MLR, 35 (July), 341-49.
   Discusses Drayton's deposition "in the Chancery suit
   of Engelbert v. Saunders" and other records which show
   "that in the winter of 1584/85, and probably for some
   time before, he was acting as servant to Sir Henry Goodere's brother, Thomas Goodere of South Collingham, Notts."
   Transcribes the deposition.

9 TILLOTSON, K[ATHLEEN MARY]. "An Untraced Drayton Quotation
   in Englands Parnassus." N&Q, 178 (27 April), 298.
   Identifies quotation 169, the only one from Drayton
   that Charles Crawford (Englands Parnassus [Oxford:
   Clarendon Press, 1913]) was unable to track down, as a
   passage from Gaveston.

10 TILLOTSON, KATHLEEN [MARY]. "William Sampson's Vow-Breaker
   (1636) and the Lost Henslowe Play Black Batman of the
   North." MLR, 35 (July), 377-78.
   Suggests that Sampson was indebted to Black Batman of
   the North, partly written by Drayton, and discusses
   possibility that Sampson knew Drayton.

11 WASSERMAN, EARL R[EEVES]. "Elizabethan Poetry 'Improved.'"
   MP, 37 (May), 357-69.
   Comments briefly on Oldmixon's handling of Drayton's
   verse in 1703.1.

*12 ZOCCA, LOUIS RALPH. "Sixteenth Century Narrative Poetry in
   England." Ph.D. dissertation, Brown University, 141 pp.
   Published verison 1950.9.

1941

1 ANON. "An Englishman's Home." <u>TLS</u> (4 October), p. 495.
Suggests "reasons . . . why 'Poly-Olbion' should win
large numbers of new admirers in a Great Britain that is
fighting for its life for the second time in less than
thirty years."

2 ANON. "Michael Drayton's Victory: 'The Delight of Blessed
Soules': Poet of England's Past Greatness." <u>TLS</u> (4 October), pp. 494, 497.
In review of 1931.4, 1932.6, 1932.7, 1933.4, 1941.4, and
1941.8, offers an appreciative overview of Drayton's life
and works.

3 BATESON, F[REDERICK] W[ILSE], ed. <u>The Cambridge Bibliography
of English Literature, I: 600-1660</u>. Cambridge: Cambridge
University Press, 952 pp.
Provides selective list of works by and about Drayton.
H. J. Byrom contributed the section on Drayton (pp. 423-
25, passim). Revised 1974.16.

4 DRAYTON, MICHAEL. <u>The Works of Michael Drayton</u>. Vol. V.
Edited by J[ohn] William Hebel, Kathleen [Mary] Tillotson,
and Bernard H[enry] Newdigate. Oxford: Basil Blackwell
for the Shakespeare Head Press, 348 pp.
Includes: Hoyt H[opewell] Hudson, "In Memoriam
J. W. H."; Newdigate, "The Printer to the Reader" (history
of the edition); Tillotson, "Introduction"; "A Chronology
of Michael Drayton's Life and Writings"; critical introduction and explanatory and textual notes for each work;
"Index to <u>Poly-Olbion</u>"; Geoffrey Tillotson, "Bibliography";
glossary; "Finding List for Drayton's Sonnets"; and "Index
to the Introductions and Notes." (After Hebel's death,
Tillotson and Newdigate edited the volume.) Portions revised 1961.2. Reviewed in Oliver Elton, <u>RES</u>, 18 (January
1942), 111-15; C[harles] J[asper] Sisson, <u>MLR</u>, 37 (July
1942), 372-76; 1941.2; 1941.9.

*5 HUNT, JAMES CLAY. "The Beginnings of the Neo-Classic Movement
in Elizabethan Poetry." Ph.D. dissertation, Johns Hopkins
University, 438 pp.
<u>See</u> 1941.6.

6 HUNT, [JAMES] CLAY. "The Elizabethan Background of Neo-
Classic Polite Verse." <u>ELH</u>, 8 (December), 273-304.
Discusses Drayton's <u>Odes</u>, dedicatory poems, and <u>Elegies</u>
in a survey of Renaissance "familiar verse," observing

that some of his verse "is informal and conversational in style and has the social quality of much neo-classic poetry." Finds that "To Henry Reynolds" "is as near to the polite verse of the neo-classicists as anything the Renaissance produced." In surveying Renaissance poetry "which clearly anticipates the kind of light verse [vers de société] the neo-classicists wrote," discusses Idea, Nymphidia, and Odes: of the latter two, notes that "[i]n their light-hearted mood these poems . . . suggest particularly such neo-classic light verse as that of Gay."

7   NEWDIGATE, B[ERNARD] H[ENRY]. "Cotswold Sheep in Poly-Olbion." N&Q, 181 (13 September), 142.
     Provides information on present-day existence of the kind of sheep Drayton described in Song 14.

8   NEWDIGATE, BERNARD H[ENRY]. Michael Drayton and His Circle. Oxford: Shakespeare Head Press, 255 pp.
     In a biography designed to supplement 1941.4, which originally was to have included a life, discusses: ancestors; education; relationship with patrons (especially the Goodere family, Countess of Bedford, and Walter Aston); circle of literary acquaintances (particularly Jonson, Shakespeare, and Drummond of Hawthornden); composition, sources, and publication of Polyolbion; and career as a playwright. Suggests reasons for the estrangement between Drayton and the Countess of Bedford, examines causes for his loss of favor at the court of James I, and "trace[s] the course of . . . [his] life-long devotion to Anne Goodere." "[Q]uestion[s] whether there was really such close friendship between . . . [Shakespeare and Drayton, and Drayton and Jonson] as is generally assumed" and considers arguments for Drayton as the Rival Poet. Reprinted 1961.8. Reviewed in Oliver Elton, RES, 18 (January 1942), 111–15; David Mathew, "Poly-Olbion," Spectator, 167 (17 October 1941), 386; C[harles] J[asper] Sisson, MLR, 37 (July 1942), 372–76; 1941.2, 1941.9.

9   ROWSE, A[LFRED] L[ESLIE]. "A Topographical Elizabethan." New Statesman and Nation (8 November), p. 412.
     In review of 1931.4, 1932.6, 1932.7, 1933.4, 1941.4, and 1941.8, stresses how "readable" Drayton is and points out that "the discerning reader will discover a discreet and rewarding pleasure in the poetry of Drayton, a note cool and silvery, and for the most part calm and detached." Argues that Drayton is not the Rival Poet.

1941

10 TANNENBAUM, SAMUEL A[ARON]. Michael Drayton (A Concise Bib-
     liography). Elizabethan Bibliographies, no. 22. New York:
     Samuel A. Tannenbaum, 64 pp.
         Provides classified list of works by and about Drayton
     (983 entries). In "Foreword" (pp. vii-viii), gives a brief
     overview of his work and reputation. Continued 1967.7;
     reprinted 1967.15.

11 YATES, FRANCES A[MELIA]. "The Emblematic Conceit in Giordano
     Bruno's De gli eroici furori and in the Elizabethan Sonnet
     Sequences." JWCI, 6: 101-21.
         Analyzes some of the "emblem-conceits" in Idea's Mirror
     to suggest that Eroici furori "provide[s] a clue to Dray-
     ton's anti-Petrarchist Petrarchism" in the sequence and
     that Idea's Mirror is possibly "a translation of the
     Canticle into Petrarchan emblems."

                              1942

1   ABRAMS, WILLIAM AMOS. "Introduction," in his edition of "The
     Merry Devil of Edmonton," 1608. Durham: Duke University
     Press, pp. 3-103.
         Argues that Drayton is not the author (pp. 69-70,
     passim).

2   CRUNDELL, H. W. "Love's Labour's Lost: A New Shakespeare
     Allusion." N&Q, 183 (18 July), 45-46.
         Points out Drayton's debt to the play in England's
     Heroical Epistles (Shore to Edward IV, 11. 35-37, 41-44).

3   DAVENPORT, A. "The Seed of a Shakespeare Sonnet?" N&Q, 182
     (2 May), 242-44.
         Examines similarities between passage in Shepherd's
     Garland, Second Eclogue, and Sonnet 2; discusses possible
     relationships between the two poems.

4   TILLOTSON, GEOFFREY. "Elizabethan Decoration," in his Essays
     in Criticism and Research. Cambridge: Cambridge Univer-
     sity Press, pp. 5-16.
         Reprints 1937.9.

5   WATSON, SARA RUTH. "Milton's Ideal Day: Its Development as
     a Pastoral Theme." PMLA, 57 (June), 404-20.
         Discusses Drayton's combination of "the 'come-live-with-
     me' theme" and the description of the ideal day in Shep-
     herd's Garland, Seventh Eclogue, and Muses' Elysium, and
     comments on his use of the former theme in Quest of Cynthia.

1943

1 ADKINS, MARY GRACE MUSE. "Sixteenth-Century Religious and
   Political Implications in <u>Sir John Oldcastle</u>." <u>University</u>
   <u>of Texas Studies in English</u>, 22: 86-104.
      Examines why the authors gave Oldcastle "the political
   complexion demanded of loyal subjects of Elizabeth,
   and . . . [interpreted] his Lollard beliefs largely in
   terms of sixteenth-century Puritanism." Suggests that
   the emphasis on Oldcastle's loyalty to the sovereign is
   due to the "recognition of . . . [the] struggle for head-
   ship" of the church between Elizabeth and the Puritans.
   Discusses inconsistencies in the treatment of Puritanism,
   attributing them to multiple authorship.

2 BROOKS, ALDEN. <u>Will Shakspere and the Dyer's Hand</u>. New
   York: Charles Scribner's Sons, 724 pp.
      Interprets references to "Shakespeare" in "To Henry
   Reynolds" in light of his identification of Sir Edward
   Dyer as the author of Shakespeare's plays (pp. 398-401,
   passim).

3 HARRISON, THOMAS P[ERRIN], JR. "Drayton's Herbals." <u>Univer-</u>
   <u>sity of Texas Studies in English</u>, 22: 15-25.
      Traces Drayton's sources for his references to herbs in
   <u>Muses' Elysium</u> and <u>Polyolbion</u>. Notes that the comparison
   with sources "illustrate[s] Drayton's awkward task of
   turning into verse the practical descriptions of the herb-
   alists."

4 LE COMTE, EDWARD S[EMPLE]. "Milton: Two Verbal Parallels."
   <u>N&Q</u>, 184 (2 January), 17-18.
      Points out parallel between <u>Barons' Wars</u> (II, 451) and
   <u>Paradise Lost</u> (I, 302); also comments on Drayton's use of
   "finny" in <u>Polyolbion</u> (Song 2, 1. 439).

1944

1 LE COMTE, EDWARD S[EMPLE]. <u>Endymion in England: The Literary</u>
   <u>History of a Greek Myth</u>. New York: King's Crown Press,
   203 pp.
      Examines Drayton's use of the myth in the context of
   other English treatments. Discusses the unobtrusive Neo-
   Platonic allegory of <u>Endymion and Phoebe</u> and provides
   running commentary on the poem, noting in particular Drayton's emphasis on decorative details. Compares <u>Man in the</u>

1944

Moon, in which "the poet has definitely given way to the pedant," to the superior earlier version. Compares Endymion and Phoebe with Keats's Endymion in considering the question of Drayton's influence (pp. 85-106, passim).

*2 NEARING, HOMER. "English Historical Poetry, 1599-1641." Ph.D. dissertation, University of Pennsylvania, 314 pp. Published as 1945.4.

3 ROLLINS, HYDER EDWARD, ed. The Sonnets. 2 volumes. New Variorum Edition of Shakespeare. Philadelphia: J. B. Lippincott, 424, 539 pp.

In notes gathers commentary on parallels between Drayton's poems and the Sonnets. In various appendices provides overview of scholarship on question of influence between Drayton and Shakespeare and on identification of Drayton as the Rival Poet. Concludes that "Drayton . . . deserves no serious consideration" as the Rival Poet (passim).

1945

1 BUSH, DOUGLAS. English Literature in the Earlier Seventeenth Century, 1600-1660. Oxford History of English Literature, vol. V. Oxford: Clarendon Press, 629 pp.

Provides overview of seventeenth-century works of Drayton, who is the "chief heir of Spenser" and who "remained a stout-hearted Elizabethan." Observes that "[n]ative endowment, an ideal of 'noble poesie,' and a devoted craftsmanship which led to both persevering revision and happy experiment, these combined to produce a large body of verse of distinctive flavour and of frequent and varied beauty" (pp. 76-80, passim). Revised edition 1962.2.

*2 FORREST, J. "The Elizabethan Ovid: A Study of the Ovidian Spirit in Elizabethan Poetry, 1589 to 1616." Ph.D. dissertation, University of Edinburgh.

3 MACDONALD, CHARLOTTE. "Drayton's 'tidy' and Chaucer's 'tidif.'" RES, 21 (April), 127-33.

Identifies "tidy" (Polyolbion, Song 13, 1. 79) as "the great tit, or conceivably but improbably a small black-headed tit."

4   NEARING, HOMER, JR. English Historical Poetry, 1599-1641.
    Ph.D. dissertation, University of Pennsylvania, 1944.
    Philadelphia: n.p., 222 pp.
        In published version of 1944.2, provides detailed analy-
    sis of Drayton's historical poems in the context of Renais-
    sance historical verse. Gives a critical estimate of each
    work: examines sources, influence, purpose, and revisions.
    Calls Drayton "the historical poet of the English Renais-
    sance" (passim).

5   WILSON, F[RANK] P[ERCY]. Elizabethan and Jacobean. Oxford:
    Clarendon Press, 152 pp.
        In an appreciative overview of Drayton's poetry, dis-
    cusses his versatility, his late development particularly
    in "control over matter and rhetoric," and his perception
    of himself, even late in his career, "as the heir of
    Spenser and Sidney" (pp. 76-83, passim).

1946

*1 DRAYTON, MICHAEL. "Ode to the Virginian Voyage." Edited by
    J[ames] D. H[art]. Berkeley: Hart Press, 15 pp.
        Cited in National Union Catalog Pre-1956 Imprints, 148,
    540.

2   STEVENSON, DAVID LLOYD. The Love-Game Comedy. Columbia
    University Studies in English and Comparative Literature,
    164. Morningside Heights: Columbia University Press,
    271 pp.
        In chapter 8 ("Amorous Conflict in Elizabethan Poetry,"
    pp. 123-47), discusses Drayton's treatment of "the tradi-
    tional celebration of love as though it were a kind of
    polite fiction" in Idea's Mirror and Idea (pp. 137-41).

3   WHITMORE, J. B. "Anthony Cooke." N&Q, 191 (30 November),
    239-40.
        Identifies the Anthony Cooke who was Drayton's patron
    in response to a query by R[oderick] L[ewis] Eagle (19 Oc-
    tober, p. 170). Questions whether the title of Idea could
    "be a play on the name of the [Cooke] family seat, Gidea
    Hall."

1947

1   ATKINS, J[OHN] W[ILLIAM] H[EY]. English Literary Criticism:
    The Renascence. London: Methuen, 383 pp.
        In chapter 10 ("Later Critical Judgments: Bolton,
    Peacham, Carew, Drayton, Suckling, Jonson," pp. 291-311),
    discusses Drayton's literary criticism in "To Henry Rey-
    nolds" and Nymphidia (pp. 299-301).

2   GRIERSON, HERBERT J[OHN] C[LIFFORD], and J[AMES] C[RUICK-
    SHANKS] SMITH. A Critical History of English Poetry.
    Revised edition. London: Chatto & Windus, 547 pp. [The
    first edition, not seen, was published in 1944.]
        In chapter 8 ("Elizabethan Poetry," pp. 79-89), offer
    a general critical appreciation of Drayton and Daniel, who
    "are the best, after Spenser, of all the non-dramatic
    poets, certainly the most copious and varied" (pp. 83-85,
    passim).

3   HELTZEL, VIRGIL B[ARNEY]. Fair Rosamond: A Study of the
    Development of a Literary Theme. Northwestern University
    Studies in the Humanities, no. 16. Evanston: Northwestern
    University Studies, 143 pp.
        Examines the place of the Henry II-Rosamond epistles
    (England's Heroical Epistles) in the development of the
    Rosamond legend; notes that "[a]lthough his poems are
    meritorious in artistic conception and execution, Drayton
    really adds nothing to the plot of the story." Discusses
    influence of Daniel's Rosamond on the epistles and on
    their later imitations (passim).

4   PRAZ, MARIO. "Michael Drayton." ES, 28: 97-107.
        Provides lukewarm critical appraisal of Drayton's works,
    stressing his imitativeness and lack of poetic power and
    finding that his current appeal derives from the antiquar-
    ian interest of the poems. Discusses Drayton's use of
    the couplet in England's Heroical Epistles. Concludes:
    "Once we have read the four big volumes of Drayton's verse,
    we relegate them to the back row of our bookcase, only to
    be consulted by the curious antiquary."

5   TUVE, ROSEMOND. Elizabethan and Metaphysical Imagery: Ren-
    aissance Poetic and Twentieth-Century Critics. Chicago:
    University of Chicago Press, 448 pp.
        Draws frequently on Drayton (particularly Mortimeriados,
    Barons' Wars, Idea's Mirror, Idea, and Endymion and Phoebe)
    in analyzing the characteristics of Elizabethan imagery.

Examines <u>Mortimeriados</u> and <u>Barons' Wars</u> in discussing the
relationship between imitation and image. Analyzes revisions in the sonnets to argue against the common "generali-
zation that Drayton outgrew an earlier admiration for
intrinsically decorative images." Finds that in revising,
Drayton was concerned about the clarity of logical structure and the images sharpening meaning rather than about
the "intrinsic content of images." Also finds that the
"metaphysical" quality of his later sonnets "reside[s] not
in images but in concept, syntax, meter (especially ar-
rangement of pauses)" (pp. 34-37, 69-76, passim). <u>See</u>
1967.16.

6 WASSERMAN, EARL R[EEVES]. <u>Elizabethan Poetry in the Eighteenth Century</u>. ISLL, 32. Urbana: University of Illinois
Press, 291 pp.
    In revision of 1937.13 discusses the eighteenth-century
attitude toward and reception of Drayton. Gives particular
attention to the popularity, adaptation, and influence of
<u>England's Heroical Epistles</u> (passim).

1949

1 ALLEN, DON CAMERON. <u>The Legend of Noah: Renaissance Ration-
alism in Art, Science, and Letters</u>. ISLL, 33, nos. 3-4.
Urbana: University of Illinois Press, 229 pp.
    In chapter 7 ("Rationalism and the Literary and Artistic
Tradition of Noah," pp. 138-73), compares <u>Noah's Flood</u>
with other literary treatments of the Noah story. Notes
that Drayton, though he produces a learned poem, "makes
no attempt whatsoever to elaborate poetically on the her-
meneutic tradition" (pp. 144-47).

*2 ING, C[ATHERINE] M[ILLS]. "Metrical Theory and Practice in
the Elizabethan Lyric." Ph.D. dissertation, St. Hilda's
College, Oxford University.
    Published version 1951.3.

3 MÜLLERTZ, MOGENS. "De fire Shakespeare Folioer." <u>Bogvennen</u>,
4: 9-59.
    Suggests that the meeting between Drayton, Jonson, and
Shakespeare mentioned in John Ward's diary took place
during March 1616, and "that the reason for the said feast
was the publishing of Ben Jonson's folio." (English summary, pp. 40-41.)

1949

4   SHAPIRO, I. A.   "Drayton at Polesworth."   N&Q, 194 (12 November), 496.
    Notes discovery of an indenture of 3 December 1613 witnessed by Drayton which shows that he was at Polesworth by then.

5   WILSON, J[OHN] DOVER.   "Ben Jonson and Julius Caesar."   ShS, 2: 36–43.
    Points out, in passing, that in Barons' Wars (canto 3, stanza 40) Drayton draws from both Julius Caesar and Jonson's Every Man in His Humor.

1950

1   BIRD, DONALD ARTHUR.   "The Pronunciation of Michael Drayton." Ph.D. dissertation, University of Wisconsin, 199 pp. [Abstract in Summaries of Doctoral Dissertations, University of Wisconsin, 11 (1951), 352–53.]
    Provides "an analysis and interpretation of all the rimes of Michael Drayton": "treats the stressed vowels, the vowels of syllables with secondary stress, a small amount of evidence on unaccented vowels, and some of the consonant problems." Concludes that "though Drayton uses some traditional rimes and some eye rimes, the majority reflect his pronunciation and the pronunciation of his period with considerable accuracy."

2   BULLITT, JOHN M.   "The Use of Rhyme Link in the Sonnets of Sidney, Drayton, and Spenser."   JEGP, 49 (January), 14–32.
    Analyzes Drayton's use of rhyme links in Idea (1619) to refute Bray's claim that Drayton "revels" in rhyme linking (1938.2). Finds "only scattered examples of such linkages" and suggests that "it [is] highly doubtful that [Drayton's sonnets] . . . were originally integrated by rhyme links to form a 'flowing whole.'"

3   FIEHLER, RUDOLPH.   "Sir John Oldcastle, the Original of Falstaff."   Ph.D. dissertation, University of Texas at Austin, 302 pp.   [DAI, 31 (1970), 2341–42A.]
    Discusses Oldcastle, noting that "Puritan resentment accounted for the play . . . , which was clearly an effort to counteract an offensive impression of a clownish Oldcastle on the stage." Published version 1965.6.

4 HARRISON, THOMAS P[ERRIN]. "Drayton's Birds." <u>University of Texas Studies in English</u>, 29: 102-17.
    Traces evolution of Drayton's use and depiction of birds from the "medieval symbolism" of <u>Owl</u> through the "hybrid" <u>Man in the Moon</u> to ornithological study and observation in <u>Polyolbion</u>. Finds that "the transition in Drayton's outlook parallels the vastly more gradual growth of the New Science from the bondage of tradition." Identifies sources of Drayton's knowledge of birds and suggests that his use of books to supplement direct observation "is convincing proof of the genuineness of his interest in nature as of his desire for accuracy and fullness." Revised 1956.3.

5 HUTCHESON, W[ILLIAM] J. FRASER. <u>Shakespeare's Other Anne</u>. Glasgow: William McLellan, 128 pp.
    Identifies Idea as Anne Whately (passim).

6 MEYERSTEIN, E. H. W. "A Drayton Echo in Tennyson." <u>TLS</u> (2 June), p. 341.
    Suggests influence of "the fourth and eighth lines in the stanzas" of "Ballad of Agincourt" on the meter of "the six irregular stanzas of" "Charge of the Light Brigade."

7 THOMAS, WILLIAM BEACH. <u>Hertfordshire</u>. County Books Series. London: Robert Hale, 278 pp.
    In chapter 21 ("What Drayton Admired," pp. 236-44), discusses description of Hertfordshire in <u>Polyolbion</u>, noting that Drayton emphasized the rivers and forests.

8 WHALLEY, A[RTHUR] G[EORGE] C[UTHBERT]. "Samuel Taylor Coleridge, Library Cormorant: The History of His Use of Books; With a Consideration of Purpose and Pattern in His Reading, and an Account of the Books He Owned, Annotated, and Borrowed." Ph.D. dissertation, University of London.
    Discusses Coleridge's marginalia on Drayton in both the Dove Cottage and Victoria and Albert copies of 1793.1.

9 ZOCCA, LOUIS R[ALPH]. <u>Elizabethan Narrative Poetry</u>. New Brunswick: Rutgers University Press, 318 pp.
    In published version of 1940.12, discusses <u>Gaveston</u> as an example of the late Elizabethan <u>Mirror</u> poem and examines the Neo-Platonism and sources of <u>Endymion and Phoebe</u>; provides critical estimate of each (pp. 78-82, 262-67).

1951

1951

*1   DRAYTON, MICHAEL. "The Ballad of Agincourt": Reprinted with
      the Additional Stanza from Richard Butcher's Copy of the
      1619 Folio Edition of the "Poems." Oxford: Charles Batey.
          Cited in 1974.16, where Bent Juel-Jensen is identified
      as editor.

2   HUNTER, G. K. "The Marking of Sententiae in Elizabethan
      Printed Plays, Poems, and Romances." Library, 5th ser.,
      6 (December), 171-88.
          Draws on Drayton's works in analyzing characteristics
      of gnomic pointing.

3   ING, CATHERINE [MILLS]. Elizabethan Lyrics: A Study in the
      Development of English Metres and Their Relation to Poetic
      Effect. London: Chatto & Windus, 252 pp.
          In published version of 1949.2, examines influence of
      "the characteristics of the air" on the meter of "Ballad
      of Agincourt." Finds that although no music is extant for
      the poem, Drayton "used an equivalent for a tune--phrases
      of very strongly marked rhythmical structure occurring at
      obviously important points in the stanza" (pp. 142-47,
      passim).

4   McMANAWAY, JAMES G[ILMER]. "A New Shakespeare Document."
      SQ, 2 (April), 119-22.
          Transcribes and discusses warrant for payment for per-
      formances of twenty-one plays in 1630-1631. Argues that
      the "Olde Castle" acted on 6 January 1631 is 1 Henry IV,
      not Oldcastle.

1952

1   BRADBROOK, M[URIEL] C[LARA]. Shakespeare and Elizabethan
      Poetry: A Study of His Earlier Work in Relation to the
      Poetry of the Time. New York: Oxford University Press,
      287 pp.
          Discusses Endymion and Phoebe as an example of "Ovidian
      romance," comparing it briefly with Marlowe's Hero and
      Leander and Shakespeare's Venus and Adonis. Compares
      Oldcastle with Shakespeare's Henry plays and discusses
      treatment of Henry V in the former (pp. 70-73, 191-94).

2   SMITH, HALLETT. Elizabethan Poetry: A Study in Conventions,
      Meaning, and Expression. Cambridge: Harvard University
      Press, 367 pp.

Discusses Drayton as a pastoral poet, examines Endymion and Phoebe as an Ovidian mythological poem, places Gaveston and Matilda in the evolution of the complaint, discusses the popularity of England's Heroical Epistles and the influence of the complaint on the work, and analyzes native influences on Drayton's revisions of his sonnets (particularly the influence of Astrophel and Stella on the 1599 revisions) (passim).

3   STEVENSON, HAZEL ALLISON. "The Major Elizabethan Poets and the Doctrine of Signatures." Florida State University Studies, 5: 11-31.
    Draws frequently on Drayton in a survey of the influence of the Doctrine of Signatures, "the notion that God, in giving particular shapes and colors to leaves and flowers, had plainly taught what disease each cured."

4   TAYLOR, DICK, JR. "Drayton and the Countess of Bedford." SP, 49 (April), 214-28.
    Argues that "there was a serious and final break" between Drayton and the Countess of Bedford, perhaps before 1603. Provides detailed bibliographical analysis of England's Heroical Epistles (1602), Barons' Wars (1603), and Poems (1605) to argue that the addresses to the Countess were retained not because Drayton hoped to regain her favor but because of the printer, who "would have had to undergo considerable trouble and expense" to excise or replace them and "would have lost from his books some renowned names" valuable as advertising.

1953

1   ANON. "Drayton's Discovery of England." TLS (8 May), p. 303.
    In review of 1953.6 discusses reasons for Drayton's "failure" in Polyolbion and provides an estimate of his strengths and (especially) weaknesses as a poet. Points out that he "was not naturally a heroic poet" but "is essentially an Elizabethan pastoral poet, suffering from all the over-worked symbolism and trite conventional moods." Concludes: "The trouble with Drayton is that his talent and feeling require naturalism, while his ambition and style always strive for the heroic sonority of Chapman."

2   ANON. "Flashing Lyricism." Nation, 177 (26 September), 257.
    In review of 1953.6 points out that although "Drayton is at his best in the shorter pieces" his "lyricism flashes through time and again" in the longer poems.

1953

3   BOWERS, R. H. "Borrichius Recommends Some English Poets."
    N&Q, 198 (March), 105.
        Reprints listing of English poets (including Drayton)
    from Oluf Borch's Dissertationes Academicae de Poetis
    (1683); offers the passage an "an interesting example of
    European hack writing."

4   BUXTON, JOHN. "The Poets' Hall Called Apollo." MLR, 48
    (January), 52-54.
        Uses Richard Butcher's inscription in his copy of
    Drayton's Poems (1619) to establish that the Apollo Room
    at the Devil and St. Dunstan Tavern "was already named and
    dedicated" by 1620. Suggests that "Sacrifice to Apollo"
    was composed before Jonson's Leges Convivales and that
    both "were composed for the occasion on which the room
    was named and dedicated."

5   COHEN, J. M. "Professional Poet." Spectator, 190 (8 May),
    580.
        In review of 1953.6 discusses Drayton as "a professional
    writer of conventional feelings" and a poet of "varied
    accomplishments."

6   DRAYTON, MICHAEL. Poems of Michael Drayton. 2 volumes.
    Edited by John Buxton. Muses' Library. Cambridge: Har-
    vard University Press, 780 pp.
        Provides annotated selections. In "Introduction"
    (pp. ix-xxxiii), discusses Drayton as a "professional
    poet" and provides a critical survey, by type, of his
    poetry. Reviewed in Anon., Listener, 49 (23 April 1953),
    693; Michel Poirer, EA, 7 (April 1954), 230-31; Geoffrey
    Taylor, "One of the First Poets," Time and Tide (25 April
    1953), pp. 548-49; C[alvin] G[raham] Thayer, Books Abroad,
    28 (Autumn 1954), 485; Kathleen [Mary] Tillotson, RES,
    NS 5 (April 1954), 190-91; 1953.1; 1953.2; 1953.5;
    1953.7; 1953.9; 1953.10.

7   FRASER, G. S. "The Poet as Plain Man." New Statesman and
    Nation (9 May), p. 557.
        In review of 1953.6 questions "whether the traditional
    judgment [of Drayton as "the honest but unexciting master
    of the plain style"] ought not, in some respects, to be
    revised." Suggests "that there is occasionally in Drayton
    a remarkable, though not fully conscious, play between the
    extremely conventional morality of the Elizabethans and
    their natural admiration for vigour and even for excess."
    Draws on Barons' Wars and Muses' Elysium for examples.

8   JUEL-JENSEN, BENT. "Polyolbion, Poemes Lyrick and Pastorall,
     Poems 1619, The Owle, and a Few Other Books by Michael
     Drayton." Library, 5th ser., 8 (September), 145-62, 3
     plates.
        Provides publishing history and bibliographical analysis
     of Polyolbion (with section on the engraving of Prince
     Henry playing with a lance), Poems Lyric and Pastoral,
     Poems (1619), Owl, and England's Heroical Epistles; cor-
     rects several errors in earlier descriptions. Briefly
     discusses copies in contemporary binding or with price.
     See 1954.4 and 1955.5.

9   LEWIS, NAOMI. "A Major Minor." The Observer (14 June), p. 9.
        In review of 1953.6 offers an appreciative estimate of
     Drayton as man and poet.

10   NICHOLSON, NORMAN. Review of John Buxton, ed., Poems of
     Michael Drayton. Fortnightly, no. 1040, pp. 140-41.
        In review of 1953.6 finds "in much of Drayton's verse a
     conflict between the backward look and the forward look,
     between the art of the past and the vision of the present."
     Concludes that "Drayton is not only one of the most honest,
     most independent, most English of poets, he is also, at
     his best, one of the most delightfully readable."

1954

1   BUXTON, JOHN. Sir Philip Sidney and the English Renaissance.
     London: Macmillan; New York: St. Martin's Press, 296 pp.
        Discusses Drayton's relationship with the Countess of
     Bedford (pp. 223-27, passim). (In second edition [1964]
     makes no substantive changes in his discussion of Drayton.)

2   COLBRUNN, ETHEL B. "The Simile as a Stylistic Device in
     Elizabethan Narrative Poetry: An Analytical and Compara-
     tive Study." Ph.D. dissertation, University of Florida,
     315 pp. [DA, 14 (1954), 2064-65.]
        Discusses Endymion and Phoebe and Mortimeriados.

3   DUCLOS, PAUL-CHARLES. "Michael Drayton: Le Poète de la
     découverte élisabéthaine de l'Angleterre." RLV, 20:
     276-84.
        Provides general appreciative overview of Drayton's
     life and work.

1954

4   JUEL-JENSEN, BENT. "Michael Drayton's Owle, 1604." TLS
        (23 July), p. 473.
            In response to review ("Bibliographical Journals,"
        11 June, p. 384) of 1953.8, cites errors in STC entries
        for Owl (STC 7211-7213).

5   LEWIS, C[LIVE] S[TAPLES]. English Literature in the Sixteenth
        Century (Excluding Drama). Oxford History of English
        Literature, vol. III. Oxford: Clarendon Press, 704 pp.
            Classifies Drayton as a "half Golden" poet--one who
        began in the "Drab" tradition but ended in the "Golden."
        Discusses Idea's Mirror and Idea in section on sonnet
        sequences and provides a critical overview of Drayton's
        other sixteenth-century works. Praises Sirena and Muses'
        Elysium, in particular, but observes that Drayton "was in
        a sense too poetical to be a sound poet" (pp. 495-97,
        531-35, passim).

6   POTTER, JAMES LAIN. "The Development of Sonnet-Patterns in
        the Sixteenth Century." Ph.D. dissertation, Harvard Uni-
        versity, 185 pp.
            Includes Idea's Mirror and Idea in an examination of
        the "forms of the sonnet used by" Elizabethan poets. Of
        1619 Idea, notes that it "consisted largely of Shake-
        spearian sonnets, and seems mature and logically clear,
        though Drayton evidently had become less concerned with
        formal internal structure."

1955

1   BATES, PAUL A. "Elizabethan Amorous Pastorals." Ph.D. dis-
        sertation, University of Kansas, 930 pp.
            Discusses Eclogues, Endymion and Phoebe, and Gaveston
        in an investigation of the "pastoral love-lay."

2   EVANS, MAURICE. English Poetry in the Sixteenth Century.
        Hutchinson's University Library, English Literature.
        London: Hutchinson's University Library, 183 pp.
            Examines characteristics and evolution of Drayton's
        historical poetry; emphasizes his change in "attitude
        to history" by 1605 (pp. 125-31, passim). (The discussion
        of Drayton is unrevised in the second edition, 1967.)

3   GROOM, BERNARD. The Diction of Poetry from Spenser to
        Bridges. Toronto: University of Toronto Press, 294 pp.
            In chapter 3 ("The Spenserian Tradition and Its Rivals
        up to 1660," pp. 48-73), analyzes Drayton's "picturesque"

style ("a modified Spenserian style") and its links with
Keats in Endymion and Phoebe as well as the style of "his
later poetry [wherein] he appears rather as a judicious
artist in the choice of diction than an inventor of new
effects." Observes that "[i]f one had to select from the
later Elizabethans the author whose judgment was most
surely rooted in the good work of the past and most marked
in its anticipation of the future, Drayton might well be
that man." Draws upon Barons' Wars for examples of diction
(pp. 58-60, passim).

4   JUEL-JENSEN, BENT. "A Drayton Collection." BC, 4 (1955),
    133-43.
        Provides overview of his collection--"the most consid-
    erable in private hands"--with much information on states
    and issues, rarity, and provenance. Points out that
    "Drayton had been collected for a very long time" before
    1941, when he began. See 1966.5.

5   _____. "Isaac Oliver's Portrait of Prince Henry and Polyol-
    bion: A Footnote." Library, 5th ser., 10 (September),
    206-207.
        Notes an additional version of the portrait (see
    1953.8) in John Taylor's Great Britain All in Black,
    pointing out that the verses below it were "obviously in-
    spired" by Drayton's verses accompanying the portrait in
    Polyolbion.

6   SELLS, A[RTHUR] LYTTON. The Italian Influence in English
    Poetry from Chaucer to Southwell. London: George Allen
    & Unwin, 346 pp.
        Devotes chapter 12 (pp. 264-85), to an overview of
    Drayton's work to illustrate "the sometimes hardly per-
    ceptible manner in which the currents of Italian poetry
    entered the main stream of English." Discusses Italian
    (as well as French and Classical) influences on and
    parallels to Idea's Mirror, Endymion and Phoebe, England's
    Heroical Epistles, and Muses' Elysium.

                            1956

1   BENNETT, JOSEPHINE WATERS. "Britain among the Fortunate
    Isles." SP, 53 (April), 114-40.
        Discusses Drayton's use of the tradition that Great
    Britain was one of the Fortunate Isles (in Polyolbion,
    Shepherd's Garland, and Muses' Elysium).

Michael Drayton

2   COHEN, HENNIG. "Michael Drayton's Poly-Olbion (Part I)."
    RenP 1956: 110-11.
        Describes contents and bibliographical features of the
    University of South Carolina copy of 1612 edition.

3   HARRISON, THOMAS P[ERRIN]. They Tell of Birds: Chaucer,
    Spenser, Milton, Drayton. Austin: University of Texas
    Press, 178 pp.
        As chapter 5 ("Drayton," pp. 109-31), provides a slight-
    ly expanded, revised version of 1950.4. In "Conclusion"
    (chapter 6, pp. 132-34), notes that in his description of
    birds "Drayton's triumph lies in the revelation that
    poetry is capable of serving a new end in objective and
    intimate descriptions of bird life. In this art Drayton
    is remote from his contemporaries; he is much nearer
    Chaucer, who had divorced nature from morality, and he
    anticipates John Clare." Includes "Index to Birds Named
    by Chaucer, Spenser, Milton, and Drayton" (pp. 135-59);
    notes that Drayton names ninety-four different species.

4   HEFFNER, RAY LORENZO. "Michael Drayton as Pastoral Poet."
    Ph.D. dissertation, Yale University, 307 pp. [DAI, 31
    (1970), 389A.]
        Traces the evolution of Drayton's pastoral poetry from
    his early imitation of Spenser to his anticipation of
    eighteenth-century pastoral. Examines changes in style
    and subject matter.

5   JUEL-JENSEN, BENT. "Drayton and His Patron." TLS (7 Decem-
    ber), p. 731.
        Describes copy of 1619 Poems which was probably owned
    by Henry Goodere, the younger; also describes presentation
    copies to Richard Butcher and Thomas Bond.

6   LEVER, J[ULIUS] W[ALTER]. The Elizabethan Love Sonnet.
    London: Methuen, 292 pp.
        In chapter 7 ("The Late Elizabethan Sonnet," pp. 139-
    61), provides estimate of Drayton's importance in the
    development of the Elizabethan sonnet, particularly as he
    "resuscitated the wit and idiomatic force of Wyatt and
    Sidney." Examines Drayton's sonnets as "a kind of poeti-
    cized journalism that mirrored the everyday activities and
    intellectual interests of his time" and discusses his
    style, diction, imitativeness, and revisions. Compares
    Drayton with Daniel (pp. 154-60). (The discussion of
    Drayton is unrevised in the second edition, 1966.)

7   MAXWELL, BALDWIN. Studies in the Shakespeare Apocrypha.
    New York: King's Crown Press, Columbia University,
    237 pp.
        In chapter 2 ("The True Chronicle History of Thomas
    Lord Cromwell," pp. 72–108), argues against Fleay's
    (1891.5) ascription of the play to Drayton (pp. 95–98).

8   PEET, CHARLES DONALD, JR. "The Pastoral and Heroic Poetry of
    Michael Drayton." Ph.D. dissertation, Princeton Univer-
    sity, 310 pp. [DA, 17 (1957), 1341–42.]
        Examines Shepherd's Garland, Eclogues, Muses' Elysium,
    Mortimeriados, Barons' Wars, Battle of Agincourt, and
    Margaret "to provide a thorough account of Drayton's
    achievement in" pastoral and historical poetry. Focuses
    on style.

9   PETER, JOHN. Complaint and Satire in Early English Litera-
    ture. Oxford: Clarendon Press, 331 pp.
        In chapter 10 ("The Legacy of Satire," pp. 288–300),
    discusses the influence of satiric verse on Drayton's
    revisions of Idea (pp. 295–97).

*10 SCOULAR, K[ITTY] W. "Studies in the Presentation of Nature
    in English Poetry from Spenser to Marvell." Ph.D. disser-
    tation, St. Hugh's College, Oxford University.
        Published version 1965.17.

11 WIATT, WILLIAM HAUTE. "Englands Heroicall Epistles: A Criti-
    cal Study." Ph.D. dissertation, University of North
    Carolina. [Abstract in University of North Carolina Rec-
    ord, no. 576 (October 1957), pp. 110–13.]
        Analyzes England's Heroical Epistles as "a peculiarly
    Elizabethan product of the interaction of Drayton's mate-
    rial and Ovid's form." Compares Drayton and Ovid to show
    that Drayton worked for "a variety of effects," "paid more
    attention . . . to the demands of verisimilitude," and
    "was more concerned . . . with the problems of unity."
    Analyzes influence of the Mirror tradition on the work to
    show "that the major differences between Englands Heroicall
    Epistles and the Heroides are explained by the fact that
    Drayton's material came from or was affected by the Mir-
    ror tradition" and "that the Mirror tradition had estab-
    lished . . . a favorable climate for Drayton's imitation
    of the Heroides."

1956

12   WILKES, G[ERALD] A[LFRED]. "Poetry of Moral Reflection at
     the Turn of the Sixteenth Century." Ph.D. dissertation,
     Merton College, Oxford University.
          Discusses Drayton as he "illustrates reflective verse
     of the 'marginal' and occasional type, and the entangle-
     ment of the reflective strain in other modes and fashions."

                              1957

1   FRIEDRICH, GERHARD. "The Genesis of Michael Drayton's Ode
    'To the Virginian Voyage.'" MLN, 72 (June), 401-406.
         Supplements Adams's examination (1918.1) of Drayton's
    indebtedness to Hakluyt's Principal Navigations.

*2 MADDISON, CAROL HOPKINS. "Apollo and the Nine: The Renais-
    sance Baroque Ode in Italy, France, and England." Ph.D.
    dissertation, Johns Hopkins University.
         Published version 1960.4.

3   RIBNER, IRVING. The English History Play in the Age of
    Shakespeare. Princeton: Princeton University Press,
    365 pp.
         Examines Oldcastle as an example of a biographical
    play: discusses the historical Oldcastle and events sur-
    rounding the impetus for the play and its political
    purpose (pp. 199-205). (The discussion of Oldcastle in
    the revised edition [London: Methuen, 1965, pp. 200-205]
    is unchanged.)

4   THOMPSON, RANDALL. "Ode to the Virginian Voyage," Michael
    Drayton (1563-1631): Set to Music for Chorus of Mixed
    Voices with Piano or Orchestral Accompaniment. No. 2433.
    Boston: E. C. Schirmer, 67 pp.
         "[C]omposed at the invitation of the Virginia 350th
    Anniversary Commission, in honour of the" settlement of
    Jamestown and "first performed in Williamsburg, Virginia,
    on the occasion of the opening day of the Jamestown Festi-
    val, April 1, 1957."

                              1958

1   HEFFNER, RAY L[ORENZO], JR. "Drayton's 'Lady I.S.'" N&Q,
    NS 5 (September), 376-81.
         Identifies I. S. as "Isabella, supposed daughter of
    Robert Rich, first Earl of Warwick, and Penelope Dev-
    ereux . . . , who in 1618 married Sir John Smith."

2   LaBRANCHE, ANTHONY [SPAHR]. "Drayton's Historical Poetry:
     The Barons Warres." Ph.D. dissertation, Yale University.
         In attempting "to define the nature of one kind of
     historical poetry, most clearly illustrated by Drayton's
     The Barons Warres," examines "[t]he poetical, as well as
     historical, development of" the poem. Analyzes the "dis-
     advantageous influence" of Mirror for Magistrates and
     "the highly ornamented domestic complaint" on Drayton's
     early legends, and the influence of Daniel's Civil Wars,
     Lucan's Pharsalia, and Holinshed's Chronicles on Barons'
     Wars. Finds that the poem "depends upon oratorical pro-
     cedures in its 'set' scenes . . . [and] is less well
     integrated and less thoughtful, but more vigorous, than
     Daniel's" Civil Wars.

3   MINER, PAUL. "William Blake: Two Notes on Sources." BNYPL,
     62: 203-207.
         In the second note ("A Source for Blake's Enion?"),
     suggests that Blake took the name from the river Enion in
     Polyolbion, Song 6.

4   MORGAN, FLORENCE H. "A Biography of Lucy, Countess of Bed-
     ford, the Last Great Literary Patroness." Ph.D. disser-
     tation, University of Southern California. [Abstract in
     University of Southern California Abstracts of Disserta-
     tions, 1956, pp. 30-34.]
         Discusses the Countess's patronage of Drayton. Sug-
     gests that the "relationship . . . did not thrive" because
     of differences in political allegiances and because of
     Drayton's "temperament" ("conservative, moralistic, and
     old-fashioned"), which was "different from that of most
     of the literary men associated with the Countess."

5   MORRIS, HELEN. Elizabethan Literature. Home University
     Library of Modern Knowledge, 233. London: Oxford Uni-
     versity Press, 249 pp.
         Offers appreciative estimate of Drayton. In comparing
     him to Daniel, finds that "Drayton is far more 'Eliza-
     bethan.' . . . His verse is more energetic[,] fanciful
     and conceited, and though sometimes he sinks lower, his
     heights surpass Daniel's more level achievement: his
     long poems are enlivened by vigorous outbursts and happy
     phrases" (pp. 69-74, passim).

Michael Drayton

1959

1   ACKERMAN, CATHERINE A.   "Drayton's Revision of The Shepheards
    Garland."   CLAJ, 3 (December), 106-13.
         Analyzes revisions of 1606 (Eclogues) and 1619 (Pas-
    torals), particularly in the "biographical detail that
    sheds light on the circumstances and aspirations" of a
    late-Elizabethan, early-Jacobean poet.   Examines how the
    changes result in "greater specification."   Concludes:
    "His revision of The Shepheards Garland provides a fasci-
    nating study of the Elizabethan poet engaged in the
    evaluation of his own work, toning down the exuberance
    characteristic of his age, pruning and rewriting as his
    maturing Muse directed, and preparing the way for the
    smooth gracefulness of the Caroline lyric."

2   BENJAMIN, EDWIN B.   "Fame, Poetry, and the Order of History
    in the Literature of the English Renaissance."   Studies
    in the Renaissance, 6: 64-84.
         Discusses Drayton's treatment of fame in Robert and
    "To the Virginian Voyage."

3   BRIGGS, KATHARINE M[ARY].   The Anatomy of Puck: An Examina-
    tion of Fairy Beliefs among Shakespeare's Contemporaries
    and Successors.   London: Routledge and Kegan Paul, 296 pp.
         Examines Nymphidia as an example of "the fashion for
    the miniature" in Jacobean fairy poetry.   Discusses the
    work as "a parody of the romances," the influence of folk
    tradition and Shakespeare's Midsummer Night's Dream on
    the poem, and the significance of some of the names.
    Comments briefly on Muses' Elysium, Eighth Nymphal
    (pp. 56-62, passim).

4   CAMPBELL, LILY B[ESS].   Divine Poetry and Drama in Sixteenth-
    Century England.   Cambridge: Cambridge University Press;
    Berkeley: University of California Press, 276 pp.
         Discusses Harmony of the Church in examining transla-
    tions of the Song of Solomon, and Moses in a Map of His
    Miracles, Noah's Flood, and David and Goliath in examining
    biblical epics.   Comments on influence of Du Bartas and
    Sylvester on the latter group (pp. 61-62, 102-106).

5   MILLER, EDWIN HAVILAND.   The Professional Writer in Eliza-
    bethan England: A Study of Nondramatic Literature.
    Cambridge: Harvard University Press, 298 pp.
         Draws frequently on Drayton's life and works in analyz-
    ing various aspects (e.g., audience, patronage, censor-
    ship) of the career of the Elizabethan professional writer
    (passim).

1960

6   NICOLSON, MARJORIE HOPE. Mountain Gloom and Mountain Glory:
    The Development of the Aesthetics of the Infinite. Ithaca:
    Cornell University Press, 417 pp.
         In an analysis "of the change in English taste toward
    mountains," examines "the literary conventions stemming
    from classics and Scripture" behind Drayton's description
    of mountains in Polyolbion (pp. 53-55, passim).

7   SCHRODER, WILLIAM THOMAS. "Michael Drayton: A Study of the
    Idea Sonnet Revisions." Ph.D. dissertation, Northwestern
    University, 213 pp. [DA, 20 (1959), 2277-78.]
         Analyzes changes in "subject matter, prosody, and
    rhetoric" in Drayton's revisions and examines the effect
    of "literary, social-political, and religious atmospheres"
    on the revisions.

                              1960

1   BARNES, RICHARD GORDON. "The Effect of the New World on
    English Poetry, 1600-1625." Ph.D. dissertation, Claremont
    Graduate School, 281 pp. [DA, 21 (1961), 3086.]
         Analyzes Drayton's response "in action, thought and
    feeling as well as in . . . [his] poetry" to America.

2   HILLYER, ROBERT [SILLIMAN]. In Pursuit of Poetry. New York:
    McGraw-Hill, 243 pp.
         Comments frequently on Idea, "the most interesting
    sequence in the language except for Shakespeare's." Be-
    lieves that the sonnets are autobiographical and "that
    there is little doubt that Shakespeare and Drayton were
    friends." Points out that in spite of the "wretched syn-
    tax" the sonnets in Idea "are wonderfully alive" (pp. 92-
    94, 98, 101-102, passim).

3   JUEL-JENSEN, BENT. "Three Lost Drayton Items." BC, 9: 78-79.
         Request location of Drayton's copy of Robert Cotton's
    A Short View of . . . Henry III, a presentation copy to
    Thomas Holl of Polyolbion, and Thomas Corser's copy of
    Idea's Mirror.

4   MADDISON, CAROL [HOPKINS]. Apollo and the Nine: A History
    of the Ode. Baltimore: Johns Hopkins University Press,
    437 pp.
         In revision of 1957.2 examines Drayton's place in the
    development of the ode, calling him "the first proper
    ode writer in English." Discusses form of and influences
    on several of his odes. Concludes: "[A]lthough his

1960

definition of the ode is in many ways perceptive, his all-
inclusive use of the term does much to destroy its value.
His practice of the ode, which makes no distinction between
the new classically inspired and the old familiar lyric
poetry; between typical songs and love poems flaunting
only Petrarchan conceits, and formal poems on public
events . . . do[es] little to establish it as a new genre
in English poetry. Drayton represents the first stage of
the introduction of the ode into English literature, when
the fashionable new term is used for almost everything
that is in any sense lyric" (pp. 290-96).

5   MILES, JOSPEHINE. Renaissance, Eighteenth-Century, and Mod-
    ern Language in English Poetry: A Tabular View. Berkeley:
    University of California Press, 77 pp.
        Includes Idea and Pastorals in tabular analyses of
    adjectives, nouns, and verbs; mode; types of measures;
    and major adjectives, nouns, and verbs in order of innova-
    tion (passim).

6   SERONSY, CECIL C. "Daniel's Complaint of Rosamond: Origins
    and Influence of an Elizabethan Poem." Lock Haven Bulle-
    tin, 1st ser., no. 2, pp. 39-57.
        Traces influence of Rosamond on Gaveston, Matilda,
    Mortimeriados, Robert, and England's Heroical Epistles
    (Henry II-Rosamond). Observes that "Peirs Gaveston in
    its narrative framework and diction appears to borrow
    more heavily than any other poem of the period from
    Rosamond."

<h2 style="text-align:center">1961</h2>

*1   CAREY, J. "The Ovidian Love Elegy in England." D. Phil.
     thesis, Christ's Church, Oxford University.

2   DRAYTON, MICHAEL. The Works of Michael Drayton. 5 volumes.
     Edited by J[ohn] William Hebel, Kathleen [Mary] Tillotson,
     and Bernard H[enry] Newdigate. Oxford: Basil Blackwell
     for the Shakespeare Head Press, 519, 600, 447, 621, 372
     pp.
         Provides corrected reprint of 1931.4, 1932.6, 1932.7,
     1933.4, and 1941.4, with revised "Bibliography" by Bent
     Juel-Jensen (V, 265-306).

1961

3   FOAKES, R. A., and R. T. RICKERT, eds. <u>Henslowe's Diary</u>.
Cambridge: Cambridge University Press, 428 pp.
    Provide transcription of the Diary, which includes
several entries of payments to Drayton for various plays
(passim).

4   JUEL-JENSEN, BENT. "An Oxford Variant of Drayton's <u>Polyol</u>-<u>bion</u>." <u>Library</u>, 5th ser., 16 (March), 53–54, plate ix.
    Describes copy of parts I and II bound up with a "'half-title'" reading "The Faerie Land." Speculates on reasons
behind the leaf.

5   LEISHMAN, J[AMES] B[LAIR]. <u>Themes and Variations in Shake</u>-<u>speare's Sonnets</u>. New York: Hillary House, 254 pp.
    Analyzes Drayton's treatment of "the theme of poetic
immortality" in five sonnets, comparing his treatment
with that of Shakespeare (pp. 85–91).

6   LEVÝ, JIRÍ. "The Development of Rhyme-Scheme and of Syntac-tic Pattern in the English Renaissance Sonnet." <u>Acta</u>
<u>Universitatis Palackianae Olomucensis, Philologica</u>, 4:
167–85.
    In an analysis of "the syntactic patterns and arrange-ment of ideas" in the sonnet, provides a statistical
analysis of the "clause-limits" in Drayton's sonnets (as
printed in 1904.2). Observes that Drayton was "[t]he
only poet among the Elizabethan eclectics [Sidney, Barnes,
and Constable] whose thought-pattern was intrinsically
English."

7   NELSON, MALCOLM ANTHONY. "The Robin Hood Tradition in Eng-lish Literature in the Sixteenth and Seventeenth Centuries."
Ph.D dissertation, Northwestern University, 274 pp. [<u>DA</u>,
22 (1962), 2398–99.]
    Discusses how "Drayton's <u>Poly-Olbion</u> shows Robin Hood
as an outlaw, not an earl, and makes Maid Marian into an
English Diana." Published 1973.10.

8   NEWDIGATE, BERNARD H[ENRY]. <u>Michael Drayton and His Circle</u>.
Oxford: Basil Blackwell for the Shakespeare Head Press,
255 pp.
    Reprints 1941.8.

<u>1962</u>

1   BERTHELOT, JOSEPH ALFRED. "A Handbook of the Poetical Works
of Michael Drayton, with Critical Interpretations."
Ph.D. dissertation, University of Denver, 276 pp. [<u>DA</u>,
23 (1962), 1681.]

1962

Traces "[i]n handbook format . . . Drayton's literary development"; analyzes his revisions and provides critical commentary on each work. Concludes: "From a relatively second-rate Petrarchist in his early years he became in his later days a highly diversified and accomplished, if not great, poet."

2   BUSH, DOUGLAS. English Literature in the Earlier Seventeenth Century, 1600-1660. Second edition, revised. Oxford History of English Literature, vol. V. New York: Oxford University Press, 688 pp.
       In revision of 1945.1 makes only minor changes in discussion of Drayton (pp. 76-80, passim).

*3   ENZENSBERGER, CHRISTIAN. Sonett und Poetik: Die Aussagen der elisabethanischen Sonettzyklen über das Dichten im Vergleich mit der zeitgenössischen Dichtungslehre. Ph.D. dissertation, University of Munich. Munich: n.p., 269 pp.
       Cited in Hans Walter Gabler, English Renaissance Studies in German, 1945-1967: A Check-List of German, Austrian, and Swiss Academic Theses, Monographs, and Book Publications on English Language and Literature, c. 1500-1650. Schriftenreihe der Deutschen Shakespeare-Gesellschaft West, NS 11 (Heidelberg: Quelle & Meyer, 1971), p. 12, item 9.

4   FRIEDMAN, STANLEY. "Drayton and His Elizabethan Epic." Ph.D. dissertation, Columbia University, 203 pp. [DA, 24 (1964), 5384.]
       Examines problems of character and unity in Mortimeriados and Barons' Wars. Analyzes the relationship between the two, finding that "the two poems, despite differences in style and emphasis, are basically alike in structure, characterization, and effect." Analyzes techniques Drayton uses to give "heroic stature" to Mortimer, who is both "tragic victim" and "epic protagonist." Concludes: "In both Mortimeriados and The Barons Warres Drayton was writing not versified chronicles, as some scholars misleadingly suggest, but historical-tragical-epics, poems which manifest care and skill in construction, fuse history and realism with mythology and symbolism, and take the record of the past as a source but morality and art as guides."

*5   LOGAN, ROBERT ALEXANDER. "The Renaissance Epyllion." Ph.D. dissertation, Harvard University.

*6   LUDWIG, HEINZ. Der Einfluss römischer Dichter auf das Werk
     Michael Draytons: Unter besonderer Berücksichtigung von
     Ovid und Horaz. Ph.D. dissertation, University of Cologne,
     Cologne: n.p., 219 pp.
         Cited in Hans Walter Gabler, English Renaissance
     Studies in German, 1945-1967: A Check-List of German,
     Austrian, and Swiss Academic Theses, Monographs, and Book
     Publications on English Language and Literature, c. 1500-
     1650, Schriftenreihe der Deutschen Shakespeare-Gesell-
     schaft West, NS 11 (Heidelberg: Quelle & Meyer, 1971),
     p. 24, item 102.

7   McCOY, DOROTHY SCHUCHMAN. "Tradition and Convention: A
     Study of Periphrasis in English Pastoral Poetry from 1557-
     1715." Ph.D. dissertation, University of Pittsburgh,
     402 pp. [DA, 23 (1963), 3888-89.]
         See published version 1965.11.

8   OWEN, A. L. The Famous Druids: A Survey of Three Centuries
     of English Literature on the Druids. Oxford: Clarendon
     Press, 276 pp.
         Discusses Drayton's representation of the Druids and
     his sources in England's Heroical Epistles and Polyolbion
     (pp. 46-51).

9   SCHAAR, CLAES. Elizabethan Sonnet Themes and the Dating of
     Shakespeare's "Sonnets." LSE, 32. Lund: C. W. K.
     Gleerup; Copenhagen: Ejnar Munksgaard, 199 pp.
         Argues that Drayton had no influence on the Sonnets and
     that Shakespeare had only "limited influence" on Drayton's
     sonnets. Provides detailed analysis of influence of Son-
     net 144 on Idea 20 (pp. 74-83).

10   WHITFIELD, CHRISTOPHER, ed. Robert Dover and the Cotswold
     Games; "Annalia Dubrensia." London: Henry Sotheran;
     Ossining, N.Y.: William Salloch, 256 pp.
         Discusses Drayton's knowledge of the games and his
     association with Dover, examines his relationship to the
     collection (he was possibly "the initiator"), comments on
     his relationships with and influence on other contribu-
     tors, and provides an annotated reprint of Drayton's
     contribution (pp. 99-103, passim).

1963

1963

1   BUSH, DOUGLAS. Mythology and the Renaissance Tradition in
    English Poetry. Revised edition. New York: W. W.
    Norton, 385 pp.
        In revision of 1932.5 makes only minor changes in dis-
    cussion of Drayton (pp. 156-66, passim).

2   BUXTON, JOHN. Elizabethan Taste. London: Macmillan, 384 pp.
        Discusses Drayton's criticism of private, as opposed to
    public, poetry; contrasts his attitude with Donne's
    (pp. 317-23).

3   DRAYTON, MICHAEL. Endimion and Phoebe: Ideas Latmus, in
    Elizabethan Minor Epics. Edited by Elizabeth Story Donno.
    New York: Columbia University Press; London: Routledge &
    Kegan Paul, pp. 180-206.
        Reprints 1595 edition. In "Introduction" (pp. 1-20),
    briefly discusses the poem in an overview of the minor
    epic.

4   LaBRANCHE, ANTHONY [SPAHR]. "Drayton's The Barons Warres and
    the Rhetoric of Historical Poetry." JEGP, 62 (January),
    82-95.
        In showing how an understanding of rhetoric "will
    sharpen our appreciation of the poetic element in" Barons'
    Wars, analyzes Drayton's use of rhetorical figures and
    their relationship to the historical narrative, the ora-
    torical structure of the work, and the influence of Lucan
    on the rhetoric of the poem.

5   _____. "The 'Twofold Vitality' of Drayton's Odes." CL, 15
    (Spring), 116-29.
        Examines the native and classical elements in Drayton's
    Odes to show how "they represent, at their best moments,
    an original vitality joined to vigorous imitation."
    Discusses "how Drayton conceived historically of his task
    of 'musical' imitation," his "attempt to define the
    poet's place and his attitude to his art," and the rela-
    tionship of his use of native and historical elements to
    the Horatian spirit. Draws frequently on Ronsard for
    comparison.

6   MOORE, WILLIAM HAMILTON. "The Fusion of History and Poetry
    in Drayton's Poly-Olbion." Ph.D. dissertation, Harvard
    University.
        Examines Polyolbion "in relation to the other histori-
    cal poems by Drayton and his contemporaries and in

relation to the serious historical thought and writing of
Renaissance England." Analyzes structure, themes, and
tone of the work, and comments on "the most important
virtues of . . . [Drayton's] style and the essential nature of his hexameter couplets." Concludes that the poem
"is a panegyric, and it is the fullest expression of
Drayton's patriotism. It also reveals his reasonableness
in controversy, his keen perception of beauty, and his
tolerant appreciation of all things of value."

7   PERRINE, LAURENCE. "A Drayton Sonnet." CEA, 25 (June), 8.
     Argues contra Phillipson (1963.8) that in Idea 61 "the
     speaker . . . is threatening to end a love affair that he
     wishes to continue . . . and that the 'circumstance' is
     fully indicated in the poem." Identifies the "circum-
     stance" as the woman's refusal to satisfy sexually the
     speaker. See 1973.6, 1974.4, 1974.14, and 1974.15.

8   PHILLIPSON, JOHN S. "A Drayton Sonnet." CEA, 25 (April), 3.
     Observes "that classroom interest in [Idea 61] . . .
     can be considerably stimulated by suggesting that it may
     be read as a dialogue." Identifies lines which might be
     assigned to a male and female speaker. See 1963.7,
     1973.6, 1974.4, 1974.14, and 1974.15.

9   WILKES, G[ERALD] A[LFRED]. "Paradise Regained and the Con-
     ventions of the Sacred Epic." ES, 44 (February), 35-38.
     Draws on Noah's Flood in discussing "'the oration from
     a given moral standpoint,'" one of the conventions of the
     minor sacred epic. Calls Noah's Flood, Moses, and David
     and Goliath "the best examples of the type [i.e., sacred
     epic] in English verse before Milton."

1964

1   BUCHLOH, PAUL GERHARD. Michael Drayton, Bard und Historiker--
     Politiker und Prophet: Ein Beitrag zur Behandlung und
     Beurteilung der nationalen Frühgeschichte Grossbritanniens
     in der englischen Dichtung der Spätrenaissance. KBAA,
     vol. 1. Neumünster: Karl Wachholtz, 390 pp.
     Provides detailed analysis of the evolution of Drayton's
     historical poetry, especially Polyolbion. Examines his
     techniques and methods of representing early history,
     particularly his poetic, historic, and political treatment
     of early English history. Also examines his treatment of
     biblical history. Places Drayton's historical verse in
     the context of the social and political concerns of his

1964

age. Reviewed in Ludwig Borinski, Anglia, 84, no. 2
(1966), 227-31; Claes Schaar, ES, 49 (April 1968), 162-63.

2 CURTIS, MARK H. "Shakespeare and Other English Dramatists
at Cambridge, ca. 1700." SQ, 15 (Autumn), 445-46.
Notes that Drayton was among the six dramatists recom-
mended by Joshua Barnes, Regius Professor of Greek, to
his students.

3 GOLDMAN, LLOYD NATHANIEL. "Attitudes Toward the Mistress
in Five Elizabethan Sonnet Sequences." Ph.D. dissertation, University of Illinois, 297 pp. [DA, 25 (1965),
6590-91.]
Analyzes Drayton's attitude toward Idea "by examining
his attitude toward his conceits"; finds that Drayton,
Sidney, and Shakespeare "employ their sonnets as tools for
the logical examination of the attitudes of their per-
sonae." Shows how Drayton "constructed his sequence in
a manner which shows his attitude toward his Lady evolving
through four different stages, which are finally united in
his last sonnets." Concludes that "Drayton was presenting
the maturation of a lover courting his Lady."

4 GRUNDY, JOAN. "'Brave translunary things.'" MLR, 59 (October), 501-10.
Analyzes "Drayton's use of 'clear'" as a complex critical term which implies "something knowledgeable, visionary,
heroic in theme and spirit, perspicuous, and shiningly
beautiful"; relates the use of the term to Drayton's Neo-
Platonic views of poetry and the poet, particularly in the
passage on Marlowe in "To Henry Reynolds" and Endymion and
Phoebe (wherein Endymion is "a type of the poet" and
Phoebe "may to some extent be identified with the Heaven-
ly Muse").

5 JUEL-JENSEN, BENT. "Fine and Large-Paper Copies of S.T.C.
Books, and Particularly of Drayton's Poems (1619) and The
Battaile of Agincourt (1627)." Library, 5th ser., 19:
226-30, 6 plates.
Provides bibliographical description of fine and large-
paper copies of STC 7190 and 7222. See 1968.8.

6 ORUCH, JACK BERNARD. "Topography in the Prose and Poetry of
the English Renaissance." Ph.D. dissertation, Indiana
University, 303 pp. [DA, 25 (1964), 2966.]
Discusses Polyolbion and topographical passages in
Drayton's other works in a survey of the topic.

260

7   RICHMOND, H[UGH] M. The School of Love: The Evolution of
    the Stuart Love Lyric. Princeton: Princeton University
    Press, 350 pp.
        In chapter 3 ("The New Style," pp. 99-173), discusses
    Drayton's "syntactical rhythm" and use of the motif of
    rejecting the mistress as an excuse for the catalogue of
    her charms in "To His Coy Love" (pp. 112-15).

                            1965

1   APPELBE, JANE LUND. "An Inquiry into the Rehabilitation of
    Certain Seventeenth-Century Poets, 1800-1832." Ph.D.
    dissertation, University of Toronto. [DA, 27 (1966),
    1777-78A.]
        Discusses the revival of interest in Drayton.

2   BARKER, J. R. "A Pendant to Drummond of Hawthornden's Con-
    versations." RES, NS 16 (August), 284-88.
        Points out that Drummond's marginalia in his copy of
    Jonson's Works (1616) establishes that Daniel, not Dray-
    ton, was the "better verser" of Forest, Epistle 12, ll.
    68-70.

3   BRAND, C[HARLES] P[ETER]. Torquato Tasso: A Study of the
    Poet and of His Contribution to English Literature.
    Cambridge: Cambridge University Press, 356 pp.
        Comments on influence of Gerusalemme liberata on Robert,
    Barons' Wars, and Muses' Elysium (pp. 247-48).

4   DRAYTON, MICHAEL. The Harmony of the Church. Edited by
    Alexander Dyce. Percy Society, vol. 7. New York:
    Johnson Reprint, 77 pp. [Separately paginated.]
        Reprint of 1843.1.

5   EAGLE, RODERICK L[EWIS]. The Secrets of the Shakespeare
    Sonnets. London: Mitre Press, 148 pp.
        Cites several parallels between Idea and Sonnets to
    argue that Drayton was the Rival Poet (passim).

6   FIEHLER, RUDOLPH. The Strange History of Sir John Oldcastle.
    New York: American Press, 243 pp.
        In revision of 1950.3 provides scene-by-scene commentary
    on Oldcastle, with emphasis on sources. Concludes that the
    authors "continually lapsed into imitation" of Shake-
    speare's Henry plays, that Holinshed's Chronicles was a
    main source, and that the play was "hastily cobbled to-
    gether out of piecemeal knowledge, and filled in with
    imagination" (pp. 187-207).

1965

7 GILDE, HELEN CHENEY. "The Castalian Fount: The Development
   and Decline of the Mythological Narrative Poem in the
   English Renaissance." Ph.D. dissertation, University of
   Chicago.
       Discusses Endymion and Phoebe in "a study of the his-
   tory of the" type. Finds that Drayton's poem "differs
   from most contemporary poems of the same kind in eschewing
   eroticism, wit, and irony in favor of didactic allegory
   and pseudo-Platonic theorizing" and that the "work is, to
   a degree, an attempt to return to the morally serious
   mythological poetry of an earlier age and at the same
   time to exploit the rich pictorial style of the 1590's."

8 HILLER, GEOFFREY G. "Robert White and Michael Drayton." N&Q,
   NS 12 (October), 384.
       Requests information on the possible acquaintance be-
   tween Drayton and White and on Drayton's knowledge of
   White's Cupid's Banishment, a possible source of Muses'
   Elysium. See 1970.10.

9 HOBSBAUM, PHILIP. "Elizabethan Poetry." PoetryR, 56: 80-97.
       Argues that "it is high time that we ceased to see the
   [late Elizabethan] period as that of Sidney, Spenser,
   Daniel and Drayton; rather its key figures are Chapman,
   Jonson, Marston, Donne, Raleigh and Greville--together
   with the great translators, Stanyhurst, Golding and Harington." Characterizes Drayton and Daniel as "dull sticks
   that sometimes rub up against a few sparks of poetry."

10 LEVINE, JOSEPH MARTIN. "From Caxton to Camden: The Quest
   for Historical Truth in Sixteenth Century England." Ph.D.
   dissertation, Columbia University, 624 pp. [DA, 29
   (1968), 200-201A.]
       Discusses "Drayton's choice of the historian Selden to
   annotate (and correct) his historical fictions" in Polyolbion as an example of the "self-conscious separation between history and historical fiction" which developed in
   the latter part of the sixteenth century.

11 McCOY, DOROTHY SCHUCHMAN. Tradition and Convention: A Study
   of Periphrasis in English Pastoral Poetry from 1557-1715.
   SEngL, 5. The Hague: Mouton, 289 pp.
       In revision of 1962.7 draws frequently on Pastorals and
   and Muses' Elysium in analyzing the characteristics and
   uses of periphrasis (pp. 144-47, 197-98, passim).

12 PRATT, SAMUEL M[AXON]. "Shakespeare and Humphrey Duke of
     Gloucester: A Study in Myth." SQ, 16 (Spring), 201-16.
          Discusses place of England's Heroical Epistles
     (Gloucester-Cobham and Queen Margaret-Suffolk) and
     Margaret (briefly) in the development of the myth of the
     Duke. Isolates Drayton's characterization of Humphrey,
     "a man who can get outside himself to become genuinely
     concerned about another [i.e., his wife]," as his "major
     contribution to the myth." Notes that Drayton, like
     Ferrers and Shakespeare, "presented . . . [the Duke] in
     such ways as to elevate him, morally and intellectually,
     above the normal level of the English nobility."

13 RIDLON, HAROLD GUY, JR. "Michael Drayton as a Satirist."
     Ph.D. dissertation, Harvard University.
          In arguing that "there seethes under the surface of a
     surprisingly large percentage of Drayton's work a tone
     reflecting an attitude which can only be called satiric,"
     attempts "to discover, identify, and trace the influence
     of satire on Drayton's work." Finds that in most of the
     genres in which he writes there is a "pattern of imita-
     tion, rebellion, and reconciliation, and in each case the
     adaptation of genuine feeling to conventional form--
     especially when that feeling is one of bitterness, frus-
     tration, disappointment, and protest--strengthens the
     impuse toward vivid communication. In elegy, in Biblical
     narrative, in ode, and in pastoral idyll, the transforma-
     tions constantly reveal the salutary effect of satire in
     providing focus and energy."

14 RIGGS, E. S. "A Little Learning." AN&Q, 3 (May), 135.
          Suggests "To Henry Reynolds" as Pope's source for Essay
     on Criticism (I.215-16).

15 ROBERTSON, JEAN. "Drayton and the Countess of Pembroke."
     RES, NS 16 (February), 49.
          Identifies "Meridianis" in Idea's Mirror 51 and "Mere-
     dian's" in Gaveston (ll. 1735-38) as anagrams for "Mari
     Sidnei."

16 SALMON, VIVIAN. "The Family of Ithamaria (Reginolles)
     Reynolds Pell, Grandmother of Thomas Pell II, Third Lord
     of the Manor of Pelham." Pelliana, NS 1, no. 3, 1-24.
          Identifies and provides brief biography of the Henry
     Reynolds of "To Henry Reynolds."

1965

17   SCOULAR, KITTY W.   Natural Magic: Studies in the Presenta-
     tion of Nature in English Poetry from Spenser to Marvell.
     Oxford: Clarendon Press, 208 pp.
          In published version of 1956.10, draws frequently on
     Drayton to illustrate various aspects of the treatment of
     nature in the pastoral; in particular notes his use of
     "the debate between hill and valley" in Polyolbion (pas-
     sim).

18   STÜRZL, ERWIN [ANTON].   Der Zeitbegriff in der elisabethan-
     ischen Literatur: The Lackey of Eternity.   WBEP, 69.
     Vienna: Wilhelm Braumüller, 536 pp.
          Draws frequently on Drayton's works in a wide-ranging
     analysis of the concept of time in Elizabethan literature
     (passim).

19   WHITFIELD, CHRISTOPHER.   "Clifford Chambers: The Muses Quiet
     Port." N&Q, NS 12 (October), 362-75.
          Discusses Drayton's references to and association with
     the Rainsford and Goodere families.

1966

1   BRISTOL, MICHAEL DAVID.   "Structural and Thematic Patterns
     in Michael Drayton's The Shepheards Garland." Ph.D. dis-
     sertation, Princeton University, 192 pp. [DA, 28 (1967),
     1046-47A.]
          "[A]ttempts to define the principal thematic preoccupa-
     tions of the eclogue sequence and to point out the charac-
     teristic structure of the genre through a critical inter-
     pretation of" Shepherd's Garland. Analyzes how Drayton,
     influenced by Virgil's Bucolics, uses "a pattern of
     reciprocal pairing and symmetrical placing" to structure
     the work.

2   CURTIS, JARED R.   "William Wordsworth and English Poetry of
     the Sixteenth and Seventeenth Centuries." Cornell Library
     Journal, no. 1, pp. 28-39.
          Traces several references to Drayton in Wordsworth's
     works and manuscripts.

3   ELTON, OLIVER.   Michael Drayton: A Critical Study.   New
     York: Russell & Russell, 232 pp.
          Reprint of 1905.3.

4   HARDIN, RICHARD FRANCIS. "Michael Drayton and the Ovidian
     Tradition." Ph.D. dissertation, University of Texas,
     320 pp. [DA, 27 (1967), 3248A.]
         Examines "the background of Drayton's Ovidian works and
     the manner in which these poems reflect Ovidian conven-
     tions." Discusses Gaveston, Matilda, Endymion and Phoebe,
     Man in the Moon, Quest of Cynthia, England's Heroical
     Epistles, and Polyolbion.

5   JUEL-JENSEN, BENT. "Contemporary Collectors XLIII." BC, 15
     (Summer), 152-74.
         Includes a description of his Drayton collection, with
     particular emphasis on items acquired since 1955. See
     1955.4.

6   _____. "Michael Drayton and William Drummond of Hawthornden:
     A Lost Autograph Letter Rediscovered." Library, 5th ser.,
     21 (December), 328-30, 1 plate.
         Describes and transcribes Drayton's letter of 22 Novem-
     ber 1620, which disappeared after being published in the
     1711 edition of Drummond's Works.

7   PAPAJEWSKI, HELMUT. "An Lucanus Sit Poeta." DVLG, 40,
     no. 4, 485-508.
         Draws frequently on Drayton in examining the question
     in English literary criticism of whether Lucan was a poet
     or historian. Discusses the blurring of history and
     poetry in Drayton's works.

8   ROWAN, D. F. "Shore's Wife." SEL, 6 (Summer), 447-64.
         Discusses Edward IV-Shore epistles (England's Heroical
     Epistles) as representatives of the "literary tradition"
     (as opposed to the "popular tradition") in the Renaissance
     treatments of the Shore story. Concludes that in "Dray-
     ton's poem[s] there is no tragedy, and only a very little
     pathos. There are no moral judgments . . . , but only a
     typical Elizabethan delight in love and in words and their
     ways."

1967

1   ALPERS, PAUL J. The Poetry of "The Faerie Queene." Prince-
     ton: Princeton University Press, 425 pp.
         In analyzing the relationship between sentence and
     stanza in Faerie Queene, compares Drayton's practice in

1967

> Barons' Wars. Finds that reading Drayton's poem "requires
> a distinct consciousness of the sentence structure" and
> that there is a "conflict between verse form and sentence
> structure" in the work (pp. 78-81).

2　BALDWIN, ANNE WILFONG. "Thomas Berthelet and Tudor Propa-
　　ganda." Ph.D. dissertation, University of Illinois,
　　482 pp. [DA, 28 (1968), 5005-5006A.]
　　　Discusses Barons' Wars in analyzing the possible influ-
　　ence in later Renaissance literature of Henrican propa-
　　ganda about "the nature of kingship."

3　BERTHELOT, JOSEPH A[LFRED]. Michael Drayton. TEAS, 52. New
　　York: Twayne, 172 pp.
　　　Traces Drayton's evolution "[f]rom a relatively second-
　　rate Petrarchist . . . [to] a highly diversified and ac-
　　complished, if not great, poet." Places particular
　　emphasis on revisions of Idea as representative of his
　　"growth as a poet." Devotes chapters to Idea; pastoral
　　and fairy poems; historical verse; Polyolbion; religious
　　and occasional poems, satires, odes, and elegies; and
　　poetic theory and reputation. For most works gives a
　　running commentary with brief discussion of prosody,
　　theme(s), literary background, revision(s), and influence.
　　Concludes that Drayton did not remain "an Elizabethan
　　throughout his entire poetic career" but "moved with the
　　changing times in his poetic techniques"--he "was an in-
　　veterate experimenter both in genre and prosody." Sug-
　　gests that Drayton's name "might be advanced for the title
　　of 'the complete Renaissance Poet.'" Includes selected
　　bibliography.

4　BUXTON, JOHN. A Tradition of Poetry. London: Macmillan;
　　New York: St. Martin's Press, 200 pp.
　　　In chapter 4 ("Michael Drayton," pp. 59-86), provides
　　critical overview of his life and work to illustrate how
　　Drayton, as the "dedicated professional poet," responded
　　"to the literary modes and manners of his time." Examines
　　how he experimented and revised "until he had brought . . .
　　[a form] to the greatest excellence of which he was capa-
　　ble" and analyzes how the love of England, poetry, and
　　history animate his work.

5　DRAYTON, MICHAEL. Poemes, Lyrick and Pastorall. Burt Frank-
　　lin Research and Source Works Series, no. 150. New York:
　　Burt Franklin, 122 pp.
　　　Reprint of 1891.3.

6 _____ . Poems: By Michael Draiton, Esquire. Burt Franklin
   Research and Source Works Series, no. 150. New York:
   Burt Franklin, 504 pp.
       Reprint of 1888.2.

7 GUFFEY, GEORGE ROBERT. "Michael Drayton, 1941-1965," in his
   Elizabethan Bibliographies Supplements, VII: Samuel Daniel, 1942-1965; Michael Drayton, 1941-1965; Sir Philip
   Sidney, 1941-1965. London: Nether Press, pp. 23-29.
       Continues 1941.10, providing a chronological list of
   seventy-eight works published 1941-1965.

*8 HILLER, G[EOFFREY] G. "The Pastoral Poetry of Michael Dray-
   ton and His Age." Ph.D. dissertation, Cambridge University.

9 HOLLOWAY, JOHN. Widening Horizons in English Verse. Evans-
   ton: Northwestern University Press, 125 pp.
       Examines Drayton's knowledge of Celtic poetic art,
   especially as it represents "a knowledge of non-English
   and at the same time non-classical culture first truly
   imping[ing] on English literature and taste" (pp. 5-9,
   passim).

10 LEVY, F[RED] J[ACOB]. Tudor Historical Thought. San Marino:
   Huntington Library, 317 pp.
       In chapter 6 ("The Popularization of History," pp. 202-
   36), surveys Drayton's historical poetry; finds Battle of
   Agincourt his "most successful" historical poem (pp. 220-
   23).

11 LOGAN, GEORGE MEREDITH. "Lucan in England: The Influence
   of the Pharsalia on English Letters from the Beginnings
   through the Sixteenth Century." Ph.D. dissertation,
   Harvard University.
       Examines influence of Pharsalia on Barons' Wars and
   Mortimeriados.

12 MUIR, KENNETH. Introduction to Elizabethan Literature.
   New York: Random House, 213 pp.
       In chapter 4 ("Two Professional Poets," pp. 64-83),
   provides a general critical overview of Drayton's works
   (pp. 75-83).

13 SCHÖNERT, JÖRG. "Draytons Sonett-Revisionen: Zum Problem
   des Übergangsdichters.'" Anglia, 85: 161-83.
       Provides detailed analysis of style, form, and content
   of Drayton's revisions of Idea to show him moving toward
   a metaphysical style.

1967

14   SHEAVYN, PHOEBE. The Literary Profession in the Elizabethan
      Age. Second edition, revised by J[ohn] W[hiteside]
      Saunders. Manchester: Manchester University Press;
      New York: Barnes & Noble, 258 pp.
         In revision of 1909.5 draws frequently on Drayton in
      analyzing various aspects of the profession of letters
      (passim).

15   TANNENBAUM, SAMUEL A[ARON]. Michael Drayton, in Samuel
      A[aron] Tannenbaum and Dorothy R[osenzweig] Tannenbaum,
      Elizabethan Bibliographies. Vol. II. Port Washington,
      N.Y.: Kennikat Press, 64 pp. [Separately paginated.]
         Reprint of 1941.10.

16   TUVE, ROSEMOND. "'Imitation' and Images," in Elizabethan
      Poetry: Modern Essays in Criticism. Edited by Paul J.
      Alpers. New York: Oxford University Press, pp. 41-62.
         Reprints chapter of 1947.5 in which Tuve discusses
      Mortimeriados and Barons' Wars.

17   WINTERS, YVOR. "Aspects of the Short Poem in the English
      Renaissance," in his Forms of Discovery: Critical &
      Historical Essays on the Forms of the Short Poem in
      English. Chicago: Alan Swallow, pp. 1-120.
         In revision of 1939.13 omits comparison with Sidney
      and points out that Drayton's "genius--a remarkable
      genius--shows itself in great lines and passages." In-
      cludes a list of his best poems.

18   _____ . "The 16th Century Lyric in England: A Critical and
      Historical Reinterpretation," in Elizabethan Poetry:
      Modern Essays in Criticism. Edited by Paul J. Alpers.
      New York: Oxford University Press, pp. 93-125.
         Reprints 1939.13.

                              1968

1   ALEXANDER, NIGEL, ed. Elizabethan Narrative Verse.
      Stratford-upon-Avon Library, 3. Cambridge: Harvard Uni-
      versity Press, 348 pp.
         In "Introduction" (pp. 1-26), discusses several of
      Drayton's poems in a survey of Elizabethan narrative verse.
      Suggests that "[i]t could be argued that England's Hero-
      icall Epistles is not only Drayton's most popular poem
      but his most decisive contribution towards that epic his-
      tory of England which he and Daniel laboured all their
      lives to write." Includes annotated reprint of Henry II-
      Rosamond epistles (1597), pp. 237-47.

2   BEVINGTON, DAVID. <u>Tudor Drama and Politics: A Critical Ap-</u>
    <u>proach to Topical Meaning</u>. Cambridge: Harvard University
    Press, 372 pp.
        Discusses <u>Oldcastle</u> as "the moderate Puritans' warning
    to extremists of their own party" and places the work in
    its historical and religious context (pp. 256-59).

3   BROICH, ULRICH. "Michael Drayton," in <u>Die englische Lyrik:</u>
    <u>Von der Renaissance bis zur Gegenwart</u>. Vol. I. Edited
    by Karl Heinz Göller. Dusseldorf: August Bagel, pp. 65-
    75.
        Explicates <u>Idea</u> 62 (titling it "The Paradox") and
    places the sonnet in the tradition of the paradox of un-
    fulfilled love from Petrarch through the Renaissance.
    Also briefly discusses the relationship of the poem to
    the use of paradox in religious poetry.

4   DÖRRIE, HEINRICH. <u>Der heroische Brief: Bestandsaufnahme,</u>
    <u>Geschichte, Kritik einer humanistisch-barocken Literatur-</u>
    <u>gattung</u>. Berlin: Walter de Gruyter, 594 pp.
        In "Die heroische Briefdichtung in England: Michael
    Drayton" (pp. 158-62), provides annotated list of verse
    epistles c. 1542-1753. Includes list of works influenced
    by <u>England's Heroical Epistles</u>.

5   DRAYTON, MICHAEL. <u>Endymion and Phoebe: Idea's Latmus</u>, in
    <u>Elizabethan Verse Romances</u>. Edited by M[ax] M[eredith]
    Reese. Routledge English Texts. London: Routledge &
    Kegan Paul, pp. 159-87.
        Provides modernized, annotated reprint. In "Introduc-
    tion" (pp. 1-23), discusses the poem as an attempt "to
    show that an erotic romance did not have to be lewd" and
    provides brief overview of Drayton's career with a criti-
    cal estimate of his poetry.

6   HARDIN, RICHARD F[RANCIS]. "The Composition of <u>Poly-Olbion</u>
    and <u>The Muses Elizium</u>." <u>Anglia</u>, 86, nos. 1-2, 160-62.
        Points out that if Meres's and Jonson's statements
    about <u>Polyolbion</u> are accurate "between 1598 and 1612
    Drayton contemplated at least two different lines of
    development for his work: one descriptive, the other
    narrative." Suggests that some of the unused passages in
    the revision of <u>Polyolbion</u> were incorporated in <u>Muses'</u>
    <u>Elysium</u>.

1968

7   _____. "Convention and Design in Drayton's <u>Heroicall</u>
     <u>Epistles</u>." <u>PMLA</u>, 83 (March), 35-41.
         Analyzes influence of the tragic complaint, structure,
     contrasts with Ovid's <u>Heroides</u>, and purpose ("to convey
     to the reader . . . [the] spirit of confident patriotism")
     to demonstrate that Drayton created "a wholly new, thor-
     oughly English heroic epistle."

8   JUEL-JENSEN, BENT. "Fine and Large-Paper Copies of <u>STC</u>
     Books: A Further Note." <u>Library</u>, 5th ser., 23 (Septem-
     ber), 239-40.
         Describes two more fine and large-paper copies of <u>Poems</u>
     (1619); <u>see</u> 1964.5.

9   MOORE, WILLIAM H[AMILTON]. "Sources of Drayton's Conception
     of <u>Poly-Olbion</u>." <u>SP</u>, 65 (October), 783-803.
         Places <u>Polyolbion</u> in the tradition of Elizabethan anti-
     quarian works and examines the influence of Leland, Cam-
     den, cartography, John Price, Llwyd, Richard Verstegan,
     Churchyard, William Vallans, Edmund Spenser, and Ausonius
     on the "general conception" of and techniques in the poem.
     Gives particular attention to identifying Drayton's speci-
     fic indebtedness to Verstegan, Churchyard, Vallans, and
     Ausonius.

10   NAGY, N[ICLAS] CHRISTOPH DE. <u>Michael Drayton's "England's</u>
     <u>Heroical Epistles:" A Study in Themes and Compositional</u>
     <u>Devices</u>. Cooper Monographs, 14. Bern: Francke, 67 pp.
         Defines "primary aim" as "the elucidation of the themes
     and some of the formal elements" in the work as they are
     conditioned by Drayton's attempt "to imitate Ovid 'partly'
     and to disseminate historical information at the same
     time." Divides epistles into the historical, the erotic,
     and a group "falling somewhere between the two" and at-
     tempts "to delineate the Ovidian and the non-Ovidian in
     the" poems. Examines place of <u>England's Heroical Epistles</u>
     in Drayton's work, themes and composition, influences on
     the work, the chief compositional devices, structure,
     style, and use of narrative. Finds that Drayton's "compo-
     sition" of the work is "defective" largely because "of the
     lack of transitions within the various elements . . . that
     constitute his epistles." Reviewed in A[lice] d'Haussy,
     <u>EA</u>, 22 (April-June 1969), 186-87; Joan Rees, <u>YES</u>, 1
     (1971), 235-36.

11   PARSONS, D. S. J. "The Odes of Drayton and Jonson." <u>QQ</u>, 75
     (Winter), 675-84.

In discussing the two as the first poets "not only to capture the spirit of the ode but to master its intrinsic classical requirements," surveys the changes in style, sensibility, and form in Drayton's odes as "he moved from a humanist-medieval to a Cavalier form of expression."

1969

1   BONI, JOHN MICHAEL. "Two Epics of English History: Samuel Daniel's Civile Wars and Michael Drayton's Barons Wars." Ph.D. dissertation, University of Denver, 214 pp. [DAI, 30 (1970), 4398A.]
    Analyzes the "grave weaknesses" of the poems in terms of the "three traditions from which . . . [they] spring: sixteenth century English history writing, The Mirror for Magistrates, and the epic tradition."

2   DAVIS, JOYCE OUTTEN. "Robert Davenport's King John and Matilda: A Critical Edition." Ph.D. dissertation, Tulane University, 303 pp. [DAI, 30 (1969), 2478-79A.]
    Discusses Davenport's indebtedness to England's Heroical Epistles (King John-Matilda) and Matilda.

3   DAVIS, WALTER R[ICHARDSON]. "'Fantastickly I sing': Drayton's Idea of 1619." SP, 66 (April), 204-16.
    Argues "that Idea [1619] is essentially a comic sonnet-sequence, its subject the unsuccessful attempt to avoid conventionality." Concludes: "The plot of Idea is the attempt to establish the uniqueness of individual experience and its failure, the attempt to escape from standard passionate suffering into a libertine pose and its failure, the attempt to range sportively inside an offhand fantastic style and its failure in returning to sighs and tears and all the rest of the Petrarchan panoply of emotions. Drayton's plot is in this way essentially a comic plot, its butt the lover himself who refuses to accept the everyday world of romantic cliché for what it is, but who must at length--sonnet by sonnet--realize his involvement in it and side with the readers who laugh at him."

4   DONOW, HERBERT S. "Concordance and Stylistic Analysis of Six Elizabethan Sonnet Sequences." CHum, 3 (March), 205-208.
    Describes "stylistic tests" on data in and the making of 1969.5.

1969

5   _____ . A Concordance to the Sonnet Sequences of Daniel,
     Drayton, Shakespeare, Sidney, and Spenser. Carbondale:
     Southern Illinois University Press; London: Feffer &
     Simons, 784 pp.
         Includes Idea's Mirror (from 1931.4) and Idea (from
     1932.6) in a computer-generated "single merged index."
     Provides word frequency list for each work in appendix
     (pp. 728-42). In preface (pp. vi-xi), suggests possible
     applications of the concordance to stylistic studies.

6   DRAYTON, MICHAEL. A Gratulatorie Poem. English Experience,
     no. 169. New York: Da Capo Press; Amsterdam: Theatrvm
     Orbis Terrarvm, n.p.
         Provides facsimile reprint of 1603 edition of Majesty
     of King James.

7   _____ . "Poems," [1619]. Menston: Scolar Press, 487 pp.
         Provides facsimile reprint of 1619 edition.

8   FRIEDMAN, STANLEY. "Antony and Cleopatra and Drayton's
     Mortimeriados." SQ, 20 (Autumn), 481-84.
         Notes parallels between Drayton's account of the "love
     affair between Mortimer and Isabella" and Shakespeare's
     play; points out that the resemblances do not suggest that
     Drayton influenced Shakespeare but that they "are signi-
     ficant in revealing the two poets' interest in similar
     historical situations and in characters who command ad-
     miration despite the ambiguity of their moral natures."
     Concludes that Drayton provided an "extremely eulogistic
     treatment of historical characters known to have partici-
     pated in a morally questionable love affair."

9   GRUNDY, JOAN. The Spenserian Poets: A Study in Elizabethan
     and Jacobean Poetry. London: Edward Arnold, 232 pp.
         Includes extensive discussion of Drayton in an attempt
     to rescue the Spenserians from their current "undeserved"
     neglect. Examines Drayton's attitude toward and concep-
     tion of poetry, his conception of the pastoral and use of
     it as an embodiment of his poetic, and his transmutation
     of the influence of Spenser. Devotes chapters to Dray-
     ton's presentation of the heroic ideal and to the tech-
     niques he uses to organize, unify, and dignify the subject
     matter of Polyolbion (passim).

10   LaBRANCHE, ANTHONY [SPAHR]. "Poetry, History, and Oratory:
     The Renaissance Historical Poem." SEL, 9 (Winter), 1-19.
         In examining "how and with what modifications the con-
     ventional rhetorical training of Shakespeare's day was

put to use in some historical poetry and what accommoda-
tions were made there between rhetorical conventions and
historical conventions," focuses on Barons' Wars "to dem-
onstrate what may be the poetic uses of source material
and of rhetorical amplification, resulting in the 'fic-
tionalizing' of the historical events." Also discusses
England's Heroical Epistles as it "reveal[s] Drayton's
basic method of combining personal with political events."

11   PIPER, WILLIAM BOWMAN. The Heroic Couplet. Cleveland:
     Press of Case Western Reserve University, 466 pp.
          In chapter 4 ("Early Developments," pp. 49-82), anal-
     yzes Drayton's ineffective use of the "enjambed romance
     couplet" in Man in the Moon; and in a separate essay
     ("Michael Drayton [1563-1631]," pp. 189-92), surveys
     Drayton's use of the couplet in Elegies, England's Heroi-
     cal Epistles, Endymion and Phoebe, Man in the Moon, and
     Moon-Calf. Observes that Drayton's use of the couplet
     illustrates both "the range of poetic opportunities the
     form offered . . . and . . . the dangers"--particularly
     the "problem [of] . . . working it into a coherent poetic
     medium" (pp. 50-55, 189-92).

12   RHINEHART, RAYMOND PATRICK. "The Elizabethan Ovidian Epyl-
     lion: A Definition and Re-Evaluation." Ph.D. disserta-
     tion, Princeton University, 452 pp. [DAI, 30 (1969),
     2040A.]
          Includes Endymion and Phoebe in a survey and definition
     of the genre.

13   SCHABERT, IRMGARD. "Ideas Mirrour" und "Idea," Sonette,
     1594-1619: Vollständige und kommentierte Textausgabe.
     Ph.D. dissertation, Ludwig-Maximilians-Universität.
     Augsburg: W. Blasaditsch, 250 pp.
          Provides critical edition of all of the sonnets from
     Idea's Mirror and the various editions of Idea. Offers
     detailed commentary, along with textual and explanatory
     notes, for each sonnet. In introduction (pp. 1-33),
     discusses the various editions, the significance (bio-
     graphical, Petrarchan, and Platonic) of Idea, the poet's
     representation of himself in the sequence, the handling
     of the relationship between the poet and the lady, and
     the relationship of Drayton's sequence to other sonnets
     and lyrics of the period.

1970

1970

*1   AKAGAWA, YUTAKA. "Renaissance no Sonnets [Sonnets in the Renaissance]." <u>Ronso</u> (Meijigakuin Daigaku), no. 164 (October), pp. 71–116
      Cited in [Kazuyoshi Enozawa and Sister Miyo Takano,] "The 1970 Bibliography," <u>RenB</u>, 5 (1978), 19, item 7.

2   BERLETH, RICHARD JOHN. "In the Field of the Muses: A Reading of Michael Drayton." Ph.D. dissertation, Rutgers University, 287 pp. [<u>DAI</u>, 31 (1971), 6045A.]
      Analyzes Drayton's relationship to Spenser and the Spenserians in "elucidat[ing] the order underlying Drayton's varied work." In successive chapters "suggests that . . . stylistic affinities [with Spenser and the Spenserians] account for Drayton's loss of popularity and difficulties with the Court of King James"; "demonstrates the emphasis placed upon the Muse throughout the works and considers the theory of inspiration symbolized by this convention"; examines the dependence of Drayton's "conventional and unconventional uses of the catalogue and <u>blazon</u> . . . upon his theory of inspiration"; analyzes his topographical imagery; and demonstrates how "Drayton's usual concerns and artifice are adapted to new poetic models."

3   BRISTOL, MICHAEL D[AVID]. "Structural Patterns in Two Elizabethan Pastorals." <u>SEL</u>, 10 (Winter), 33–48.
      Analyzes Drayton's use of "Virgil's scheme of symmetrical pairing" to structure <u>Shepherd's Garland</u>. Examines relationship of the subtitle and the importance of Eclogue 5 (and its subject, Idea) to the structure of the work.

4   DRAYTON, MICHAEL. <u>Ideas Mirrovr</u>, in <u>Elizabethan Sonnet Sequences</u>. Edited by Herbert Grabes. English Texts, 3. Tübingen: Max Niemeyer, pp. 89–117.
      Provides unannotated reprint of 1594 edition.

5   _____. <u>The Mvses Elizivm</u>. Burt Franklin Research and Source Works Series, no. 150. New York: Burt Franklin, 215 pp.
      Reprint of 1892.2.

6   _____. <u>The Poly-Olbion: A Chorographical Description of Great Britain</u>. Burt Franklin Research and Source Works Series, no. 150. New York: Burt Franklin, 507 pp.
      Reprint of 1889.3.

1970

7   [DRAYTON, MICHAEL, ANTHONY MUNDAY, RICHARD HATHAWAY, and ROB-
     ERT WILSON]. "Sir John Oldcastle": "Written by William
     Shakespeare," 1600. Edited by John S[tephen] Farmer.
     Tudor Facsimile Texts, 89. New York: AMS Press, n.p.
          Reprints 1911.2.

8   DRISKILL, LINDA LORANE PHILLIPS. "Cyclic Structure in Ren-
     aissance Pastoral Poetry." Ph.D. dissertation, Rice Uni-
     versity, 406 pp. [DAI, 31 (1970), 2872-73A.]
          Devotes chapters 7 and 8 to Shepherd's Garland: exam-
     ines the "world view of the poem," the importance of time
     as a concept, and the structure of the eclogues (particu-
     larly "Drayton's use of repetition and planned variation").
     Compares structure of the work to Spenser's Shepherd's
     Calendar.

*9   HAUSSY, ALICE d'. "Michael Drayton, poète de l'Angleterre
     elisabéthaine." Ph.D. dissertation, Paris.
          Published version 1972.7. Cited in Gernot U. Gabel and
     Gisela R. Gabel, Dissertations in English and American
     Literature: Theses Accepted by Austrian, French, and
     Swiss Universities, 1875-1970 (Hamburg: Gernot Gabel,
     1977), p. 23, item 276.

10   HILLER, GEOFFREY G. "Drayton's Muses Elizium: 'A New Way
     over Parnassus.'" RES, NS 21 (February), 1-13.
          Argues that Drayton used Robert White's masque Cupid's
     Banishment as a source and discusses the strong possibil-
     ity that he originally wrote Muses' Elysium "as some form
     of dramatic entertainment," likely for the Sackvilles at
     Knole. Analyzes "the originality and novelty" of the
     work.

*11 JEHMLICH, REIMER. Die Bildlichkeit in der Liebeslyrik Sir
     Philip Sidneys, Michael Draytons und John Donnes ("Astro-
     phel and Stella, Idea, Songs and Sonnets"). Ph.D. dis-
     sertation, University of Kiel. Kiel: n.p., 202 pp.
          Provides comparative analysis of the use of metaphor in
     the three works in examining "Donne's 'modernism' and his
     alleged revolt against Elizabethan conventions." Finds
     that "Drayton, who rather rigidly adheres to the conven-
     tional conception of Neoplatonic love and indulges in
     panegyrics and laments, shows a preference for elaborately

1970

expanded metaphors, similes and concatenations. Since he varies the themes and situations of Petrarchan poetry only very slightly, his metaphors often have a certain sterility." (Abstract in English and American Studies in German: Summaries of Theses and Monographs, 1970, edited by Werner Habicht [Tübingen: Max Niemeyer, 1971], pp. 31-33.)

12   LELL, VIRGIL GORDON. "The Rape of Ganymede: Greek-Love Themes in Elizabethan Friendship Literature." Ph.D. dissertation, University of Nebraska, 303 pp. [DAI, 31 (1971), 5367-68A.]
Discusses Drayton's "generally critical" attitude toward Greek love in Gaveston.

13   PALMER, D[AVID] J[OHN]. "The Verse Epistle," in Metaphysical Poetry. Edited by D[avid] J[ohn] Palmer and Malcolm Bradbury. Stratford-upon-Avon Studies, 11. New York: St. Martin's Press, pp. 72-99.
Examines Drayton's verse epistles (noting in particular how they "reveal a man out of sympathy with the trends of a new age") in an overview of the Renaissance verse epistle.

14   PATTERSON, ANNABEL M. Hermogenes and the Renaissance: Seven Ideas of Style. Princeton: Princeton University Press, 256 pp.
Analyzes influence of Hermogenes' Seven Ideas of Style on "Sacrifice to Apollo" and Barons' Wars. Of the latter work, concludes that "it seems more than likely that" many of its rhetorical effects are the result of "a deliberate application . . . of Hermogenic Ideas" (pp. 79-81, 197-200).

15   SAUNDERS, J[OHN] W[HITESIDE]. "The Social Situation of Seventeenth-Century Poetry," in Metaphysical Poetry. Edited by D[avid] J[ohn] Palmer and Malcolm Bradbury. Stratford-upon-Avon Studies, 11. New York: St. Martin's Press, pp. 236-76.
Discusses Drayton's discontent with the literary climate in a survey of the "social context" of poetry, 1600-1660. Points out that he "wanted a social context which did not exist at the time."

16   STRZETELSKI, JERZY. The English Sonnet: Syntax and Style. Zeszyty Naukowe Uniwersytetu Jagiellońskiego, 213: Prace Jezykoznawcze, 27. Kraków: Nakładem Uniwersytetu Jagiellońskiego, 149 pp.

Includes selected sonnets from Idea in investigating
"what describable formal syntactic features of the sonnets
differentiate the style of English sonneteers from one
another." Concludes that in the overall development of
the English sonnet "Drayton's structure is nearly as
elaborate as was the syntax of Spenser but he is not so
much looking backwards as forwards, towards the Metaphysical Poets. This may be seen in the lesser stress he puts
on belating sentence elements and in his more extensive
use of split coordinate afterthought structure" (passim).

1971

1 BAZERMAN, CHARLES. "Verse Occasioned by the Death of Queen
   Elizabeth I and the Accession of King James I." Ph.D.
   dissertation, Brandeis University, 118 pp. [DAI, 32
   (1971), 2674A.]
      Includes Majesty of King James and Paean Triumphal in
   a survey of verse on the topics. Notes similarity of
   Majesty of King James to An Excellent New Ballad, Showing
   the Pedigree of . . . King James (Revised STC 14423).

2 BEITH-HALAHMI, ESTHER YAËL. "Angell Fayre or Strumpet Lewd:
   The Theme of Jane Shore's Disgrace in Ten Sixteenth Century Works." Ph.D. dissertation, Boston University,
   444 pp. [DAI, 32 (1971), 2050A.]
      Published as 1974.2.

3 BENTLEY, GERALD EADES. The Profession of Dramatist in Shakespeare's Time, 1590-1642. Princeton: Princeton University
   Press, 343 pp.
      Draws frequently on Drayton's career as a dramatist in
   tracing "the general outlines of the normal professional
   life of a writer of plays" during 1590-1642 (passim).

4 BOHLMEYER, BEVERLY JEANNINE. "Michael Drayton: Moral Cer-
   tainty in Poetic Diversity." Ph.D. dissertation, University of Minnesota, 265 pp. [DAI, 33 (1972), 1159A.]
      Argues that despite the diversity of his poetry "Dray-
   ton's work has an internal consistency, largely the result
   of his moral vision." Defines his moral vision, showing
   that he "symbolizes the excellencies of this world in the
   figure of a totally beautiful and virtuous woman, the
   Idea whose presence pervades his life and work."
   "[T]races Drayton's vision and his increasing skill in
   embodying that vision in verse." Omits Polyolbion.

1971

5   CARTER, KATHERINE DAVIS. "Drayton and Decorum: A Stylistic
     Study of the Relation of Ornament to Subject in Peirs
     Gaveston (1593) and Englands Heroicall Epistles (1619)."
     Ph.D. dissertation, University of Southern California,
     286 pp. [DAI, 32 (1971), 957A.]
        Analyzes how "the stylistic changes from the early
     historical poem Peirs Gaveston to the later more success-
     ful Englands Heroicall Epistles show 'not a simple out-
     growing of "rhetoric"' but rather reflect a 'mature
     attention to the Decorum which governed the relation of
     ornament to subject.'" Examines Drayton's use of various
     rhetorical devices in the works.

6   CLARY, FRANK NICHOLAS, JR. "Drayton, Greville, and Shake-
     speare: Sonneteers in an Age of Satire." Ph.D. disser-
     tation, University of Notre Dame, 269 pp. [DAI, 32
     (1971), 2634A.]
        In an analysis of how the "sonnet sequences of Drayton,
     Greville, and Shakespeare . . . represent diverse methods
     of adapting the sonnet to the shift in aesthetics from
     idealism to realism," examines how the "various editions
     of Idea express an evolving new aesthetic for the sonnet."
     Traces Drayton's evolution from the Petrarchism of Idea's
     Mirror through the "satiric attitude and style" of Idea,
     1599, to the "comic and nonamorous sequence" of 1619.

7   CRAUN, EDWIN DAVID. "The De Casibus Complaint in Elizabethan
     England, 1559-1593." Ph.D. dissertation, Princeton Uni-
     versity, 354 pp. [DAI, 32 (1972), 6420-21A.]
        Devotes chapter to Gaveston: places the work in its
     historical context and examines Drayton's "use of rhetoric."
     Also discusses Matilda.

8   DAY, W. G. "The Athenian Society: Poets' Reputations,
     1692-1710." N&Q, NS 18 (September), 329.
        Notes that Drayton and Daniel were among "recommended
     authors" in "An Essay upon All Sorts of Learning, Written
     by the Athenian Society" (1962); when the essay was re-
     printed in 1710, Drayton's name was dropped.

9   DEUBEL, VOLKER. Tradierte Bauformen und lyrische Struktur:
     Die Veränderung elisabethanischer Gedichtschemata bei
     John Donne. SPGL, 14. Stuttgart: W. Kohlhammer, 168 pp.
        Draws frequently on Drayton's works (especially Idea)
     to illustrate various structural devices in Elizabethan
     poetry (passim).

10   FREDIN, LOWELL EDWARD. "The Variant Muse: A Study of Hero
      and Leander and the Elizabethan Love Narrative." Ph.D.
      dissertation, Ohio University, 153 pp. [DAI, 32 (1972),
      5180-81A.]
           Discusses Endymion and Phoebe in chapter on "the Love
      Narrative as a genre."

11   McKENZIE, STANLEY DON. "Drayton's Heroical Epistles: A
      Study in Passions." Ph.D. dissertation, University of
      Rochester, 454 pp. [DAI, 32 (1971), 3260A.]
           Provides "an introductory essay on the theme of pas-
      sion" and on the "rhetorical techniques Drayton uses to
      illustrate passion in action" as well as "a set of ex-
      planatory Notes to the Epistles," with particular emphasis
      on illustrating the "historical irony" in the work.

*12   TANIFUJI, ISAMU. "The Life of Sir John Oldcastle no Kenkyu--
      Shakespeare, Henry IV ni Kankei aru Geki to shite [A Study
      of The Life of Sir John Oldcastle as a Play Related to
      Shakespeare's Henry IV]." Ronshu [Eigo/Eibungaku]
      (Tohokugakuin Daigaku), no. 58 (December), pp. 19-47.
           Cited in [Kazuyoshi Enozawa and Sister Miyo Takano,]
      "The 1971 Bibliography," RenB, 5 (1978), 56, item 165.

13   WEST, MICHAEL D. "Drayton's 'To the Virginian Voyage':
      From Heroic Pastoral to Mock Heroic." RenQ, 24 (Winter),
      501-506.
           Analyzes "the curious inconsistency that results when
      Drayton tries to combine the attractions of both pastor-
      alism and heroism in the . . . poem."

14   WHITE, RITA ANN SIZEMORE. "The Prosody of Michael Drayton's
      Pastorals." Ph.D. dissertation, University of Tennessee,
      198 pp. [DAI, 32 (1972), 4583A.]
           Examines revisions of Shepherd's Garland, Quest of
      Cynthia, Sirena, and Muses' Elysium to study the matura-
      tion of Drayton's prosody. Finds that he excised "Eliza-
      bethan ornamental stanzas and redundancies in favor of a
      more delicate and precise prosodic style that is almost
      neoclassic in effect" and that his "prosodic development
      in the pastoral not only parallels and illustrates his
      changing theory of the purpose of pastoral from Eliza-
      bethan didacticism to Augustan delight, but is also
      representative of the prosodic change taking place in
      English poetry from 1590 to 1630."

1972

1972

1   BIRLEY, ROBERT. "Jane Shore, Part II: Jane Shore in Litera-
     ture." Etoniana, no. 125 (4 June), pp. 391-97.
            Includes Edward IV-Shore epistles (England's Heroical
     Epistles) in an overview of literary treatments of the
     Shore story.

2   BOLIEU, LOUIS SHERMAN, JR. "Michael Drayton, Transitional
     Sonneteer: The Place of Drayton in English Renaissance
     Sonnet Development." Ph.D. dissertation, Texas A & M
     University, 218 pp. [DAI, 33 (1973), 6301-6302A.]
            Analyzes Idea "to characterize the devices that
     give . . . [the sonnets] dramatic force, and thus to de-
     termine, by comparing Drayton's practice in sonnet writing
     to that of his contemporaries, whether Drayton made a
     unique contribution to the sonnet form." In successive
     chapters, "assesses Drayton's current status as a sonnet
     writer"; "relates Idea to European and English sonnet
     traditions, showing Drayton to be both an innovator and
     an improver on existing models"; characterizes his drama-
     tic techniques, especially his use of the dramatic mono-
     logue; and compares Idea to Sidney's Astrophel and Stella
     and Donne's Holy Sonnets. Concludes: "Drayton's contri-
     bution to the sonnet is an advance . . . in the possibil-
     ities for external drama."

*3   COOPER, ELIZABETH HELEN. "The Medieval Background of English
     Renaissance Pastoral Literature." Ph.D. dissertation,
     Cambridge University.
            Published version 1977.1.

4   CURRENT, RANDALL DEAN. "The Curious Art: A Study of Lit-
     erary Criticism in Verse in the Seventeenth Century."
     Ph.D. dissertation, University of California, Los Angeles,
     402 pp. [DAI, 33 (1972), 304A.]
            Includes Drayton in "an analytical survey of the variety
     of poems throughout the century which concern the art of
     poetry."

5   DRAYTON, MICHAEL. "The Battle of Agincourt," 1627. Menston:
     Scolar Press, 234 pp.
            Provides facsimile reprint of 1627 edition.

6   HARNER, JAMES LOWELL. "Jane Shore: A Biography of a Theme
     in Renaissance Literature." Ph.D. dissertation, Univer-
     sity of Illinois, 177 pp. [DAI, 33 (1972), 274A.]

Places Edward IV–Shore epistles (England's Heroical Epistles) in the development of the Shore legend in Renaissance literature. Examines the influence of Anthony Chute's Beauty Dishonored and Heywood's Edward IV on the two epistles.

7　HAUSSY, ALICE d'. "Poly-Olbion" ou l'Angleterre vue par un élisabéthain. Publications de l'Université de Paris X, Lettres et Sciences Humaines, Série A: Thèses et Travaux, no. 13. Paris: Klincksieck, 187 pp.

In published version of 1970.9, analyzes Polyolbion as Drayton's attempt to preserve for posterity an accurate representation of his Great Britain. Devotes chapters to the conception and composition of the poem; to Drayton's treatment of the history of the island; to the influence of voyages and discoveries on the work as well as his representation of them; to his depiction of the physical geography; to his handling of social and economic life; and to the value and importance of the poem. Also examines sources and analyzes various structural techniques. Reviewed in John Buxton, EA, 26, no. 3 (1973), 356–57; Glyn P. Norton, SCN, 31 (Fall–Winter 1973), 83–84.

8　JAHN, JERALD DUANE. "The Elizabethan Epyllion: Its Art and Narrative Conventions." Ph.D. dissertation, Indiana University, 416 pp. [DAI, 33 (1972), 2331A.]

Discusses how Drayton "superimpose[s] . . . [his] metaphysic of love on the amorous tragedy."

9　MARTIN, PHILIP. Shakespeare's Sonnets: Self, Love and Art. Cambridge: Cambridge University Press, 179 pp.

In chapter 4 ("The Sonnet and the Sonneteers," pp. 100–21), observes that in Idea there is "a robust, sardonic common sense, with a humour that can make a better job of the anecdotal conceit than Sidney could." Concludes: "On the one hand Drayton's poetry must seem limited by being derivative; on the other his awareness of what greater poets were doing was a means by which . . . he strengthened his own work" (pp. 115–17, passim).

10　MILLS, LLOYD. "English Origin of 'still-born' and 'dumb-born' in Mauberley." AN&Q, 10 (January), 67.

Points out Drayton's use of "dumb-born" in Idea's Mirror 12.

1972

11 NORTON, RICTOR CARL. "Studies of the Union of Love and
        Death: I. Heracles and Hylas: The Homosexual Archetype;
        II. The Pursuit of Ganymede in Renaissance Pastoral Lit-
        erature; III. Folklore and Myth in Who's Afraid of Vir-
        ginia Woolf ?; IV. The Turn of the Screw: Coincidentia
        Oppositorum." Ph.D. dissertation, Florida State Univer-
        sity, 275 pp. [DAI, 33 (1973), 5190-91A.]
            Includes Drayton in examination of the "Hylas Ritual"
        in section II.

12 ORUCH, JACK B[ERNARD]. "Imitation and Invention in the
        Sabrina Myths of Drayton and Milton." Anglia, 90, nos. 1-
        2, 60-70.
            Discusses Drayton's contribution to and treatment of
        the Sabrina myth and the influence of his version in
        Polyolbion on Comus.

13 PINEAS, RAINER. Tudor and Early Stuart Anti-Catholic Drama.
        Bibliotheca Humanistica & Reformatorica, 5. Nieuwkoop:
        B. de Graff, 48 pp.
            Draws frequently on Oldcastle in a survey of anti-
        Catholic drama, its relationship to contemporary polemics,
        and its techniques. Points out that the "main purpose"
        of the play is not to answer Shakespeare's depiction of
        Falstaff but "to clear Oldcastle and the Lollards--and
        consequently their Tudor coreligionists--of the charge
        that Protestantism leads to treason" (passim).

14 ROGERS, PAT. "Drayton Modernis'd: An Augustan Version of
        Englands Heroicall Epistles." ES, 53 (April), 112-23.
            Examines characteristics of Oldmixon's reworking of
        England's Heroical Epistles in Amores Britannici (1703.1).

15 ROWSE, A[LFRED] L[ESLIE]. The Elizabethan Renaissance: The
        Cultural Achievement. New York: Charles Scribner's Sons,
        428 pp.
            Provides appreciative estimate of Drayton, noting in
        particular his love of England (pp. 67-69, passim).

16 RUTTER, RUSSELL KEENAN. "Shakespeare's Troilus and Cressida:
        Mythical History and Renaissance Satire in a Theological
        Framework." Ph.D. dissertation, University of Wisconsin,
        208 pp. [DAI, 33 (1972), 2342A.]
            Discusses Polyolbion as a representative of the liter-
        ary treatment of the legendary founding of Britain by the
        Trojans.

17   WOLFF, HERMANN. Das Charakterbild Heinrichs VIII in der
     englischen Literatur bis Shakespeare. Ph.D. dissertation,
     Albert-Ludwigs-Universität. Freiburg: n.p., 238 pp.
         Devotes section to an analysis of Drayton's characteri-
     zation of Henry as a "corrupt prince" in Cromwell (pp. 136-
     40, passim).

1973

1   BJORK, GARY FLOYD. "The Renaissance Mirror for Fair Ladies:
     Samuel Daniel's Complaint of Rosamond and the Tradition of
     the Feminine Complaint." Ph.D. dissertation, University
     of California, Irvine, 232 pp. [DAI, 34 (1974), 7698A.]
         Discusses place of Matilda in the evolution of the
     genre. Notes that Drayton "emphasizes the theme of chas-
     tity" unlike Daniel and Chute, who "had focused upon the
     beauty and the amoral nature of their heroines." Concludes
     that Drayton's "concern with morality rather than character
     results in didactic complaint, thin in characterization
     and reactionary in nature."

2   BUGGE-HANSEN, NIELS. That Pleasant Place: The Representa-
     tion of Ideal Landscape in English Literature from the
     14th to the 17th Century. Copenhagen: Akademisk Forlag,
     171 pp.
         Examines Drayton's description of ideal landscape in
     his pastoral poems. Concludes that his "use of pastoral
     for the representation of an ideal land which was not only
     a rural retreat from the vicissitudes of everyday life,
     but an imaginary other world on a different plane was not,
     however, typical of the development of pastoral poetry and
     the type of landscape to be found in works of this kind"
     (pp. 113-19, passim).

3   COLLINS, MICHAEL JOHN. "Comedy in the Love Poetry of Sidney,
     Drayton, Shakespeare, and Donne." Ph.D. dissertation,
     New York University, 211 pp. [DAI, 34 (1974), 7743A.]
         Analyzes comic elements--ending "a sonnet with a humor-
     ous, aphoristic comment on the way of the world; . . .
     point[ing] up the comedy of the lover's situation and of
     his relationship with the lady"--in Idea. Gives particu-
     lar attention to Idea 61. Concludes: "Although we do
     not get from Idea the same sense of multiplicity and
     playful exuberance that we do from Astrophil and Stella,
     we still find in it several good comic poems and one
     great one."

1973

4   GRABES, HERBERT. Speculum, Mirror und Looking-Glass: Kon-
    tinuität und Originalität der Spiegelmetapher in den
    Buchtiteln des Mittelalters und der englischen Literatur
    des 13. bis. 17. Jahrhunderts. Buchreihe der Anglia,
    Zeitschrift für Englische Philologie, 16. Tübingen: Max
    Niemeyer, 425 pp.
        Draws heavily on Drayton for examples in a detailed
    analysis of the appearance of the looking-glass metaphor
    in Renaissance literature (passim).

5   HARDIN, RICHARD F[RANCIS]. Michael Drayton and the Passing
    of Elizabethan England. Lawrence: University Press of
    Kansas, 193 pp.
        Intends "to impart a sense of . . . [Drayton's] iden-
    tity as a poet, particularly to explain how he is dis-
    tinguished among his contemporaries by the intensity of
    his devotion to England and English traditions." Examines
    Drayton's historical, satiric, and pastoral works and
    establishes interrelationships among the three kinds.
    Identifies "the motives underlying almost all of Drayton's
    work: the desire to place English poetry in competition
    with that of the ancients and moderns of other countries;
    to revere the past and praise the natural beauty of Eng-
    land; to make clear to his English readers their virtues
    as a people." Argues that the point of view of the "con-
    servative rural gentry" permeates his poetry and that he
    "represents a large number of his countrymen in his grow-
    ing aversion to" James I. Discusses relationship between
    Drayton and Jonson in Appendix B (pp. 147-51). Reviewed
    in P. C. Bayley, DUJ, 36 (1974), 114-15; John Buxton, RES,
    NS 25 (November 1974), 468-70; Annabel [M.] Patterson,
    Ren&R, 11, no. 2 (1975), 133-34; W. Gordon Zeeveld,
    American Historical Review, 79 (June 1974), 781; 1975.5;
    1976.7.

6   HIGDON, DAVID LEON. "Love's Deathbed Revisited." CEA, 36
    (November), 35.
        Responds to 1963.7 and 1963.8, arguing that Idea 61 is
    a dialogue, with lines 1 and 9-14 belonging to one voice,
    lines 2-8 to another. Does not determine whether the
    voices represent two individuals or the "private and pub-
    lic" aspects of one speaker. Also argues that the sonnet
    is not a seduction poem. See 1974.4, 1974.14, and 1974.15.

7   HOBBS, MARY. "Drayton's 'Most Dearely-Loved Friend Henery
    Reynolds Esq.'" RES, NS 24 (November), 414-28.
        Offers study of the life and work of Reynolds; includes
    transcripts of his poems from various manuscripts.

8   HÜLSBERGEN, HELMUT E.   "Michael Draytons Englands Heroicall
     Epistles und Hofmann von Hofmannswaldaus Helden-Briefe:
     Geschichte und galante Liebe," in Europäische Tradition
     und deutscher Literaturbarock: Internationale Beiträge
     zum Problem von Überlieferung and Umgestaltung.   Edited by
     Gerhart Hoffmeister.   Bern: Francke, pp. 427-48.
          Examines influence of England's Heroical Epistles on
     Hofmannswaldau's work and compares treatment of love and
     history in the two poems.   Finds that Drayton subordinates
     love to history.

9   MELCHIORI, GIORGIO.   L'uomo e il potere: Indagine sulle
     strutture profonde dei "Sonetti" di Shakespeare.   Einaudi
     Paperbacks, 42.   Turin: Giulio Einaudi, 248 pp.
          Includes Idea's Mirror in tabular analyses of words
     most frequently used, pronouns, and frequency of terms
     related to love in five Elizabethan sonnet sequences
     (Sidney, Daniel, Spenser, and Shakespeare).   Compares
     Drayton's usage with that of the others (passim).   Revised
     1976.5.

10 NELSON, MALCOLM A[NTHONY].   The Robin Hood Tradition in the
     English Renaissance.   ElizS, 14.   Salzburg: Institut für
     Englische Sprache und Literatur, Universität Salzburg,
     269 pp.
          In published version of 1961.7, examines Drayton's
     treatment of Robin Hood in Polyolbion; suggests that his
     account "is probably a good summation of what the serious
     Renaissance man of letters knew and thought about Robin
     Hood."   Discusses sources, relationship to other Renais-
     sance treatments, and contribution (especially in the
     characterization of Maid Marian) to the legend.   Concludes
     that Drayton's "has remained one of the best and most in-
     fluential treatments of the Robin Hood tradition (pp.
     175-82).

11 ORAM, WILLIAM ALLAN.   "The Disappearance of Pan: Some Uses
     of Myth in Three Seventeenth-Century Poets."   Ph.D. dis-
     sertation, Yale University, 324 pp.   [DAI, 34 (1973),
     3423A.]
          In examining how "[t]he secularization of thought
     that characterizes the seventeenth century alters the use
     of mythology in poetry," discusses how "Drayton follows
     Spenser in using mythology extensively, but . . . under-
     cuts his own myth-making by his desire to adhere to a
     standard of truth based on empirical fact.   His poetry--
     from Endimion & Phoebe through Polyolbion--mirrors this
     split between the desire for factual 'truth' and the 'de-
     lights' of poetic mythology."

1973

12 OZARK, JOAN MARY. "Faery Court Poetry of the Early Seven-
    teenth Century." Ph.D dissertation, Princeton University,
    504 pp. [DAI, 34 (1974), 5115-16A.]
        Interprets Muses' Elysium, Eighth Nymphal, as "a fairy
    prothalamion in which Drayton may be fancifully proclaim-
    ing a real marriage of English nobility, paying a compli-
    ment to his patron, Edward Sackville." Examines sources
    and analogues of Nymphidia and "its mock heroic form and
    generic parody of fairy literature and the romance epic."
    Also suggests "that the poem satirizes the early marital
    difficulties of Charles and Henrietta Maria."

13 RICHMOND, HUGH M. Renaissance Landscapes: English Lyrics in
    a European Tradition. DPL, Series Practica, 52. The
    Hague: Mouton, 156 pp.
        Points out that "Drayton comes closest in temper and
    range to Ronsard's . . . achievement" and uses Polyolbion
    and "An Ode Written in the Peak" to illustrate the French
    poet's influence on English verse, particularly landscape
    poetry (pp. 77-84).

14 STEVENS, IRMA NED RILEY. "Ronsard and Stuart Lyric Poetry."
    Ph.D. dissertation, Florida State University, 270 pp.
    [DAI, 34 (1973), 3432-33A.]
        Discusses how "Drayton echoes Ronsard in the strong
    sense of geography in some of his odes."

15 WEBBER, JANET McRAE. "The English Renaissance Epyllion."
    Ph.D. dissertation, Yale University, 259 pp. [DAI, 34
    (1974), 7252A.]
        Discusses Drayton's attempt "to reshape the genre ac-
    cording to the doctrine of the utility of poetry and to
    devote it to the celebration of Truth." Finds that of
    the "moral epyllia" only Endymion and Phoebe "succeeds
    fully in expressing a serious moral message within the
    epyllion form."

1974

1   ADKINS, BETTY JEAN VanNUS. "A Critical Analysis of the
    Erotic, Mythological Narrative Poem, 1598-1598." Ph.D.
    dissertation, University of Miami, 141 pp. [DAI, 35
    (1974), 2211A.]
        Includes Endymion and Phoebe in analyzing the popular-
    ity, sources, "characteristic structural and decorative
    elements, and . . . theme and characters" of the type.

2   BEITH-HALAHMI, ESTHER YAËL. Angell Fayre or Strumpet Lewd:
     Jane Shore as an Example of Erring Beauty in 16th Century
     Literature. 2 volumes. ElizS, 26-27. Salzburg: Insti-
     tut für Englische Sprache und Literatur, Universität
     Salzburg, 367 pp.
          In published version (unrevised) of 1971.2, places
     Edward IV-Shore epistles (England's Heroical Epistles) in
     the development of the Shore legend. Analyzes how Drayton
     "focuses on the moment of courtship to characterize an
     essentially immoral relationship in a tone of gay in-
     souciance" (passim).

3   BERTHOLD, MARY HAINES. "The Meaning and Function of the
     'Speaking Picture': Description of Pictures in English
     Narrative Poetry, 1590-1606." Ph.D. dissertation, Uni-
     versity of Wisconsin, Madison, 398 pp. [DAI, 35 (1975),
     7859A.]
          Examines how "Drayton use[s] pictures as moral exempla
     which express and universalize the fate of Rosamond" in
     Henry II-Rosamond epistles (England's Heroical Epistles);
     how pictures in Man in the Moon "function to bring variety
     and particularity to [the] . . . philosophical poem"; and
     how in Barons' Wars "the description of paintings ampli-
     fies Mortimer's pride and thus intensifies the effect of
     his fall."

4   CLARK, PAUL O. "Other Visits to Love's Deathbed." CEA, 37
     (November), 30-31.
          In reply to 1973.6 argues that Idea 61 is a monologue
     and a seduction poem. Discusses consistency of tone and
     psychological subtleness in the sonnet and comments on
     its relationship to others in the sequence. See 1963.7,
     1963.8, 1974.14, and 1974.15.

5   DORANGEON, SIMONE. L'Églogue anglaise de Spenser à Milton.
     Études Anglaises, 49. Paris: Didier, 594 pp.
          Traces evolution of Drayton as a writer of pastoral
     poetry. Offers extensive examination--frequently an
     eclogue-by-eclogue analysis--of Shepherd's Garland (with
     particular emphasis on the influence of Spenser on themes
     and motifs); of the 1606 Eclogues (with emphasis on satire
     and stylistic revisions); of Sirena (with emphasis on
     problems of interpretation); of 1619 Pastorals (with em-
     phasis on Drayton's conception of the pastoral); of Nymph-
     idia (with emphasis on the work as a parody of chivalric
     romances and its baroque qualities); and of Muses' Elysium
     (with emphasis on Drayton's conception of the Golden Age
     and his humor). Throughout the discussions examines

1974

Drayton's emphasis on virtue, his attitude toward society,
and his changing style. Concludes that his pastoral poetry reflects the changing modes from 1593 to 1630
(pp. 184-213, 260-70, 331-36, 386-97, 449-505, passim).

6   DRAYTON, MICHAEL, ANTHONY MUNDAY, RICHARD HATHAWAY, and ROB-
    ERT WILSON. First Part of Sir John Oldcastle, in Disputed
    Plays of William Shakespeare. Edited by William Kozlenko.
    New York: Hawthorn Books, pp. 326-68.
        Reproduces text and notes from 1860 edition of 1850.4.
    In introductory note (pp. 326-32), characterizes Oldcastle
    as "a tiresome but presumably veracious history of" Old-
    castle and discusses the events surrounding the composition
    of the play.

7   EWELL, BARBARA C., S.S.N.D. "Art and Experience in the Poetry
    of Michael Drayton." Ph.D. dissertation, University of
    Notre Dame, 335 pp. [DAI, 35 (1974), 2264-65A.]
        "[T]races the changing relationship between art and
    experience that is manifest as a central concern of the
    poetry of Michael Drayton." Analyzes evolution of the
    "aesthetic which governs the themes and methods of his
    poetry" from Idea's Mirror and Endymion and Phoebe (where-
    in "[e]xperience . . . is virtually irrelevant to art"),
    through England's Heroical Epistles (where "the actual
    process of recording experience . . . becomes the content
    of the poem"), Idea, 1599-1619 (which is infused with a
    "sense of process and experience"), and Polyolbion (where
    the "notion of art as the shaper of experience is extended
    to include the property of transforming unity"), to Muses'
    Elysium (where "art is re-defined as the means by which
    experience is totally transfigured").

8   GUERRIN, ROBERT T. "The Historical Background to Henry V,
    I.i." UDR, 10 (Summer), 15-28.
        Discusses alteration of historical facts in the presen-
    tation of Henry V "as an admirable Protestant" in Old-
    castle.

9   HULSE, SHIRLEY CLARK, III. "Myth and Narrative in Elizabethan
    Poetry." Ph.D. dissertation, Claremont Graduate School,
    255 pp. [DAI, 35 (1975), 5408-5409A.]
        Includes Gaveston, Endymion and Phoebe, and Barons'
    Wars in an analysis of mythological and historical narra-
    tive poems. Discusses how Drayton "develops his Piers
    Gaveston into a meditation on the corruption of love and
    beauty by decorating his chronicle with astrological and

mythological imagery" and how he develops "a new, plain
style of historical narrative" in revising his early historical poems.

10   KLEIN, GEORGE JAY.   "Theme and Form in English Landscape
        Poetry: Eighth to Eighteenth Centuries." Ph.D. disserta-
        tion, University of Oregon, 210 pp. [DAI, 35 (1975),
        5350-51A.]
            Discusses Polyolbion as it "established the precedent"
        for the "particular, named landscape" in landscape poetry.

11   LEVER, J[ULIUS] W[ALTER], ed. Sonnets of the English Renais-
        sance. Athlone Renaissance Library. London: Athlone
        Press, 202 pp.
            Includes annotated selection from Idea. In "Introduc-
        tion" (pp. 1-30), briefly discusses the distinctive quali-
        ties of Drayton's sonnets.

12   McKERROW, RONALD BRUNLEES. "The Supposed Calling-In of Dray-
        ton's Harmony of the Church, 1591," in Ronald Brunlees
        McKerrow: A Selection of His Essays. Compiled by John
        Phillip Immroth. Great Bibliographers Series, 1. Metu-
        chen, N.J.: Scarecrow Press, pp. 39-40.
            Reprints 1910.6.

13   MARCHESANI, JOSEPH JOHN, JR. "The Revisions of Michael Dray-
        ton's Four Legends." Ph.D. dissertation, University of
        Rochester, 340 pp. [DAI, 36 (1975), 905A.]
            Provides detailed examination of revisions of Gaveston,
        Robert, Matilda, and Cromwell "to define Drayton's devel-
        opment as a poet and to show how his development reflects
        a transition from Elizabeth [sic] to Jacobean poetic atti-
        tudes." Finds "first, that the progress of the revisions
        is marked by an increasing integration of technique; sec-
        ond, that the progress develops in two stages; third, that
        the revisions in syntax and rhetoric provide a sensitive
        gauge for changes in structure and attitudes throughout
        the legends."

14   REAMER, OWEN J. "Come Back to Love's Deathbed." CEA, 37
        (November), 28-29.
            In reply to 1973.6 argues that Idea 61 "is an obvious
        monologue to anyone familiar with the customs and behavior

1974

of young lovers from the 16th Century to about 1940."
Sees the speaker attempting "to save face" after having
been "given . . . the brush. See 1963.7, 1963.8, 1974.4,
and 1974.15.

15   STRINGER, GARY. "Love's Deathbed One More Time: A Reply to
Mr. Leon Higdon." CEA, 37 (November), 27–28.
In reply to 1963.7, 1963.8, and 1973.6, argues that
Idea 61 is a "dramatic monologue in which a lover, with
cool premeditation, attempts a rhetorical (if not holy)
rape upon the will of the mistress to whom he speaks."
Also discusses the placement of "yet" in line 14. See
1974.4 and 1974.14

16   WATSON, GEORGE, ed. The New Cambridge Bibliography of Eng-
lish Literature, I: 600–1660. Cambridge: Cambridge
University Press, 56 pp., 2476 columns.
Revises selective list of works by and about Drayton
in 1941.3; William A. Ringler contributed the section on
Drayton as a poet (columns 1065–69).

17   WESTLING, LOUISE HUTCHINGS. The Evolution of Michael Drayton's "Idea." ElizS, 37. Salzburg: Institut für Englische Sprache und Literatur, Universität Salzburg,
195 pp.
In published version of 1974.18, examines Drayton's
use of "the pose of the libertine" as a "structural
principle" and "as a defense against the mocking criticism which Drayton felt was aimed at Ideas Mirrour." Devotes chapters to a review of scholarship on the sonnets,
a critical analysis of Idea's Mirror (notes Drayton's
problems in syntax and control of sonnet form), the
revisions in the 1599 edition (argues for influence of
Wyatt) and the creation of the libertine pose, the 1619
Idea, and the place of Idea in "the development of the
English lyric." Concludes: "What Drayton has created in
Idea . . . is a persona who masks himself as a libertine
and then proceeds to report the story of his love,
gradually lowering his mask as the end of the sequence
approaches." Reviewed in James L[owell] Harner, SCN, 34
(Winter 1976), 84–85.

18 ＿＿＿. "The Pose of the Libertine in Michael Drayton's
Idea." Ph.D. dissertation, University of Oregon, 197 pp.
[DAI, 35 (1974), 3706A.]
Published version 1974.17.

19 WILSON, KATHARINE M[ARGARET]. Shakespeare's Sugared Sonnets.
New York: Barnes & Noble, 238 pp.
Argues for Shakespeare's influence on Idea's Mirror and
comments on Sir John Davies's parody of Drayton's sonnets
in Gulling Sonnets (passim).

20 WINDT, JUDITH HANNA. "'Not Cast in Other Womens Mold':
Strong Women Characters in Shakespeare's Henry VI Trilogy,
Drayton's Englands Heroicall Epistles, and Jonson's
Poems to Ladies." Ph.D. dissertation, Stanford University,
325 pp. [DAI, 35 (1974), 3777-78A.]
Discusses how Drayton "reveals . . . that the female
writers of these paired verse letters are frequently more
concerned with public life and government than with
private life and romance, and that they often possess
greater political wisdom than the men."

1975

1 BARTON, ANNE. "The King Disguised: Shakespeare's Henry V
and the Comical History," in The Triple Bond: Plays,
Mainly Shakespearean, in Performance. Edited by Joseph G.
Price. University Park: Pennsylvania State University
Press, pp. 92-117.
Discusses Oldcastle as "a work especially commissioned
as an answer to the Falstaff plays," the authors' use of
Shakespeare's Henry plays and Greene's George a Greene as
sources, the influence of the ballad and folk traditions
on the play, and "the religious difficulties posed by
their subject matter." Sees the play as "a detailed dem-
onstration of how to turn a tragical into a comical history."

2 CARTER, KATHERINE D[AVIS]. "Drayton's Craftsmanship: The
Encomium and the Blazon in Englands Heroicall Epistles."
HLQ, 38 (August), 297-314.
Examines Drayton's use of the encomium and blazon to
show his "competence as a poetic craftsman." Illustrates
"Drayton's care in fitting the encomium into the argument
and theme of the individual epistle and his skill in
using it as a means of" integrating pairs of epistles;
discusses his use of encomia to make "the poem heroical

and historical." Examines how "Drayton accommodate[s] his blazons generally to the character or station of his speaker, [and] . . . use[s] the blazon as a precise instrument for characterization of the speakers."

3   CHRISTOPHER, ROBERT J.   "The Emergence of Story: The Relationship of Fiction and History in English Historical Poetry, 1559-1621." Ph.D. dissertation, University of California, Berkeley, 299 pp. [DAI, 37 (1976), 2891A.]
    Examines Gaveston, Matilda, Robert, Cromwell, Mortimeriados, Barons' Wars, and Polyolbion in tracing "the gradual movement [during 1590-1620] of story from an historical category to a literary one." Discusses influence of "Daniel's modifications of style and historical purpose in the historical legend" on Drayton's legends and Mortimeriados; examines how in the revisions of his legends and Mortimeriados "Drayton suppressed his earlier hyperbolic style and introduced a stronger analytic and historical perspective"; analyzes importance of the collaboration of Selden and Drayton in Polyolbion, finding that the result "is . . . a significant demarcation in the development of story and history as independent terms."

*4   DUCHEMIN, H. P. "Michael Drayton's Poly-Olbion: A Critical and Historical Study." Ph.D. dissertation, Birbeck College, University of London.
    Cited in 1975 MHRA Annual Bibliography, item 5477.

5   FRIEDMAN, STANLEY. Review of Richard F[rancis] Hardin, Michael Drayton and the Passing of Elizabethan England. RenQ, 28 (Autumn), 414-15.
    Favorably reviews 1973.5, but objects to Hardin's choice of the four odes in his opening chapter as "'poems containing the essence of Drayton.'"

6   HARDIN, RICHARD F[RANCIS]. "Michael Drayton," in The Popular School: A Survey and Bibliography of Recent Studies in English Renaissance Drama. Edited by Terence P. Logan and Denzell S. Smith. Lincoln: University of Nebraska Press, pp. 136-47.
    Provides essay review of scholarship, c. 1923-1973.

7   _____. "A Variant Text of Drayton's 'The Heart' in an 'Unknown' Miscellany." PBSA, 69 (Third Quarter), 393-94.
    Discusses variants of "The Heart" as printed in Poems, Written by the Right Honorable William Earl of Pembroke (1660); suggests that the source of the text is one of Drayton's early manuscript versions.

8   HAUSSY, ALICE d', [SIMONE] DORANGEON, GISÈLE VENET, and
    PIERRE LEGOUIS. "Table ronde sur tradition et innovation
    dans les notions de temps et d'instant au dix-septième
    siècle," in Tradition et innovation: Littérature et
    paralittérature: Actes du Congrès de Nancy (1972).
    Société des Anglicistes de l'Enseignement Supérieur.
    Paris: Marcel Didier, pp. 95-98.
        In a discussion of a paper by Robert Ellrodt, D'Haussy
    comments on Drayton's handling of time, especially in
    Polyolbion; and Dorangeon comments on Drayton's represen-
    tation of the triumph over time in Muses' Elysium. (Ell-
    rodt's paper, which does not appear in the volume and
    which does not discuss Drayton, was published as "De Platon
    à Traherne: L'Intuition de l'instant chez les poètes méta-
    physiques anglais du dix-septième siècle," in Mouvements
    premiers: Études critiques offertes à Georges Poulet
    [Paris: José Corti, 1972], pp. 9-25.)

9   HUNTER, WILLIAM B[RIDGES], JR. "The Date of Michael Drayton's
    First Elegy." N&Q, NS 22 (July), 306.
        Argues for 1614 as the date of "Of His Lady's not Coming
    to London" (Elegy 1).

10 LEIDIG, HEINZ-DIETER. Das Historiengedicht in der englischen
    Literaturtheorie: Die Rezeption von Lucans "Pharsalia"
    von der Renaissance bis zum Ausgang des achtzehnten
    Jahrhunderts. Eüropäische Hochschulschriften, 26. Bern:
    Herbert Lang; Frankfurt; Peter Lang, 200 pp.
        Examines influence of Pharsalia on Drayton's treatment
    of history in Barons' Wars (pp. 78-79, 84-88, passim).

11 LOVE, JOHN MICHAEL. "'To varietie inclin'd': A Study of
    Michael Drayton's Idea." Ph.D. dissertation, University
    of North Carolina at Chapel Hill, 158 pp. [DAI, 36
    (1975), 3732-33A.]
        Analyzes versions of Idea to define Drayton's "substan-
    tial contribution to Petrarchism in England." Discusses
    how in Idea's Mirror "Drayton's metaphors of praise and use
    of the brutal and ugly aspects of Elizabethan life to
    convey the poet-lover's anger demonstrate an originality
    of vision and anticipate later achievements"; finds
    "[h]is most important addition of 1599 is the portrayal
    of Idea and Love as familiar, sixteenth-century criminals,
    a technique of metaphor implying a substantial redefini-
    tion of the" lover-lady relationship; examines, in 1600
    and 1602, the "dialectical structure of the sonnets" and
    "the prominence of paradox and metaphoric fools and

1975

madmen"; in 1605 analyzes how "Drayton has shifted attention from those qualities of Idea deserving love to those
difficulties in despite of which one loves, defining
Petrarchan love . . . by dissociation or disjunction"; and,
in 1619 discusses how Drayton "dramatizes the dissociation,
inherent in the Petrarchan relationship, of justice from
selfless love."

12 POISSON, RODNEY. "Othello's 'Base Indian': A Better Source
    for the Allusion." SQ, 26 (Autumn), 462-66.
    Suggests that Richard Eden's Second English Book on
    America is the source of Matilda, 1. 287.

13 WRIGHT, ELLEN FABER. "'Rhethoricke to deceive': The Eliza-
    bethan Epyllia." Ph.D. dissertation, Indiana University,
    199 pp. [DAI, 36 (1976), 7449-50A.]
    Discusses "[t]he emphatic reassertions of the importance
    of an ordered society" in Endymion and Phoebe (one of the
    "'counter-epyllia'") in tentatively suggesting that "the
    epyllia . . . may imply a challenging of the stable,
    basically knowable world of the Christian humanist."

<u>1976</u>

1   BEHR, EUGENE THOMAS. "Structure and Meaning in the Sonnet
    Sequences of Michael Drayton, 1594-1619." Ph.D. disserta-
    tion, Princeton University, 288 pp. [DAI, 37 (1977),
    5135A.]
    In successive chapters "describes the poetic and histor-
    ical background of Drayton's sequences, with particular
    attention to . . . emblematic imagery and . . . ironic
    language"; analyzes the "numerological organization of
    Drayton's sequences and the operation of individual poems
    within number patterns"; examines "structure and thematic
    organization in Ideas Mirrour"; "examines the revisions of
    Drayton's pastoral poetry as a key to his re-working of
    the sonnet sequences and to his developing characteriza-
    tion of Idea"; describes revisions in Idea, 1599; and
    discusses development of Drayton's "approach to writing
    sonnets as it finally resulted in Idea 1619." Concludes
    that the sequences "are about the 'idea' of proper, vir-
    tuous love" and that they are structured through the "use
    of symbolic number" and a "developing focus on Idea . . .
    as the embodiment of virtuous love within any woman."

2   BRUCE, DUANE F.   "Drayton's Use of Epic and De Casibus Materi-
     als in Historical Poetry from 1593 to 1603." Ph.D. disser-
     tation, University of North Carolina at Chapel Hill,
     221 pp. [DAI, 37 (1977), 5136A.]
        "[E]xamines the ways in which Drayton combined epic and
     de casibus elements in" Gaveston, Robert, Mortimeriados,
     and Barons' Wars.

3   HULSE, S[HIRLEY] CLARK.   "Elizabethan Minor Epic: Toward a
     Definition of Genre." SP, 73 (July), 302-19.
        Draws frequently on Gaveston in analyzing the character-
     istics of various "overlapping families" of poems which
     make up the genre. Concludes: "The genre of minor epic,
     like any uncanonical genre, must remain loosely defined,
     embracing a number of subgroupings with different bases."

4   JONES, ANN ROSALIND.   "The Lyric Sequence: Poetic Performance
     as Plot (Dante's Vita nuova, Scève's Délie, Sidney's
     Astrophil and Stella, Drayton's Idea, La Ceppède's
     Théorèmes)." Ph.D. dissertation, Cornell University,
     327 pp. [DAI, 37 (1977), 6464-65A.]
        In analyzing the "organizational principles and poetic
     implication shared by [the] five early lyric sequences,"
     examines how Drayton juxtaposes "violently diverse sonnets
     to dramatize the connection between amorous and poetic
     schizophrenia" and exploits "the sudden turnabouts of
     comedy, the rough diction of satire, and the dramatic im-
     plications of ambiguous or unresolved endings."

5   MELCHIORI, GIORGIO.   Shakespeare's Dramatic Meditations:
     An Experiment in Criticism. Oxford: Clarendon Press,
     218 pp.
        In revision of 1973.9 includes Idea's Mirror in a com-
     parative statistical analysis of word-frequency, personal
     pronominal forms, and frequencies of connotative words in
     five Elizabethan sonnet sequences (Daniel, Sidney, Spenser,
     and Shakespeare). Points out that in the sonnets of
     Drayton and Daniel, data from word-frequency analysis
     "confirm their relative linguistic and lexical poverty,
     their greater monotony; their faithful following of con-
     vention is demonstrated also by the fact that they show no
     outstanding variations from the norm." Further observes
     that in Idea's Mirror the incidence of "first person
     pronominal forms . . . exceeds . . . 50 per cent of the
     total number of pronouns employed" and that "the high
     incidence . . . of words less commonly used by other
     authors . . . is merely further evidence of the stereotyped
     character of . . . [Drayton's] poetry" (passim).

1976

6 PLATZER, RONALD M. "Causation and Character in Samuel Daniel's The Civil Wars." Ph.D. dissertation, Columbia University, 158 pp. [DAI, 37 (1977), 6509A.]
        Contrasts Drayton's "greater interest in the heroic
   than the historical" in Barons' Wars and Mortimeriados
   with Daniel's subordination of the heroic to an analysis
   of "the effects of men's deeds on the nation" in Civil
   Wars.

7 REES, JOAN. Review of Richard F[rancis] Hardin, Michael
   Drayton and the Passing of Elizabethan England. N&Q, NS
   23 (May-June), 268-69.
        Finds 1973.5 a generally "intelligent and lively essay"
   but objects to Hardin's emphasis on Drayton's political
   ideas and "conservative temperament, increasingly reac-
   tionary in outlook as the years pass." Suggests instead
   that "Drayton, in his criticism of James and his satire
   on Jacobean society, was following a common trend and,
   for all his love of country, he contributes nothing on
   social and political topics which is likely to make him
   read for the quality of his thought."

8 SCOTT, PETER N. "Michael Drayton: Poet and Mapmaker."
   Country Life, 160 (30 December), 1966-67.
        Offers brief popular overview of Drayton as man and
   poet. Asserts that current interest in Polyolbion is on
   the maps, which he attributes to Drayton and characterizes
   as "the strangest maps of the English and Welsh counties
   ever produced."

*9 TURNER, J[AMES] G. "Topographia and Topographical Poetry."
   D. Phil. thesis, Oxford University.
        Published version 1979.5.

                            1977

1 COOPER, [ELIZABETH] HELEN. Pastoral: Mediaeval into Renaissance. Ipswich: D. S. Brewer; Totowa, N.J.: Rowman and
   Littlefield, 263 pp.
        In published version of 1972.3, examines Drayton as a
   pastoral poet; emphasizes his "pastoral theory," themes,
   and the influence of medieval pastoral conventions on his
   poetry, especially in his use of realistic detail (pp. 166-
   69, passim).

2   DRAYTON, MICHAEL. Idea, in Elizabethan Sonnets. Edited by
     Maurice Evans. London: Dent; Totowa, N.J.: Rowman and
     Littlefield, pp. 87–113.
         Provides annotated reprint of 1619 edition. In "Intro-
     duction" (pp. vii–xxxi), offers a brief critical estimate
     of Drayton as a sonneteer, noting that "[i]n Idea, the
     sonnet comes nearest to the poetry of the Metaphysicals."

3   _____. "Michael Drayton," in The English Spenserians: The
     Poetry of Giles Fletcher, George Wither, Michael Drayton,
     Phineas Fletcher, and Henry More. Edited by William
     B[ridges] Hunter, Jr. Salt Lake City: University of Utah
     Press, pp. 197–309.
         Provides annotated texts of Elegies (1627), Nymphidia
     (1627), and Odes (1619). In introductory comments offers
     a brief critical estimate of each, emphasizing prosody.

4   _____. Selected Poems. Edited by Vivien Thomas. Manchester:
     Carcanet, 96 pp.
         Provides annotated, modernized selection based largely
     on the 1619 Poems. In "Introduction" (pp. 7–12), gives an
     overview of the forms and genres Drayton used and stresses
     his versatility and "capacity for growth and change."

5   GILES, MARY DOOLEY. "The Elizabethan Sonnet Sequence: Seg-
     mented Form in Its Earliest Appearances, Astrophil and
     Stella, Hekatompathia, and Delia." Ph.D. dissertation,
     University of Virginia, 261 pp. [DAI, 39 (1978), 872–73A.]
         Discusses Drayton in arguing that "[p]eriodic analogy,
     a common feature of Renaissance music, best describes the
     structural principle . . . in the Elizabethan sequence."

6   MUTH, MARCIA FINLEY. "Elizabethan Praise of the Queen:
     Dramatic Interaction in Royal Panegyric." Ph.D. disserta-
     tion, Ohio State University, 264 pp. [DAI, 38 (1978),
     4850A.]
         Discusses Shepherd's Garland, Eclogue 3, as a work in
     which the "Queen is absorbed into her writer's fictional
     realm."

7   PEACOCK, A. J. "Drayton and Horace." N&Q, NS 24 (December),
     542.
         Points out that lines 1–8 of "To Henry Reynolds" "are
     an adaptation of a poem by Catullus on a literary evening
     spent with the poet Licinius Calvus." Discusses Drayton's
     "'Horatian' transformation" of the passage.

1977

8 REVARD, STELLA P. "The Design of Nature in Drayton's Poly-
Olbion." SEL, 17 (Winter), 105-17.
Argues that "Drayton has hierarchically organized the
world of Poly-Olbion so that it mirrors English society,
wherein sovereigns reign and subjects offer obedience"
and that his "aim . . . was to create . . . a tableau in
which the geography of the land becomes one with the history, the morality, the aesthetics of the people who
inhabit it."

9 SCHABERT, INA. Die Lyrik der Spenserianer: Ansätze zu einer
absoluten Dichtung in England, 1590-1660. Buchreihe der
Anglia, 18. Tübingen: Max Niemeyer, 228 pp.
Draws frequently on Drayton in analyzing how the Spenserians "developed a poetic creed and, if only to a certain
degree, modes of poetic composition which foreshadow
Mallarmé" and the invention of pure poetry. Examines how,
by "selecting and combining ideas from Christian neo-
Platonism, from Du Bartas, Sidney, and Henry Reynolds,
the Spenserians worked out the concept of a poem which is
epistrophe, i.e., purification, dematerialization, and
'illumination' of reality and language." Provides detailed
analysis of Endymion and Phoebe as an example of the
poetics of the group, observing that, as with the others,
Drayton's poem moves "from an enthusiastic beginning to
the final, necessary defeat of the poetic ambition which
refuses to give a local habitation and a name to its crea-
tions" (pp. 86-99, passim). (English summary in English
and American Studies in German: Summaries of Theses and
Monographs, 1977, edited by Werner Habicht [Tübingen: Max
Niemeyer, 1978,] pp. 76-77.

10 SPIKES, JUDITH DOOLIN. "The Jacobean History Play and the
Myth of the Elect Nation." RenD, NS 8: 117-049.
Discusses Oldcastle as it embodies the myth of the Elect
Nation.

11 SWEENEY, KEVIN McCONNELL. "The Structural Importance of the
First Quatrain in the Sequence Sonnets of Michael Drayton:
A Study of the 4-10 Sonnet." Ph.D. dissertation, Catholic
University of America, 235 pp. [DAI, 38 (1977), 2147A.]
Analyzes "Drayton's practice of according the first
quatrain of a sonnet a structural importance that exceeds
conventional expectation" in "an attempt to understand
more clearly the nature of the sonnet, specifically the
4-10."

12   THOMAS, W. K.   "Mors Amoris: When Is Love Really Dead?" DR,
        57 (Winter), 737-56.
            Discusses Idea 61 in a survey of English poems on the
        topic of when is love really dead. Points out that in
        Drayton's sonnet love is not really dead since the speaker
        is willing to take back the woman; observes that the
        "separation of the woman from faith and innocence suggests
        that she has had neither, that her lack of them has caused
        the break."

13   WOODEN, WARREN W.   "Michael Drayton's Nymphidia: A Renais-
        sance Children's Classic?" ChildL, 6: 34-41.
            Suggests "that much of the sustained popularity . . .
        [of Nymphidia] lies in its particular appeal to children"
        and "analyze[s] the elements [particularly the fairy lore
        and "descriptive technique"] . . . which contribute to
        this appeal." Argues that "Nymphidia is designed not to
        instruct but to delight by giving pleasure to different
        types of readers of widely diverse literary intelligence
        and comprehension" and concludes that the poem "deserves
        a prominent place not just in the annals of fairy poetry,
        but in the history of early English children's literature."

14   ZACHARASIEWICZ, WALDEMAR.   Die Klimatheorie in der englischen
        Literatur und Literaturkritik von der Mitte des 16. bis
        zum frühen 18. Jahrhundert. WBEP, 77. Vienna: Wilhelm
        Braumüller, 678 pp.
            Discusses Drayton's allusions to climate theory in
        Polyolbion and England's Heroical Epistles in an historical
        survey of the subject (pp. 187-90).

1978

1   EWELL, BARBARA C.   "Drayton's Poly-Olbion: England's Body
        Immortalized." SP, 75 (July), 297-315.
            Analyzes how Drayton, by "[u]sing the controlling meta-
        phor of the body, . . . constantly reinforces the structur-
        al and thematic unity of the poem through the techniques of
        symmetry and contrast, the motif of the journey, and the
        integrating forces of prosopopoeia." Concludes: "The
        very act of unifying becomes the transforming act of poetry
        by which mere experience is transfigured into an immortal
        idea [i.e, Albion]. Out of the variety of England Drayton
        has thus shaped not only a poem, but a poem about poetry."
        (See SCN, 35 [Spring-Summer 1977], 15, for an abstract of
        the paper as presented at the 1976 MLA meeting.)

Michael Drayton

1978

2 JOHNSON, PAULA. "Michael Drayton, Prophet without Audience."
   SLitI, 11 (Spring), 45-55.
      Discusses structural function of the Muse, relation-
   ships among geographic features, and audience in an analysis of Polyolbion. Suggests, in passing, that of major
   writers Drayton most resembles Jonson. (See SCN, 35
   [Spring-Summer 1977], 15, for an abstract of the paper as
   presented at the 1976 MLA meeting.)

3 KOPPEL, CATHERINE CONSTANTINO. "'Of Poets and Poesy': The
   English Verse Epistle, 1595-1640." Ph.D. dissertation,
   University of Rochester, 285 pp. [DAI, 39 (1978), 2292-
   93A.]
      Draws frequently on Drayton in an attempt to define the
   genre and trace its evolution. Examines, in particular,
   the relationship between Drayton's poetic theories and his
   verse epistles.

4 NEELY, CAROL THOMAS. "The Structure of English Renaissance
   Sonnet Sequences." ELH, 45 (Fall), 359-89.
      Draws frequently on Idea's Mirror and Idea in arguing
   that English Renaissance sonnet sequences share "a charac-
   teristic overall structure," one adopted with modifications
   from Petrarch and Dante. Analyzes the generation of the
   sequences (pointing out "that fragmentary composition over
   a long period of time is compatible with a deliberately
   ordered structure" and noting that "Drayton's extensive
   revisions . . . offer the most detailed picture of the
   generation of an English sequence and . . . offer the
   closest parallels with Petrarch's method of composition");
   characteristics of the beginnings (noting the importance
   of "the metaphor of breeding"); strategies of development;
   the two-part division; and characteristics of the endings.

5 ORAM, WILLIAM A[LLAN]. "The Muses Elizium: A Late Golden
   World." SP, 75 (January), 10-31.
      "[E]xplores the boundaries of Elizium, noting particu-
   larly Drayton's significant modification of the ecologue-
   tradition and his friendly critique of a poetry of
   imaginative retreat." Analyzes how his "reexamination of
   the materials and purposes of" pastoral "forms part of a
   larger inquiry into the nature of all imaginative fiction-
   making."

6 ROSS, DONALD, JR. "Stylistics and the Testing of Literary
   Hypotheses." Poetics, 7 (December), 389-416.
      Provides tabular analyses of various stylistic elements
   of selected Idea sonnets in comparing stylistic features of
   Keats, Coleridge, Wordsworth, and Blake with those of
   Elizabethan sonnets.

7   WINK, SUSAN WADE. "Traditional Contexts and Imagistic Modes
         in the Amatory-Philosophical Narratives of George Chapman
         and Michael Drayton." Ph.D. dissertation, University of
         Arkansas, 155 pp. [DAI, 39 (1978), 3609A.]
             Argues that Endymion and Phoebe, misunderstood because
         studied as a part of the Ovidian-mythological tradition,
         should be read as a philosophical poem. Reviews traditions
         behind Endymion and Phoebe, analyzes Drayton's imagery,
         and examines the structural unity of the poem.

                              1979

1   CORBETT, MARGERY, and RONALD LIGHTBOWN. The Comely Frontis-
         piece: The Emblematic Title-Page in England, 1550-1660.
         London: Routledge & Kegan Paul, 256 pp.
             In chapter 13 ("Michael Drayton," pp. 152-61), provide
         a detailed analysis of the engraved title page to Polyol-
         bion. Emphasize the sources for the figures and point
         out that "[t]he influence of . . . [Selden's] learning and
         antiquarian fervour is apparent in the details of the
         title-page."

2   HELGERSON, RICHARD. "The Elizabethan Laureate: Self-Presen-
         tation and the Literary System." ELH, 46 (Summer), 193-
         220.
             Draws frequently on Drayton in analyzing the evolution
         of the laureate (as distinct from amateur and professional)
         poet and the techniques of "literary self-presentation"
         and "self-definition" accompanying the creation of the
         role.

3   JUNGMAN, ROBERT E., and EDWARD C. JACOBS. "The Sestet in
         Drayton's Sonnet 61." Renaissance and Renascences in
         Western Literature, 1 (Summer), 1-4.
             Show that although Drayton's use of the "Love-as-
         Physician motif" in Idea 61 is not new, his "method of
         presentation"--dramatizing the motif--is. Conclude:
         "Within the context of . . . [the] poem, . . . the Speaker
         has developed such an image in order to 'possesse . . .
         the soul' (or more likely the body) of his mistress."

4   MEANS, JAMES A. "Drayton and Pope: An Unrecorded Parallel."
         N&Q, NS 26 (February), 23.
             Notes parallel between "To Henry Reynolds" (11. 129-30)
         and Pope's Essay on Criticism.

1979

5 TURNER, JAMES [G.]. The Politics of Landscape: Rural Scenery and Society in English Poetry, 1630–1660. Oxford: Basil Blackwell, 251 pp.
   In published version of 1976.9, draws frequently on Drayton (especially Polyolbion) for comparison with later landscape poets (passim).

6 WISE, VALERIE M. "Metaphors for the Imagination in Ovid, Ariosto, and Drayton." Ph.D. dissertation, Harvard University.
   In examining the use of flight as "a metaphorical expression for the vision of the poet and for the creative imagination itself," analyzes Drayton's use of the metaphor in Endymion and Phoebe. Concludes that "Endymion's flight in the arms of his beloved Phoebe images the Neo-Platonic ascent of the soul toward the contemplation of Ideas. Drayton also points to the analogies between poets and lovers and between the poetic and erotic imagination through the metaphor of flight. Hence, the shepherd's ascent and the concomitant vision express the aspirations of poets and lovers toward the intuitive knowledge of Ideas."

Indexes

Samuel Daniel

A., F. S., 1888.2
Aboul-Enein, A. M., 1953.1
Adamany, Richard George, 1963.1
Adler, Thomas P., 1974.1
Agamemnon (Shakespeare, Troilus
    and Cressida), 1904.3
Ahern, Matthew Joseph, 1963.2
Aiken, Pauline, 1932.1
Akagawa, Yutaka, 1970.1
Albright, Evelyn May, 1927.1
Alcon (Queen's Arcadia), 1931.1
Alden, Raymond Macdonald, 1916.1
Alexander, Nigel, 1968.3
Alexander, William, Earl of
    Stirling, 1924.11; 1968.9
Allott, Robert, 1908.2
Alpers, Paul J., 1967.19
Altman, Joel B., 1978.1
Anders, Henry R. D., 1904.1
Anderson, Robert, 1793.1
Anne of Denmark, 1967.5
Anonymous, 1718.1; 1823.1;
    1854.1; 1893.1; 1892.2, 3;
    1896.1; 1899.1, 5; 1919.1;
    1925.2; 1930.1; 1949.1;
    1951.1; 1958.1; 1959.1;
    1965.1
Antonius, Marcus, 1955.1;
    1957.2; 1958.10; 1971.3;
    1974.13
Appel, Louis David, 1949.2
Appelbe, Jane Lund, 1965.2
Arber, Edward, 1877.1; 1880.1;
    1904.2
Ardinger, Barbara R., 1976.1
Arnold, Matthew, 1909.4
Atkins, John William Hey, 1947.1

Attridge, Derek, 1974.2
Aue, Wilhelm, 1961.1

B., C. C., 1899.2, 9
Bacon, Francis, 1938.2
Bald, Robert Cecil, 1924.1
Baldwin, Anne Wilfong, 1967.1
Baldwin, Thomas Whitfield, 1949.3
Ball, Lewis Franklin, 1933.1;
    1934.1
Ballweg, Oskar, 1909.1
Bambas, Rudolph Charles, 1941.1
Barker, J. R., 1965.3
Barkstead, William, 1968.8
Barnes, Barnabe, 1923.3
Barroll, John Leeds, 1958.2
Bartlett, Henrietta Collins,
    1922.1; 1929.1
Barton, Anne, 1973.1
Bateson, Frederick Wilse, 1941.2
Bazerman, Charles, 1971.1
Beall, Julianne, 1974.3
Beatty, Richmond Croom, 1935.1
Beauchamp, Virginia Walcott,
    1955.1
Bedford, Lucy Harington, Countess
    of, 1899.10; 1954.1; 1963.3
Beeching, Henry Charles, 1899.3-
    5, 8, 9
Beith-Halahmi, Esther Yaël,
    1971.1; 1974.4
Bell, Robert, 1839.1
Berringer, Ralph W., 1943.1
Berthold, Mary Haines, 1974.5
Bjork, Gary Floyd, 1973.2
Black, Matthew Wilson, 1955.2
Blake, William, 1978.8

Drummond, William, of Hawthorn-
den, 1920.2; 1965.3, 12
Dryden, John, 1925.5; 1928.1;
1940.3; 1958.1; 1974.10
Du Bartas, Guillaume de Salluste,
1924.5; 1934.4; 1935.2;
1953.10
Du Bellay, Joachim, 1904.2;
1908.5; 1908.9; 1909.6;
1978.7
Du Bos, Abbé, 1912.3
Duls, Louisa Desaussure, 1962.5;
1975.2
Duncan-Jones, Katherine, 1971.7
Dunn, Catherine Mary, 1967.4
Dunn, Esther Cloudman, 1936.3
Dyer, Edward, 1943.2
Dymoke, Edward, 1937.3; 1938.3

Eagle, Roderick Lewis, 1918.1, 2
Eccles, Mark, 1937.3
Eckhardt, Eduard, 1928.2
Edward II, 1964.5
Edwards, Edward, 1868.1
Egerton, Thomas, 1808.1; 1904.8;
1948.2
Eliot, Thomas Stearns, 1927.5
Elizabeth I, 1921.1; 1936.6, 8;
1937.2
Ellis, Oliver Coligny de Champ-
fleur, 1947.2
Elton, Oliver, 1904.5; 1907.1;
1924.3
Emperor, John Bernard, 1928.3
Emulo (Patient Grissil), 1913.4
Endicott, Norman J., 1974.18
Enozawa, Kazuyoshi, 1970.1
Enzensberger, Christian, 1962.6
Erondelle, Pierre, 1916.4
Erskine, John, 1903.4
Esdaile, Arundell James Kennedy,
1908.3
Espiner, Janet Girvan Scott (See
also Scott, Janet Girvan),
1935.2
Esplin, Ross Stolworthy, 1970.6
Essex, Robert Devereux, Second
Earl of, 1927.1; 1937.2;
1942.1, 2; 1949.3; 1951.10;

1956.6; 1962.14, 15; 1964.11;
1967.3; 1970.5
Evans, G. Blakemore, 1958.5
Evans, Herbert Arthur, 1897.2
Evans, Maurice, 1977.2
Ewig, Wilhelm, 1899.6

Fairfax, Edward, 1737.1
Falls, Cyril, 1956.1
Farmer, Norman K., Jr., 1976.3
Farnham, Willard, 1936.4; 1950.3
Farrand, Margaret L., 1930.4
Ferguson, Arthur B., 1971.8
Fink, Lila Ruth, 1976.2
Fleay, Frederick Gard, 1889.2;
1891.1; 1899.10; 1926.2
Flood, W. H. Grattan, 1926.1
Florio, John, 1865.1; 1916.4;
1921.2; 1933.6; 1934.5;
1957.5
Forbis, John F., 1924.4
Ford, Boris, 1955.10
Forrest, Henry Telford Stonor,
1923.3
Fowler, William, 1968.9
Frank, Rudolph, 1913.2
Freeman, Arthur, 1970.7; 1973.7
Froissart, Jean, 1915.3
Frowde, Philip, 1942.1; 1949.3

Gabel, Gernot U., 1900.1; 1913.2
Gabel, Gisela R., 1900.1; 1913.2
Gabler, Hans Walter, 1961.1;
1962.6
Gardner, Helen, 1959.4
Gardner, Thomas, 1967.5
Garnier, Robert, 1909.1; 1924.11;
1928.2; 1949.3; 1952.3;
1960.4
Genouy, Hector, 1928.4
Giles, Mary Dooley, 1977.4
Gill, R. B., 1977.5
Giovio, Paolo, 1970.8, 9; 1971.7,
9; 1976.3; 1979.1
Godshalk, William Leigh, 1964.5,
6; 1967.15; 1977.6
Golding, Arthur, 1965.10
Golding, S. R., 1926.2
Goldman, Lloyd Nathaniel, 1964.7;
1968.5

Michael Drayton

Abrams, William Amos, 1942.1
Ackerman, Catherine A., 1959.1
Adams, Joseph Quincy, 1917.1;
    1918.1; 1957.1
Adkins, Betty Jean VanNus,
    1974.1
Adkins, Mary Grace Muse, 1943.1
Aeschylus, 1910.2
Aetion (Edmund Spenser, Colin
    Clout), 1874.2; 1935.7
Aiken, Pauline, 1932.1
Akagawa, Yutaka, 1970.1
Albright, Evelyn May, 1915.1
Alden, Raymond Macdonald, 1916.1
Alexander, Nigel, 1968.1
Alexander, William, Earl of
    Stirling, 1857.3
Alfred (Aelfred), 1908.10
Allen, Don Cameron, 1937.1;
    1938.1, 5; 1949.1
Allott, Robert, 1908.3; 1940.9
Alpers, Paul J., 1967.1, 16, 18
Anderson, Robert, 1793.1
Androwes, George, 1888.3
Anonymous, 1753.1; 1785.1;
    1788.1; 1806.1; 1813.1;
    1849.1; 1854.1; 1876.1;
    1883.1; 1884.1, 2; 1891.1;
    1893.1; 1895.1; 1897.1, 2;
    1898.1; 1899.1, 3; 1905.3;
    1910.1; 1921.1; 1924.1;
    1925.3, 11; 1931.1; 1932.2;
    1933.1; 1941.1, 2; 1953.1, 2,
    6
Appelbe, Jane Lund, 1965.1
Arber, Edward, 1883.2; 1896.3;
    1904.2

Askew, H., 1928.3
Aston, Walter, 1933.7; 1941.8
Atkins, John William Hey, 1947.1
Atkins, Sidney H., 1936.1
Aubin, Robert Arnold, 1927.1;
    1936.2
Ausonius, Decimus Magnus, 1968.9

B., A., 1877.3
B., C. C., 1909.1, 2
B., H. A., 1872.1
Baeske, Wilhelm, 1905.1
Bainton, Edgar Leslie, 1926.1
Baldwin, Anne Wilfong, 1967.2
Ball, Lewis Franklin, 1933.2;
    1934.1
Barker, J. R., 1965.2
Barnes, Barnabe, 1961.6
Barnes, Joshua, 1964.2
Barnes, Richard Gordon, 1960.1
Bartlett, Henrietta Collins,
    1922.1
Barton, Anne, 1975.1
Bates, Paul A., 1955.1
Bateson, Frederick Wilse, 1941.3
Baxter, Nathaniel, 1850.1;
    1873.5
Bayley, P. C., 1973.5
Bayne, Thomas, 1909.2
Bazerman, Charles, 1971.1
Beaumont, George, 1931.3
Beaumont, John, 1894.2
Bedford, Lucy Harington, Countess
    of, 1899.4; 1903.1; 1905.3;
    1907.4; 1923.7; 1924.7;
    1940.4; 1941.8; 1952.4;
    1954.1; 1958.4

1941.6; 1947.1; 1959.3;
1973.12; 1974.5; 1977.3,
13
--Odes, 1752.1; 1793.1;
1896.3; 1903.3; 1918.2;
1931.4; 1932.6; 1941.6;
1960.4; 1963.5; 1968.11;
1973.14; 1975.5; 1977.3
--"Ballad of Agincourt,"
1872.1; 1884.2; 1891.2,
6; 1893.2; 1903.5;
1926.3; 1935.4; 1950.6;
1951.1, 3--"The Heart,"
1975.7--"An Ode Written
in the Peak," 1973.13--
"Sacrifice to Appolo,"
1937.6; 1939.7; 1953.4;
1970.14--"To His Coy
Love," 1964.7--"To His
Valentine," 1909.1, 2
--"To John Savage,"
1823.1--"To Sir Henry
Goodere," 1814.1--"To
the Virginian Voyage,"
1918.1; 1926.1, 3;
1946.1; 1957.1, 4, 1959.2;
1971.13
--Oldcastle, 1709.1; 1780.1;
1810.2; 1836.1; 1840.1,
2; 1850.4; 1852.1;
1855.1; 1887.2; 1892.4;
1894.1; 1900.2; 1902.3;
1905.1; 1906.5; 1907.1,
5, 1908.7, 8, 9; 1909.4;
1911.2, 3; 1913.2, 3;
1915.1; 1922.1; 1923.2;
1928.2; 1930.1; 1931.4;
1935.5; 1939.3; 1943.1;
1950.3; 1951.4; 1952.1;
1957.3; 1965.6; 1968.2;
1970.7; 1971.12; 1972.13;
1974.6, 8; 1975.1;
1977.10
--Owl, 1752.1; 1793.1;
1837.1; 1877.1; 1893.1;
1932.6; 1940.1; 1950.4;
1953.8; 1954.4
--Paean Triumphal, 1828.1;
1931.4; 1971.1

--Pastorals, 1752.1; 1793.1;
1910.3; 1932.6; 1936.4;
1959.1; 1960.5; 1965.11;
1971.14; 1974.5
--Poems (1605), 1877.1;
1888.2; 1893.1; 1933.7;
1952.4; 1967.6
--Poems (1608), 1877.1
--Poems (1609?), 1893.1
--Poems (1610), 1849.3;
1877.1; 1893.1
--Poems (1613), 1877.1
--Poems (1619), 1837.1;
1849.1; 1893.1; 1932.6;
1940.1; 1953.4, 8;
1956.5; 1964.5; 1968.8;
1969.7; 1977.4
--Poems (1630), 1877.1;
1893.1
--Poems (1637), 1877.1
--Poems Lyric and Pastoral,
1856.1; 1859.1; 1877.1;
1891.3; 1931.4; 1953.8;
1967.5
--Polyolbion, 1748.1;
1788.1; 1793.1; 1827.1;
1831.1; 1834.2; 1839.1;
1841.1; 1845.1; 1851.1;
1854.1; 1870.4; 1873.3;
1876.1, 4; 1877.1-3;
1879.2; 1884.2; 1889.1, 3-
5; 1890.1; 1893.1;
1896.1; 1897.2; 1903.2,
6, 9; 1906.6, 7; 1907.2;
1908.10; 1910.2; 1911.4;
1920.3; 1922.2; 1923.1;
1924.9, 11; 1925.1, 2;
1926.2, 8, 16; 1927.1;
1928.4, 5; 1929.3;
1930.5, 6; 1931.1, 5;
1932.4, 8, 13; 1933.1, 2,
4; 1934.1, 3; 1935.2, 4;
1936.2, 9; 1937.2, 7;
1938.3, 7; 1940.1, 2, 6;
1941.1, 4, 7, 8; 1943.3,
4; 1945.3; 1950.4, 7;
1953.1, 8; 1955.5;
1956.1, 2; 1958.3;
1959.6; 1960.3; 1961.4,
7; 1962.8; 1963.6;

Hart, James D., 1946.1
Haskell, Glenn Percival, 1936.14
Haslewood, Joseph, 1815.2
Hasselkuss, Hermann Karl, 1927.3
Hathaway, Richard (See also
    Drayton, Michael, Oldcastle),
    1709.1; 1780.1; 1810.2;
    1836.1; 1840.1, 2; 1850.4;
    1852.1; 1855.1; 1887.2;
    1894.1; 1907.1; 1908.7, 8;
    1911.2; 1913.2; 1970.7;
    1974.6
Haussy, Alice d', 1968.10;
    1970.9; 1972.7; 1975.8
Hayward, John, 1939.10
Hazlitt, William, 1852.1; 1854.2;
    1887.2
Hazlitt, William Carew, 1862.1, 2;
    1867.2; 1876.3; 1887.3; 1903.7
Headley, Henry, 1787.1; 1819.2;
    1851.1
Hebel, John William, 1923.4;
    1924.7, 8; 1925.3; 1926.6;
    1927.4; 1931.4; 1932.6, 7;
    1933.4; 1941.4; 1961.2
Heffner, Ray, 1932.8
Heffner, Ray Lorenzo, 1956.4;
    1958.1
Helgerson, Richard, 1979.2
Heltzel, Virgil Barney, 1947.3
Henrietta Maria, 1973.12
Henry V, 1952.1; 1974.8
Henry VIII, 1939.11; 1972.17
Henryson, Robert, 1906.4
Henslowe, Philip, 1903.11;
    1904.3; 1961.3
Herbert, Mary, Countess of Pem-
    broke. See Pembroke, Mary
    Herbert, Countess of.
Herbert, William, Third Earl of
    Pembroke. See Pembroke,
    William Herbert, Third Earl
    of.
Hermogenes, 1970.14
Hewlett, Maurice, 1920.3
Heywood, Thomas, 1923.2; 1939.1;
    1972.6
Hibernicus, 1938.3
Higdon, David Leon, 1973.6
Hillebrand, Harold Newcomb,
    1922.8; 1926.7

Hiller, Geoffrey G., 1965.8;
    1967.8; 1970.10
Hillyer, Robert, 1923.5
Hillyer, Robert Silliman, 1960.2
Hitchcock, Ethan Allan, 1865.1
Hobbs, Mary, 1973.7
Hobsbaum, Philip, 1965.9
Hoffmeister, Gerhart, 1973.8
Hofmann von Hofmannswaldau,
    Christian, 1891.4; 1936.8;
    1973.8
Höhna, Heinrich, 1930.7
Holinshed, Raphael, 1926.9;
    1958.2; 1965.6
Holl, Thomas, 1960.3
Holland, Abraham, 1931.2
Holland, Philemon, 1930.6;
    1931.2
Holloway, John, 1967.9
Holmes, Urban Tigner, 1937.2;
    1938.7
Hood, Eu., 1823.1; 1827.1
Hookes, Nicholas, 1923.6
Hooper, Richard, 1872.1, 2;
    1873.3; 1876.1, 2
Hopkinson, Arthur Frederic,
    1894.1; 1900.2; 1914.2
Horace (Quintus Horatius Flaccus),
    1962.6; 1977.7
Howard, Claud, 1910.4
Howard, Henry, Earl of Surrey.
    See Surrey, Henry Howard,
    Earl of.
Hudson, Hoyt Hopewell, 1941.4
Hughes, Thomas, 1758.1
Hughes, William John, 1924.9
Hull, Vernam Edward Nunnemacher,
    1926.8
Hülsbergen, Helmut E., 1973.8
Hulse, Shirley Clark, III,
    1974.9; 1976.3
Hunt, James Clay, 1941.5, 6
Hunter, G. K., 1951.2
Hunter, William Bridges, Jr.,
    1975.9; 1977.3
Hurdis, James, 1788.2
Hutcheson, William J. Fraser,
    1950.5

Idea, 1889.4; 1903.1; 1905.3;
    1907.6; 1926.13; 1937.8;

3 5282 00069 1066